ANNUAL OF THE AMERICAN SCHOOLS OF ORIENTAL RESEARCH

THE ANNUAL
OF THE
AMERICAN SCHOOLS
OF ORIENTAL RESEARCH

VOL. XX
FOR 1940-1941

EDITED FOR THE TRUSTEES BY
MILLAR BURROWS AND E. A. SPEISER

INTRODUCTION TO HURRIAN

E. A. SPEISER
Professor of Semitics in the University of Pennsylvania

WIPF & STOCK · Eugene, Oregon

Wipf and Stock Publishers
199 W 8th Ave, Suite 3
Eugene, OR 97401

Introduction to Hurrian
By Speiser, E. A.
ISBN 13: 978-1-4982-8811-8
Publication date 2/11/2016
Previously published by New Haven: ASOR, 1941

AMERICAN SCHOOLS OF ORIENTAL RESEARCH

Founded 1900, incorporated under the laws of the District of Columbia, 1921

Henry J. Cadbury, Secretary, Harvard University, Cambridge, Mass.
Warren J. Moulton, Treasurer, Bangor Theological Seminary, Bangor, Maine
The Provident Trust Company, Assistant Treasurer, Philadelphia, Pa.
Pepper, Bodine, Stokes & Schoch, Counsel, Philadelphia, Pa.

EXECUTIVE COMMITTEE

The President, Secretary, and Treasurer, *ex officio*, Professors W. F. Albright, C. R. Morey, and Nelson Glueck

FINANCE COMMITTEE

The Treasurer, *ex officio*; Messrs. Frank Altschul and Kingsley Kunhardt

CORPORATION MEMBERS

American University of Beirut, Dr. S. B. L. Penrose, Jr.
Andover Newton Theological School, Professor Winfred N. Donovan
Augustana College and Theological Seminary, Professor Carl A. Anderson
Bangor Theological Seminary, President Emeritus Warren J. Moulton
Beloit College, President Irving Maurer
Berkeley Divinity School, Professor Robert C. Dentan
Birmingham-Southern College, Professor Charles D. Matthews
Boston University School of Theology, Professor Elmer A. Leslie
Brown University, Professor R. P. Casey
Bryn Mawr College, President Marion E. Park
Butler University, Professor T. W. Nakarai
Catholic University of America, Rev. Fr. E. P. Arbez
Central Conference of American Rabbis, Rabbi Jonah B. Wise
Colgate–Rochester Divinity School, Professor Earle B. Cross
Columbia University, Professor A. Jeffery
Cornell University, Professor A. H. Detweiler
Crozer Theological Seminary, Professor I. G. Matthews
Drew University, Professor J. Newton Davies
Dropsie College, President Abraham A. Neuman
Duke University, Professor W. F. Stinespring
Eastern Baptist Theological Seminary, Professor W. E. Griffiths
Episcopal Theological School, Professor W. H. P. Hatch

Garrett Biblical Institute, Professor Otto J. Baab
General Theological Seminary, Professor C. A. Simpson
Goucher College, President D. A. Robertson
Hartford Theological Seminary, Professor Moses Bailey
Harvard University, Professor R. H. Pfeiffer
Haverford College, Professor John Flight
Hebrew Union College, President Julian Morgenstern
Institute for Advanced Study, Professor Ernst Herzfeld
Jewish Institute of Religion, President Stephen S. Wise
Jewish Theological Seminary, President Louis Finkelstein
Johns Hopkins University, Professor W. F. Albright
Kenyon College, Professor C. C. Roach
Lutheran Theological Seminary (Gettysburg), Professor H. C. Alleman
Mount Holyoke College, Professor David E. Adams
New Brunswick Theological Seminary, President John W. Beardslee, Jr.
Oberlin Graduate School of Theology, Professor Herbert G. May
Pacific School of Religion, Professor Chester C. McCown
Presbyterian Theological Seminary (Chicago), Professor Floyd V. Filson
Princeton Theological Seminary, Professor Henry S. Gehman
Princeton University, Professor P. K. Hitti
San Francisco Theological Seminary, Professor E. A. Wicher
Smith College, Professor Margaret B. Crook
Southern Methodist University, Professor Wesley C. Davis
Syracuse University, Professor I. J. Peritz
Union Theological Seminary, Professor Julius A. Bewer
University of California, Professor William S. Popper
University of Chicago, Professor A. T. Olmstead
University of Cincinnati, Professor W. T. Semple
University of Michigan, Professor Leroy Waterman
University of Pennsylvania, Professor James A. Montgomery
University of Toronto, Professor W. R. Taylor
Wellesley College, Professor Louise P. Smith
Western Theological Seminary (Pittsburgh), President James A. Kelso
Wheaton College, Professor Joseph P. Free
Yale University, Professor Charles C. Torrey
Zion Research Foundation, Miss A. Marguerite Smith
The President of the Archaeological Institute, *ex officio*
President Emeritus Warren J. Moulton, representing the Society of Biblical Literature
Professor Ovid R. Sellers, representing the American Oriental Society

HONORARY MEMBERS

Mr. R. S. Cooke, *London*
Mrs. Morris S. Jastrow, Jr., *Philadelphia*

BENEFACTORS

† Dr. James B. Nies
† Mrs. James B. Nies
† Mr. Felix M. Warburg
Mrs. Felix M. Warburg
The Rockefeller Foundation

LIFE MEMBERS

Mrs. W. F. Albright, *Baltimore, Md.*
Dr. Ludlow Bull, *New York, N. Y.*
Professor Elihu Grant, *Stamford, Conn.*
Miss Caroline Hazard, *Peace Dale, R. I.*
Professor James R. Jewett, *Cambridge, Mass.*
Dr. Warren J. Moulton, *Bangor, Maine*
Miss Julia Rogers, *Baltimore, Md.*
Professor W. T. Semple, *Cincinnati, Ohio*
Mrs. J. C. Stodder, *Bangor, Maine*
† Mrs. Charles S. Thayer, *Hartford, Conn.*
† Mr. George H. Warrington, *Cincinnati, Ohio*

PATRONS

Mr. Loomis Burrell, *Little Falls, N. Y.*
Mr. Samuel F. Houston, *Philadelphia, Pa.*

STAFF OF THE SCHOOL IN JERUSALEM

1940–1941

* Dr. Robert M. Engberg, *Director*
† Professor Clarence S. Fisher, *Acting Director and Professor of Archaeology*
* Professor Clarence T. Craig (Oberlin Graduate School of Theology), *Annual Professor*

† Deceased.
* Appointed but unable to go.

* Mr. Ronald J. Williams (University of Toronto), *Joseph Henry Thayer Fellow*
* Mr. John C. Trever (Yale University), *Two Brothers Fellow*

1941–1942

* Dr. Robert M. Engberg, *Director*

STAFF OF THE SCHOOL IN BAGHDAD

1940–1941

Professor E. A. Speiser (University of Pennsylvania), *Director*
* Professor T. J. Meek (University of Toronto), *Annual Professor*
* Mr. D. W. Lockard (Harvard University), *Albert T. Clay Fellow*

1941–1942

Professor E. A. Speiser, *Director*

* Appointed but unable to go.

INTRODUCTION TO HURRIAN

E. A. SPEISER

PREFACE

In our recovery of the past there is probably no parallel to the rapid emergence of the Hurrians as a vital factor in the history of a large portion of the Ancient Near East. Their political relations with Egypt have been known, it is true, for some time. But the profound cultural influence of the Hurrians upon the Assyrians, the Hebrews, and the Hittites has come in only recently for due recognition. With the growing understanding of the significance of the people there has come about also an increased interest in their language. This book owes its origin to that interest.

To the linguist Hurrian has an independent appeal which need have no relation to historical and cultural considerations. The language has no genetic connection with the major linguistic families or branches of that area, such as Hamito-Semitic, Sumerian, and Hittite. In type and structure Hurrian presents intricate problems of classification and analysis. It thus holds out the promise of possible contributions to the study of language in general.

The wisdom of an attempt at a comprehensive study of Hurrian at this time is not beyond questioning. The material at our disposal is scanty and fragmentary. Unpublished texts are known to exist and their eventual appearance is bound to have a bearing on conclusions limited to the accessible sources. Nevertheless, we have today a body of data regarding the phonology, morphology, and syntax of Hurrian which seem to justify a tentative correlation.

In venturing such a correlation I have had the important advantage of results achieved by previous workers in this field, notably Messerschmidt, Thureau-Dangin, Friedrich, and Goetze. If most of what the present work contains is still very definitely "stuff for transforming," the fault is certainly not theirs. It is rather due to my effort to hazard an analysis of the entire material. This has entailed a discussion of a large number of forms not previously isolated or interpreted, and a statement of the syntax of Hurrian which is at variance with the position held by my colleagues. In these circumstances it is probable that in evaluating the individual details I may have expressed myself all too often with more confidence than the evidence at hand might warrant. I feel more hopeful about the relative validity of the general outline of the language here offered because its structure permits frequent independent checks of the results obtained. Thus the analysis of the morphologic elements of the noun or the verb has to agree with various collateral features of the syntax. The more numerous such agreements are, the greater is the presumption of the approximate correctness of the solution proposed.

The method of presentation is not wholly in accordance with the requirements of the subject matter. A strictly descriptive account of Hurrian is precluded for the time being by the necessity of determining first the great majority of the facts. For this reason many details have had to be cited out of their logical place, not without some speculation and argument. Furthermore, it has seemed advisable not to add to existing difficulties by departing radically from traditional terminology, prejudicial as this may be to a language like Hurrian. I have made an exception, however, in the matter of arrangement since the traditional mode of grammatical treatment could not possibly serve the needs of Hurrian.

The scope of the book as originally announced called for a brief account of the grammar followed by a chrestomathy and a complete glossary. But the grammar alone has proved to require more space than had first been contemplated for all three parts. A suitably annotated chrestomathy would at least have doubled the present size. Since the two omitted parts are practically ready for publication, having been prepared before the grammatical analysis was undertaken, they may appear as a separate volume at some future date.

The preparation of this volume was facilitated by much generous assistance. To my wife I am indebted for transcribing and filing the glossary and indices of elements used in the progress of the work. Professor Zellig S. Harris was able to read part of the manuscript and to contribute valuable suggestions. For the help which I was fortunate to receive from Professor Albrecht Goetze it is difficult to make adequate acknowledgment. He found time to study all of the text and to give me the benefit of his judgment concerning virtually every section of this book. I owe to him many corrections and improvements. Above all, however, I am grateful to him for the quality and stimulus of his opposition in matters on which we do not see eye to eye; quite possibly, I may come to regret my own stand in more instances than one.

Finally, I wish to express my gratitude to the American Schools of Oriental Research for publishing the book and for the patience and consideration of their officers during the delay which attended its completion.

E. A. Speiser

Wynnewood, Pennsylvania
September 19, 1941

TABLE OF CONTENTS

IV. MORPHOLOGIC ELEMENTS

ABBREVIATIONS

AASOR = Annual of the American Schools of Oriental Research
Aḫḫ.-Urk. = F. Sommer, Die Aḫḫijavā-Urkunden (Abhandlungen der Bayerischen Akademie der Wissenschaften, phil.-hist. Abteilung, Munich, 1932)
AJSL = American Journal of Semitic Languages and Literatures
AfO = Archiv für Orientforschung, Berlin
Anal(ecta) Orient(alia), Pontifical Biblical Institute, Rome
AOr. = Archiv Orientalní, Prague
BA = Beiträge zur Assyriologie und Semitischen Sprachwissenschaft, Leipzig
BASOR = Bulletin of the American Schools of Oriental Research
BChG = J. Friedrich, Kleine Beiträge zur Churritischen Grammatik, MVAeG 42/2
BoTU = E. Forrer, Die Boghazköi-Texte in Umschrift, Leipzig
Br. = C-G. v. Brandenstein, Zum Churrischen aus den Ras-Schamra-Texten, ZDMG 91 (1937) 555 ff.
CT = Cuneiform Texts in the British Museum
EA = J. A. Knudtzon, Die El-Amarna-Tafeln
Gadd = C. J Gadd, Tablets from Kirkuk, RA 23. 49 ff.
H(SS) = Harvard Semitic Series
HG = E. H. Sturtevant, A Comparative Grammar of the Hittite Language
Hr. = B. Hrozný, AOr. 4. 118-29
HT = Hittite Texts in the Cuneiform Character, London
Iraq = Journal of the British School of Archaeology in Iraq
JAOS = Journal of the American Oriental Society
JPOS = Journal of the Palestine Oriental Society
KBo = Keilschrifttexte aus Boghazköi
Kleinas. Sprachdenkm. = J. Friedrich, Kleinasiatische Sprachdenkmäler (Kleine Texte . . Hans Lietzman 163)
KUB = Keilschrifturkunden aus Boghazköi
Kulturfragen, ed. A. Ungnad, Breslau
Lang. = Language, Journal of the Linguistic Society of America
Lang. Dissert. 23 = M. Berkooz, The Nuzi Dialect of Akkadian, Language Dissertations 23 (1937)
MAOG = Mitteilungen der Altorientalischen Gesellschaft
Mâri = F. Thureau-Dangin, Tablettes Ḫurrites provenant de Mâri, RA 36. 1-28
MDOG = Mitteilungen der Deutschen Orient-Gesellschaft
MVAG = Mitteilungen der Vorderasiatischen Gesellschaft
MVAeG = Mitteilungen der Vorderasiatisch-Aegyptischen Gesellschaft
Mit. = Mitanni Letter (Text: O. Schroeder, VS 200; transliteration: J. Friedrich, Kleinas. Sprachdenkm.)

Mitannisprache = F. Bork, Die Mitannisprache, MVAG 1909 1/2
Mit(anni)-Studien = L. Messerschmidt, MVAG 1899 4
N = Publications of the Baghdad School, Joint Expedition with the Iraq Museum
Nuzi = R. F. S. Starr, Nuzi, Harvard University Press
OLZ = Orientalistische Literaturzeitung
Orientalia, Journal of the Pontifical Biblical Institute
PBS = Publications of the Babylonian Section, University of Pennsylvania Museum
RA = Revue d'Assyriologie et d'Archéologie Orientale
RES = Revue des Études Sémitiques
RHA = Revue Hittite et Asianique
RŠ = Ras Shamra: X = Syria 10 plates 61 ff.; XX = Syria 20. 126 f.
RŠ Voc. = Ras Shamra Vocabulary, Syria 12. 225 ff.
SA = F. Thureau-Dangin, Le Syllabaire Accadien
SMN = Nuzi texts (unpublished) in the Semitic Museum, Harvard
Subartu = A. Ungnad, Subartu, Beiträge zur Kulturgeschichte und Völkerkunde Vorderasiens
Syria, Revue d'Art Orientale et d'Archéologie, Paris
TCL = Textes Cunéiformes, Musée du Louvre
Tunnawi = A. Goetze, The Hittite Ritual of Tunnawi
VBoT = A. Götze, Verstreute Boghazköi-Texte, Marburg
VS = Vorderasiatische Schriftdenkmäler
WZKM = Wiener Zeitschrift für die Kunde des Morgenlandes
ZA = Zeitschrift für Assyriologie
ZDMG = Zeitschrift der Deutschen Morgenländischen Gesellschaft

Other titles are cited in full. Cross-references are enclosed in square brackets. Phonetic transcription and supplemented passages are also indicated by square brackets. Roman numerals which are not preceded by an abbreviated reference indicate respective volumes of KUB.

In literal translations from Hurrian bound morphemes are marked by means of hyphens. Elsewhere the English rendering does not follow the exact order of the Hurrian bound forms.

METHOD OF NORMALIZED TRANSCRIPTION

In analyzing the complex linguistic forms of Hurrian it is often necessary to break up the given word into its component morphologic elements. However, such a division has little in common with the sequence of signs which the syllabary had to employ in order to represent that word. E. g., the spelling *ge-pa-a-nu-u-ša-aš-še-na* contains the morphologic elements *keb-an-oz̄-a-s̄e-na.* The underlying distinctions of voice and vowel-quality are conveyed by the syllabary in a consistent manner although the method employed for the purpose differs from that of the late Akkadian texts on which the direct transliterations are based. To ignore the distinctions thus reflected would be to obscure the known facts of the language. But our knowledge of the sounds of Hurrian is as yet far from sufficient to permit adequate normalization in all instances. For this reason the great majority of citations will be given in direct transliteration, while transcription will be reserved for morphologic analysis. To avoid confusion between transliterated and normalized forms plus-signs will be used for purposes of analysis whenever the elements involved might otherwise be mistaken for actual syllabic readings.

It should be pointed out at this time that the normalized forms are not meant as a phonemic transcription. The discussion of the sounds of Hurrian in Chapter II will contain the evidence for setting up such pairs as *s̄* : *z̄*, *p* : *b*, *k* : *g*, *t* : *d*, *f* : *v*, and *u* : *o*. But the symbol *s̄*, e. g., implies only a sound that differed from *z̄* with regard to voice and was distinct also from *s* in some unknown way; the pair *f* : *v* indicates labial spirants, voiceless and voiced respectively, without implying any further phonetic qualification.

The incomplete nature of the evidence at hand will be reflected by the following limitations:

Syllabic *š* is retained where there is no way of deciding between *s̄* and *z̄*; e. g., *šue* for *šu-e.*

Single intervocalic *ḫ* of the syllabic texts is not transcribed as *ġ* because the available evidence is as yet not wholly free from ambiguity; hence syllabic *Ḫalbaḫe* alongside alphabetic *ḫlbġ*.

The consonant in the genitive and dative suffixes is written *-w-* because that is the regular writing in Mitanni; e. g., *ašti* + *we.* In the other syllabic sources the writing of that consonant varies between *w* and *b*, which would seem to suggest [v]. But the orthography of Mitanni has to be our standard for the time being and consistency demands that we follow it also in this instance.

When the syllabic texts use single *b* or *p* after a vowel, the transcription is *b* unless we have independent evidence in favor of *v*.

Before the ambiguous spirant-form *ḫ* stops are arbitrarily represented as voiceless. But in a sequence of vowel + stop + stop the first stop is marked as voiced, the second as voiceless; cf. RŠ *lbtġ* and perhaps Mâri *ki-ib-ti-en*. This conventional procedure does not imply a definitive phonetic interpretation.

Double writing of stops in the syllabic sources is represented in transcription by the corresponding double voiceless stops although we cannot be sure that the sounds in question were invariably long or doubled; e. g., *ittummi*.

Since there is no clear evidence for etymological long vowels in Hurrian the transcription *-*ān* for written -*a-an* would be misleading. I have used -*àn* instead, as an arbitrary marker of full spelling and not as an indication of a particular form of stress.

The normalized forms, subject to the foregoing restrictions, will be employed when necessary after the required evidence has been furnishd in Chapter II. It cannot be emphasized too strongly that the adopted method is strictly schematic and applicable only to a limited number of instances. It has the advantage of presenting a better picture of the variety of the sounds of Hurrian than could be obtained from direct transliterations alone. Without some such method grammatical analysis would be seriously impeded. At all events, the reader need never have any difficulty in visualizing the underlying orthography: normalized *s̄* represents double intervocalic *š* of the syllabic texts; elsewhere this transcription has to have the independent support of the alphabetic material; *o* stands for the sign *U* attested in Mitanni; and the like.

. . . . . .

In direct transliteration, which will be the rule rather than the exception, the system followed is that of Thureau-Dangin's Le Syllabaire Accadien and Les Homophones Sumériens. I write, however, *ya* instead of *ia* and I give preference to the commonest sign-values, namely, those without diacritics and subnumerals. Thus, e. g., I write *pa* instead of *bá*, *tu* instead of *dú* even where the evidence calls for a voiced consonant. This is done in order to present the true state of the orthographic evidence. An exception to this procedure is the use of *pí* and *pè* initially and after consonants, mainly because these forms have come into common use in recent transliterations of Hurrian, apart from being phonetically preferable. Where the system of Thureau-Dangin offers a choice of free variants (without calling for diacritics or subnumerals) the variant closest to the required form has been used. The sign IB appears thus in several of its permissible variants in *ew-ri*, *at-ta-ip-pa*, *pa-ši-ib*; ID is found in *aš-te-ni-*wa_a*-ni-id*, *it-ta-in-na-a-an*, *ú-ni-e-et-ta*; and GI of the main syllabary is consistently transliterated as *ge*. The sign T/DIN is transliterated *ten* without differentiating *t* from *d*.

AR-ZAVA

I. INTRODUCTION

1. The name Hurrian is applied today to that ancient language which modern scholars first called "Mitannian" and later came to designate as "Subarean." These changes in terminology have marked successive stages of progress in the study of the subject.

2. Among the cuneiform tablets from Tell el-Amarna, brought to light in 1887, the one which was the largest in the group happened also to be composed in an unknown language.[1] Only the introductory paragraph, which takes up seven out of nearly 500 lines, was written in Akkadian. From that introduction it was learned that the document was a letter addressed to Amenophis III by Tushratta, king of Mitanni. It was logical, therefore, at the time to assume that the rest of the letter was in the principal language of the Kingdom of Mitanni; the use of the term "Mitannian" was the natural consequence of that assumption.

This name was employed by all the early students of the subject, including P. Jensen (cf. his articles in ZA 5 [1890] 166 ff., 6 [1891] 34 ff., and 14 [1899] 173 ff.); L. Messerschmidt, Mitanni-Studien (MVAG 4 [1899] No. 4); F. Bork, Die Mitannisprache (MVAG 14 [1909] Nos. 1/2. Current usage restricts the term, as a rule, to the material in the non-Akkadian letter of Tushratta. This is done in order to maintain a special dialectal position for the language of that letter (e. g., by Bork, who would separate it from Ras Shamra Hurrian and from the linguistic substratum at Nuzi); more commonly, however, "Mitanni" refers (when used in a linguistic sense) to the orthography and vocabulary of the Tushratta letter, without further dialectal connotation. In the present monograph the abbreviation Mit. will be employed in the latter sense.

3. Related linguistic material was discovered subsequently in the form of glosses included in other Amarna letters and in the form of proper names preserved in the same correspondence.[2] Far more extensive, however, was to prove a flow of pertinent onomastic material from another source: this time not from Syria and Palestine, but from Mesopotamia, where the main language was abundantly established as Akkadian. A. Ungnad, who was the first to subject the material in question to careful study (following earlier attempts by Clay, Bork, and Gustavs), showed reason for connecting the bearers of

[1] Two other cuneiform documents from Amarna proved to be in a language which was unknown at the time of their discovery, but different from that of the tablet mentioned above. They are the so-called Arzawa letters, now known to be Hittite; cf. E. Sturtevant, HG 29, and B. Hrozný, Journal Asiatique 1931. 307 ff., and for the text see A. Götze, Verstreute Boghazköi-Texte (1930) 1-2.

[2] For "Mitanni" glosses see the early statement by Messerschmidt, op. cit. 119 ff.

those names with the land Subartu. He recognized also the relation between the onomastic elements which he had analyzed and the language of the Mitanni letter. Since "Mitannian" could be applied properly only to certain Syrian sources, Ungnad proceeded to set up "Subarean" as a common designation which was free from the limitations of "Mitannian." In this he was followed later by a majority of scholars. His objections to the earlier usage were to be borne out by discoveries yet to come.

Ungnad first established his position on the basis of proper names from Dilbat, cf. BA 6 (1909) No. 5; he followed up his argument in Kulturfragen 1 (Breslau, 1923); his most exhaustive treatment has been presented recently in his comprehensive work Subartu (1936).

4. The problem took a new turn with the study of the cuneiform records from Boghazköi. In 1915 Hrozný called attention to the fact that among the passages in languages other than Hittite which had been included in the Hittite texts a number were introduced by the adverb *ḫurlili*.[3] It was determined subsequently that (1) this adverb was based on a nominal form *ḫurla-* which (2) could be used appellatively as a substitute for *mit(t)anni*; (3) the corresponding form in Akkadian texts is *ḫurri* which is equated independently with *mitanni*; Tushratta applies to his land the terms *ḫurroḫe* and *ḫurwoḫe*, which are adjectives in -(*o*)*ḫe* based on the stem *ḫurr-* or *ḫurw-*, while in his Akkadian introduction he calls himself "king of the land Mitanni."[4] It follows that there is a close correspondence between Hittite *ḫurl-*, Akkadian *ḫurr-*, and Tushratta's *ḫurr/w-* on the one hand, and *mitanni* on the other. Added to this is the linguistic correspondence between the Boghazköi passages marked as *ḫurlili* and the language of the Mitanni letter.[5] Since "Mitannian" is inadequate as a designation for the whole of the linguistic material in question, the choice lies between "Subarean" and the name which is reflected in Hittite *ḫurlili*.

A full discussion of the problems arising from the Hittite uses of *ḫurla-* and *ḫurlili* is given by F. Sommer in Die Aḫḫiyavā-Urkunden (1932) 42 ff., 385 ff. Sommer sees in *ḫurla-* (whose *-l-* as against the *-w-* of the native *ḫurw-* is manifestly a Hittite development) an appellative which became specialized as an ethnic designation. The geographical connotation is incidental: "Ḫurla-land" is not the same thing as "the land Ḫurla." It is significant that Tushratta's *ḫurw/ḫurr-* does not occur without the

---

[3] Cf. MDOG 56 (1915) 40 ff.; see also E. Forrer, ZDMG 1922. 224 ff.

[4] For *ḫurw-* and *ḫurr-* cf. Mit. I 11, 14, 19; II 68, 72; III 6, 113; IV 127; for the Akk. phrase see Mit. I 3.

[5] Emphasized by Ungnad himself in ZA 1923. 133 ff. The awkwardness of "Subaräer" as against "Ḫurriter," where Anatolian material is concerned, is admitted by Ungnad in Kulturfragen 1. 8. n. 1.

adjectival ending -(*o*)*ḫe*; i. e., Ḫurr(w)ian" ("land" *omini*), not "the land Ḫurri." It follows that the native stem, too, does not point to a geographical meaning.

5. The Boghazköi material helped to show that *Mitanni* had only a limited political application and never served as a comprehensive ethnic or linguistic designation. Similar restrictions apply, however, to *Subartu* and its Sumerian equivalents.[6] This name started out as a geographical term for territories north of Akkad. In course of time it came to serve as a basis for ethnic and even linguistic uses, but these were not always consistent.[7] Moreover, they are known to us only through speakers of Akkadian.[8] On the other hand, "Hurrian" represents a name which Tushratta, writing in the language of his country, applied to the people of that country. The Hittites used it for the same people as well as for its language, which they record as far away as Central Anatolia. The Ras Shamra texts have preserved the same basic name in Ugaritic *ḫry*,[9] in addition to furnishing pertinent linguistic material both in syllabic and alphabetic form. Other witnesses of this term are the biblical ethnicon "Horite" (Hebrew *ḥorî*, Greek Χορραῖος) and the Egyptian land-name *Ḫr*.[10] In view of this abundant testimony from a number of independent sources the use of "Hurrian" can no longer be open to dispute, not only with regard to the respective Boghazköi documents but also the rest of the related and widely scattered sources.

The argument in favor of "Hurri" was presented by E. Chiera and E. A. Speiser in AASOR 6 (1926) 75 ff.; cf. also Hrozný, AOr. 1 (1929) 104; ibid. 3 (1931) 289. New material made possible a fuller statement on my part in AASOR 13 (1933) 13 ff. The use of "Subarean," especially for linguistic purposes, has been declining steadily. J. Friedrich, who still favored the term in 1932 (cf. his Kleinasiatische Sprachdenkmäler 7 f.), gave it up in his Kleine Beiträge zur churritischen Grammatik (1939).[11] Ungnad's

---

[6] Cf. Ungnad, Subartu 24 ff.

[7] *Subartu* may refer to Assyria (op. cit. 61); the description "man from Su (= Subartu) may take in proper names that are not Hurrian (ibid. 106); and glosses marked as Subarean include Akkadian words (ibid. 98 f.).

[8] The alleged representation of an ethnicon **Šubari* in the alphabetic texts from Ras Shamra (cf. Br. 570) remains to be proved. RŠ X 2 (= Syria X pl. 62) 12, 23, 30 cites *šbr* after the ethnica *ḫry* "Hurrian," *ḫty* "Hittite," and *alšy* "Alashian" (= Cyprian). But the sibilant in question is not [š]; it is a Hurrian sound which configurates with Semitic *ṯ* [44]. Now this sound is expressed invariably in the syllabic writing as *š*, not *s* (cf. JAOS 58 [1938] 192). The [s] of *Subartu* militates, therefore, against this identification of *šbr*. C. G. v. Brandenstein may be right in comparing *šbr* with *Šabarra*, which occurs in a Hittite context as a land name (Br. 570 n. 1). But the further equation *Šabarra* = *Šubari* (cf. also Orientalia 8 [1939] 84 n. 2) is very doubtful.

[9] See the above note.

[10] Cf. AASOR 13 (1933) 27 ff.

[11] See also Die Welt als Geschichte 3 (Stuttgart, 1937) 60.

defense of *Subartu*, in his book by the same title (1936), has resulted in a valuable collection of sources; but the work does not alter the general position on the question of terminology.

Since the Sumerian equivalents of *Subartu* include *subir* and *ḫubur* (Ungnad, Subartu 26 f.), there is a remote possibility that these Sumerian names are reflexes of the native term which is contained in Tushratta's *ḫurw-oḫe*, provided that the labial of both Sumerian synonyms stands for [w].[12] But there is nothing to prove that such a relationship really existed. At best, *Subartu* would be the result of an old borrowing from a foreign source, traceable ultimately, through **suwr̥* and **ḫuwr̥*, to the native *ḫurw-*. It is not a constructive speculation.

6. An attempt to establish the etymology of *Ḫurri* was made by Hrozný.[13] He would connect the name with Akk. *ḫurru* "hole." But apart from the inherent improbability that the Hurrians had borrowed an Akkadian word for their national designation, this etymology is refuted by the fact that the basic stem was *ḫurw-*, a patently un-Akkadian combination.[14] Ungnad recognizes the Hurrian character of this stem. His suggestion that the name may have meant originally something like "alliance, union"[15] lacks, however, the slightest support. All that we can surmise at present is that the name was based on an appellative of unknown meaning.

The earlier readings of the two cuneiform signs with which *Ḫurri* is written, viz., as *Ḫarri* and *Murri* respectively, have today only a historical interest. These readings were made possible by the fact that the first sign has as its common values in the Akkadian syllabary not only ḪUR but also ḪAR and MUR. The forms based on the two latter readings were due to etymologizing tendencies which sought to equate *ḪAR-ri* with the Aryans and *MUR-ri* with Amurru. The value ḪUR is not only made probable in the present instance by the prevailing usage in the Hittite syllabary (cf. Sommer, Aḫḫ.-Urk. 42 n. 1) but is supported also by Heb. *ḥorî* = Χορραῖος; note also Albright's syllabic reading of the Eg. group *Ḫr* as *ḫu-ru*, The Vocalization of the Egyptian Syllabic Orthography (1934) 54. The Egyptian name *P3-Ḫr*, "the Syrian," is transcribed *Pa(i,u)ḫuru(a)* in the Amarna texts. Finally, the place-name *Ḫu-ur-ra*, esp. with the Hurrian gen. *Ḫu-ur-ra-we*KI, which occurs in the Mâri texts (RES 1937. 102), may prove pertinent in this connection.

7. The Hurrian material published so far varies considerably as to contents, date, and provenience. It consists of the following groups:

7a. Connected texts, which include

(1) The Mitanni letter. This document, dating from ca. 1400 B. C., takes

[12] Cf. A. Goetze, JAOS 57 (1937) 108.

[13] AOr. 3 (1931) 287.

[14] Curiously enough, the same derivation used to be maintained for the biblical Horites, viz., from Heb. *ḥor* "hole," a cognate of Akk. *ḫurru*. It is possible that Hebrews and Akkadians alike amused themselves with such puns on the name of another people. On Semitic grounds alone these combinations are ruled out as serious etymologies by the fact that "troglodytes" go not with "holes," but "caves," for which Semitic employs special stems.

[15] Subartu 131.

up four lengthy columns, which total nearly 500 lines averaging more than twenty cuneiform signs. For the most part the letter is well preserved. It constitutes our principal source for the study of Hurrian in spite of the great amount of new material which has come to light since 1887, the year when the letter was discovered. This is due to the continuous nature of its subject matter and the presence of other letters from Tushratta to Amenophis III, which deal with similar topics but are recorded in Akkadian.[16]

The latest publication of the text is given in a copy by O. Schroeder, Vorderasiatische Schriftdenkmäler XII (1915) No. 200. The latest available transliteration is that of Friedrich, Kleinasiatische Sprachdenkmäler (1932) 9-32 [17]; it is based on an independent study of the original text.

(2) The material from Boghazköi. This group consists of Hurrian passages scattered among the Hittite texts; longer Hurrian documents with brief passages in Hittite; and a few purely Hurrian texts.[18] The date is the same as that of the Boghazköi archives in general, i. e., the Amarna period approximately, with some margin both ways; the majority is probably close to the time of the Mitanni letter. Only part of the extant material has been published so far. The contents are chiefly of a religious nature, with rituals predominating; there are also epic and historic-mythological passages. The published material takes up well over a thousand lines. A number of passages of considerable length are well preserved, but many others are in fragments, often with a single word, or only part of one, to a line. Moreover, with one exception,[19] the number of signs to a line averages less than in the Mitanni letter. The result is that the total amount of Hurrian material from Boghazköi is below that of the single letter of Tushratta. Nor does our understanding of the Boghazköi material compare with our present knowledge of the letter. The

[16] EA 17-23, 25. Other letters from Tushratta to the Egyptian court are: ibid. No. 26 (to the widow of Amenophis III); Nos. 27-29 (to Amenophis IV).

[17] Abbr. Kleinas. Sprachdenkm. I have not been able to obtain a copy of Bork's latest study of the letter, which was announced for the year 1939. [See now J. Friedrich's adverse criticism of Bork's Der Mitanibrief une seine Sprache in WZKM 46. 195-204.] His earlier transliteration and translation of the document, included in Mitannisprache (1909), can no longer be accepted. The recent translation by S. A. B. Mercer, The Tell El-Amarna Tablets (1939) No. 24, is a wasted effort.

[18] Examples of Hurrian texts with brief passages in Hittite: KUB XXVII 38 (ritual followed by a historic-mythological passage [col. iv]); 42 (ritual for the king and queen); XXIX 8 ii 29 ff. (ritual for the "washing of the mouth"); straight Hurrian texts: VIII 61 (= KBo. VI 33 [fragment of the Gilgamesh epic; cf. also VIII 60 rev.]); XXVII 46 ("Teshub and the River"); XXXI 3 (mentions Sargon of Akkad); and many other fragments.

[19] XXVII 42.

discontinuous contexts of the religious documents coupled with their specialized vocabulary present serious obstacles to a satisfactory interpretation. It is probable that the language of rituals, myths, and epics was more archaic than the every-day speech which the practical Tushratta employed.[20] But each new publication promises further gains.

Hurrian passages occur in all the principal publications of Hittite texts: the two series KBo. = Keilschrifttexte aus Boghazköi (1921-3) and KUB = Keilschrifturkunden aus Boghazköi (1921 ff.), the latest being vol. XXXI (1939); and the single volumes HT = Hittite Texts (London, 1920) and VBoT = Versteute Boghazköi-Texte (Marburg, 1930). The bulk of the material is presented in KUB XXVII (1934); note especially Nos. 1, 38, 42, and 46. KUB XXIX (1938) gives a long Hurrian passage, excellently preserved, in No. 8 (ii 29-31; 34-52; iii 4-54; 59-61; iv 1-35). Occasional duplicates, complete or partial, furnish valuable assistance; cf., e. g., XXVII 1 iii 34 ff.: 6 i 3 ff.; 23 ii: 24 iv; 23 iii: 24 i; 42 rev. 12-13: XXIX 8 iii 30-33; XXVII ibid. 17-19: XXIX ibid. 34-38; XXVII ibid. 21-23: XXIX ibid. 39-43; and others.

(3) The texts from Mâri. The very extensive cuneiform archives from this ancient center on the Middle Euphrates have been found to include short Hurrian texts which date from the period of Hammurabi. This material antedates, therefore, all the other connected records in Hurrian by four to five centuries and provides a starting point for a historical approach to the language. Of the six relevant documents published so far four are in Hurrian alone, while two contain Akkadian material on the obverse, plainly independent from the Hurrian context on the reverse. The texts are poetic in form and religious in content. The system of writing differs from the Mitanni-Boghazköi syllabary. Progress in the interpretation of these difficult religious poems promises to bring out other instructive differences.

These texts have been published and analyzed by F. Thureau-Dangin, Tablettes ḫurrites provenant de Mâri, RA 36 (1939) 1-28.

(4) The alphabetic material from Ras Shamra. Still another group of religious texts comes from Ras Shamra (ancient Ugarit), in the northern part of the Syrian coast. The date (shortly after 1500 B. C.[21]) compares with that of the Mitanni-Boghazköi material. But the script is consonantal, not syllabic, differing only slightly from the cuneiform alphabet employed for the local dialect of Semitic.[22] The principal text in the group (RŠ X 4) contains 62

[20] Cf. Friedrich, Der gegenwärtige Stand unseres Wissens von der churritischen Sprache, Ex Oriente Lux 6 (1939) 93.

[21] For the date see Z. Harris, The Smithsonian Report for 1937 (publ. 1938) 491.

[22] In the form of *z̄* (/Ugar. *š*) and *s̄* (<Ugar. *ṯ*, but often resembling Ugar. ʿ [44]). The Ras Shamra signs *'a*, *'i/e*, *'u* may have been used in the Hurrian texts for the respective vowels alone.

lines divided into 17 paragraphs each of which presents an invocation to a deity or deities. For the most part this text is well preserved. The remaining Hurrian passages are short and mostly fragmentary. One of them [23] gives a list of deities. Lack of vocalic representation makes the Hurrian material from Ras Shamra particularly difficult to interpret.

A valuable study of RŠ X 4 (= Syria 10 [1929] pl. 64 [tablet 4]) was contributed by v. Brandenstein, ZDMG 91 (1937) 555 ff. (= Br.). The only serious objection to his treatment results from Brandenstein's interpretation of the symbol ġ as a special form of š [58]. For a photograph of RŠ X 4 see the publication by Th. H. Gaster, in the M. Gaster Anniversary Volume 154 ff. Bork's individualistic view of the same material, to which he has devoted a monograph with an impressive title (Das Ukirutische, Die unbekannte Sprache von Ras Schamra, Die Grundlagen der Entzifferung [Leipzig, 1938]) is of little use. For other Hurrian material from Ras Shamra cf. Friedrich, Analecta Orientalia 12 (1935) 128 ff., and add now Syria 20 (1939) 127 (= RŠ XX A, B).

7b. The Sumero-Hurrian vocabulary. Ras Shamra has yielded also a vocabulary in syllabic cuneiform (of the same date as the alphabetic texts) in the form of the second tablet of the Sumero-Akkadian series known as ḪAR.ra : *ḫubullu*; but the Sumerian entries are translated here into Hurrian instead of Akkadian. Most of the 135 lines of this bilingual text are well preserved. Thus far, however, the vocabulary has been of less assistance than one would expect. Its words and phrases are derived from legal and economic usage which otherwise figures little in the extant Hurrian material. The Sumerian is often faulty so that the accuracy of the corresponding Hurrian cannot be taken for granted. Dialectal peculiarities seem to be present.[24] It is likely, moreover, that Hurrian words would appear more variable as abstract lexical items than in the concrete framework of a sentence [230].

The vocabulary was published and fully analyzed by Thureau-Dangin in Syria 12 (1931) 225-66. For additional remarks by B. Landsberger cf. AfO 12 (1938) 136.

7c. Proper names. This is a particularly extensive source of Hurrian linguistic elements even though they are restricted in variety by the conditions of onomastic usage. They span a longer period and cover a larger area than do the extant connected texts and they help to establish the penetration of Hurrian into territories which were dominated by other languages. Names of demonstrably Hurrian origin occur shortly after the middle of the third millennium in a region northeast of Akkad.[25] At the turn of that millennium they are on the increase in Babylonia and at the beginning of the

[23] Syria 12 (1931) 389 ff. and AOr. 4 (1933) 118 f. (abbr. Hr.).

[24] Cf. Friedrich, Ex Oriente Lux 6. 92.

[25] Cf. Ungnad, Subartu 141 f. Still earlier is the name *Puttim-adal* (not *Putti-madal*, as analyzed by Ungnad, ibid. 144) borne by a contemporary of Narâm-Sin; but it has come down in a late copy (RA 16 [1919] 161 ff.).

next they appear in considerable numbers as far north as Chagar Bazar in the Ḫabûr Valley; in the succeeding centuries Hurrian names are attested abundantly in widely separated areas. The largest group by far, embracing thousands of occurrences, comes from the Arrapḫa area (modern Kirkuk), east of the Tigris, primarily from the site of ancient Nuzi.[26] Many others are scattered over a wide area, from Southern Mesopotamia to Cappadocia, Syria, and Palestine. A few are recorded in the Boghazköi texts. Some are as late as the end of the second millennium.[27] All of these occurrences are attested in the cuneiform syllabic writing. In addition, there are Hurrian names in the alphabetic texts from Ras Shamra, a few probable examples in the Old Testament, and one or two possible instances in Egypt.

This extensive onomastic material has contributed to our knowledge of the vocabulary of Hurrian. The meaning of many individual elements has been established. From a grammatical standpoint, however, the names still present unusual difficulties [241].

An exhaustive study of the Nuzi names and their component elements has been prepared by P. M. Purves and will appear soon in the Oriental Institute Publications. For recent discussions on the subject cf. L. Oppenheim, AfO 12 (1937) 29 ff.; Purves, JAOS 58 (1938) 462 ff. and AJSL 57 (1940) 162 ff. (orthography). The names from Chagar Bazar (which date from the Hammurabi period) are included in a study by C. J. Gadd, Iraq 7 (1940) 35 ff. The Palestinian material from Taanach was presented by A. Gustavs in Zeit. d. deut. Pal. Ver. 57 (1927) 1 ff. and ibid. 58 (1928) 169 ff. Mesopotamian sources are cited in Ungnad, Subartu 138 ff. and G. R. Meyer, AfO 12 (1939) 366 ff.; Cappadocia: Ungnad, op. cit. 150 f.; L. Oppenheim, RHA 33 (1938) 7 ff.; other brief discussions are scattered in numerous recent publications.

7d. Other material. Here may be listed (1) the few so-called glosses from the Amarna letters.[28] (2) Numerous Hurrian terms from Nuzi, which occur as independent words or in periphrastic expressions formed with the aid of Akk. *epēšu* "do." To the same category of quasi-loanwords [29] belong many of the technical terms found in the Akkadian lists of presents from Tushratta to the Egyptian court; [30] also a number of terms in the long Qatna tablet.

[26] For the form of this place-name cf. [62].

[27] In the annals of Tiglathpileser I (ca. 1100), cf. Ungnad, op. cit. 162 (note already C. J. Gadd, RA 23 [1926] 77). In outlying mountain districts Hurrian names survive into the first millennium; one can hardly separate the Median Deioces (ca. 715), cuneif. *Dayaukku*, from Nuzi *Tay(a)uki*; cf. G. G. Cameron, History of Early Iran (1936) 153.

[28] Messerschmidt, Mitanni-Studien 119 ff.; Friedrich, BChG 22, 31 f. Goetze has demonstrated, however, that not all the alleged glosses are accompanied by Akkadian equivalents; cf. RHA 35 (1939) 103 ff.

[29] They are not loanwords proper because they occur in texts which are traceable to speakers of the language in question.

[30] EA 22, 25. For the Qatna tablet (380 lines) cf. Virolleaud, Syria 11 (1930) 311 ff.

(3) True Hurrian loanwords have frequently been noted or suspected in Hittite inscriptions and they may turn up in Ugaritic. Some are demonstrable in good Akkadian. (4) Lastly, non-Akkadian constructions in the Nuzi texts which betray the influence of Hurrian syntax.

(2) For the Hurrian material from Nuzi cf. C. H. Gordon, BASOR 64 (1936) 23 ff. and Orientalia 7 (1938) 51 ff.; add also Goetze, Lang. 16 (1940) 168 ff. (3) For the Hurrian (and not ultimately Akkadian) origin of *ambašši keldi* see Friedrich, AfO 10 (1935) 294 and v. Brandenstein, AfO 13 (1939) 58; for *iwaru* cf. Speiser, JAOS 55 (1935) 436 n. 17. On *tišan* "very" in Hittite see [131]. The common Akk. *papāḫu* "cella, sacred precinct, etc." appears to have a Hurrian etymology [62]: of Hurrian origin seems to be also the agrarian term *šiluḫli* (gen.) which occurs in the Assyrian Laws B ii 8. (4) For Hurrianized syntax in Nuzi Akkadian see Speiser, AASOR 16 (1936) 136 ff. and Leo Oppenheim, AfO 11 (1936) 56 ff.; the latter study ascribes these foreign constructions to Elamite influence, but Oppenheim has since recognized the linguistic substratum at Nuzi as Hurrian; cf. now RHA 26 (1937) 58 ff.; ibid. 33 (1938) 7 ff.

8. The foregoing survey of the Hurrian material presupposes that all these disparate sources, spread over a wide area much of which was dominated by speakers of other and unrelated languages, and extending over many centuries, were linguistically homogeneous. This assumption will be substantiated in the succeeding chapters by examples from the entire field. In the meantime it is necessary to state that all the students concerned did not admit at once the essential unity of this material as it was gradually coming to light. The skepticism which they expressed had its basis in the comparative paucity of the material as a whole, the variety of subject matter, and the manifest differences in scripts and systems of writing. Recent progress in the study of Hurrian has served to overcome these obstacles. The problem reduces itself now chiefly to dialectal peculiarities. They are the inevitable corollary of the length of period and size of area affected, coupled with the remoteness of the respective Hurrian groups from their original centers and from one another.

A cautious attitude with regard the Ras Shamra vocabulary [7b] was voiced by Friedrich, Kleinasiatische Sprachdenkmäler (1932) 149. For a more recent view on the question of Hurrian dialects cf. Speiser, AASOR 16 (1936) 141 f. in line with earlier opinions expressed by Thureau-Dangin, Syria 12 (1931) 264 ff., and others. Bork's dissenting interpretation, Das Ukirutische (1938) 38 ff., called forth a thorough refutation by Friedrich, BChG (1939) 45 ff., who in withdrawing his previous objections gives the most complete statement on the subject yet published.

9. The question of the relation of Hurrian to other languages is as old as the initial studies of the Mitanni letter. It was clear, however, to scholars like Messerschmidt that substantial results by the combinatory method from within must precede any serious attempt at outside comparisons. For such results the Mitanni letter alone did not suffice. Bork's venturesome effort,

Mitannisprache (1909) 68 ff., was therefore doomed to failure; it operated with too many unknown quantities. Now that the situation has altered appreciably a tentative statement is not out of order.

Of the ancient languages of the Near East, Elamite was the first to be compared with Hurrian. Today it is necessary to deny the existence of a direct relationship between the two. As for Hattic, the language of Central Anatolia which preceded Hittite, too little is known as yet for any purposes. At all events, its predominantly prefixing character,[31] as compared with the exclusively suffixing structure of Hurrian, points to important underlying differences.

Conditions are much more encouraging with regard to Urartian, the pre-Indo-European language of Armenia. Correspondences in morphology, syntax,[32] and vocabulary bespeak a close connection with Hurrian. Since the extant records of Hurrian and Urartian respectively differ considerably in age, contents, and systems of writing, the grammatical differences which have been noted so far are not inconsistent with the above assumption.

Conclusive comparisons with modern Caucasic, in so far as these languages may be regarded as uniform in type,[33] are ruled out on chronological grounds and by the inchoate status of Caucasic linguistics. Die " Suffixübertragung," or repetition of the suffixes of the head with the dependent noun, a characteristic feature of Hurrian, is present also in Caucasic.[34] Moreover, I expect to demonstrate that the concept of the verb in Hurrian was passival, just as in Urartian and in Caucasic. Such correspondences suggest an ultimate similarity in the type of the languages concerned. But a direct relationship between Hurrian and any single group of Caucasic cannot be upheld at present, any more than it can be established between Hurrian and Elamite.

The connections between Hurrian and Urartian are summed up by Friedrich in ch. 9 of his BChG; see now also Orientalia 9 (1940) 211 ff. For a sketch of the grammar of Urartian see Friedrich, Einführung ins Urartäische (MVAeG 37.3 [1933]).

The Caucasic character of " Mitanni " was maintained by Bork (op. cit.) on insufficient and methodologically inadmissible grounds. It can be seen today, however, that he was on the right track. He erred in making his claims too sweeping and in basing them in part on unprovable correspondences between individual formatives.

For the concept of the Hurrian verb see Speiser, Studies in Hurrian Grammar, JAOS 59 (1939) 289 ff. The dissenting opinion of Goetze is presented in Lang. 16 (1940) 125 ff. The argument is reviewed in [246].

---

[31] Not entirely so, as is often asserted; cf. Friedrich, AfO 11 (1936) 78.

[32] In the passival orientation of the verb; for the situation in Urartian cf. Friedrich, Einführung ins Urartäische §§ 50, 82.

[33] Cf. A. Dirr, Einführung in das Studium der kaukasischen Sprachen (1928).

[34] Ibid. 355; cf. also Ex Oriente Lux 6.95. For its operation in Hurrian see [238].

II. ORTHOGRAPHIES AND PRONUNCIATION

10. The unusually wide distribution of Hurrian linguistic elements led to the recording of this material in a corresponding variety of forms. Today we are confronted with Hurrian sources preserved in such basically distinct systems of writing as the alphabetic script of Ras Shamra and the cuneiform syllabic script. What is more, the syllabic material is not uniform in itself as regards orthography. Unlike the case of the Hittite documents, e. g., we have to contend in the Hurrian texts with the individual characteristics of the Mâri syllabary and the Nuzi, Amarna, and Boghazköi syllabaries, not to mention sources of minor importance. An attempt at a reconstruction of the sounds of Hurrian must proceed, therefore, from the combined evidence of all these separate systems. It is a laborious task, but the situation has its advantages in the independent nature of the respective sources. In fact, recent progress in the study of Hurrian phonetics, and consequently also Hurrian phonology and morphology, is due in large measure to the heterogeneous character of the given orthographies.

Before the phonetic results are stated a few facts about the systems of writing concerned will have to be examined. We begin with the syllabaries.

11. A common feature of all Hurrian syllabic texts is their relative avoidance of ideograms, except in some proper names, and their sparing use of determinatives. Even the determinative for "god" may be omitted; it is lacking notably in the Mâri material. This custom introduces a sharp distinction between the Hurrian texts, including those from Boghazköi, and the Hittite documents. The modern student is deprived thereby of a valuable aid to the understanding of the context, which proved so important in the early stages of Hittite studies.

For the cuneiform syllabary and its subdivisions see Thureau-Dangin, Le Syllabaire Accadien (1926). The system here employed for transliterating syllabic values is that proposed ibid. and in its companion work, Les Homophones Sumériens (1929); accents and subnumerals are employed only to separate given homophones.

For the Hittite system of writing cf. Sturtevant, HG 34-86.

12. The Hurrian texts from Mâri show the same orthography as the local Akkadian documents. The sign BE has the value *úš*. Stop-signs are differentiated according to voice, just as in Old Babylonian. A minor departure is the writing of the sign Ú with four horizontal wedges alone, without the crossing verticals; the normal form appears, however, in Mâri 6. 7, 20.

12a. With the Akkadianizing system of the Mâri documents should be grouped the scattered systems employed for Hurrian proper names in (1) Babylonia up to and including the Hammurabi period; (2) Chagar Bazar, in the Hammurabi period; (3) early Nuzi, in a small number of texts which represent the first generation of the local Hurrian settlers (ca. 1500). Here belongs also (4) the vocabulary from Ras Shamra [7b]. All these groups agree in differentiating between voiced and voiceless stops and in employing the vowel sign Ú to the exclusion of U [28]. On the other hand, we have to subdivide Mâri and (4) as against the first three groups in the matter of expressing Hurrian *z̄* [45]. Whereas the former subdivision favors for this purpose *š*-signs, the latter prefers *z*-signs, at least in intervocalic position.

For the names from Babylonia and the first-generation names from Nuzi see now P. M. Purves, AJSL 57 (1940) 162 ff. Hurrian names from Chagar Bazar are included in the list compiled by C. J. Gadd, Iraq 7 (1940) 35 ff.

The use of Ú to the exclusion of U is reflected, as Goetze reminds me, in Old Babylonian, where there are very few exceptions to this rule.

For the Mâri forms cf. Thureau-Dangin, RA 36 (1939) 25. The tablets are numbered according to the order of their presentation, ibid. 2-21.

13. The remaining larger subdivisions of the main Hurrian syllabary may be regarded roughly as a single system which comprises the rest of the material from Nuzi, Amarna, and Boghazköi. This is not to minimize the existing differences among these three important groups. For our present purposes, however, these differences are less significant than the manifest correspondences which set apart the system as a whole not only from the orthography of Mâri but also from that of classical Old Babylonian. The common features include (1) virtual absence of special signs for the emphatics,[1] the sign QA being merely a homophone of *ka*; (2) rearrangement of the values attached to the signs for labials and sibilants;[2] and, most important of all, (3) indiscriminate use of the signs for stops in respect to voice. To be sure, such correspondences may be due in part to common underlying linguistic conditions. But the Mâri texts show that this is not a necessary corollary, and independent considerations suggest another reason for the orthographic connections just noted.

[1] The later sign ṢI (Berkooz 11) certainly has the old value *zé* in genuinely Hurrian elements from Nuzi: cf. *-zé-ni* (= normal *šenni*), AASOR 16 95. 21. Mit. employs ṢU/ZUM in the obscure word *ú-ú-*ZUM*-ki* (II 73-4, III 5-6), which Bork, Mitannisprache 20 n. 1) reads *u-u-rik-ki*.

[2] Labials: use of *p* in the value of *w* [52]; medial *b/w* for *-m-*, and conversely (Goetze, Lang. 14 134-5), note esp. ^{d}*Dab-ki-in-na-* KUB XXVII 42 rev. 13 for ^{d}*Damkina*. Sibilants: common use of double *š* for Hurrian *s̄* [44]; use of *š* for Hittite *s*, and interchange of *s/z* with one type of *š* in Nuzi (cf. JAOS 58 [1938] 189-92).

The reasons advanced by Thureau-Dangin (SA IV-V) for setting up his "syllabaire accado-hittite" apply also to the material from Nuzi, which was unknown at the time. For the Nuzi syllabary see M. Berkooz, The Nuzi Dialect of Akkadian: Orthography and Phonology, Language Dissertations 23 (1937) 9 ff. and Goetze, Lang. 14 (1938) 134-7; and now especially P. M. Purves, loc. cit.[3]

14. Paleographic arguments lead to the conclusion that the "Akkado-Hittite" syllabary goes back to a form which antedates the Old Babylonian script.[4] On orthographic-phonetic grounds the date of the prototype required must be pushed back to the Old Akkadian period. For it was then that signs with an initial *š*-value were used for the Akkadian descendant of the Semitic interdental spirant [ṯ], but not the sibilants [ś] and [š]; the same correlation is paralleled later in the case of Hurrian *š* [44].[5] The *s*-signs, which represent Semitic Samekh [s] in Old Babylonian, are used in Old Akkadian for [ś] and [š]; the same use is demonstrable in the Akkadian material from Nuzi, Amarna, and Boghazköi.[6] Finally, the Old Akkadian syllabary fails to differentiate with consistency between voiced and voiceless stops,[7] and lacks special signs for the emphatics. In short, the main characteristics of the Hurrian syllabary can be traced back to Old Akkadian times. They are not found in Old Babylonian, where the inherited system had been modified to suit the requirements of records in a Semitic language.

15. Since there are no conceivable grounds for postulating any Hittites in Lower Mesopotamia back in the third millennium, the Hittites must have learned their cuneiform script from some intermediate group.[8] We have seen that Hurrian names occur in the neighborhood of Akkad near the middle of the third millennium [7c]. Furthermore, the Hittite syllabary shows many significant correspondences with the Hurrian syllabary, not only from Boghazköi—which is natural—but from Amarna and, to a

[3] Purves has shown in this article that the earlier Nuzi scribes followed Akkadian principles of orthography (probably under the influence of an Akkadian school), whereas the later scribes, who constitute an overwhelming majority, employ an essentially un-Semitic system. The rest of the Nuzi material agrees substantially with the Amarna-Boghazköi system.

[4] Cf. E. Forrer, BoTU 1. 3; Goetze, ZA 40 (1931) 72 f.; B. Landsberger and H. G. Güterbock, AfO 12 (1937) 55 ff.

[5] Cf. Goetze, Lang. 14 (1938) 137, and Speiser, JAOS 58 (1938) 188-93.

[6] Ibid.

[7] Cf. Thureau-Dangin, SA V.

[8] It is an established fact that the Hittites did not get the cuneiform system from their nearest Akkadian neighbors, viz., the writers of the so-called Cappadocian documents, as might have been expected; cf. Sturtevant, HG 34-6; Götze, Kleinasien (1933) 63. The above evidence of Hurrian mediation supplies now a positive answer to the question. It is in full accord also with the known cultural facts; cf. Götze, Hethiter, Churriter und Assyrer (1936).

lesser degree, from Nuzi as well. Finally, it is now very probable that the Hittites borrowed from the Hurrians the method of distinguishing in writing between voiced and voiceless stops [79]. It follows that the Hittite syllabary is an adaptation of the Hurrian system of writing.

16. The Hurrian and Mâri syllabaries share the use of the sign PI for *w* followed by a vowel. When the next syllable begins with a consonant the vowel after *w* is often ambiguous; it is marked in such cases in the present transliteration by the symbol *ə*; e. g., *wə-ri-e-(e-)ta* Mit. III 13, 15; IV 39 "will know, see" (3 p. sg.). The texts from Boghazköi avoid this ambiguity by using the ligatures WA + A, WE + E, etc. The determining vowel is represented usually as a subscript sign; e. g., *ti-wi*$_i$*-na* "words, things" KUB VIII 61 obv. 8. Signs which represent a vowel followed by *b* (IB, UB) frequently indicate a syllable-closing *w*; e. g., I*Im-ma-aš-ku-un* IB-*ri e-we*$_e$*-er-ne* (14) [KUR] *Lu-ul-lu-e-ne-we*$_e$ "King Immashku, the king of the Lullu [-land] KUB XXVII 38 iv 13-4, where IB-*ri* is meant clearly for *ew-ri,* as is shown by the following *ewerne* and the Nuzi cognate *erwi.*

By the side of *w*$_u$ we find also the ligatures (marked as such by the smaller and subscript writing of the determining sign) *wu*$_{ú}$ and even *wu*$_{bu}$; cf d*Ku-li-it-ta-wu*$_{ú}$*-na* XXVII 37. 13, [*w*]*u*$_{ú}$*-ut-ti-la-a-e* ibid. 38 iv 21, and *ḫu-wu*$_{bu}$*-ur-ra-aḫ-ḫi-na* KBo. II 21. 3. For the special implications with regard to the Hurrian vowel system which result from the use of Ú and GU in the Mitanni letter see below [29].

17. From the standpoint of textual criticism the Mitanni letter is by far our most reliable source. This is due in part to the circumstance that large portions of this lengthy document are in an excellent state of preservation. Even more significant, however, is the fact that so large a portion of our total connected material [7a] is from the hand of a single scribe. When it is borne in mind that the Hurrian passages from Boghazköi—which at this writing do not equal the amount of material contained in the Mitanni letter [7a (2)]—are spread over many separate texts and betray the hand of more than one scribe, the textual value of the Tushratta letter assumes much added importance. Special emphasis must be placed, therefore, on the evidence from this source.

18. The survey of the available orthographies of Hurrian is concluded with a brief reference to the alphabetic material from Ras Shamra [7a (4)]. The system as a whole corresponds closely to that employed for the Ugaritic texts. Vowels are indicated only in connection with the three Aleph-signs (*'a, 'i/e, 'u*). The Hurrian passages use a special form of the consonant-sign *š* to represent a Hurrian sibilant or affricate which will be transcribed here as *ẑ*.[9] The voice-

[9] See Z. S. Harris, JAOS 55 (1935) 95 ff.

less counterpart of this sound [44] is introduced in the form of Ugaritic ṯ (also transcribed by some as s̈ and *θ*)[10]; in this study it will be rendered by s̄. The ambiguous Ugaritic sign *x*, which is employed for both *ġ* and *ż*, has in Hurrian only the value *ġ* [58]. Finally, the Hurrian alphabetic texts write the name of the goddess *Ša(w)uška* with the symbols *s̄ws̄k* and *s̄us̄k*[11]; the latter writing shows the use of (')*u* for *w*, i. e., the '*u*-sign is employed here as the second element in what seems to be the diphthong [aw].

For the script of Ras Shamra cf. Friedrich, Ras Shamra (Der Alte Orient 33. 1/2 [1933]) 18 ff. and J. A. Montgomery and Z. S. Harris, The Ras Shamra Mythological Texts (1935) 13-16.

19. The combined evidence of the orthographies noted above will now be consulted with a view to determining the speech-sounds of Hurrian so far as is possible at present. The difficulties inherent in the uneven nature of the available material and the variety of systems in which it has come down to us are increased by yet another factor. None of the orthographies before us had been intended originally for the use of Hurrian. The syllabic systems represent in each instance a second adjustment of the original Sumerian method of writing, following earlier modifications which had been made for the purposes of the Akkadian dialects involved. The Ras Shamra alphabet, on the other hand, had been devised for the use of Canaanite. What we have now, therefore, is a record of Hurrian sounds expressed through Semitic, or Semitized, symbols. Since the isolated position of Hurrian precludes for the present any external assistance from related quarters, our phonetic conclusions have to be of a general nature.

VOWELS

20. First we have to note that the syllabic texts employ pleonastic vowels for several purposes. For instance, there is a tendency in words beginning with a vowel to prefix the vowel-sign to a syllabic sign with initial vowel.[12] This is obvious in the name ^{URU}*A-ak-ka-te-ne-wə* "of Akkad" XXXI 3 rev. 8, and in such forms as *a-am-mu-li(-eš)* XXVII 42 obv. 14, rev. 14, 16 by the side of *am-mu-u-u-ša* Mit. I 95. More common is the pleonastic writing of *i*

[10] Cf. Speiser, JAOS 58 (1938) 175. I now write s̄ in place of *θ* because (1) s̄ does not imply a specific phonetic interpretation while (2) it marks suitably the voiceless counterpart of z̄.

[11] For the Ras Shamra occurrences of this name see Br. 570 and add RŠ XX B 8. The syllabic forms include, by the side of ^{d}*Ša-uš-kaš* Mit. I 76 and ^{d}*Ša-uš-ka-a-wə* Mit. III 98, such writings as ^{d}*IŠTAR-bu-uš-ga* XXVII 1 ii 44 and ^{d}*Ša-wu$_{u}$-uš-ga-an* ibid. 29 iv 15. For Nuzi *Šamuška* in proper names cf. [73].

[12] For similar conditions in Hittite cf. Sturtevant, HG 46.

or *e* in connection with syllable signs involving *i/e*. The Mitanni letter, e. g., which uses LI, NI, RI, IT, etc. ambiguously (to be read either with *i* or *e*), seeks to indicate the proper reading in a given instance—especially in medial position—by means of an additional vowel sign; cf. *ti-i-ḫa*-NI-*i-ten-na-a-an* III 27, alongside *ti-i-ḫa-ni-ten* III 24; *ú*-NI-*e*-IT-*ta* III 21 (the same writing of the suffix -*etta* [182] also in III 22, 29; IV 59, 60, 109). Accordingly, the unvarying orthography *pa-aš-ši-i*-IT- in the very common *pašitḫe* "envoy" Mit. I 53, 59, etc. may simply guard against a reading **pašetḫe*. The Boghazköi texts, on the other hand, prefer such guiding vowels initially. A case in point is *ewri* "lord, king"; cf. *e*-IB-*ri* (XXVII 43. 21, 46 i 13 ff., XXXI 3 rev. 7, 8, etc.) as against IB-*ri*- Mit. (I 85, III 48, etc.).

21. Another type of inorganic vowel appears in the writing of consonant-groups for which there could be only limited means of expression in a syllabary with an Akkadian background.[13] The pair ᵈ*Ku-ú-šu-uḫ* (XXVII 38 ii 11) and ᵈ*Ku-ú-ša-aḫ* (ibid. 16) shows that the name of this moon-god should be normalized as **Kušḫ*. Similarly, such spellings as *e-we$_e$-er-ne* (XXVII 38 iv 10 ff.), *e-bi-ir-ni* (ibid. 14), and *e-we-er-ni* (Mit. IV 127-8), contrasted with *e-bar-ni* (Br. 571 n. 1) and the simple stem *ewri* [20], point to an underlying **ewrne* "lordly." In proper names we get variant forms like *Ta-ḫab-* (AJSL 57 [1940] 175 n. 60), *Te-ḫib-*, *It-ḫib-*, and *Ut-ḫab-* (Nuzi passim), which may reflect an initial **tḫ*- (with -*ḫ*- representing apparently the voiced spirant *ġ* [58]).[14] It is logical therefore to suspect Hurrian of other similar consonant combinations, and also of other types of inorganic and indistinct vowels, but we have little positive evidence to go beyond surmises.

22. The question of vowel-quantity is a difficult one. We have seen [20] that double writing of vowels need not indicate vowel-length, contrary to the later usage in Akkadian. The same conclusion is indicated by variant spellings which mark a given vowel either by double or single writing. An interesting example is furnished by the word for "pure." The vowel of the first syllable occurs as follows: (1) double *e*, in *še-e-ḫa-la* XXVII 23 ii 5, iii 1; also (in other forms of this word) XXVII 24 i 5, 46 i 22, iv 22, 24-5, XXIX 8 ii 48-9, iv 23, 31; (2) single *e*, in *še-ḫa-a-la* XXVII 25. 15; *še-ḫa-la-a* XXIX 8 iv 8; also XXVII 23 ii 10; 46 i 15 ff., 28, iv 8, 10, XXIX 8 iii 53, iv 9, 25; (3) *i* in *ši-ḫa-a-la* XXIX 8 iv 27 and *ši-ḫa-la-am* XXVII 23 iii 7; (4) *a* in *ša-ḫa-la-šu* RŠ Voc. II 31, also 32.[15] It is significant that *še-e-ḫa-la*, *še-ḫa-a-la*, *še-ḫa-la-a*, and *ši-ḫa-a-la* are all found in precisely the same context, so that differences of stress cannot be held responsible for these particular variants.

[13] Cf. Sturtevant, HG 47.

[14] The variant forms which are indicated by the second group of letters (*ḫab*, *ḫib*; also *ḫub*) are not graphic, however, but morphologic [171]. For the possibility of other inorganic vowels in Hurrian cf. Friedrich, BChG 18 n. 3.

[15] For the meaning of this stem cf. Goetze, RHA 35 (1939) 106 n. 15.

We are thus forced to assume that the double *e* was in this case one of several efforts to indicate the quality of the vowel in question and that the writing had nothing to do with quantity.

The word *eni* "god" is written regularly with double (or triple) *e* in Boghazköi and in the Mitanni letter (cf. Mitanni-Studien 125), except in Mit. I 105. On the other hand, the Mâri texts write this word with single *e*, cf. 1. 32; 2. 12, 16; 6. 10 ff., 15, 19 f., 21. Since double writing of vowels is found in other Hurrian words from Mâri,[16] we have reason to doubt whether the *e* of *eni* was long (especially when *-nn-* follows, cf. *e-e-en-na-šu-uš* Mit. I 78, II 52, IV 117; cf. the analogous sequence in *an-za-a-an-nu-* [56]). It is significant, however, that the initial *e* of the very common word *e-ti* "sake, behalf" appears in the Mitanni letter invariably in single writing (Mitanni-Studien 125). As against this, Boghazköi furnishes one occurrence with *e* (VIII 61 obv. 6), the rest with *i*: *i-ti* XXIX 8 iv 11, 25; *i-ti-ib* XXVII 23 iii 7, 9, XXIX 8 ii 29, 31, 35, iii 34; *i-ti-pa* XXIX 8 ii 36, iv 12, 18; *i-te-pa* ibid. ii 41; *i-ti-ta* XXVII 24 iv 2, 42 rev. 14, 16; XXIX 8 iii 29, iv 3; here may belong also Mâri *i-te-ni* 1. 9 and *i-te-ni-e* 1. 6. It would appear that we have one quality of the vowel in Mit. *e-e-*: Mâri-Bogh. *e*, and another in Mit. *e*: Mâri-Bogh. *i*. There is thus reason for doubt that other double writings of vowels in the Mitanni letter need have special reference to quantity.

That the Mitanni letter observed some method in the writing of double vowels is shown by the following curious correlation. The pronominal elements *-tilla-* "we" and *-lla-* "they" are found with single *l* whenever the *-a* of the attached connective "and," which normally is written *-a-an*, appears single.[17] We get accordingly either *-til-la-a-an* or *-ti-la-an*; cf. the five occurrences in Mit. I 76-7 of which two are with double *l* and *a* while three show reduction of both the consonant and the vowel; for other occurrences of *-ti-la-an* cf. II 11, III 16, 108. Analogously, we read *ur-ḫal-la-a-an pal-ta-a-la-an* "they (are) true and authentic" IV 23, (29).[18] The same rule is reflected in *ma-a-*

[16] Mostly, however, with a known or probable semivowel. In 1. 17 *ša-ú-úš-a-an* is almost certainly a form of *Ša(w)uška*, cf. ibid. p. 10; the name is introduced by the epithet *al-la-a-e-en* "the lady" (1. 16), where the double *a* may represent *ay* (stem *allay*); *i-wa-a-ru* (3 rev. 20) is meant apparently to indicate the *a* after *w*; the *ú* in *a-ga-ú-um* (2. 4) and *šu-ú-wa-r*[*i*] (2. 13) seems to mark *w*-diphthongs, and the *i* in *ši-i-wə-ni* (5. 21) goes back to *y*, as is shown by other occurrences of *šey*(*a*) "river" (cf. Br. 563 n. 2); cf. also the single writing of the vowel in *ši-wə-na-šu-úš* (Mâri 5. 9). Distinctive double vowels are confined to the final syllables of *al-la-a-e-en* and *ša-ú-úš-a-an* (above, and *tu-wə-la-an-e-en* (Mâri 1. 31, 33, 37).

[17] Noted by Friedrich, BChG 27; but note *kàr-kut-tiš-ti-la-a-an* Mit. IV 120, *ya-ti--la-a-an* II 74.

[18] An exception to this rule is *ag-ge-la-a-an* Mit. IV 70, provided that we have here the same enclitic elements.

4

-an-na-a-an I 84: *ma-a-na-an* I 92 (in identical context). Even the suffix *-š*, which requires double writing in intervocalic position [44], is subject to reduction under the above conditions; contrast *še-e-ni-iw-wu-uš-ša-a-an* (II 12, 103, III 1, 13, 24, 49, IV 56, 59, 109) with *še-e-ni-iw-wə-ša-an* (IV 14 [?], 57) and *še-e-na-wə-ša-an* (I 84). This interdependence between consonant and vowel writing obviously cannot be without special significance; we do not know as yet, however, what that is; cf. [88].

Lastly, it is to be noted that vowels may be written triple. As examples of such writing (note also *e-e-en-na-šu-uš*, above) we have a number of perfect-forms of the third person singular in *-u-u-ša,* preceded by a third *-u-* which is written with the last consonant of the root; e.g., *gu-lu-u-u-ša* √"say" Mit. I 83, *ú-nu-u-u-ša* √"come" Mit. I 86, alongside *ta-a-(a)-nu-u-ša* √"do, make" Mit. I 85, III 106, *a-ku-u-ša* √"direct, grant" Mit. I 87, etc.; also *šu-ú-ú-ta* "to me" Mit. III 113, IV 24; *šu-u-u-wə* "of me" Mit. III 115; *e-ti-i-i-ta* "for (his) sake" Mit. I 82, III 53. It is important for an evaluation of such triple writings that all of the above types are paralleled in the Mitanni letter with double vowel only.[19] Internal evidence discourages the assumption that quantity was involved. The perfect-element *-ož/uš-*, which shows a repeated *u* in the third person, may be written with single *u* in the first person; cf. *ša-a-ru-ša-a-ú* √"request" Mit. III 91, *ta-a-nu-ša-a-ú* Mit. I 58, 70, IV 32. There is here no suggestion of etymological length. At best, we may suspect secondary length in the third person, which would have to be ascribed in that case to accentual conditions. In *e-ti-i-i-ta* original length is unlikely on account of Bogh. *i-ti-ta* (see above).[20] As for the pronominal forms of *šu-*, it is significant that double writing is also attested; cf. *šu-ú-ta* Mit. I 50 and *šu-u-wə* Mit. III 99.[21] Moreover, in the Mitanni letter *ú* and *u* reflect qualitative distinctions [31], so that the triple writing may simply be a means of emphasizing in each case a particular vocalic quality without any regard to quantity.

To sum up, there is no clear evidence that Hurrian possessed original long vowels. If such vowels did exist the syllabary failed to mark them in an unambiguous way. It is probable, however, that secondary length was indicated by triple writing, and perhaps also by some of the double forms.[22]

[19] Cf. Mitanni-Studien index ad loc.

[20] Messerschmidt 103 sees in the double (and triple) *i* of instances like *e-ti-i-i-ta* an infixed possessive pronoun of the third person singular. Friedrich, BChG 30, signifies his acceptance of this view by translating *e-ni-i-wə at-ta-i-i-wə* "seines Gottes, seines Vaters" (Mit. I 105 f.). The length indicated by the repeated writing of the vowel would result from contraction of the final vowel of the stem with *-*i* "his" [146].

[21] Little can be said at present about *šu-u-we-e* XXIX 8 iii 5 and *šu-u-wa-a-e* ibid. 14.

[22] A possible connection between stress-accent and double writing may be indicated by

It follows that a sequence like *a-a-i-i-e-e* Mit. IV 50 need have nothing to do with **āīē*, or **āyyē* [23] and probably indicates a simple *aye*. But the curious succession of three double vowels serves to emphasize the existing problem as to the real purpose of such combinations. The assumption of a strong stress accent cannot account by itself for pleonastic vowels in contiguous syllables. Considerations of quality are not likely to affect the writing of *a*. One other possible reason of pleonastic writing has yet to be suggested: to mark the full grade of a given vowel as against reduced grade or even writing of silent vowels to express consonant groups. The latter possibility has to be kept in mind when in a sequence of two open syllables the vowel of the first is consistently written double; e. g., *ti-i-ḫa-nu/i-* Mit. III 8, 20, 22, 24, 27, IV 49 may mark *tiḫ-* as opposed to *te-ḫu-u-u-ša* Mit. II 100 (prob. with initial **tḫ-* [/tǵ], cf. [21]. Similarly, the invariable writing of *šena* "brother" in the Mitanni letter as *še-e-na/i-* may have been a means of expressing a full-grade *e*, especially in the longer forms of this very common word; cf. also Friedrich, BChG 18 f. n. 3.[24]

23. For the expression of individual vowels the syllabary inherited signs for *a, e, i,* and *u* (separate or in combination with consonant values). The Ras Shamra alphabet was capable of indicating *a, i/e,*[25] and *u* in association with the glottal stop (ʾ). Since there is no evidence for assuming such a stop in Hurrian [26] the above Aleph-symbols are transliterated as plain vowels. It is worth noting that the Hurrian alphabetic texts use *a* and *u* initially, except for the single instance of *šušk* [18]; *i* occurs also medially.[27]

a

24. For initial *a* we have now a number of instances both in the alphabetic and the syllabic texts. Cf., e. g.,

aln "the Lady" [28] RŠ X 4. 51 = *al-la-a-e-en* Mâri 1. 16; *al-la-i* Mit. I 63; AASOR 16 49. 30 (and in Nuzi proper names).

awr- "field" RŠ X 4. 4, 30 = *a-wə-ri* RŠ Voc. IV 25; XXVII 1 iii 46 (also

d*Dab-ki-in-na* XXVII 42 rev. 13 for the normal d*Dam-ki-na*. There is certainly no other reason for the double *n*.

[23] A clear case of *i/y* is *a-ta-i-ta* "to (his) father" Mâri 5. 5; the form has to be analyzed as *atay-ta* on account of *t/d* in the suffix, cf. [33, 52]; note also *at-ta-ya-na-pa* Br. 560 and *atynpd* RŠ X 4. 4.

[24] In the Nuzi names this word appears normally as *še-en-ni* (prob. not the stem form, cf. [86a]), less often as *še-ni*; cf., e. g., AASOR 16 159 (under *Puḫi-še(n)ni*).

[25] The value *e* is assured for the Hurrian texts by RŠ *in* "god(s) = *eni, enna*; cf. Br. 559 f.

[26] The name d*Te-eš-šu-ub-ʾa-ri* (VS VII 72. 10), in the tablets from Dilbat dating from the Hammurabi period, is not evidence of Hurrian ʾ, cf. [78].

[27] Br. 574. The new material in RŠ XX does not alter this statement.

[28] For the meaning of this noun see Br. 571 n. 1; for other examples of initial *a* cf. ibid.

ILU or ÉL-Ú (same)

a number of instances with the particle *-ne* assimilated [66], e. g., *a-wa-ar-ri-we*$_e$ XXVII 1 ii 12); prob. also *a-wi-i-ru* Nuzi 101. 3.[29]

Medial and final *a*: *ta-a-(a-)nu-u-ša* √ "give" Mit. I 85, III 106; *ša-a-ru-u-ša* √ "request" Mit. III 1; *ka-ti-ya* √ "speak" VIII 61 rev. 7.

For the question of the quality of Hurrian *a* there may be a clue in the following parallel forms of three important stems: (1) *-me-/-ma-* "he," cf. *i-nu(-ú)-me-e-ni-i-in* Mit. I 13, II 123, 125, etc.: *i-nu-ú-ma-a-ni-i-in* Mit. IV 108; *in-na-me-e-ni-i-in* Mit. III 21: *in-na-ma-a-ni-i-in* Mit. II 6, 14, 16, etc.; (2) *-lla-/-lle-* "they," e. g., *i-i-al-la-a-ni-i-in* Mit. I 96, 104, etc.: *i-i-al-li-e-ni-i-in* Mit. I 98, II 19, etc.; (3) the relative particle *ya-/ye-*, cf. the examples just cited and *ya-me-e-ni-i-in*[[-*in*]] Mit. III 91: *i-i-e-me-e-ni-i-in* Mit. II 62. These forms occur frequently in parallel contexts and may be ultimately orthographic.[30] It is certain that there can be no other reason for the interchange of *a* and *e* in the variant writings of identical proper names from Nuzi, such as *E-kam-a-šu*: *E-kam-me-šu, Ḫu-bi-ta*: *Ḫu-bi-te,* and the like.[31] It appears therefore that Hurrian *a,* or at least one kind of *a* under certain conditions, inclined toward [e].[32]

e and *i*

25. It was indicated above [20, 22] that variant writings involving *e* and *i* do not imply that these vowels were not distinguished in pronunciation. On the contrary, the care with which the Mitanni letter differentiates between full-grade *e* and *i* (usually by means of double writing) establishes their individual character. Thus *eni* "god" definitely begins with *e,* as is shown by the double writing in Mit., the consistent use of *e* and not *i* in the entire syllabary (a possible exception is the derivative *i-ni-pa-a-i* XXIX 8 iii 39: *e-ne-[pa-]a-i* XXVII 42 rev. 21), and the significant *e-ne* which is glossed in an Akk. entry (CT XXV 18 ii 11) with *ilu* "god." Alphabetic *in* [23 n. 25] shows only that the sign (')*i* was used also for (')*e*. Cases like Mit. *e-ti* "behalf" (with one *e*) as against Bogh. *i-ti* [22] may imply that certain types of Hurrian *e* constituted a very close sound. Even then, however, that sound was

[29] Cf. C. H. Gordon, Orientalia 7 (1938) 21.

[30] Cf. Friedrich, BChG 24; but the sign IA may have the value *ye* as in Hittite; cf. Sturtevant, HG 54; see, however, 254.

[31] Cf. M. Berkooz, Lang. Dissert. 23 (1937) 26 f. See also below, n. 51.

[32] The interchange of *a* and *u* in Nuzi (Berkooz, op. cit. 28; cf. also Nuzi ᵈ*Ku-mu-ur-wə* AASOR 16 48. 1, 49. 1 and Bogh. ᵈ*Kumarbi*) and in the RŠ Voc. (cf. Thureau-Dangin, Syria 12 [1931] 262) may reflect an *o*-vowel which, unlike Mit., neither of these systems had a means of expressing; cf. [31].

[Cf. also v. Brandenstein, ZA 46. 88 and ibid. notes 1-2.]

different from Hurrian *i*. We need only contrast the verbal termination *-e-ta* (3 p. sg. of the future tense) with *-i-ta* (directive case with *i*-stems) to appreciate that difference. On orthographic grounds alone the verbal form *wə-ri-e-ta* √ "know" Mit. III 13, 16, IV 39 has to be kept apart from the nominal form *wə-ri-i-ta* Mit. I 91, III 94, and syntactic considerations bear out this analysis.[33] It may be stated as a general rule that writing with *i* does not preclude the reading *e* whereas even an occasional use of *e* eliminates the reading *i*.[34] Thus the common ᵈ*Ni-na-*(*at-*)*ta-* XXVII 1 ii 46 f., etc. (for occurrences in Hittite texts cf. Götze, Kleinasien 123) has to be read with *e* on account of ᵈ*Ne-na-at-ta-* XXV 42 v 2, in spite of ᵈ*Ni-i-na-at-ta* XXVII 16 iii 11.

This orthographic ambiguity is due in part to the fact that the syllabary inherited from Akkadian a number of signs (e. g., RI, LI) which could be read either with *i* or *e*. Even where unambiguous substitutes were available, as in the case of *ne* for NI, Hurrian prefers the more common but polyphonous sign; cf. e. g., the normal writing of the particle *-ne* with NI (*ti-iš-ni* "the heart" RŠ Voc. II 27) or NI-*e* (*ti-we-e-ni-e-wə* "of the word" Mit. I 110, and passim) as against the rare *-ne* (e. g., *e-we*$_e$*-er-ne* XXVII 38 iv 10 ff.). But in instances like *idi/edi* it is the quality of the initial vowel and not the orthography that must be held responsible for the variants.

26. After *k* and *g* the Hurrian syllabary could indicate an *e*-vowel by means of the sign GI with the values *ge* or *ke*. In other words, GI may be ambiguous as to the voiced or voiceless character of the consonant, but the vowel in question is *e* and not *i*. This usage was pointed out for the Mitanni letter by Bork (Mitannisprache 17) and for the Nuzi material by Berkooz (Lang. Dissert. 23. 10 f.; cf. also P. M. Purves, AJSL 57 [1940] 171). For examples from Bogh. cf. *ge-e-lu-* VII 30 7, 13; *ge-e-a-ši* XXVII 42 rev. 22; *ge-e-wa*$_a$ XXVII 38 i 11 and LUGAL-*ge-wa*$_a$*-a* XXXI rev. 10.

27. It follows that indisputable examples with *i* are not easy to establish unless the orthography comes to our aid with frequent use of the double writing. Even then we have to discount initial occurrences as instances of *y-* or *yi-*. Medially, *i* is well represented in the common element *-ni-i-in* (perh. "indeed"[35]) Mit. I 74 f., etc.; cf. also *u-u-mi-i-ni* "land" Mit. I 90, II 69 etc., and for the Bogh. occurrences see XXVII p. III.[36] The rare final double *i* is exemplified in *pa-li-i* Mit. II 56, *pa-a-ḫi-i*, XXVII 44. 4.

[33] Verbs in *-e-ta* require a subject in the *š*-case [195] which is not necessary, of course, with *wə-ri-i-ta*.

[34] For the same orthographic principle in Hittite cf. Sturtevant, HG 51. That Hurrian *e* was a close sound is suggested by the *e/i* interchange in the onomastic material; cf. Purves, AJSL 57. 181 n. 96.

[35] Cf. JAOS 59 (1939) 303.

[36] The form *ú-me-in-ni-bi-na* XXVII 1 ii 29 (with *e/i*) cannot be used as an argument against the reading with *i* in view of the invariable double *i* in the Mitanni letter (over

Since Hurrian *e*, or at least some forms of it, inclined toward [i], the question about the quality of Hurrian *i* is in order. Frequent interchange of *i* and *u* may throw some light on this point. Examples of this variation are given by Thureau-Dangin (Syria 12 [1931] 262—fr. RŠ Voc.), Goetze, Lang. 14 (1938) 139 n. 45, and Berkooz (op. cit. 34f.—Nuzi names); cf. also P. M. Purves, loc. cit. 175 n. 60. It is true that cases like *ti-bu-ša* (RŠ Voc. I 21) and *tu-bu-e* (ibid. II 23), both from a root meaning "strong," may indicate no more than a Shwa in the first syllable; but *I-ri̯-ya* alongside *I-ru̯-ya* (Berkooz, op. cit. 35) cannot be dismissed on similar grounds. Berkooz draws, therefore, the conclusion that an underlying sound [ü] may have to be assumed in such cases (ibid. 35). This assumption seems to be supported by the very interesting juxtaposition of *nu-i-wa*$_a$*-al-la* XXVII 42 rev. 12 and *nu-u-ya-al* XXIX 8 iii 30, in parallel contexts. The orthographic variants *-uiwa-*: *-uuya-* favor a sequence [-ü-a], or the like. If this supposition is correct, it is probable that Hurrian *i* in general was close to the sound [ü]. Note also especially the changes listed in [61] and for *i/unu-* cf. [127]. For the present, however, these deductions constitute no more than a working hypothesis.[38]

u and *o*

28. In addition to a number of syllabic signs containing *u* Hurrian took over from the Akkadian syllabary the vowel-signs Ú and U, both of which had the value *u*. There is no example with U in the extant Mâri texts, the proper names from Chagar Bazar,[39] and the vocabulary from Ras Shamra[40]; in the Nuzi names the sign is exceedingly rare.[41] It follows that none of these

40 examples). All that the Bogh. writing shows is that the sign ME had also the value *mi*, or that before *-nn- i* changed to *e*. For a clear indication of *e* we should require a form **u-me-e-*.

[37] The question as to the precise nature of the vowel in *e/i*-stems does not admit as yet of a clear-cut answer. With *ti-we* "word," e. g., we get in Mit. *ti-we-e-e* I 80, *ti-we-e-ni-en* IV 33, *ti-we-e-ma-a-an* IV 1, *ti-we-e-e-na* I 73, 99, etc.; but *ti-wi-i-wa-an* II 84; cf. also *ti-wi*$_i$*-na* VIII 61 obv. 8. Before the suffix *-ta* we get *i*, e. g., *e-ti-i-i-ta* Mit. I 82, 99, etc.; the same holds of *-wə*: *e-ti-i-wə* Mit III 55; cf. also *i-ti-pa*: *i-te-pa* [22]. It is a question therefore whether some cases take *-e* while others take *-i*, and whether this distribution is due to morphologic or phonetic causes. Some of the above examples of repeated *-i-* are due, however, to a special suffix, cf. [69], [104 n. 19], and [146]. See also [104].

[38] Another case in point is ^{d}*Na-ra-am-zu-un* XXVII 38 iii 18 for Akk. *Narâm-Sin.* The variant is easily explained on the assumption that the Hurrians pronounced foreign [i] as [ü], which they would write either *u* or *i*.

[39] Iraq 7 (1940) 35 ff. To judge from the copies at the end of the article, Gadd transcribes Ú as *u*, which does not invalidate the above statement.

[40] In other words, the syllabaries which differentiate between voiced and voiceless stops also employ Ú to the exclusion of U; cf. [12a].

[41] Cf. Berkooz, Lang. Dissert. 23. 12. The Nuzi texts use also the sign Ù (ibid. 12 f.) in a small number of special cases, e. g., *Ḫa-ni-ù*, *Ki-ik-ki-ù*, *Ta-a-a-ù-ki*. Berkooz regards these writings as evidence for a glottal stop in Hurrian. This interpretation is unduly specific. There are no grounds for positing an etymological [']. Moreover, other

groups differentiated in writing between *u* and *o*. The Boghazköi documents employ both Ú and U; as a rule, the former sign is used initially, the latter medially, while no preference for either sign is apparent in final position.[42] This distribution does not suggest a difference in the pronunciation of the two signs, and occasional variant writings bear this out; note *ú-mi-ni-*: *u-mi-ni-* "land" (cf. v. Brandenstein, XXVII p. III) and *ši-i-u-um-mi-ni* XXVII 23 ii 5, 8: *ši-ú-um-mi-ni* ibid. 7; see also [30 n. 47].

Attention should be called also to the form of the complementary *u*-sign in ligatures with *wu*. By the side of the usual *wu*$_u$ we get *ú* in *ᵈKu-li-it-ta-wu*$_u$*-na* XXVII 37. 13 and [*w*]*u*$_{ú}$*-ut-ti-la-a-e* XXVII 38 iv 21 [16]; for the reading of the latter see [166 n. 152].

[The interchange of U and Ú in Bogh. is apparently responsible for v. Brandenstein's mistaken assertion (cf. ZA 46. 84 n. 2) that these writings were non-distinctive throughout; see below [44].

29. The situation is different, however, in the Mitanni letter. Here too both signs are used and, owing to the prevalence of double writing, both occur frequently. Yet there are no variant writings in forms which constitute exact duplicates.[43] On the other hand, in a number of stems and grammatical elements we find consistent employment either of Ú or U with not a single exception. Moreover, the syllabic sign KU invariably takes U as a complementary vowel, never Ú, wheras GU can be augmented only by Ú; obviously, therefore, KU and GU differed not so much in the value of the initial consonant as in that of the following vowel, thus behaving analogously to KI: GI [26]. For this reason Bork concluded as far back as 1909 that Ú and U represented two distinct vocalic values and that the latter was in all likelihood *o*.[44] Today we are in a position to corroborate Bork's view and give it additional support.

writings of the last-cited name (*Ta-a-a-ú-ki*; cf. AASOR 16 163 and see above [7c n. 27]) point to a reading *Tayug/ki*. Nuzi Ú may indicate the glide between an *u*-vowel and a preceding vowel, the nature of this glide depending on the quality of the first vowel. Cf. also *nu-i-wa*$_a$*-al-la* XXVII 42 rev. 12: *nu-u-ya-al* XXIX 8 iii 30 [27]; *ḫi-*(*i-*)*ya-ru-un-na* XXV 45. 6, XXVII 14 iii 4: *ḫé-pa-ru-un-na* XXVII 16 iii 12 [32], and note alphabetic *šwšk*: *šušk* [18].

42 Both signs occur at the end of the form *a-ša-aš-te-du-u-ú* VIII 61 obv. 7. The distribution and interchange of the *u*-signs in Boghazköi Hurrian are paralleled in the Hittite texts; cf. Sturtevant HG 52 ff.

43 Bork (Mitannisprache 14 f.) cites two exceptions to this rule. One is *u-u-lu-Ú-ḫa-a-ti-la-an* Mit. III 16, alongside *u-u-lu-u̯-ḫe-wa-a-ti-la-an* II 11; the tablet gives, however, *u* in both instances. The other is *šu-uk-ku-u̯-ut-ti* II 68, contrasted with *šug-gu-ú̯-ud-du-u-ḫa* II 70, III 108. Here the variants are cited correctly, but the latter form contains an added adverbial element -(*o*)*ḫa* which might well account for the vocalic change involved.

44 Ibid. 14-9.

30. A few representative examples will first be in order. For initial *u* we may adduce once more *u-u-mi-i-ni* "land" which occurs (with double *u*) over 40 times (including plural forms); cf., e. g., Mit. III 6, 7. Another good example is *u-u-li* "other," pl. *u-u-ul-la* (12 sure instances) II 79, 82, etc. Medial *u* is abundantly evidenced in the perfect-element *-ož-* (over 20 cases with repeated *u*); cf. *a-ru-u-u-ša* √"give" I 46, *pa-aš-šu-u-u-ša* √"send" II 108, *ta-a-nu-u-ša-a-aš-še-na* √"do" I 100, 105, etc. Final *u* is implied in the *-ku* of forms like *ú-ru-uk-ku* √"be present (?)"[45] II 99, 101, III 46, 123; cf. [29]

For initial *ú* cf. the common *ú-(ú-)n-* "go"[46] I 86, II 14, etc. Medial *ú* is represented in *i-nu-ú-* "as" I 74 f., etc.; furthermore, before the suffix *-šš-* (e. g., II 25, 91, III 95 f., IV 38), and the pronominal enclitics *-tta-* and *-lla-* when these enclitics are added to a nominal form in *-iwwu(š)* "meus"; e. g., *še-e-ni-iw-wu-ú-ul-la-a-an* I 107, 113, etc. For final *ú* we have numerous examples in the ending of the 1. p. sg. of transitive verbs; e. g., *pa-la-a-ú* √"ask" (pres.) III 91, 93; *ka-te-e-ta-ú* √"tell" (fut.) III 99; *ta-a-nu-ša-a-ú* √"do" (pret.) I 58, IV 32.

In none of these groups do we find variant forms with the other *u*-vowel. The same stem may appear with *ú* or *u*, but only one or the other may be used with a given suffix; e. g., the oblique stem of the pronoun "I," viz., *šu-*, appears with *-ú-* in *šu-ú-(ú-)ta* "to me" I 50, III 113, IV 24 (also *šu-ú-ú-ra* "with me" II 93), but *šu-u-(u-)we* "of me" III 99, 115.[47] Here the choice of the vowel obviously depends on the following suffix.[48]

31. When we next inquire about the nature of the vowels which are written *ú* and *u* respectively, the problem with regard to the former can be solved promptly by virtue of the fact that *ú* is used at times for the semivowel *w* (cf. [35]), whereas *u* is never so employed. It follows that *ú* can be nothing other than a sound close to [u]. This will explain the exclusive, or all but exclusive,

[45] Cf. JAOS 58 (1938) 301.

[46] See Goetze, Lang. 15 (1939) 215 ff.

[47] Cf. Speiser, JAOS 60 (1940) 264 ff. If *šu-u-ta* VBoT 59 ii 12 and *šu-ú-wə* ibid. 14 are also pertinent in this connection, we may have here additional proof that Bogh. and Mit. differed in the writing of *u/o*-vowels. Note also *a-ru-ú-ši-ik-ki* (loc. cit. 13) as against the invariable Mit. *u* in the same formative (*-uš*).

[48] The consistency with which given consonants take either a preceding *ú* or *u*, to the exclusion of the alternate writing, enables us in some instances to restore breaks in the text. Thus the current restoration *še-e-ni-iw-wu-ú-š[a-a-a]n* Mit. I 9 (similarly II 83 f.), which is made by Friedrich and his predecessors, is rendered suspect by the fact that we find otherwise the sequences *ú-šš* and *u-š*, but not the reverse. But *ú* is permissible before *r*, and a careful study of the copy and the context will show that the supplementation *-r[a-* "with" is not only possible textually but also preferable contextually.

use of *ú* in Mâri, Chagar Bazar, Nuzi, and the Ras Shamra syllabary [28]; for in syllabaries under Akkadian influence we expect a reflection of Akkadian usage, which recognized [u] but not any specific form of *o*.

Less simple is a decision with regard to *u*. Since the Boghazköi orthography points, by its interchange of *ú* and *u* and by the employment of *ú* for Mit. *u*, to a value for Mit. *u* that was close to [u], the obvious choice lies between [ü] and some form of *o*. The former may now be eliminated on the ground that this vowel suggests itself for the sound represented by *i* and *i-i* [27]. We are left therefore with *o* as the most likely alternative.

In partial support of this assumption may be cited the interchange of *a* and *u* in Nuzi and in the vocabulary from Ras Shamra (see above, note 32). Another bit of indirect evidence is furnished by the use of Ú for *u* and U for *o* in Nippur; cf. most recently A. Poebel, Studies in Akkadian Grammar (1939) 117 n. 1. We would thus have here another link between the Hurrian syllabary and an old Akkadian source; cf. [14].

If Mitanni Hurrian made extensive use of the *o*-sound, it is improbable that this sound was absent from the other Hurrian groups. We should have to assume strong foreign influence in order to account for so serious a modification of the inherited sound-pattern. It follows that Bogh. Hurrian cannot be charged with the lack of *o* solely on the ground that its orthography followed the Hittite usage in interchanging the vowel signs *ú* and *u*. The probability remains that the Hurrian dialect from Anatolia, and perhaps also other Hurrian dialects in outlying territories, had the same basic vowel-pattern as Mitanni Hurrian. The latter had developed, however, methods of reducing that pattern to writing which proved to be more effective than the methods elsewhere employed.

Semivowels and Diphthongs

32. At the beginning of a syllable *y* followed by *a* could be expressed by the syllabic sign *ya*; e. g., *ya-(a-)la-an* "those which" Mit. II 73, 82, 92. The corresponding form *i-i-al-la/e-* Mit. I 96, 98, 104, etc. shows that *y-* could be also written *i-i-*. Accordingly, *i-i-e-ma-a-ni-i-in* Mit. II 101, IV 27 contains *ye-*. The juxtaposition of *i-i-im-ma-ma-an* Mit. II 98: *i-i-um-mi-im-ma-ma-an* ibid. 99 yields the values *yi-* and *yu-*.

33. Medial *-i-i-* and *-i-*, when accompanied by a dissimilar vowel, represents a syllable-closing or ambisyllabic *y*. E. g., *at-ta-i-i-wə* Mit. I 87, 106, *at-ta-i-wu-uš* Mit. III 67; *a-ta-i-ta* Mâri 5. 5; alphabetic *atynp-* RŠ X 4. 4, all from *a(t)tay-* "father." The Bogh. form *at-ta-ya-na-pa* (Br. 560 shows that [-ay] could be written *-a-ya-*, with a silent *a* at the end. For *y* : *w* (wr. *p*) cf. wr. *ḫiyarunna* : *ḫeparunna* [28 n. 41].

34. In the case of *w* the situation is complicated by the fact that signs containing *w*, *b*, and *p* may be used interchangeably. Thus we get ^{d}*Ša-uš-ka-* Mit. I 76, III 98, ^{d}*Ša-wu*$_{u}$*-uš-ga-* XXVII 29 iv 15, *IŠTAR-bu-uš-ga* XXVII 1 ii 44, alongside RŠ *šušk* and *šwšk,* cf. [18]; here the semivowel is assured by the alphabetic variants, as it is also in *awari* "field" and *ewri* "lord" (for examples from RŠ see Br. 571). Consistent writing with *w* in *ḫawur-* "earth" (Mâri 6. 16; XXVII 28 iv 7, 38 ii 10, 15, iv 30, etc.) also suggests a semivowel.[49] But the nature of the labial in *ḫu-bu-u-ur-ra* KBo. II 21 2: *ḫu-wu*$_{bu}$*-ur-ra-* ibid. 3, or in *ni-bu-u-ši-* XXVII 42 rev. 22: *ni-wu*$_{u}$*-u-ši-* XXIX 8 iii 42 is doubtful, and a labial spirant is virtually certain in *p/waḫru* "good" on account of the orthographic variation *pa*: *wə* [50]; the same may be said of *p/wand-* "right"; cf. *pa-an-ti-* XXVII 42 rev. 23, XXIX 8 iii 43: *Wandi-* in proper names (e. g., AASOR 16 167).[51] The same uncertainty attaches, of course, to forms written with syllabic signs which express a final labial, inasmuch as there is no distinction in such instances among *-p, -b,* and *-w.*

35. There was, however, another method to represent the semivowel [w] and apparently also the spirant [f]. The nominal suffixes *-we* and *-wa* are expressed after [u] by means of the sign *-ú*; e. g., *a-gu-ú-e* "of the other" Mit. IV 123; *a-gu-ú-a* "to the other" Mit. I 81; *an-du-ú-e*(*-e*)- "of that" Mit. II 63, 100, III 9. Since the same suffixes appear as [y] after *-i,* e. g., *e-ti-i-e-e* Mit. IV 19, 22, 25, 28, cf. [33], it follows that the above *ú* also represents a semivowel, hence [w].

The value [f] is possible in the numerous occurrences of *ú* after the digraph *-iw-wə* "mine," which represents a single syllable ending in a voiceless labial spirant [53]. Similarly, the suffix of transitives referring to an agent in 1 p. was in all probability [-af]; it is written *-a-ú* [30, 195].

As for initial *ú* followed by a dissimilar vowel, e. g., *ú-a-du-ra-an-* Mit. I 65, II 15, III 68 f., either [w] or [f] is possible. The latter phoneme is a distinct probability with written *ú-ú* (i. e., [fu]). Cf. initially the verb *ú-ú-r-* "hold fast, desire," which is distinct from the intransitive *ú-r-* "take place, be present";[52] medially, in forms like *a-ru-u-ša-ú-ú-un* Mit. III 2 (for *-afun*), cf. [195].

[49] The Bogh. form *ḫa-!-ur-ni-ya* Br. 571 n. 1 may simply be an error due to an accidental omission of *-wu-*. If the form is correct, however, the omission would serve to establish the semivowel, since a spirant could scarcely be left out. The form *ḫa-bur-ni-wi*$_{i}$ VII 58 ii 11 employs the sign BUR in the value *wur*; see below, note 92. [For a fuller list of occurrences see now ZA 46. 86 f.]

[50] For the meaning and occurrences of this common word see v. Brandenstein, Orientalia 8 (1939) 82 ff. New examples are SAL*Pa-aḫ-ri-še-ḫi-ir-ni* and SAL*Pa-aḫ-ri-u-zu-wa* from Chagar Bazar (Iraq 7 [1940] 40).

[51] Here belongs also the name *Bi-en-te-ši-na/Ba-an-di-ši-*(*in-*)*ni* (E. Weidner, Boghazköi-Studien 8 [1923] 126 n. 3 = Nuzi *Wandi-ženni*; because of this variation the form *pend-* (Mit. I 103, II 5; XXVII 46 obv. i 22) may also be adduced; cf. Friedrich, RHA 35 (1939) 99 n. 19. Note also Goetze, Kizzuratna (1940) 6 n. 23.

[52] Cf. JAOS 59 (1939) 299 ff.

Liquids and Nasals

36. The Hurrian liquids *l* and *r* and the nasals *m* and *n* pattern with the vowels, but against the other consonants and the semivowels, in that they cause an immediately following stop to become voiced. This is clear from instances in the alphabetic texts in which the absence of an intervening vowel is established by syllabic equivalents. Cf., e. g., *ard-* "city" = *arde*; *ḫlb* = URU*Ḫalba*;[53] in these examples the alphabetic writing is explicit with regard to the voiced character of the stops, while the syllabic orthography is ambiguous on that point but decisive as to lack of vowels. The same conditions are observed in those syllabic texts which recognize dichotomy of stops with regard to voice (documents of the Hammurabi period and before; early Nuzi texts[54]; the vocabulary from Ras Shamra [12a]); e. g., *ši-in-di ša-la-ar-di* Mâri 5. 11 *nu-du-un-da* 5. 9; Nuzi *Túr-ma-ar-di, A-ri-lu-um-di,* and *Pa-an-di-ya*[55]; *zu-bal-gi* RŠ Voc. II 33. To this extent at least we have to regard the Hurrian liquids and nasals as vocalic sonants.

37. Interchange between *l* and *n* or *r* is attested frequently in proper names.[56] Variant writings of the same name occur at times on the same tablet. This shows that the variation was orthographic and not phonologic; it must have been due to a close phonetic connection between the sounds involved—more so than was the case in Akkadian. The same conclusion has been drawn from the occurrence of *t*[*e*]*-u-u-la-e* Mit. IV 130, alongside the common *te-u-u-na-e* "much" Mit. 49, 55, etc; but see [175 (3)].

It is possible, but by no means certain, that the Boghazköi documents furnish similar indications of orthographic variation. Interchange between *n* and *l* is found, e. g., in *ni-bu-u-ši-in-na-a-in* XXVII 42 rev. 22: *ni-wu*$_u$*-u-ši-el-la-an-ti-in* XXIX 8 iii 42; [*ḫu-u*]*-ši-in-na-an-ti* XXVII 42 rev. 19: *ḫu-u-ši-el-la-an-ti-in* XXIX 8 iii 38; *a-*[*ru-ši-*]*-in-na-a-in* XXVII 42 rev. 13: *a-ru-ši-el-la-a-im* XXIX 8 iii 34. For each *-nn-* in one text we have *-ll-* in the other. A difference in number (such as is found in *šu*(*w*)*annaman* [sg.]: *šu*(*w*)*allaman* [pl., cf. Friedrich, BChG 4 f.]) seems to be precluded by the second pair of examples, both of which have the same subjects in the plural (*enna*^{na}*-šu-uš* etc.). Since the passages in question are otherwise parallel a difference in tense is scarcely likely; cf. [189-90] for further discussion of these elements. See also [71].

For d*Nu-pa-ti-ig* = d*Lu-pa-ki-ta* (XXVII 13 i 6) cf. Br. 566.

38. In initial position both *l* and *r* are very rare in Hurrian. This is true

[53] For these equivalents see Br. 570 ff. and Friedrich, Analecta Orientalia 12 (1935) 130. The above pattern was first observed by the latter, loc. cit.

[54] See P. M. Purves, AJSL 57 (1940) 174 ff.

[55] Ibid. 180. Goetze's statement (Orientalia 9 [1940] 223) that the voicing of stops after *n* is not proved is now answered by the evidence from Mâri and Nuzi.

[56] Cf. Berkooz, Lang. Dissert. 23. 57 ff.

especially of *r*, which cannot be identified with certainty as an initial element in proper names. The fact that initial *r* is absent in Hittite [57] has been cited as an apparent parallel.[58] The correspondence is not complete, however, since we do find clear instances of initial RI in Boghazköi. To be sure, this sign is used in the Hurrian syllabary for *t/dal* as well as *ri* and so the reading of this sign in RI-*ta-an* XII 44 ii 11 is rightly regarded as uncertain.[59] But RI-*ip-pa* XXVII 46 iv 21 (unless it is incomplete; cf. *a-a-ri-ip-pa* XXVII 42 rev. 17) seems to point to an initial *ri-* rather than *dal-*. Nevertheless, it cannot be asserted as yet that the presence of *r-* may be taken for granted in words of unquestionably Hurrian origin. It is clear, of course, that *rapšu* "wide" RŠ Voc. iv 14 is a loanword from Akkadian.

39. Consistent double writing of liquids and nasals indicates length. This is evident from the fact that the result of assimilation [66] is invariably written double. Elsewhere double and single writings may vary; cf. [22] and note in connection with *-til(l)a* "we" the new example *š[a]-a[t]-ti-la* "we together(?)" [60] Mâri 6. 13.[61] For similar variation in Boghazköi note, e. g., *a-za-mi-na* XXVII 8 rev. 5: *a-za-am-mi-na* ibid. 4 and XXVII 4. 5; [*ša*]*-la--a-ni* XXVII 4. 8: *ša-(a-)la-an-ni* XXVII 1 iii 7, 8 rev. 8. That these writings need not indicate necessarily etymological length is evident from ^{d}*Dab-ki-in-na-aš* XXVII 42 rev. 13 as against ^{d}*Dam-ki-na-aš* XXV 42 v 6, XXIX 8 iii 33. But Mâri *al-la-a-e-en* (1. 16) and *ḫi-il-li-in* (6. 10 f.), alongside the consistent double *ll* in *allay* throughout the syllabary and the common and invariable *ḫill-* in Mit. (but *ḫi-li-šu* RŠ Voc. I 150) suggests long *l* in the middle of stems.

Sibilants

40. The combined Hurrian material yields clear evidence of four distinct sounds within the sibilant range; there are transcribed here as *s*, *z*, *š*, and *ž* respectively. A fifth member of this group, viz., *ṣ*, seems to occur in the alphabetic texts from Ras Shamra; cf. ibid. X 7. 6; XX A 13-15. But the first of these instances may be due to scribal error [62] and the remaining

[57] Cf. Sturtevant, HG 136.

[58] See Berkooz, op. cit. 57 n. 113.

[59] Cf. Friedrich, Kleinasiatische Sprachdenkmäler 33 n. 9. The same is true of RI-*mi-el-k*[*u*?] VBoT 59 iii 8; cf. Br. 576.

[60] Cf. Speiser, JAOS 59 (1939) 306 n. 52.

[61] Thureau-Dangin (RA 36 [1939] 23) analyzes this form as *ša-a-at-ti*+ the pronoun *-la* of the third person pl. I would see in it the enclitic *-ti(l)la-* of the first person pl., with haplologic loss of *-ti-*, in view of the fact that "they together" is expressed by *ša-⟨at-⟩ta̱-a-al-la-(an)* Mit. IV 62. Cf. [91].

[62] Cf. H̱. Bauer, OLZ 1934. 475 n. 2; for the Hurrian sibilants in general cf. Speiser, JAOS 58 (1938) 175-93.

occurrences are found in a fragmentary passage on which we cannot base any conclusions whatever. Since unambiguous examples of *ṣ* are lacking in the available syllabic texts,[63] we have to leave to the future to decide whether such a sound was indeed present in Hurrian.

41. Only the alphabetic texts have individual symbols for the four Hurrian sibilants established thus far. To represent these sounds, the syllabary had but three sets of signs at its disposal: those containing *s, z,* and *š*; a fourth possible set, viz., the emphatics, had not come into use at the time of the formation of the Hurrian syllabary [14]. The need to render four separate sounds with only three sets of signs led to compromise-orthographies which differ with the individual sources. In Chagar Bazar *z*-signs were used for [z] as well as *z̄*. In the names from Babylonia and Nuzi *z̄* may be written either *š* or *z*; the sound [z] is rendered, of course, with *z*-signs, but *s*-signs may also be used for the same purpose [43]. In Mâri, the Mitanni letter, the vocabulary from Ras Shamra, and the Boghazköi texts *š*-signs are employed both for *s̄* and *z̄*, so that the *z*-set is freed for the exclusive representation of [z]

These crossing orthographies may seem confusing at first glance, but they are not inconsistent within themselves. Each has to be evaluated according to its own prevailing usage and the results can then be checked against the independent evidence of other Hurrian systems of writing.

For an earlier account of this subject see above, note 62; for the Nuzi system cf. also Goetze, Lang. 14 (1938) 136.

s

42. To judge from the available material, this sound was relatively rare in Hurrian. For alphabetic occurrences cf. *psm* RŠ X 4 53; *usgr* RŠ XX A 3; for the uncertain *sbl* RŠ X 4. 8 cf. JAOS 58 (1938) 177. Mâri furnishes a (verbal?) stem with *s* in *i-si* 5. 1, 5 and *i-su-di-iš* 5. 6; note also *ma-ru-sa* 5. 15. In Mit. we get the fairly common verb *pis-* "rejoice," cf. I 79, II 55, etc.; also the stem *ḫisuḫ-* "vex" III 76, 85, etc. both with invariable *s*.

We have no way at present to establish the underlying phonetic value. In the Nuzi texts *s*-signs are used as variant writings of Akk. *š* < Sem. [š/ś], but never for š < Sem. [ṯ].[64] On the other hand, Sem. [s] is written in Nuzi with *z*-signs.[65] It appears, therefore, that original Sem. [s] was pronounced in Nuzi as a voiced sibilant or perhaps an affricate [ts], whereas the pronunciation of *s*-signs inclined towards [š] or [ś]; there is no evidence that a pure [s] was recognized by the Nuzians. The same need not be true, of course, of Hurrian sounds in Mâri, Mitanni, or Ugarit. Nevertheless, it is

[63] See above [13 n. 1].

[64] Cf. Speiser, JAOS 58 (1938) 187 ff.

[65] Cf. Goetze, Lang. 14 (1938) 136.

probable that Hurrian *s*, as recorded in those centers, was different from Semitic [s].

There is nothing to show how Hurrian *s* was represented in Boghazköi. It is logical, however, to assume that in such close contact with the Hittites both *s* and *š* would be expressed by means of *š*-signs.[66] That Akkadian [s] was written *z* (as in the Nuzi texts) may be seen from ᵈ*Na-ra-am-zu-un* XXVII 38 iii 18 for Akk. Narâm-Sin.

There are no instances of double *s*. Whether any phonetic significance attaches to this fact cannot be decided at present in view of the scarcity of examples which show this sound even in single writing.

z

43. This sound is reflected in all the Hurrian sources. Where the writing is unambiguous there is, of course, no confusion with other sibilants. This is true of the following sources: (a) The alphabetic texts; cf. e. g., *ḫzḫz* RŠ X 4. 24. (b) The Mitanni letter; e. g., *zu-gán* II 11, III 16, etc., *še-e-ni-iw-wu-ú-uz-zi* III 43. (c) Apparently, also the Boghazköi documents, e. g., *za-a-az-za-ri* XXVII 38 ii 25; (d) Mâri, cf. *ḫi-in-zu-ru-úš* 6. 7 (with parallels from Boghazköi and Nuzi, cf. RA 36 [1939] 22; and (e) the vocabulary from Ras Shamra, e. g., *zu-gi* II 19.

In Nuzi we find a number of proper names in which *z* appears consistently; e. g., *Zigi, Zili-*, etc.[67] Other names share a suffix which is characterized by *-zz-*, e. g., *A-pa-az-zi-ya, Tup-ki-iz-za*.[68] The occupational term *zi(l)lik-uḫlu* " witness "[69] likewise appears with *z* in all its occurrences. In all these instances the writing points obviously to the same kind of *z* which is reflected above under (a)-(e).

But *z* could serve also as a variant writing for *š*, e. g., in *I-š/zi-ib-ḫa-lu*,[70] both forms having as their purpose to render Hurrian *ž* [45]. The same method was employed in the texts from Chagar Bazar, as we shall see presently. Finally, Nuzi *z* represented Semitic [s], and this has its counterpart in the writing of Hurrian *-zz-* as *-ss-* in *A-gi-is-si* (BE XV 190 ii 31, an example from Nippur where the orthography is comparable to early Nuzi)[71] alongside Amarna *A-ki-iz-zi* (EA. p. 1557). It is clear, therefore, that in Nuzi and its analogues *z*-signs cannot be regarded as reflexes of the sound *z* without sufficient statistical or comparative evidence.

There is no proof that in the syllabic texts *-zz-* represented a phoneme dis-

[66] For the situation in Hittite see Sturtevant, HG 70.

[67] Cf. Berkooz, Lang. Dissert. 23. 61 f.

[68] See L. Oppenheim, WZKM 44 (1936) 206; cf. below [160].

[69] See C. H. Gordon, Orientalia 7 (1938) 60; Speiser, Lang. 14 (1938) 308; Goetze, Lang. 16 (1940) 170 f.

[70] Cf. JAOS 58 (1938) 190.

[71] See Purves, AJSL 57 (1940) 172.

tinct from *-z-*. Since we find *ḫa-az-zi-zi* XXIX 8 30 and *ḫa-zi-iz-*[*z*]*i-bal* XXVII 42 rev. 12 in parallel passages, it is reasonable to assume that with this particular sound double writing indicated length, and in this instance evidently secondary length.

It should be noted that v. Brandenstein, AfO 13 (1939) 58 ff. derives *ḫa-az-zi-zi* from Akk. *ḫss*. In that case one source of Hurrian *z* would have been Akk. Samekh.

With regard to pronunciation, *z* was probably a sound which resembled Semitic [z], to judge from the use of the corresponding symbols of the Akkadian and Ugaritic systems. If the only difference between Semitic [z] and [s] was one of voice, then Hurrian *z* : *s* did not constitute a similar pair of opposites; cf. [42].

s̄

44. This symbol is used here for a Hurrian sound which the alphabetic texts wrote with the sign for Ugaritic *ṯ* (transcribed thus far as *ṡ* or *θ*). The syllabic texts write the same sound regularly with *š*-signs. The present symbol may be taken to indicate that the underlying sound was intermediate between [ṯ] and [š], an assumption which will be justified later on [46]. What is more, it serves to associate the sound in question with its voiced counterpart *z̄* [45]. In direct transliteration of syllabic occurrences *š* will have to be retained, but *s̄* can be used conveniently both for the Ras Shamra material and for normalized transcription of the syllabic instances; e. g., RŠ *ts̄b* = [d]*Te-eš-šu-ub* (*Tes̄ub*, properly *Tes̄ob*).

The equation of alphabetic *s̄* with syllabic *š* is established by a number of definite correspondences; e. g.,

RŠ *s̄mg* "Shimige" Br. 570 = [d]*Ši-mi-*(*i-*)*ge* Mâri 1. 36, 5. 10; Mit. I 77, 86 f., etc.; also *Ši-mi-g/ka* in proper names, e. g., AASOR 16 58. 45, 52 (Nuzi), and Iraq 7 (1940) 38 (from Chagar Bazar under [SAL]*Ḫa-zi-ib-Si*[72]*-mi-ga*)

RŠ *s̄u*(*w*)*s̄k* "Shaushka" Br. 570, RŠ XX B 8 = *Ša-uš-ka-* Mit. I 76, III 98 (cf. also [18 n. 11] and add *Ša-ú-úš-a-* Mâri 1. 17)

RŠ *ts̄b-s̄* "Teshub" (in the agentive case [150]) XX B 10, 11 = [d]*Te-e-eš-šu-pa-aš* Mit. I 76, II 65, IV 118; this very common name is attested in Mâri (*Te-šu-ba-* 1. 34), Boghazköi (e. g., [d]*Te-eš-šu-ub-* XXVII 38 ii

[72] Since this name is given in transliteration only it is impossible to determine at present whether *si* is merely a typographical error for *ši*. If *si* should prove to be correct (which appears doubtful), the orthography of Chagar Bazar will have to be listed as exceptional in this particular respect.

14, 20, etc.) and is especially prominent in proper names. The same writing is found in Hittite contexts, e. g., *E-ḫal-Te-eš-š[u-ub]* XXVI 41 rev. 11; cf. Goetze, Kizzuwatna 44.

The above examples illustrate the occurrences and syllabic correspondences of *s̄* in all positions. They show also that intervocalic *s̄* was written *-šš-* in the Mitanni letter and in the Boghazköi texts (at least in the name Teshub), whereas Mâri used *-š-* for the same purpose. Further examination shows that the principles which are apparent in these examples apply to the entire syllabic material: (a) Hurrian *s̄* was expressed by *š*-signs throughout (and not by signs containing *z* or *s*); (b) intervocalic *s̄* was indicated by *-šš-* in the Hurrian syllabary proper (Mitanni, Boghazköi, later Nuzi); (c) the "Akkadianizing" syllabary [12a] used *-š-* in identical cases.

(a) This point was established in previous publications and requires no further demonstration.[73]

(b) On this question the evidence is abundant and uniform. The suffix found in *ts̄b-s̄* becomes intervocalic when followed by another grammatical element consisting of, or beginning with, a vowel. Of the frequent combinations which thus result we need cite only a few; e. g., *i-ša-aš-ša-a-an* "I, by me" Mit. I 69; *we-e-eš-ša-a-an*[74] "thou, by thee" Mit. III 68; *še-e-ni-iw-wu-uš-ša-a-an* "my brother" (in the agentive case) II 12, 103, III 1, etc.[75] It follows that *-šš-* must reflect Hurrian *s̄* in all the other instances for which direct alphabetic-syllabic correspondences are lacking. Indeed, double writing is found consistently in a long list of words and grammatical elements. I shall mention only the abstract suffix *-šš/i*; cf., e. g., *ta-a-nu-ša-a-aš-se* "done" Mit. II 99; *šar-ra-aš-ši-* "pertaining to the ruler" XXVII 42 rev. 8, 9, 15, 18, 25; *er-wi-iš-š-* "feudal service" N 28. 24, 33. 19, 89. 10, 221. 19.

(c) In addition to *Te-šu-ba-* note also *Ša-ú-úš-a-an* Mâri 1. 17, obviously for

[73] Cf. JAOS 58 (1938) 189 ff. No importance attaches to the writing with *s* in late Assyrian (cf. Thureau-Dangin, Syria 12 (1931) 253 n. 2, since that is the normal treatment of *š* in Assyrian. The rare exceptions of *-š-/-šš-* in Bogh. are exemplified by *te-šu-ḫa-a-i* XXIX 8 ii 50: *te-eš-šu-ḫa-a-i* ibid. iv 33). Cf. also the note at the end of this section.

[74] In these examples the syntactical element *-an* has been left untranslated; for its function cf. [211].

[75] For three exceptional forms with *-š-*, which are due to special conditions, cf. [22]. In proper names we get either *Te-šub* or *Te-eš-šu-ub*. In the former writing the syllable *šub* may have the value of **s̄ub*, since we should expect otherwise a form *Te-šu-ub*, precisely as in Middle Assyrian names which use the "Akkadianizing" orthography; cf. Purves, AJSL 57 (1940) 178.

" Shaushka," and yet with single *š* although this sound is intervocalic in this particular form.

It can be seen from the use of single *š* in Mâri where Hurrian *š̄* was involved that the double writing in the main syllabary did not represent length; for otherwise Mâri too would have resorted to double writing; cf. [39]. It follows, therefore, that *-šš-* in *Te-eš-šu-ub-* and the like marks a special phoneme and not a particular quantity. From other considerations it will become apparent that the phoneme in question was voiceless [46], a counterpart of Hurrian *z̄*, which the main syllabary records as *-š-*. In other words, double writing was used in certain definite instances to indicate lack of voice.

I have developed the principle involved in this method in an article on Phonetic Method in Hurrian Orthography, Lang. 16 (1940) 319-40. The subject has an important bearing on the whole question of the sounds of Hurrian. The article gives a fuller discussion and a more representative list of examples than is possible in the present study.

[In view of v. Brandenstein's recent assertion (ZA 46. 84 n. 2 and 85 n. 3) that doubling of consonants is " in most instances without significance " it is necessary to state that (1) this is true within certain limitations [39] only of the liquids and nasals; (2) with the stops, *š*, *w*, and probably also *ḫ*, double writing was qualitatively distinctive in the system of the main Hurrian syllabary; (3) on this point Mit. is conclusive while Bogh. presents a small number of exceptions which are insufficient to offset the evidence of prevailing usage; (4) v. Brandenstein's statement fails to take into account the difference between the Akkadianizing and the main syllabary on the one hand, and the established consistency of the Mit. orthography on the other; it also fails to recognize that sounds which were not distinguished as to voice were separated by the orthography of the main syllabary from those sounds where such a dichotomy is attested by the independent evidence of the alphabetic sources.]

z̄

45. Instead of the consonant-sign *š* which the Ugaritic alphabet represents with three wedges, the Hurrian alphabetic texts employ a modified form of that sign (with two wedges); it is transcribed here as *z̄*.[76] The normal syllabic equivalent is contained in *š*-signs. We have two external aids for distinguishing between syllabic *š*: alphabetic *z̄* on the one hand, and syllabic *š*: alphabetic *š̄* on the other: (a) In certain groups of the Akkandianizing syllabary (cf. [12a]) *š*/*z̄* exhibits variant writings with *z*-signs, alongside the usual orthography with *š*; one such variant is sufficient ordinarily to establish the presence of the sound *z̄*.[77] (b) The main Hurrian syllabary indicates *z̄* by means of single *š* in intervocalic position; contrast [44]. Hereafter, the

[76] Following Z. S. Harris, JAOS 55 (1935) 95 ff.

[77] As postulated in JAOS 58 (1938) 190 ff. The names from Chagar Bazar have since confirmed this rule.

5

symbol *ẑ* will be used for the alphabetic material and for normalized transcriptions of syllabic occurrences; *š* will be retained initially when a choice between *ŝ* and *ẑ* is impossible; and, of course, in direct transliteration.

For alphabetic-syllabic correspondences cf., e. g.,

RŠ *pẑẑpḫ* (name of a god) Br. 570 = ᵈ*W/Pí-ša-(i-)ša-ap-ḫi* KBo. V 2 iii 4, XXV 46 iii 9, XXVII 42 obv. 31, etc.

RŠ *ḫẑ-lẑ* XX 4 1 ff. = *ḫa-a-šu-li-e-(e-)eš* XXVII 42 rev. 21 f.; XXVIII 85. 1; XXIX 8 iii 22 ff.; for other occurrences of the stem *ḫaẑ-* "hear" cf., in addition to Mit. and Bogh., the proper names with *Ḫa-ši-ib-*, e. g., AASOR 16 151 (very common in this writing in the later Nuzi texts); for the rarer *Ḫa-zi-ib-* cf. AJSL 57 (1940) 181 and (for Chagar Bazar) Iraq 7 (1940) 38.

RŠ *ar-ẑ-* X 4 9 ff., XX B 7, 11, 15 = *a-ru-(u-)ša/i-* Mit. I 46, II 87, etc.; XXIX 8 iii 34. These forms consist of *ar* "give" + *-oẑ-* (perf. element).

The orthography in group (b) enables us to recognize *ẑ* in a large number of words and grammatical elements for which alphabetic correspondences are lacking. Since the perf. element *-uš-*/RŠ *-ẑ-* is written consistently with single *š* in scores of instances, it is safe to assume an underlying *ẑ* in all the other occurrences of single intervocalic *š* throughout the main Hurrian syllabary. Thus the first *š* of the pl. agentive suffix (*-na*)*-šu-uš* is always written single in such examples as *e-e-en-na-šu-uš* "by our gods" Mit. I 78, II 52, IV 117; cf. also XXVII 42 rev. 9, 18, XXIX 8 iii 37; *ew-ri-e/in-na-šu-uš* "by our lords" Mit. III 48; XXIX 8 ii 37.[78] Variant writings in (b) as against (a) provide occasionally an independent check. This is illustrated in connection with *ḫaẑ* "hear"; another good example is ᵈ*Ku-ú-šu-uḫ* XXVII 38 ii 11, ᵈ*Ku-ú-ša-aḫ* ibid. 16 (similarly in Nuzi names, cf. L. Oppenheim, AfO 12 [1937] 33)[79] as against ˢᴬᴸ*Ḫa-zi-ib-ku-zu-uḫ, Ku-zu-uḫ-a-*RI (cf. Chagar Bazar, cf. Iraq 7 [1940] 38 f.).

In Mâri and RŠ Voc. the orthography is ambiguous in that both *-ŝ-* and *-ẑ-* appear there as *-š-*; cf. *Te-šu-ba-am* (= *Teŝubam*) Mâri 1. 17; *pa-pa-na-šu-uš* "the mountains" *ši-we-na-šu-uš* "the rivers," (both in the agentive case with suffix *-ẑu-ŝ*) ibid. 5. 8-9; *ti-bu-ša* "strengthened" (with perf.-element) RŠ Voc. I 21.

[78] The exceptional *pa-a-pa-an-na-aš-šu-uš* XXVII 38 iii 2 seems to be due to dittography of the first horizontal stroke of ŠU, which would yield AŠ; the normal writing with single *š* is found ibid. ii 13, 19.

[79] Oppenheim's suggestion (ibid.) that *Kušuḫ* may be merely a variant of ᵈ*Ka-aš-šu-ú/Ku-uš-ši*, from which we get "Kassite," is ruled out by the double writing of the sibilant in the latter pair of forms.

46. The precise phonetic values of *s̄* and *z̄* are difficult to determine. Their syllabic equivalents (-*šš*- and -*š*- respectively) tell us only that these sounds were differentiated according to voice. The Ugaritic homograph of *s̄* was *ṯ*, a reflex of primitive Semitic [ṯ] which was a voiceless interdental spirant. But Egyptian *Tí-su-pi* for "Teshub" (cf. W. F. Albright, The Vocalization of the Egyptian Syllabic Orthography [1934] 56) makes it unlikely that Hurrian *s̄* was an interdental spirant. Now the use of *š*-signs in the syllabary to express *s̄*, combined with the fact that *š*-signs are used also for the exclusive indication of Akk. *š* < Sem. [ṯ], would seem to suggest that there was little difference between *s̄* and [š]. But in that case we could not account at all for the presence of the *s̄*-symbol in RŠ Hurrian, since Ugaritic *š* would have furnished the necessary consonant sign. Under these circumstances it is best to regard *s̄* as a sound patterned between [ṯ] and [š], and *z̄* as the corresponding voiced sound.

It is highly suggestive in this connection that Semitic [ṯ] became [š] in Canaanite just as in Akkadian. A phonetic explanation of this type of change requires an intermediate [s], for which there is no evidence whatever in contemporary Semitic. The alternative would be to ascribe the Canaanite shift to Hurrian and the Akkadian shift to Sumerian influence. If this hypothesis is right, Hurrian *s̄* may have been a factor in the Canaanite shift.

Stops

47. The outstanding feature about the writing of stops in the main Hurrian syllabary [13] is this: in intervocalic position single writing indicates voiced sounds (undoubled) while double writing marks voiceless stops (regardless of quantity). This system represents a radical difference from traditional Akkadian orthography. In Akkadian texts, e. g., *at-ta* "thou" cannot be confused with *ad-da* (the god) "Adad." On the other hand, in Mitanni, Boghazköi, and all but the earliest Nuzi texts either writing may represent correctly the Hurrian word for "father,"[80] whereas *a-da-/a-ta-*[81] gives us a different stem. The phonetic factor was bound up with the contrast between *tt/dd* and *d̄/t*, and not *t* : *d* or *tt* : *dd*.

It follows that (a) Hurrian did not reflect in its prevailing orthography

[80] The principle followed by the Hurrian orthography is carried out rigidly in Mit. and only slightly less so in Bogh., where there are some rare exceptions. The instances of the above word for "father" are a case in point. Mit. writes invariably *at-ta-* (e. g., I 87, 106, etc.). Bogh. has *at-ta-* (X 27 iii 7; XX 93 vi 9, etc.) and *ad-da-* XXVII 1 i 71 f.; 2 ii 4, etc.); note, however, the exceptional (*e-en-na-aš*) *a-da-an-nu-uš* XX 42 v 6. In the Nuzi texts we find *at-ta-aš-ši-ḫu* (256. 7; 641. 29); cf. Goetze, Lang. 16 (1940) 168.

[81] This element is found in *a-d/ta-*(*a-*)*ni*, which is used in association with *g/k/ḫešḫ/ki* "throne" (cf. Br. 569), e. g., XXV 44 ii 5; XXVII 1 ii 30 f., 70; 6 i 31; 8 rev. 7.

the Akkadian (or rather Old Babylonian) distinction between voiced and voiceless stops, although (b) its own stops were differentiated, nevertheless, as to voice. These differences of orthography point to a considerable disparity between the underlying sound-patterns. Inasmuch as the relation between the voiced and voiceless stops of Hurrian was primarily phonologic, a fuller statement on the subject will be reserved for the next chapter. What matters at present is the fact that the Hurrian syllabary does show under certain specific conditions the existence of more than one set of stops and that the mechanism employed for the purpose can be utilized today as phonetic evidence.

Conclusive proof of the dichotomy of stops in Hurrian is furnished by the alphabetic texts where the series *b g d* is used alongside *p k t*. Independent confirmation is provided by the Akkadianizing syllabary [12a]; there stop-signs are written in accordance with normal Akkadian usage.[82]

Our results concerning the stops rest thus on the same two distinctive and mutually complementary systems of orthography that have been utilized so far in the treatment of *s̄* and *z̄*: the Hurrian, as embodied in the main syllabary; and the Semitic, as reflected in the alphabetic texts and the Akkadianizing syllabary.[83] It will be pointed out below that the Hurrian system had its origin, in all probability, in the non-phonetic positional variation of the stops [79]. But it was extended later to independent phonemes, notably sibilants, as we have just seen. There is also clear proof that the same method of writing was applied to labial spirants. It will be our task to differentiate in the following brief account between labial stops and the corresponding spirants, and to add a special section dealing with this latter group.

Doubts about the earlier assumption that Hurrian knew but a single set of mutes were voiced by Thureau-Dangin, Syria 12 (1931) 252. The evidence of the alphabetic texts was first discussed by Friedrich, Analecta Orientalia 12 (1935) 128-31; cf. also Br. 574 f. For the Nuzi orthography see Berkooz, Lang. Dissert. 23. 39 ff., and Purves, AJSL 57 (1940) 172 ff. The characteristics of the Hurrian system are presented in my article in Lang. 16 (1940) 319-40.

p : *b*

48. Because of the presence of labial spirants in Hurrian [52] and the lack of an adequate mechanism, both in the alphabetic and the syllabic systems, to represent these sounds, we have to rely largely on circumstantial evidence for reasonably clear instances of labial stops. That syllabic signs containing *p/b* could be used for the semivowel [w] is shown by the variant writings of the name Shaushka, viz., ^d^*Ša-uš-ka-*, ^d^*Ša-wu$_u$-uš-ga-*, and ^d^*IŠTAR-bu-uš-ga* (cf. [18

[82] I. e., with the sign TA; cf. *a-ta-i-ta* Mâri 5. 5; for the alphabetic *at* cf. Br. 571.

[83] The Semitic character of this orthography is stressed by Purves, loc. cit. 162 ff.

n. 11]), alongside RŠ *šw(u)šk*. We shall see later that elsewhere the inter-syllabic variation *p/b* : *w* may reflect some such spirant as [v]; for it is difficult to interpret in any other way the correspondence of RŠ *kmrb* by the side of Bogh. ^{d}*Kumarb/wi*, Mâri *Ku-ma-ar-wə* and Nuzi ^{d}*Ku-mu-ur-wə* [50]. It follows that alphabetic *b* could be used for a voiced labial spirant. In addition, the Ras Shamra alphabet lacked a symbol for the voiceless labial spirant which is implied by the Mit. digraph *-ww-* [53]; this sound was expressed presumably by alphabetic *p*. The problem then is to distinguish between the labial spirants and the corresponding stops; it is the latter group that remains to be established.

Presumptive evidence for the presence of labial stops is provided by the Hurrian stop pattern [76]. Since the other stops show in the alphabetic texts a definite positional relationship, we expect the same to be true of *p* : *b*. The latter symbols point to such a relationship by their distribution, so that some of them, at least, evidently stand for stops. Moreover, a number of common words occur in the syllabic sources with stop-signs only, without variant writings with *w*; some of these words have alphabetic equivalents, and here too only stop-signs are used. Our examples of labial stops will be restricted to such unvarying occurrences.

49. (a) Initially the alphabetic texts use *p*; the syllabic writings are non-distinctive, except for *pa* : *ba*; this distinction is ignored in the main syllabary but maintained in Mâri and its analogues [12a]. E. g., RŠ *pb* = *pa-pa* "mountain" (cf. Br. 568); *pġ-d-* RŠ X 4. 3 = (?)*pa-a-ḫi-(i-)ta* Mit. I 61; XXIX 8 iii 9, 12, 18, cf. [58]. Other forms of *paḫi/e* are written consistently with *pa-*, as above, and not *wa-*; cf. XXVII 1 ii 4, 44. 4, etc. Accordingly, the invariable *pa-* in the verb *paš* "send" and its derivative *pašitḫe* "envoy" (Mit. passim) may safely be taken to mark a voiceless labial stop, in contrast to *paḫru/a* : *waḫru* [52], where the variant writings indicate a spirant.

(b) Medially, RŠ writes *b*, except for the conditions noted below, under (c) and (d). We know from syllabic correspondences that the rule applied after vowels, liquids (and nasals). The syllabic equivalent of RŠ *b* appears regularly in single writing; furthermore, in the Akkadianizing syllabary *-ba* is contrasted in such instances with *pa-*. E. g., RŠ *tšb* = *Te-šu-ba-* Mâri 1. 34 and cf. [44]; RŠ *ḫbt* = ^{d}*Ḫebat*, and RŠ *ndbg* = ^{d}*Nubadig* (cf. Br. 570); RŠ *ḫlb-* = ^{URU}*Ḫal-pa* [58]. Consistent single writing of *-pa-* in intervocalic position, especially in Mit., may be taken as proof of a voiced stop; e. g., *ge-pa-a-nu/e-* "send" Mit. II 16, 54, etc.

(c) Medial *p* in RŠ corresponds to *-pp-* in the syllabary; in other words, the stop was voiceless when doubled. E. g., RŠ *iržp* (X 4. 42) = ^{d}*Iršappi* XXVII

1 ii 23 [84]; contrast RŠ *aštb* = ^{d}*Aštabi* (Br. 570). Note also that Akk. *-pp-* is written identically in the loanword *tup-pè* "tablet" Mit. III 36, 38, etc.

(d) But RŠ *p* may also represent a spirant, hence necessarily a voiceless one. This is indicated both in initial and medial position by syllabic ^{d}*W/Pí-ša-(i-)ša-ap-ḫi* [45] as compared with RŠ *pžžpḫ*. The first *p* is shown to be a spirant by the interchange of *w* and *p* in the syllabic orthography. As for the medial labial in this instance, a stop would have been expressed in RŠ by *b*, since a vowel precedes. Failure to conform to the pattern of positional variation betrays thus a spirant and the alphabetic *p* proves it to be voiceless. Similar instances of spirant *p* may be found in the suffix-clusters of *aty-npš̄* and *aty-npd* (RŠ X 4. 3 f.); for the subject as a whole see [53]

(e) More difficult to interpret is the second labial in *pa-pa-na-šu-uš* Mâri 5. 8. It is plain from the context that we have here a form of the word for "mountain," cf. RA 36 (1939) 19. Since the sign *pa* indicates a voiceless labial in the Mâri system of writing, Thureau-Dangin (ibid.) would separate this form and its many parallels in Bogh. from RŠ *pb-*. But this will not solve the problem, because the normal orthography in Bogh. is *pa-(a-)pa-*, e. g., XII 44 ii 23; XXVII 38 i 6, 13, ii 13, 19, iii 2; we know now that the single writing of the syllabary is equivalent to alphabetic *-b*; note also SAL*Pa*(?)*-ba-ḫi*, Iraq 7. 40 (in the Akkadianizing orthography of Chagar Bazar). On the other hand, the Mâri writing with *-pa-* has its analogues in Bogh. *pa-ap-pí-en-na* XX 95 obv. 2, 5, 8; XXVII 48 iv 1 ff., where the double writing marks a voiceless labial. All of the occurrences here cited favor "mountain," but they show also a variation in the second labial which v. Brandenstein (Br. 568) has failed to recognize. We cannot tell at present whether the problem is essentially one of phonetics or whether we have before us etymological doublets.

(f) The phonetic value of *-b* will be discussed later in connection with the other voiced stops, after the phonologic process involved in this positional variation has been clarified; cf. [78].

k : *g*

50. (a) Of this pair of sounds only *k* is represented initially in the alphabetic texts.[85] In Mâri, where the orthography was likewise distinctive, we get a number of instances with *k-* (cf. 1. 4, 2. 20, 3. 2 f., etc.), none with *g-*. In the other syllabic texts *k*-signs predominate initially, except for Nuzi QA, which was merely a more convenient homophone for *ka* [13]. It was pointed out above that in the main syllabary GI and GU are distinctive only with

[84] I cannot follow v. Brandenstein in restoring *ir*[*šb*] in RŠ X 4. 41 (cf. Br. 558 n. 49) since there is a clear instance of *iršp-* ibid. 42 (in both instances *š* is Br.'s transcription which corresponds to our *ž*). Traces in a broken part of a tablet can scarcely outweigh the testimony of an undamaged passage in an immediately following line.

[85] For the one apparent exception in the material now available see below under (d).

regard to specific vocalic qualities, but do not imply a voiced consonant; cf. [26], [29]. There is thus ample evidence, direct and circumstantial, for *k*-, and no clear evidence for its voiced variant at the beginning of a word.

A good illustration of the use of *k*- is furnished by RŠ *kmrb* = ^{d}*Kumarbi* (cf. Friedrich, Analecta Orientalia 12 [1935] 130); ^{d}*Ku-ma-ar-wi/e* KBo. V 2 ii 60; XXVII 38 iv. 21; *Ku-mar-ar-wə* Mâri 5. 4; Nuzi ^{d}*Ku-mu-ur-wə* AASOR 16 48. 1, 49. 1. Note also RŠ *kld-*, which is perhaps the same word as Bogh. *keldi* "forest" (Br. 561, 571). From Mit. may be cited the common *kad-* "tell" I 96, II 50 etc., which is paralleled in VIII 61 obv. 10.

(b) In medial and final positions, after vowels, liquids, and nasals, only *g* is found, provided that the consonant was not doubled. Common to all the Hurrian sources is the name of the sun god: RŠ *šmg* (Br. 570), Bogh.-Mit.-Mâri $^{(d)}$*Ši-mi-(i-)ge* (cf. [44] and RA 36 [1940] 8); in proper names the usual form is *Ši-mi-q/ga* (with *-ga* in the Akkadianizing orthography of Chagar Bazar, Iraq 7 [1940] 38. An example of final *g* is RŠ *nbdg* = Bogh. ^{d}*Nubadig* (Br. 570). Note also the *-g-* in Mâri *a-ga-ú-m* (2. 4), Nippur *A-ga-a-*, *A-ga-ab-*, *A-gi-ya*, etc. (Purves, AJSL 57 [1940] 172), RŠ Voc. *te-gi-še, e-gi-di, zu-bal-gi* (II, 24, 26, 33), i. e., in three distinct branches of the Akkadianizing syllabary. The main syllabary marks the voiced consonant in question by consistent single writing. We find it in all verbal forms with the element *-u-ka-(a-)r-*, e. g., Mit. II 58, 67, IV 130, etc.; *ma-ka-a-an-ni* "present" Mit. II 15, 54, III 58; and the like.

(c) On the analogy of the labials [49] and, as we shall see, the dentals [51], double writing of *k* or *g* should indicate a voiceless medial sound. That this is so is shown by the invariable double writing of the common verbal suffix *-kk-*; cf. e. g., *ú-ru-uk-ku* Mit. II 99, 101, III 46, 123; VII 56 i 24; *aš-ḫu-ši--ik-ku-un-ni* (RHA 35 [1939] 105 n. 12); Mâri *-uk-ku* RA 36 [1939] 21.

(d) The single instance of initial *g* in the alphabetic texts is *gšḫ-p* RŠ X 4. 51, which has been correlated with Bogh. *g/k/ḫešḫ/ki* "throne" (Br. 569; cf. also the Chagar Bazar names with *-kešḫi*, Iraq 7 [1940] 41). This comparison is rendered probable by the variations in orthography just noted. That the initial sound of the RŠ word was not one of the regular stops is indicated by the departure from the normal stop pattern. It appears thus that both the alphabetic and the syllabic forms in question contained a sound of a different type, perhaps a fricative. It so happens that the same variation of *k/g/ḫ* confronts us in the Nuzi name *Kušši-ḫarbe* (AASOR 16 59 ff.), which was not of Hurrian origin. Friedrich has noted (AfO 11 [1936] 78 that similar conditions may be postulated for Hattic. It is possible, therefore, that the sound under discussion was not Hurrian at all but foreign and restricted to loanwords.

Convincing evidence of the *k/b* interchange in Hurrian has not been adduced so far. That the instances cited by Berkooz, Lang. Dissert. 23. 43 f., fail to establish an intermediate or composite sound of which *k/b* would be an approximate rendering, has been pointed out by Purves, AJSL 57 (1940) 173 n. 51; the examples consist in part of foreign names and are based also to a certain extent on miscopies which Berkooz had no means of checking. It is doubtful, therefore, whether B. Landsberger (AfO 12 [1938] 136) was right in suggesting that *ḫi-ba(!)-šu* RŠ Voc. II 26 may be identical with *ki-ba-šu* ibid. I 31. Still more questionable is the connection between *ḫa-wu$_u$-ši-b(al)* XXVII 42 rev. 14 and *ka-bu-u-ši-ib* ibid. 21 (cf. also 20). These forms may be identical, but we cannot prove it as yet. Just so, *k/b* may turn out perhaps to represent a genuine Hurrian sound. For the present, however, more skepticism is called for than I have shown in Lang. 16 (1940) 332 ff.

t : *d*

51. The evidence for these sounds is more abundant than in the case of the other stops; partly because it includes grammatical elements which occur frequently and under dissimilar conditions; and partly also because the syllabary is more precise in differentiating between *t* and *d* than it can be, e. g., in indicating labials.[86]

(a) Initially *t* is the rule in the alphabetic texts and in the Akkadianizing syllabary.[87] Alphabetic-syllabic correspondences show that in the Hurrian syllabary an initial dental is to be interpreted as voiceless, even though a given sign may contain *d-*. Note especially RŠ *tr-ḫ-* "male" (cf. Br. 567) = Bogh. *tu-(u-)ru-uḫ-ḫi-* VII 56 ii 21, XXVII 3 rev. 17, alongside *du-ru-(uḫ-)ḫi-* XXVII 1 ii 27 ff., 6 i 28, 14 iii 4. The same voiceless stop is found medially if the preceding sound was a consonant other than a liquid or a nasal; cf. RŠ *as̄t-ḫ-* "female" (Br. ibid.) = *aš-tu-uḫ-ḫi-* XXV 45. 5 f., XXVII 16 iii 12, alongside *aš-du-(uḫ-)ḫi-* XXVII i ii 71, 73, iii 4 f., etc.; note also Mâri *aš-ti-* "woman" 4. 25, which establishes the *t* in the many other occurrences of this noun, e. g., Mit. III 1, 11 and passim; VIII 61 obv. 4, 6, XXVII 38 i 15 f.; and in the names from Nuzi. Cf. also Mâri *iš-ti* 1. 19; *iš-te* 3. 26,[88] *ki-ib-ti-en* 5. 20[89] for other similar instances of medial *t*.

(b) In other medial positions, i. e., after vowels, liquids, and nasals, *d* takes the place of undoubled *t*. This is best illustrated by the directive suffix "to": RŠ *-d* in a dozen instances (Br. 573 = Mâri *-da* (5. 3, 4), Mit. *-ta* (e. g.,

[86] The only unambiguous signs containing labials in our syllabaries are *pa* and *ba*. But the sign BA is so rare that we may ascribe to PA the common values *ba* and *pa* (so Goetze). In the present group we have separate signs for all vowel combinations with the exception of DE.

[87] The exceptional *ddmž* RŠ X 4. 17 is suspect; cf. Br. 562, 574.

[88] Possibly the pronoun "I," cf. Speiser, JAOS 60 (1940) 267.

[89] Thureau-Dangin's explanation of the voiceless *t* in this example (RA 36 [1939] 20) is unnecessary inasmuch as the sound is regular in this position.

šu-ú-ú-ta "to me" III 13, IV 24; *Ma-ni-e-ta* "to Mane" I 53, II 19; etc.). But the same suffix becomes *-t* in RŠ *ḫdn-š-t ḫdlr-š-t* (Br. 574) "to the Hudena and Hudelurra" and in Mâri *a-ta-i-t̲a* (5. 5), where the form is in apposition to *Ku-ma-ar-wə-ni-d̲a-* (ibid. 4). In proper names we find SAL*Ši--du-ri* (e.g., in Chagar Bazar, cf. Iraq 7 [1940] 41; this corresponds to the feminine designation *ši-du-ri-* XXVII 42 obv. 23 (note also VIII 61 obv. 4), *ši-tu-u-*[*ri*] XXVII 38 iii 8. For *-d-* after liquids and nasals cf. Mâri *ša-la--ar-di* 5. 11 and *nu-du-un-da* 5. 9; hence also *ta-di-wə an-da-an-ni* (no division after first *n*!) 3. 2.

(c) When *t* is found medially after vowels, the Hurrian syllabary marks such occurrences by double writing. The parade example is RŠ *at-* "father" (X 4. 3), Mâri *a-ta-* (5. 5), but Mit. and Nuzi *at-ta-*, Bogh. *at-ta* or *ad-da* (cf. [47 n. 80]).[90] Consequently, Mâri *ša-tu-un* 1. 6 and *ḫa-tu-di-en* 5. 19 must contain voiceless stops, which the main syllabary would write double; note indeed Mit. *ša-a-at-ti* II 67, 74 and *ša-a-at-ti-la-an* III 108 and cf. Mâri *š*[*a*]*-a*[*t*]*-ti-la* 6. 13, for which see [39 n. 61]. In Mit. *-t-* and *-tt-* are very carefully kept apart. Contrast the verbal suffix *-e-ta*, which characterizes goal-action forms, with *-e-et-ta* in actor-action forms [182]; the former is obviously to be normalized as **-eda*, the latter as **-et(t)a*. Bogh. is equally consistent on the whole; note, however, d*Ni-na-ta-* XXVII 1 ii 46-7, iii 34-5, alongside the normal d*Ni-na-at-ta-* XXVII 1 ii 45, iii 36 ff., 6 i 3 ff., 8 obv. 9 f., 16 iii 11, 29 iv 16, and d*Ne-na-at-ta-* XXV 42 v 2.

(d) Abnormal behavior of *-t* is to be noted in the name of the goddess *Ḫebat*, RŠ *ḫbt* (Br. 570 and XX B 14), or *ḫpt* (Br. ibid.). In postvocalic position we expect *-d* instead of *-t*. But this name is irregular also in other respects. Apart from the variation *b/p* noted above, the directive case appears as *ḫbt-t* in RŠ X 4. 56, but *ḫbt-d* RŠ XX B 14. Moreover, in proper names we get *-ḫé-pa* (SAL*Tadu-ḫé-pa* Mit. III 103, IV 67, 89; XXVII 23 iii 2 ff., 24 i 6; SAL*Ge-lu-ḫé-pa* EA 17. 5; the well-known king of Jerusalem ERU-*ḫi/é-ba* EA 280 ff.; etc.). All these irregularities make it probable that this name was not of Hurrian origin.[91]

Labial Spirants

52. We have so far had reason to distinguish in Hurrian a (bi)labial semi-vowel [34 f.] and the stops *p b* [48 f.]. In investigating the pertinent ortho-

[90] The single writing of the stop in the Mâri example suggests that the sound was not double etymologically; the double writing in the main syllabary need express no more than lack of voice.

[91] The dropping of the final *-t* seems to point to a Semitic origin; we should require, however, more positive evidence to establish such an assumption. At all events, Hrozný's derivation of biblical *Ḫawwa(-t)* "Eve" from Hurrian *Ḫebat* (AOr 4 [1932] 121 f.) cannot be right; the opposite process, however, is probable.

graphies we found also incidental indications of a third labial range, apparently spirant. The subject calls now for a separate presentation. The evidence at hand is indirect, since neither the alphabetic nor the syllabic writings had individual signs for three different types of labial. But the resulting compromise-orthographies vary sufficiently among themselves to furnish suggestive correlations.

It is safe to assume as a start that the use of *w* in RŠ presupposes a semivowel, especially since available syllabic equivalents also contain *w*; e.g., *awr* = *awari* "field" [24] and *iwr* = *ewri* (Nuzi *erwi*) "lord."[92] But syllabic *w* alone is not automatic evidence for [w] because of frequent intersyllabic variation between *w* and *p/b*. Where alphabetic correspondences are lacking, therefore, we require a number of consistent writings with *w*, occurring in more than one source, before we can assume the presence of [w]. For it so happens that Mit. *w* may be paralleled in Bogh. by *p*, as in *waḫr-*: *paḫr-*; uniform testimony in a single source may thus be misleading unless it is confirmed elsewhere.

It follows that the interchange of *w* and *p/b* points to a labial that was neither stop nor semivowel, hence obviously a spirant; cf. Mit. *waḫr-* I 60, 81, II 102, IV 111, 113: Bogh. *paḫr-* XXVII 42 obv. 14, rev. 26; XXIX 8 ii 40, iii 54, iv 35; cf. also *pa-ḫi-ri-e* Sum. d ù g "good" RŠ Voc. II 22,[93] and proper names with *Paḫri-* [34], Nuzi *Waḫri-* (e.g., AASOR 16 69. 3 ff.).[94] Another example of this variation in initial position is *want-*: *pant-* "right," cf. [34]. Medially we find the same kind of interchange in RŠ *kmrb* = syllabic ^{d}*Kuma/urb/wi* [50]. The last-cited instance shows that RŠ *b* could represent a spirant, in this case apparently [v]. But in *w/paḫr-* the spirant must have been voiceless on account of the Chagar Bazar form *Pa-aḫ-ri-* (cf. [34 n. 50]), since in that orthography *pa* was distinguished from *ba*. In other words, Hurrian had a voiceless spirant, probably [f], by the side of [v]. Since RŠ wrote the voiced spirant by means of *b*, it follows that its voiceless

[92] The form *e-bi-ir-ni* occurs once in XXVII 38 iv 14 as against seven clear instances of *e-we$_e$-er-ne* in the same column; cf. also *e-we-er-ni* Mit. IV 127 f. The exceptional writing may be due to the frequent use of *b* for *v*, hence less accurately also for *w*; the sign BAR in *e-bar-ni* (Br. 571 n. 1)/**ewr̥ne* evidently had the additional values V/WAR, on the analogy of IB/V/W, DAB/W, and the like; cf. above, note 49.

[93] Cf. v. Brandenstein, Orientalia 8 (1939) 82 ff. and Speiser, JAOS 59 (1939) 296.

[94] With the same metathesis of *r* and the adjacent consonant as in *erwi* [92]. The city name *Paḫarraže* (for this and similar forms cf. JAOS 29 [1929] 272) occurs in this form in the Nuzi documents, but its western origin is plain, as I have shown (ibid.). There is thus no local Nuzi variation *paḫr-*: *waḫr-* but only the orthographic and dialectal contrast between western *parḫ-* and eastern *warḫ-*.

In this connection attention is called to the frequent interchange *w/b/m* in Nuzi, cf. Berkooz, Lang. Dissert. 23. 49 ff.

counterpart was written in the alphabetic texts as *p* [49]. For this conclusion there is substantial support in the Mit. orthography; see [35].

53. The main syllabary writes *at-ta-iw-wu-uš* "by my father" (Mit. III 55, 58) and *at-ta-i-wu-uš* "by thy father" (Mit. III 67). The only difference between these two forms lies in their respective pronominal morphemes which appear, with the stem *atta*(*i*), as *-ww-* and *-w-* respectively.[95] In other words, the difference between the possessive suffixes is reduced here to the opposition of the writings *-ww-*:*-w-*. Now if we substitute for the agentive suffix -(*u*)*š*, i. e., -(*u*)*s̄* the dative suffix *-wa* we get *at-ta-iw-wə-ú-a* "to my father" (Mit. III 68) and *at-ta-i-ip-pa* "to thy father" (Mit. III 52, 58); *-ip-pa* is the product of *-iw/b* (2 p.) + *w/ba*; *-iw-wə-ú-a* represents the same suffix contracted with the preceding *-iw-wə-* (1 p.). In the case of *-ippa* we have a doubled voiceless stop, cf. [83]. The analogous *-iw-wə-ú-a* should contain, accordingly, a similar dissyllabic combination, except that the product of assimilation is conditioned in this instance by the phoneme expressed as *-ww-*. Since there is no reason whatever to suppose that the orthographic cluster in *-iw-wə-ú-a* contains a triple labial, we may regard the digraph *-iw-wə* as representing a special single sound which the syllabary could not express in any other way; *-iw-wə-ú-* would then be the double form of the same sound.

This argument from internal evidence is supported by a number of facts. (1) We have seen that *ú*/[w] is independently attested, cf. [35]. (2) The main syllabary frequently employed double writing to indicate single voiceless sounds; this is true not only of phonetic variants among the stops [47], but also of the independent phoneme *s̄* [44]. The use of *-ww-* for a voiceless labial spirant, and *-w-* for its voiced counterpart, would thus conform to the prevailing orthographic pattern. (3) There is some evidence that *-w-* was used for a voiced spirant. To the instances cited above [52] we may now add the gen. suffix, which Mit. writes consistently *-we* (cf. Mit.-Studien 97 f.), while Bogh. uses *-we/i* and *-bi*; cf., e. g., ^{d}*IŠTAR-we*$_{e}$ (XXVII 1 ii 16 ff.); ^{d}*IŠTAR-wi*$_{i}$- (X 27 iii 8, XXVII 1 ii 7, 63, iii 8, 6 i 10); ^{d}*IŠTAR*^{ga}*-bi-* XXVII 1 iii 45, 6 i 14 ff.); and the like; furthermore, the dative suffix *-w/pa*, e. g., KUR-*ni-pa* XII 44 ii 17, ^{URU}*Ša-bi-nu-wa-ḫi-ni-wa*$_{a}$ ibid. 18. The corresponding form in RŠ should be *-b*, on the analogy of *kmrb*[96]; it seems actually to occur in *ḫmr-b-n* (Br. 568). (4) The form *-ww-* is equally consistent in the numerous occurrences of the pronominal suffix of the 1 p. sg.

[95] Strictly speaking, the suffix of the first person is wr. *-iww-*, that of the second person *-w-* [144 f.]. But with a stem in *-a*(*y*) the preceding vowel is *-i-* in both instances.

[96] See above, [52]. If E. Forrer (Mélanges Franz Cumont [1936] 702) is right, *Kumarve* is itself a genitive, the form signifying "(he) of Kumar."

cited above (cf. Mit.-Studien 100 ff.).[97] (5) In the Akkadianizing syllabary this *-ww-* should be written single if the sound in question was indeed voiceless. Fortunately, we find in Mâri four instances of *e-ni-wu-úš* (6. 10, 11, 18, 19) in a religious poem which consists apparently of invocations; in such a context we expect "my god" rather than "thy god." Finally, (6) the RŠ equivalent of *-ww-* should be *-p-*. It is probable that we have this sound in *atynpš̄* (X 4. 3) and *atynpd* (ibid. 4); the context is as yet too obscure for a definite interpretation, but "my parental (gods)" would suit the passage admirably, whereas no other adequate interpretation involving a suffix *-p-* can be proposed instead. That RŠ *-p-* must represent voiceless labial spirants in *p̄z̄z̄pḫ* was indicated above, [49].

To sum up, the combined evidence of the Hurrian sources points to two labial spirants, approximately [f] and [v]. They were independent phonemes, and not positional variants as is the case with the stops, because both are attested initially as well as medially. The alphabetic texts wrote *p* for [f] and *b* for [v]. In the main syllabary these sounds are distinguished by double and single writing respectively, i. e., *-ww-* for [f] and *-w-* for [v]. The Akkadianizing syllabary does not employ this particular method. But it helps to indicate initial [f] by its use of *paḫr-* for *w/paḫr-* of the main syllabary; while medial [f] is made very likely as an undoubled sound in Mâri *e-ni-wu-úš,* in all probability "by my god."[98]

Velar Spirants

54. The problem of Hurrian velars is exceedingly involved owing to the nature of the orthographic evidence. We know that in the Hurrian syllabary signs containing *ḫ* were used for more than one phoneme. This is demonstrated in the word for "throne" [50], where the first consonant appears as

[97] The only exceptions which I have noted out of more than 200 occurrences of this suffix are *pa-aš-ši-i-it-ḫi-⟨iw-⟩wu-uš* Mit. I 83 and *še-e-ni-iw-⟨wu-⟩uš-ša-a-an* ibid. III 74. They are obvious scribal errors.

Another source of *-ww-* is found in the cluster resulting from the negating verbal infix *-wa-* + the diphthong *-a-ú* which marks the first person of transitive verbs in a goal-action construction [84]. The product is *-i-uw-wə*; cf. *ta-a-nu-ši-uw-wə* Mit. II 113, freely translated "I did not do"; *ḫi-su-ú-ḫu-ši-uw-wə* Mit. IV 33 "I did not annoy"; *ku-zu-u-ši-uw-wə-la-an* Mit. IV 46 "I did not detain them"; *ú-ú-ri-uw-wu-un-na-a-an* Mit. IV 56 "then I do not want him"; cf. [84].

[98] Ungnad and Bork read *f* indiscriminately in all instances of the *w*-sign (for references and general criticism cf. Thureau-Dangin, Syria 12 [1931] 253). It is clear now that this sign did express [f]; but it represented also [v] and [w]. Each occurrence, or each particular form, has to be evaluated individually. No single statement can possibly cover the various uses of *w* in the syllabary, which reflect in part the wealth of labial sounds in Hurrian.

k/g/ḫ, and the last as *ḫ/k*; the result is the wholly ambiguous form *k/g/ḫešḫ/-ki*; the doubtful sound in question was apparently a rare fricative. A different phoneme is reflected by the *ḫ* of $^{(d)}$*Kušuḫ*, alongside *Kušu* [99]; here weak articulation is indicated by the amissible final *ḫ*. It is possible that amissible *ḫ* in Hurrian words can be established also in intial position; but the available evidence is not conclusive.[100] For the present we need not dwell on the variant writings which involve *ḫ*. For there are enough complications in connection with those forms which appear in the syllabary with invariable *ḫ*.

55. The Ugaritic alphabet has a symbol for *ḥ* (a voiceless laryngeal spirant) and another for *ḫ* (voiceless velar spirant). Since RŠ Hurrian uses only the *ḫ*-symbol, it is evident that the corresponding sound was closer to [ḫ] than to [ḥ]. The *ḫ*-signs of the syllabary are the same that Akkadian used for its velar spirant. The Hurrian syllabary followed suit as is shown by alphabetic-syllabic correspondences; e. g., *ḫbt* = ^{d}*Ḫebat*; *ušḫr* = ^{d}*U/Išḫara*; *ḫzr ḫzlz* = *ḫa-ša-ra-i ḫa-a-šu-li-e-eš*, and the like (cf. Br. 559, 570 f.). Thus far the situation is perfectly clear. It becomes obscured, however, when we proceed to investigate whether this agreement between the alphabetic and syllabic sources applies to all occurrences of *ḫ*. Is syllabic *ḫ* invariably rendered by RŠ *ḫ*?

56. It should be pointed out first that the main syllabary is as a rule careful to observe the distinction between single and double writing. Thus the adjectival suffix *-ḫi/e* is written with single *-ḫ-* in ethnic and geographic derivations; e. g., *Ḫur-wu/ru-u-ḫé* "Hurrian" (8 times in Mit.; no example with *-ḫḫ-*); similarly *Ḫattu/oḫi/e* "Hittite," also *Kizzuwadnaḫi, Udaḫi, Illayaḫe*, etc. (cf. Friedrich, Analecta Orientalia 12 [1935] 121 ff.); from the Nuzi texts may be cited *Nuzaḫe, Nulaḫi* (= Lullubian), *Lubtuḫi* (WZKM 44 [1936] 200 [101]). Furthermore, the verbal formative *-uḫ-* appears likewise

[99] Cf. Berkooz, Lang. Dissert. 23. 44; L. Oppenheim, AfO 12 (1938) 33; cf. also [45].

[100] L. Oppenheim, WZKM 44 (1936) 187 f. and RHA 26 (1937) 63; Speiser, JAOS 58 (1937) 200 f.; Goetze, Orientalia 9 (1940) 228. Instances like *Ḫi-ya-ri-el-li*: *Ya-ri-el-li* (Oppenheim, ibid.) and the Akk. gloss *a-a-ra-ḫi* (with initial *iya-* or *ya-*) "gold" = perh. Mit. *ḫiyaruḫḫe/a* (Ungnad, Subartu 96 f.), have been interpreted as evidence for a palatal spirant. At any rate, Bogh. *i-e-ya-un-na* "all" KBo. V 2 iii 15, alongside the usual *ḫeyarunna*, cannot be cited in support of this assumption because, as Friedrich has demonstrated (RHA 35 [1939] 93 ff.), its *i* is nothing else than a simple copyist's error for *ḫé*.

[101] Oppenheim's restoration *Nu-la-a*(*ḫ-ḫi*) N 232, 22 (loc. cit.) is disproved by the traces of the third sign which indicate *a*[*n*]; the name in question was *Nu-la-a*[*n-na*], cf. Nuzi 56. 18, 313. 22, 530. 17

Of special interest are the numerous instances of KUR*Ku-uš-šu-uḫ-ḫé* and its Akk. ethnicon in *-ay-*, which have been collected from published and unpublished Nuzi sources with single *-ḫ-*; cf. *an-za-a-an-nu-u-ḫu-* "beg" Mit. I 18, III 50, 51 [102]; *ḫi-su-ú-ḫi/u-* "vex" Mit. I 110, II 52, III 76, 85, 89, 95, IV 33; finally, single *-ḫ-* is written consistently in a number of stems, e. g., *ni-ḫa-a-ri* "dowry," *ti-i-ḫa-ni/u-* "carry(?)" (cf. Mit.-Studien 128); *pa-a-ḫi-* cf. [58] Mit. I 60, 61, II 90, IV 13; VIII 61 obv. 5; XXVII 1 ii 4; 44. 4; XXIX 8 ii 36, iii 9, 12, 18, 21, iv 11, 25. The uniformity of this evidence deserves special emphasis.

57. For *-ḫḫ-* we lack the cumulative evidence of a common and established morpheme like the above *-ḫi/e*. Nevertheless, a definite orthographic pattern is apparent with *-(u)ḫ-ḫa*, a composite adverbial form marked by *-a*, signifying "according to, in the manner of." The "case" involved will be termed "stative," cf. [156].[103] Cf. *še-e-en-nu-uḫ-ḫa* Mit. IV 121 and the two similar instances in Mit. II 10; note also *ka-na-pu-ú-uš-šu-uḫ-ḫa* Mit. II 25 and *ú-ri-im-bu-ú-uš-šu-uḫ-ḫa-* Mit. III 95, but contrast *na-ḫu-ul-li-im-bu-ú-uš-šu-ḫa* (ibid. 96).[104] In conjunction with stems or bases in *-ḫ* the double writing is found in *u-ru-uḫ-ḫi-iš-til-la-a-an* Mit. IV 119 (fr. *urḫ-* "true, firm") and *an-za-a-an-nu-uḫ-ḫa-* Mit. IV 129 (fr. *anzan-oḫ* "beg"). In the Akk. loanword *ḫi-i/ya-ru-uḫ-ḫé/a-* "gold" Mit. III 66 ff. (this old derivation is accepted by Friedrich, Analecta Orientalia 12. 126), *-ḫḫ-* is ambiguous, since the *-ṣ* of the Akk. *ḫurâṣu* has been assimilated to a Hurrian element. But in another Akk. loanword, viz., *ši-(in-)ni-be-e-ru-uḫ-ḫé* "ivory" Mit. II 59, III 97 (fr. *šenni-pīri*), the final *-(u)ḫḫe* [105] must be a Hurrian adjectival suffix, hence difficult to separate from *-ḫi/e* [56].

This brings up the question of the suffix in two adjectives which are common in Bogh. For "male" we get *t/du-(u-)ru-uḫ-ḫi(-na)* VII 56 ii 21; XXVII 1 ii 27 ff., 32; 3 rev. 17; 6 i 28; 14 ii 7, iii 4; 25, 3; but XXVII 1 ii 34 writes *du-ru-ḫi-na* (with *-ḫ-*); cf. also *tu-u-ru-uḫ-ḫa-a-i* XXVII 42 rev. 23: *du-ru-ḫa-a-e* XII 44 ii 24. The corresponding form for "female" is *aš-t/du-uḫ-ḫi(-na)* XXV 45. 5 f.; XXVII 1 iii 4; 3. 13, 14(!); 6 i 28; 8 rev. 10; 16 iii

by E. R. Lacheman, BASOR 78 (1940) 21 f. At first glance they seem to invalidate the above conclusion that geographic and ethnic terms take (single) *-ḫ-*. This particular form, however, goes back to the eponymous deity *Kušši*, as is evident, among other considerations, from the name *Kušši-ḫarbe* "(the god) Kushshi is lord" AASOR 16 59 ff.; for the cognate ᵈ*Kaššu* cf. L. Oppenheim, AfO 12 (1937) 33. In other words, *Kuššuḫḫe* is a secondary derivation with the sense of "one of the people of the god Ku/ashshi." As such it constitutes an illustration of the type discussed in the next section.

[102] For *an-za-a-an-nu-uḫ-ḫa-* see below [57].

[103] Cf. also *eman-am-ḫa* "ten-fold" Mit. IV 32 (Speiser, JAOS 59 [1939] 320 f.).

[104] Likewise conflicting is *a-a-wa-ad-duḫ-ḫa* Mit. III 17 (cf. also IV 130) as against *šug-gu-ú-ud-du-u-(u-)ḫa* Mit. II 70, III 108.

[105] For the change *i>u* before *-ḫi/e* and *-ḫḫi/e* see below [61].

12; but *aš-du-ḫi-na* XXVII 1 ii 71, 73. We see thus that the normal orthography is *-ḫḫ-*, whereas single writing of the consonant is exceptional. If the ratio were reversed we could equate the present suffix with the above *-ḫi/e* without further thought. But the statistical evidence points strongly to a normal double form in *aštuḫḫi* as against the single form in *Ḫurwoḫe* and the like.

Further analysis of the occurrences in question may suggest a possible solution. We have seen [56] that single *-ḫ-* is the rule with stems that have an ethnic or geographic connotation. On the other hand, there are indications that *aštuḫḫi* and *turuḫḫi* are not based on comparable primary bases. We shall see that primary nominal stems in Hurrian end in *-a* or *-ay* [103, 107]. Consequently, *aštuḫḫi* may represent a secondary adjectival form, signified by the morpheme *-ḫḫi/e* (see above, n. 101), while direct adjectival derivation would be indicated by another morpheme, viz., *-ḫi/e*. This hypothesis is perhaps supported by *paš-ši-ḫi* "pertaining to sending, shipment" [106] (from *paš* "send") Mit. III 54, 57; whereas *i-i-ši-iḫ-ḫé-* Mit. II 59 would be a form based on a qualitative term **iži-*, just as *šinniperuḫḫe* goes back to a descriptive term for "ivory." These suppositions are all hypothetical beyond a reasonable margin of safety; they affect, furthermore, a point of morphology rather than phonetics. But ultimately bound up with this question is the problem of Hurrian *ḫ*; specifically, we are in doubt whether the Hurrian syllabary represented by means of *ḫ*-signs one or two common sounds.

We have seen that the main syllabary employs double writing for distinctions of voice where such a dichotomy existed (stops; *s̄* : *z̄*; *f* : *v*), the sound thus marked being voiceless; elsewhere (liquids and nasals, perhaps also *z*), double writing indicates quantity. Accordingly, *-ḫḫ-* may represent either a voiceless velar spirant [ḫ], as opposed to its voiced counterpart; or else, it may simply stand for a long or double sound. A definite decision would be possible if the Akkadianizing syllabary [12a], which employs double writing for quantitative purposes only, furnished a clear parallel to a form with *-ḫḫ-* in the main syllabary. The occurrence of **šinniperuḫe* in Mâri or the RŠ Voc. would tell us that the *-ḫḫ-* in Mit. marked lack of voice without specifying quantity. Unfortunately, we miss so far such revealing variants. It is barely possible, however, that *-te-ša-ḫi* "chief" RŠ Voc. III 9 and its variant -[*t*]*e-ši-ḫi* ibid. 11 give us a form which would call in the main syllabary for *-ḫḫ-*; incidentally, the other RŠ Voc. occurrences of *-ḫi*, viz., *ḫirinuḫi* and *pitiḫi* (cf. Syria 12 [1931] 260) also contain single *-ḫ-*; there are in this text no examples of *-ḫḫ-*.

58. Our doubts that syllabic *ḫ* represents only one velar phoneme in Hurrian are increased considerably by the RŠ material. In the alphabetic texts occurs the sign which is sometimes transcribed by a non-committal *x*; in Ugaritic

[106] Cf. Speiser, loc. cit.

this sign is used for Semitic ġ[107] as well as ẓ.[108] In RŠ Hurrian Hrozný (AOr. 4 [1932] 128) would limit this sign to the value ġ, and this suggestion is cautiously favored by Friedrich (Analecta Orientalia 12 [1935] 126 f., 133). On the other hand, v. Brandenstein regards the *x* of the Hurrian alphabetic texts as a mere graphic variant of *s̄* (Br. 575). This interpretation is rendered extremely doubtful by the fact that in RŠ Hurrian texts *s̄* is generally written like Ugaritic ʿ (one wedge) and is thus quite distinct from *x* (with two wedges); moreover, in the recently published texts (RŠ XX [1339]) *x* appears several times in a form that has little in common with *s̄*; Virolleaud (ibid.) transcribes it consistently as *ġ*.

Internal linguistic evidence furnishes an even stronger argument against equating *x* with *s̄*. In RŠ X 4. 10 we find the phrase *ts̄b ḫlb-x* which contains a reference to Teshub of Aleppo. It follows that the suffix here disguised as *-x* served to impart to the preceding noun, which corresponds to syllabic *Ḫalba*, the function of an adjective or a genitive; these two alternatives are illustrated in a single passage by *e-we$_e$-er-ne* [KUR] *Lu-ul-lu-e-ne-we$_e$* "the lord of the Lullu land" XXVII 38 iv 13 f. (cf. [63a]) and ^{URU}*Du-ug-ri-iš-ḫi e-bi-ir-ni* "the Tukrishite lord" (ibid.). In RŠ Hurrian the genitive is written *-b̄* [53]; "Teshub of Aleppo" would be represented by **ḫlb-b̄(n) ts̄b* on the analogy of syllabic ^{URU}*Ḫal-pa-wa$_a$-an* ^{d}*Teššub^{ub}*, for which see ZDMG 76 (1922) 226. The adjectival form, on the other hand, is found in the syllabary as *Ḫalba-ḫi*.[109] If we take alphabetic *x* in the all but generally accepted value of *ġ* (voiced velar spirant), the equation *ḫlb-ġ* = *Ḫalba-ḫi* will satisfy perfectly the phonetic requirements as well as the context; the alleged **ḫlb-s̄* (Br. 556) does neither of these things and it cannot be defended syntactically.

A suggestive parallel to the above RŠ phrase occurs ibid. 35 f., where we read in a similar context *pz̄z̄pḫ lbt-ġ*. The deity Pishashapḫi [45] is associated with a district in the neighborhood of Syria (cf. Br. 563 n. 1). In *lbt-ġ* we recognize promptly syllabic *Lu-ub-tu-ḫi* (in the Nuzi text published in Harvard Semitic Series X 231 rev. 5) "the Lubdian (Ishtar)," cf. JAOS 55 [1935] 443. Note that the two passages under discussion are strictly parallel and that the RŠ orthography presupposes just such a sequence as *Lub-tu-*, because of the voiceless medial stop (*t*); a preceding vowel would have required a *d* instead. Finally, the city Lubt/di may be located in the Middle Tigris area,[110] which accords well with the provenience of Pishashapḫi just cited.

[107] Cf. D. H. Baneth, OLZ 1932. 705; H. L. Ginsberg, OLZ 1933. 593 f.

[108] See W. F. Albright, JPOS 14 (1934) 4 f.

[109] Cf. Friedrich, Analecta Orientalia 12. 127, and add the Nuzi name *Ḫalbaḫi*; cf. SAL*Ḫa-al-pa-ḫi* SMN (= unpublished Nuzi texts, Semitic Museum, Harward) 345; SAL*Ḫal-pa-a-ḫi* SMN 352.

[110] Cf. E. Weidner, Die Inschriften der altassyrischen Könige (1926) 58 n. 4; Albright, JAOS 45 (1925) 211 f.

Of the remaining occurrences of *ġ*, one lends itself to a provisional identification. In *pġ-d-m* (RŠ X 4. 3) we may seek syllabic *paḫi*, perh. "direction(?)." The directive case *pa-a-ḫi-(i-)ta* occurs (apart from Mit. I 61) in XXIX 8 iii 9, 12, 18, passages which have much in common with the paragraphs of our alphabetic text.[111] There is also a possibility that *tġ-žnnk* (RŠ X 4. 49) reproduces syllabic *teḫ* [21], perh. "lead" or the like. By its position at the end of the paragraph the RŠ form parallels similar forms of the verbs *ar* and *ḫd*, just as syllabic *teḫ* corresponds in proper names to the verbs *ar* and *ḫud*. Cf. also [190 n. 241.]

59. The independent testimony of the RŠ material supports, therefore, the evidence of the syllabary based on the difference between -*ḫ*- and -*ḫḫ*-. These two forms may now be equated with their respective alphabetic equivalents. Single *ḫ* in intervocalic position corresponds to alphabetic *ġ*, as is shown by *Ḫalbaḫi* = *ḫlbġ* and *Lubtuḫi* = *lbtġ*. Accordingly, intervocalic -*ḫḫ*- should appear in RŠ as *ḫ*. This equation may now be illustrated by a convincing pair of instances. Alongside syllabic *turuḫḫi(na)* "male" and *aštuḫḫi(na)* "female" we get alphabetic *trḫn* and *aštḫn* (RŠ X 4. 55 ff.).[112] We see incidentally that the double writing of the main syllabary has the same purpose in the case of the velars that has previously been noted with the stops, *š ž*, and *f v*: it signifies lack of voice, while single writing marks the respective voiced sound.[113] The orthographic pattern which the syllabary discloses proves thus to embrace all consonants which were differentiated according to voice on the evidence of the alphabetic material. The origin of this pattern will be taken up in the next chapter in connection with the phonology of Hurrian.

[111] For other occurrences of this stem cf. [105].

[112] Cf. Br. 567 f.

[113] The foregoing statement about the Hurrian velars supersedes my remarks in JAOS 58 (1938) 197-201 and amplifies those in Lang. 16 (1940) 334 ff.

In view of the less consistent observance of the dichotomy *ḫ* : *ḫḫ* in the syllabic sources than we have noticed with the other sounds involved, I shall use *ġ* only for RŠ and retain *ḫ* for all pertinent syllabic forms in normalized transcription.

For an analogous situation in Hittite cf. Sturtevant, Lang. 16. 83.

III. PHONOLOGY

60. On the question of sound-change our sources are as yet less informative than they are with regard to other major problems of Hurrian linguistics. In the prerequisite field of phonetics we have barely begun to cope with the difficulties brought about by the varying orthographic traditions and the shortcomings of the inherited systems of writing; it is plain, of course, that the alphabetic texts have virtually nothing to contribute on the subject of sounds change. We shall see, moreover, that in morphology—which is no less pertinent for purposes of phonologic investigation—only a general outline can be reconstructed for the time being, with much detail obscured or lost. Added to this is the scantiness of the material as a whole, which precludes a sufficiently representative number of given phonologic correlations. As a result, no attempt at a comprehensive treatment of Hurrian phonology has been made in the present account. The presentation is restricted to several typical forms of sound-change which the available evidence allows us to assume with a reasonable measure of probability. Many individual instances have been ignored on account of their ambiguous testimony. Future results are bound to produce a fuller statement. No doubt, they will cause also a redistribution of some of the examples used in the arrangement that follows. But even at this stage it is possible to discern certain marked tendencies in the phonologic pattern of Hurrian which, in turn, have a pronounced effect on the morphologic structure.

61. The final vowel of nominal stems in *-i/e* changes to *-u/o-* before the adjectival suffixes *-ḫe* and *-ḫḫe*; e. g., *aš̄ti* "woman" : *aš̄tuḫḫe* "female," *Ḫatti* : *Ḫattoḫe* "Hittite"; similarly, *Ḫur-r/wu-u-ḫé* "Hurrian" [56-8]. The invariable orthography with -U- in the latter example indicates the phoneme [o], cf. [31], which may be due, however, to the influence of the preceding sound; it is altogether uncertain before *-ḫḫe*.

Unaffected by the foregoing change are (1) particles in *-e*; cf. KUR *Ḫur-ru-u-ḫé-ni-e-ḫé-wə* Mit. I 14 (attributive particle *-ne* [1]); *e-ew-ri-iš-ši-ḫi-* "pertaining to lordship" XXVII 42 rev. 5-6 ff., *šar-ra-aš-ši-ḫi-* "pertaining to kingship" ibid. 9, 15 ff. (abstract particle *-šše* [i. e., *-s̄e*]); (2) apparently also verbal stems, to judge from *pa-aš-ši-ḫi-iw-wə* "my shipment(s)" Mit. III 54, 57; (3) note, furthermore, the morphologically obscure *izḫḫe-*, *pitiḫi*, and *teši/aḫi* [2] [57]

[1] In instances like *še-e-ni-iw-wu-ú-e-ni-e-en-nu-uḫ-ḫa ti-ša-a-an-nu-uḫ-ḫa* "according to my brother's heart" Mit. II 10 the particle involved is not *-ne* but *-n-*; cf. [156].

[2] Not included in this group is *at-ti-ḫu* N 321. 37. Friedrich, ZDMG 91. 212 f. explains

It is uncertain whether the above change is reflected in the verbal theme in *-uḫ*, alongside the unaugmented stem in *-i*; e. g., *an-za-a-an-ni* Mit. II 66: *an-za-a-an-nu-u-ḫ-* "ask for" Mit. I 18, III 50, 51, etc. If this formation should prove pertinent, the -U- of the last verb would provide an instructive contrast to the -Ú- of *ḫi-su-ú-ḫ-* "vex"; for in that case the variation *o* : *u* could be viewed definitely as non-phonemic see [176].

Instances of *-i* + *kk-* : *-u* + *kk-*, etc. are clearly of morphologic origin; cf. [119-20; 189].

Cf. Friedrich, Analecta Orientalia 12. 126 n. 3 and ZDMG 91 (1937) 212; Speiser, JAOS 55 (1935) 443 n. 38.

62. The final vowel of *a*-stems is not changed before *-ḫe* and *-ḫḫe*. This is apparent from such adjectives based on geographic names in *-a* as *Kizzuwadnaḫe, Illayaḫe* [56], *Ḫalbaḫe* [58], and the like. Analogous instances are furnished by KUR *Pabaḫḫi* "mountain land" and IM*pabaḫḫi*, which is used in Nuzi to designate one of the points of the compass (cf. Br. 568; C. H. Gordon, RA 31 [1934] 102 f.); note also SAL*Pa*(?)*-ba-ḫi* Iraq 7. 40. This term is synonymous with Akk. *šaddânu* "eastern" (for occurrences cf. Gordon, loc. cit. 103 n. 3), a derivative from *šadû* "mountain" and thus an exact parallel to Hurrian *pap/ba-*(*ḫ*)*ḫe* < *pap/ba* "mountain." The *a*-stem appears to be assured in this case by the pl. *pabanna*, cf. [49].[3]

The regularity with which *-a* is maintained before *-ḫe*, *-ḫḫe* in known *a*-stems justifies us in postulating the same stem-ending in words whose primary form is otherwise unknown. Accordingly, forms like *Nulaḫe* "Lullubian" and *Nuzaḫe* "Nuzian(?)" [56] presuppose the primary stems **N/Lulla*[4] and **Nuza*.

the word as a hybrid Hurro-Akkadian formation meaning "thine" (< Akk. *atta* "thou" + Hur. *-ḫe*). A review of the context will show, however, that the word is not a possessive, but must mean something like "adjoining," in which case Akkadian alone will yield a satisfactory explanation: *aṭṭēḫu* < *ana ṭēḫi* "to the neighborhood, nearby."

[3] Cf. Friedrich, BChG 4. Goetze kindly suggests in a personal communication that the pl. form *pabanna* presupposes an extended stem *pap/b-an-*, cf. *Pa-pa-an-ḫ* . . . KBo II 9 iv 8; KUB XXIII 103 rev. 21. This would explain the double *n* of *pabanna*. [See, however, v. Brandenstein, ZA 46 97; for other occurrences of *pab-* cf. ibid. 94-5.]

It is not improbable that Akk. *papāḫu* "cella, sacred precinct" is to be connected with the Hurrian word before us. The semantic development remains to be established in detail, but either "east" or "mountain" could have served as the starting point.

[4] For the interchange of *n* and *l* in this name cf. Speiser, Meospotamian Origins (1930) 96 n. 35. Note also the Akk. adjective *nullâtum* which B. Landsberger interprets as "barbarous" and derives from *Lulli'ātum* "Lullubian" (fem.), cf. MAOG 4 (1929) 320; see also his article Habiru und Lulaḫḫu, Kleinasiatische Forschungen (1929) 321-34.

If the above deduction is valid, the resulting rule would give us the basic stem which underlies the adjective " Lullubian," and perhaps also that of the place-name which has come to be known as " Nuzi." For in both instances we should have stems in *-a*. With regard to **Nuza* the situation is complicated, however, by other considerations. That the current habit of writing *Nuzu* (in place of the earlier *Nuzi*) is open to dispute has been indicated in Lang. 14 (1938) 305 ff. Goetze's recent argument (Lang. 16 [1940] 171) to the effect that the gen. form *Nu-zu-e* (HSS IX 33. 2) points to a nom. *Nuzu* is inconclusive, since we find stems in *-i*, *-u*, as well as possible *a*-stems, which form genitives in *-ue* (or rather *-ú-e*, i. e., *-we*; cf. [63a-64]). Hence the gen. *Ta-az-zu-e* alongside the nom. *Ta-az-zu* (Goetze, loc. cit.) fails to prove that other genitives in *-ue* presuppose inevitably nominatives in *-u*.

In favor of **Nuza* there is the independent evidence of the spelling *Nu-ù-za* which is found in an Elamite reference to the city under discussion.[5] This would correspond to the form which underlies the adjective in *-ḫe*, as attested in *Nu-za-ḫé* N 482. 21 and *Nu-za-a-ḫi* N 625. 22. It is not absolutely certain however, that the **Nuza* of *Nuzaḫe* is identical with our city-name Nuzi. For in certain unpublished texts reference is made to *Ištar Nu-zu-ḫé* " the Nuzian Ishtar " (cf. E. R. Lacheman, Nuzi II 529). Do we have to differentiate between two place-names, *Nuzi/u* and **Nuza*, or were both forms variants of the same name?

Little importance can be attached, as yet, to the evidence of proper names like *Ar-Nuzu*, *Ithib-Nuzu*, and the like. The behavior of the individual elements in onomastic compounds still constitutes one of the most obscure phases of Hurrian linguistics. I need cite only that the well-established [d]*Šimige* (the Hurrian sun-god) becomes *-ši-mi-g/ka* (e. g., N 266. 24, AASOR 16 63. 21, etc.; note also *Ḫazib-Š!imiga* Iraq 7. 38); the common *ašti* " woman " changes its stem-ending in *Aštu(n)-naya* N 431. 6 ff., or *Ašta-meri* N 197. 1. The nature of these changes is bound up with the syntax of such compounds. It affords no automatic indication as to the nature of the respective stem-endings in uncompounded forms; cf. [241].

63. The *-a* of nominal stems is lost before the particle *-ne;* e. g., *tiža* " heart " [103] : *ti-iš-ni* RŠ Voc. II 27; *paba* " mountain " [62] : *pa-ab-ni* VIII 61 rev. 11, and apparently also Mâri 1. 13, 2. 5. Loss of the same vowel is to be assumed, in addition, before the particle *-n-*(+ *uḫḫa*), as is evident from *še-e-en-nu-uḫ-ḫa* " in a brotherly manner " Mit. IV 121 < **žena* + *n* + *uḫḫa*.[6]

For the loss of this stem-ending before the possessive suffix of the 1 p. see [144].

63a. Analogous loss of *-a* is apparent in the gen. KUR *Lu-lu-ú-e* N 466. 8 and KUR *Nu-ul-lu-e* (cf. E. R. Lacheman, BASOR 78 [1940] 23); perhaps also in the gen. [URU]*Nu-zu-e* (e. g., HSS IX 33. 2); for the stems **L/Nulla* and **Nuza* see above [62]. The normalized gen. forms would appear, then, as **Lulwe* and **Nuzwe*. In partial support of this interpretation may be

[5] Corp. Inscr. Elam. 54 II 95.

[6] This form cannot contain *-ne-* since its *-e* would not be changed to *-u-*, cf. [61] and n. 1, above. Without an intervening particle we should expect **ženaḫḫe* [62].

adduced the treatment of the stem-endings in the gen. forms of the pronouns *andi* and *agu* [64].

Another instance of the gen. *Lul(l)ue* is to be seen in the phrase *e-we$_e$-er-ne* [KUR] *Lu-ul-lu-e-ne-we$_e$* XXVII 38 iv 13-4, which is paralleled by the immediately following URU*Du-ug-ri-iš-ḫi e-bi-ir-ni* "the Tukrishite lord." For the correspondence of genitive and adjective constructions cf. [137]. The double genitive in the above instance is due to the fact that KUR "land" is in Hurrian part of the phrase. The whole phrase may be analyzed, therefore, as follows: **ewri* "king" + *ne* (attributive particle, cf. [137]) + *we* "of" + KUR (i. e., *omini*) "land" + *ue* "of" + *ne* + **Lulla*, i. e., "king of (the) land of (the) Lullu."

64. The pronouns *andi* "this," **ani/u* "that," *agu* "the other,"[7] form genitives in *-ú-e* and datives in *-ú-a*; e. g., *an-du-ú-e-* Mit. II 63, 100, III 9 and *an-du-ú-a-* Mit. III 89;[8] *a-nu-ú-a-* Mit. I 110 (cf. the pl. form *a-ni-e-na-* Mit. IV 20); *a-gu-ú-e* Mit. IV 123 and *a-gu-ú-a* Mit. I 81. The consistent writing with *-ú-* is noteworthy in that it may reflect [w], cf. [35].[9] A special pronominal genitive suffix is precluded by the forms *šu-u-(u-)we* "of me" and *we-e-we* "of thee" [109], which contain *-we*, the genitive element found with all the other nominal forms. The relation of *-ú-e* to *-we* must, therefore, be a phonetic one. Now the stem-ending of *agu* is [u], as is made clear by the use of GU (not KU), cf. [29]; the suffixes *-ú-e* and *-ú-a* reflect here the product of assimiliation of the labial in question to a preceding [u]. Since the same result confronts us with *andi*, we have to assume that (1) the stem-ending *-i* changed to [u] in this instance, or (2) the *-i* was lost and the resulting post-consonantal labial was expressed as *-ú-*.

Friedrich, to whom we owe a thorough study of *andi* (RHA 35 [1939] 98-102), holds that the genitive may be either *andue* or *andua* (ibid. 101). But the inclusion of *andua* is surely erroneous. While it is true that *an-du-ú-a-at-ta-a*[*-an*] Mit. II 54 is in the genitive, its *-a* is due to a phonetic change *e* > *a* [65]. But *an-du-ú-a-na-an* Mit. III 89 does not show the requisite conditions for this change. The case involved cannot be determined from the context, but the analogy of *a-gu-ú-a e-ti-i-i-ta* Mit. I 81-2, lit.

---

[7] This pronoun is not an opposite of *andi*, but of *akku* "the former, the first of two." In other words, *agu* means "other" in an individualizing sense; the generalizing connotation is found in *oli* "any other," cf. [110].

[8] But not *anduattàn* Mit. II 54, for which see below.

[9] A different relation *i*: *u* seems to be reflected in *a-a-wa-ru-e-ni-e-ra* Mit. III 101, from *awari* "field, land," coordinated with *e-e-še-ni-e-ra* (ibid. 100). [But v. Brandenstein, ZA 46. 85 n. 1 has corrected the reading to *ḫa-a-wa-ru-un-ni-e-ra* "with (the) earth."] Incidentally, the phrase "with heaven and earth" (as a reference to infinity) recurs in an Akkadian translation (*itti šamê ù erṣeti*) in another letter of Tushratta (EA 29. 59); cf. Speiser, JAOS 59 (1939) 296 n. 28; Goetze, Lang. 16. 139 n. 49. Cf. *e-ši ḫa-bur-ni* XXVII 6 i 13; see v. Brandenstein, RA 36 (1939) 24 n. 3.

"to the other for his sake," i.e., "for the sake of the other" argues for a dative; a clear instance of a dative with *edida* is found, e.g., in *at-ta-i-ip-pa e-ti-i-i-ta* Mit. III 52-3 "for the sake of my father."

65. Final *e* of nominal stems and case-endings may appear as *-a-* before the associative pronouns *-tta* "I" and *-lla/e* "they"; cf. *ti-w*[*a-*]*a-al-la-a-an* ibid. 16: *tiwe* "word," and cf. [214 n. 307]; *an-du-ú-a-at-ta-a*[*-an*] Mit. II 54: *andue* "of this"; *ur-ḫal*(*ḫa-al*)*-la-a-an* Mit. IV 23, 29: *urḫe* "true"; also, all occurrences of *yalla/e* "they, those," [218] from the relative particle whose stem appears as *ye-*, alongside *ya-* [130]. It is clear from these examples that we have here a phonologic process unrelated to the interchange *a/e* [24] which affects the quality of the vowel in question regardless of position. For the apparently exceptional ^{I}*Ma-ni-e-el-la-a-an* Mit. IV 27 cf. [75].

Not affected by this process are verbal stems in *-i*; e.g., *ḫi-il-lu-ši-i-it-ta-a-an* Mit. II 26, *pí-sa-an-du-ši-i-it-ta-a-an* Mit. IV 9. The vowel may have been left unchanged because it was morphologically distinctive; furthermore, it may have differed in quality from the stem-vowels of the noun of the *e/i*-class [104]. The repeated writing of *-i-* in the verbal forms just cited can scarcely be without significance.[10]

A problem is posed by *e-e-ni-il-la-a-an* "god + they" + *an* Mit. IV 65 as opposed to *tiwallan* (above).[11] Since both these phrase-words are parallel syntactically, we expect *-allan* in both instances. A difference in the respective stem-vowels cannot be involved here inasmuch as *-e* is demonstrable in both nouns [104]; cf. *ti-we-e-e* Mit. I 80; *e-ne* [25] and *e-ne-*[*pa-*]*a-i* XXVII 42 rev. 21. For a possible explanation cf. [218 n. 321].

Finally, no change *e* > *a* is involved in forms like *še-e-ni-iw-wu-ú-an*[12] Mit. II 104, and *šu-u-wa-an ti-wi-iw-wa-an* ibid. 105. Instead, we have here the loss of the *-e* of the gen. suff. before the particle *-an* (with single *a*).

66. After liquids or *n* followed by a vowel which marks the end of a stem or a grammatical element, we have syncope of the vowel in question and total progressive assimilation of the following consonant, under these conditions:

(a) With *-e/i* before the plural particle *-na*; e.g., *eni* "god": *enna* "gods" < **eni/e-na*; *omini* "land": *ominna*; *oli* "other": *olla*; ^{d}*Ḫudellurra* (RŠ *ḫdlr*) = ^{d}MAḪ^{ḪA}, where the collective determinative of the ideogram points to **-rəna*. For this rule and the above examples cf. Friedrich, BChG 5-6.

(b) With *-a* before the same particle; cf. *šawala* "year" RŠ Voc. I 13: *šawalla-* Mit. I 79; cf. Speiser, JAOS 59 [1939] 296 n. 29.

(c) With *-e/i* before the singular particle *-ne*; e.g., *niḫarre-we* < **niḫari*

[10] Cf. [187 n. 232]. This *-i-* should not be confused with the secondary vowel in *a-nam-mi-it-ta-ma-an* (: *anam*) Mit. III 64, and the like, for which see [87].

[11] I cannot accept Goetze's analysis of these two forms, JAOS 60 (1940) 222 f.; cf. [218 n. 321].

[12] Friedrich's supplementation of the next word into *ṯ*[*i-w*]*i*[*-i-*]*ṯ*[*an*] (Kleinas. Sprachdenkm. 19) has no syntactic basis; I propose *t*[*i-w*]*i*[*-i-y*]*a-*[*an*], cf. [207 n. 280].

+ *ne* + *we* "of the dowry" Mit. III 41 (established by the attribute *a-ru-u-ša-uš-še-ni-e-we*); *niḫarre-dan* Mit. II 61 (attr. *talame-ne-dan*; cf. Speiser, loc. cit. 307 n. 56); KUR *Mizirre-we* KUR *ominne-we* "of the land of Egypt" Mit. I 62 (contrast *Ḫurwoḫe-ne-we* KUR *ominne-we* Mit. II 72); *Šidurri-wa ašte-ni-wa* VIII 61 obv. 5.

(d) With *-i* before the verbal suffixes *-(i)l-ewa*: *tadugarrewa* < **tadugari-(i)l-ewa* "show affection" Mit. III 65 (in apposition to *urḫubtoži-lewa* ibid. 64); cf. Speiser, loc. cit., and see [192].

(e) In verbs ending in *-l* before the suffix *-ili/e*[13]: *kul-li* < **kul* + *ili/e*, freely "I would say" Mit. II 12, III 49, IV 1; cf. Friedrich, BChH 37.

That *m* is not involved in the process just described is shown by the following examples: *talame-ne-dan* Mit. II 61; *a-la-da-mi-ni-we* RŠ Voc. II 14; *al-du-a-mi-ni-iš* VII 56 ii 8; for the failure of *-m* to assimilate to an adjacent *n* cf. [73].

An unsyncopated form seems to occur in *ú-ra-an-ti-ḫi-ni-na* XXIX 8 ii 51. But in a parallel passage, ibid. iv 34, we get *nu(!)-ra-an-ti-ḫi-in-na*, which suggests that the sign-group *-ḫi-ni-na* is a scribal error; in this script IN appears as X + NI, so that the error lies simply in the omission of X, virtually haplographic after *-ḫi-*.

67. Stem-ending[14] *-i* may be lost in compounds before a following consonant or contracted with a following vowel; cf. the PN *Kibi-te(š)šub* as against *Kib-te(š)šub* (Purves, AJSL 57, 164 n. 4); *Ki-bu-gur/Kib(i)-ugur*, *Ki-par-ra-ap-ḫi/Kib(i)-arrapḫi* (see Oppenheim, AfO 12 [1937] 33). Note, however, *Ki-pa-ur-ḫé* N 78. 38, where *-a* may represent another stem-ending which is not contracted.

67a. The *-i-* of the verbal suffix *-ib*, which is used primarily in proper names [177], may be syncopated; e.g., *Ḫu-ud-ba-bu* for *Ḫudib-abu*; *Ar-bu--um-bi* for *Arib-umbi* (cf. Purves, loc. cit. nn. 47, 66). Note also *Ar-šaduya* for *Arib-šaduya* and *Artirm/we*, possibly for *Arib-tirm/we*; these two examples would presuppose assimilation of *-b* to the following consonant (Purves, ibid. n. 99), in which case verbal forms like **ar-* could be eliminated from serious consideration.

68. The diphthong *ai* interchanges with *ae* and *i*; e.g., *ḫa-a-ša-ra-a-i* XXIX 8 iii 39: *ḫa-ša-ra-a-e* ibid. 21: *ḫa-a-ša-ri* ibid. 23 (all in parallel passages); cf. also *ta-ku-la-a-eš, -li-e-eš, -li-iš* (Goetze, RHA 35 [1939] 106 n. 18). The

[13] Here the vowel belongs, however, not to the stem but to the suffix [196].

[14] This term is employed here for vowels which characterize given stems but may be morphologic rather than radical; cf. [102].

same type of contraction seems evident in the change of *Ma-i-ta-ni* (in the seal of Saushshatar, HSS IX 1) to the familiar *Mitanni.*[15]

A different treatment is apparent in the two *ay*-stems, viz., *attay* "father" and *allay* "lady,"[16] originally perhaps "mother (goddess).[17] In these nouns the diphthong is reduced to *a* in such forms as *attan(n)ib/wina* "those of the father" XXVII 1 i 71-2, 6 i 26, 8 obv. 16-7, 14 ii 5, 42 rev. 9; *attašiḫu* "pertaining to fatherhood," i. e., to the father's estate [47]; *allani* "lady" + attr. particle.

69. The gen. suffix *-we* becomes *-ye* in the nominalized prepositions *a-a-i-(i-)e-e* Mit. III 28, 29, IV 50 and *e-ti-i-e-e* Mit. I 91, IV 19, 22, 25, 28. A careful analysis of these occurrences will show that the forms consist of the radical element (**ai-*, perh. "face, front," *edi* "regard, sake") + pron. suffix of 3 p. sg. (*-i/ya-* [146] + gen. suff. (here [*y*]*e*). That the last element is the gen. suff. is established by such correlated phrases as (a) *še-e-ni-iw-wu-ú-e-ni-e* "brother-my-of" + *ne* (attr. particle) *a-a-i-e-e* Mit. III 28, 29; (b) *u-u-mi-i--ni-iw-wu-ú-e-ni-e e-ti-i-e-e* ibid. IV 19, 28. The significance of *-i-* may be determined from a comparison of the above examples with *šu-u-we-ni-e e-ti-iw-wu-ú-e-e* Mit. IV 22 "(what they will say) of me, of my regard," i. e., "with regard to me" (analogously ibid. 18). Hence (b) is clearly "of my land, of its regard," with regard to my land, and (a) "of my brother, his front(?)," before(?) my brother.[18] This analysis is supported by the proportional analogy:

-iw-wə "mine" : *-iw-wa-aš* "ours"
-x "his" : *-i-a-aš* "theirs"

cf. [143], where the forms are listed in normalized transcription. Here *x* yields manifestly *-y-* or *-i-*; cf. also [22 n. 20].

Our gen. form, then, is the product of *-i/y(a)-* + *we* > *-ye*. Whether the same process took place in normal nominal constructions such as "god-his-of" is

[15] For the reading *Ma-i-ta-ni* (with *-ta-*, not *-te-*) cf. Albright, BASOR 77. 29 n. 37; Lacheman, ibid. 78. 22.

[16] Cf. Br. 571 n. 1.

[17] Since *allay* shares its stem-ending *-ay* only with *attay* "father," on present evidence, the possibility should not be overlooked that the word came to mean "Lady, Queen," by way of "Mother (Goddess)." From the passages cited in Br. loc. cit. it is clear that another word for "queen" was available, namely, *ašti*, which appears paired with *žarri* "king," although its usual sense is "woman." Similarly, the plural form *aštena* is associated with *žarrena* in XXVII 38 i 1 ff., 14-6; for the meaning of the passage cf. H. G. Güterbock, ZA 44 (1938) 82 f.; Goetze, Tunnawi 74 f.

[18] It is significant that phrases of this type are contructed with the aid of the attributive particle (*-ne*) placed after the "dependent" noun; cf. [137].

not altogether certain; cf., however, *še-ḫé-el-li-we$_e$-na-ša wu$_u$-du-uš ši-i-e-na-ša* KBo V 2 ii 26-7.

For *w*: *y* note also [27].

70. Weak articulation of *-r-* is illustrated by the following examples: *ḫé!-ya-un-na* "all" (pl.) KBo V 2 iii 15, alongside the usual *ḫeyarunna* (cf. Friedrich, RHA 35 [1939] 94, 96); *ge-e-a-ši* XXVII 42 rev. 22: *ki-e-ra-ši* XXIX 8 iii 40 (cf. Goetze, RHA 35. 106 n. 19) [19]; *ta-[a-]du-ka-a-iš* Mit. IV 113 (if not a scribal error): *ta-a-du-ka-a-ri-iš* Mit. I 19, II 93, IV 121 "affectionately"; the onomastic element *ge-wa-ar*: *ge-(e-)wa* (cf. Oppenheim, AfO 12 [1937] 36).[20]

For the absence of clear instances of initial *r* in Hurrian, just as in Hittite, cf. [38]; for weakly articulated *r* in Hittite, particularly in final position, see Götze-Pedersen, Muršilis Sprachlähmung (1934) 30 f., and Goetze, The Hittite Ritual of Tunnawi (1938) 67.

71. A different problem is posed by instances of amissible *n* before *k* and *t*; e. g., *ta-a-ki-ma-a-an* Mit. IV 58: *ta-a-an-ki-ma-a-an* ibid. 60 and *ta-a-an-ki* ibid. 78; Goetze (RHA 35. 106 n. 18) has rightly connected these occurrences with Bogh. *ta-ku-la/e-eš*; cf. [189, 193]. Before *t* we get *pa-ta-ni* XXVII 1 iii 41: *pa-an-ta-ni* ibid. ii 4, 6 i 10; furthermore ᵈ*Ti-ya-bi/e-en-ti*: ᵈ*Ti-ya-p/wa-ti* (cf. Goetze, Orientalia 9 [1940] 224); finally, ᴵᴰ*Pu-ra-an-ti-* < Akk. *Purattu* "Euphrates" and *iš-pa-an-ti* < Akk. *išpatu* "quiver" (for the last two instances cf. v. Brandenstein, XXVII p. IV). These examples indicate either a secondary inorganic *-n-* or an amissible sound.[21] But in view of the difference in pattern between Akk. *t* and the corresponding Hurrian sound there may be no connection between the nasals in *iš-pa-an-ti* and *ta-a-an-ki* respectively.

72. Phonetic interchange between *m* and *n* is at best a very remote possibility in *a-ru-ši-el-la-a-im* XXIX 8 iii 34: *a-[ru-ši-]in-na-a-in* XXVII 42 rev.

[19] Note also Chagar Bazar *-ki-a-zi* Iraq 7. 40 n. 3 and Mâri *ki-ya-zi-ni* 5. 19. If this stem is connected with *ki-ra-i* "long" RŠ Voc. IV 21 (so Goetze, loc. cit.), another occurrence of it would be *ge-ra-aš-še-na* — "lasting, long") with the nominalizing *-še* [164] Mit. I 79; cf. Speiser, JAOS 59. 296 n. 29.

[20] Cf. also *Šadu-gewar* N 484. 18, 28 : *Šadu-gewa* N 403. 2, 20; HSS IX 31. 14. Note also L u g a l (= *Žarru*)*-ge-wa$_{a!}$-a* XXXI 3 rev. (6), 10 and [IL u] g a l*-ge-e-we$_e$* (gen.) XXVII 38 iv 23, the Hurrian equivalent of *Šarru-kênu* "Sargon" (of Agade). Since the second element of the compound could scarcely represent the Hurrian pronunciation of Akk. *kênu* "just," it appears that we have here the Hurrian equivalent of the Akk. adjective (the first element being identical in both languages). That this *gewa-* is not to be confused with *kib-* [67] may be seen from the name *Ki-ib-ge-wa-ar* N 255. 11.

[21] Cf. Goetze's statement (Orientalia 9. 224) that *n* "is rather indistinct in Hurrian"; but the evidence is ambiguous.

13 and *an-ti-na-mu-uš-ša-am* VII 58 ii 9: *šar-ru-mu-uš-ša-an* ibid. 10. In both instances, however, a better case can be made out for respective independent morphemes; for the element *-nn-* cf. [190], and for *-m* see [212a]. The same applies to the element *-m* in the Mâri texts [75, 212] as compared with the connective *-a(-a)-an.*[22]

73. The phoneme *m* fails to assimilate to *n* under conditions that lead to the assimilation of the other sounds with which *m* is known to pattern; cf. [66] and contrast [36]. Analogous treatment is demonstrated in *an-nu-u--un-ma-a-an* KBo V 2 ii 23 and *ú-ru-mu-um-ni-bi* XII 44 ii 11.

The interchange of *m* and *w* in proper names, e. g., *A-ga-ma-di-il* N 552. 17 for the common *Agawadil* (HSS V passim) and *Ar-šamuška* (N 76. 25, 412. 8) alongside *Ar-šawuška* (N 242. 20, 267. 26),[23] is of orthographic and not phonologic origin; cf. also [18 n. 11]. A problem is raised by the writing *Ar-ru-pa* N 419. 31 f. for *Ar-ru--um-pa* N 461. 9, 18, HSS V 27, 11, etc. Assimilation would probably have resulted in a form with *-pp-*; moreover, the writing of the name *Umb/wu* (Br. 565 f. and Goetze, Orientalia 9. 225 n. 3) speaks against it.[24]

In the loanword *zi-lu-um-pa-* "date" RŠ Voc. II 12 we have an instance of dissimilation, but the precise nature of the process is ambiguous. If the word was borrowed from the Akkadian (*suluppu*), the change was *-pp-* > *-mp-*; but if it was a direct loan from the Sumerian (s u l u m m a), we have an instance of *-mm-* > *-mp-*.

74. The phoneme *z̄* changes to *s̄* before suffixed *t* in what is obviously a process of partial assimilation. The evidence is as follows: RŠ *ḫdn-s̄-t ḫdlr--s̄-[t]* (Hr. obv. 9) end in the directive suffix (which is *-da* after vowels; note the *-d* in the remaining occurrences in the same alphabetic text). The preceding sibilant is employed to pluralize case-endings [142]; cf. the frequent *-(na-)šu-uš,* alongside the corresponding sg. *-uš*;[25] the originally voiced character of the *-š-* is established by the single writing [44]. The same plural element appears in RŠ as *z̄*, cf. *trḫ-n-z̄-r . . . as̄tḫ-n-z̄-r* (RŠ X 4. 50-1) "with the male ones . . . with the female ones." The above *-s̄-t* represents thus an original **-z̄-t* (the pl. comitative suffix); for the plural form of the names of the gods Ḫudenna-Ḫudelurra cf. Br. 563.

The resultant pl. directive *-ašta* : sg. *-da* (postvocalic) in Hurrian is strikingly paralleled in Urartian *-ašte : -di.* Cf. [*ḫu-*]*ti-i-a-di* ᵈ*Ḫal-di-e-di* ᵈIM*-di* ᵈUTU*-di*

[22] The interchange of *m* and *n* in the Nuzi name *M/Nušabu* (cf. Berkooz, Lang. Dissert. 23. 54) reflects, of course, an inner-Akkadian process.

[23] Cf. Berkooz, Lang. Dissert. 23. 50. The interchange may reflect, however, the late Old Babylonian change of intervocalic *m* to *w* (so Goetze).

[24] Berkooz, loc. cit. 51, erroneously takes *Arrupa* as the original form and *Arrumpa* as an instance of of dissimilation of *-pp-* to *-mp-*.

[25] For *-(na-)šuš* (i. e., *-(na-)z̄uš*) cf. Friedrich, BChG 10 ff.

DINGIRMEŠ-*áš-te* [*ḫa-*]*ši-a-al-me* DINGIRMEŠ "I called to Ḫaldi, Tesheba, Shiwini, the gods; the gods listened to me" (G. Tseretheli, The Urarṭean Monuments in the Georgian Museum Tbilisi [1939] 18. 10 ff.; for similar contexts cf. Friedrich, Einführung ins Urart. 55; Goetze, RHA 24 [1936] 280 f.; for the meaning of Urart. *ḫašu-* [= Hur. *ḫaž-*] cf. Goetze, ibid.; for "Shiwini" see Friedrich, Orientalia 10 [1940] 211 ff.).

It is obvious that the several singulars in *-di* are coordinated with the plural *-ašte* (Friedrich, op. cit. 57). Accidental correspondence with the respective Hurrian forms is precluded by the completeness of the parallel: sg. (postvocalic) *-d-*; pl. element *-š- : -š-*; pl. directive element *-t-*; cf. [153]. It would be difficult to adduce a more convincing single instance of linguistic interrelation.

75. The phoneme *š̄*, which occurs in the agentive suffix *-^{u}š* (after consonants) or *-š* (after vowels) is lost before (assimilated to) the pronominal elements *-tta* "I," *-til(l)a* "we," and *-lla/e* "they." E. g., *še-e-ni-iw-wu-ú-ut-ta-* (Mit. II 50, III 71, IV 41); ^{d}*A-ma-a-nu-ú-ti-la-* (Mit. I 76, cf. also 77); *še-e-ni-iw-wu-ú-ul-la-* (Mit. I 107, 113, III 61, IV 19, 39, 40, 51, 110). In all these occurrences the noun is in the agentive (logical subject): "brother-my-by-I, Amon-by-we, brother-my-they." The agentive element *-š̄* has manifestly been absorbed by the following consonant: **ženifuš̄-ta*, etc.

This assimilation of *-š̄* is confirmed by independent morphologic-phonologic evidence. The name "Mane," in the agentive case, followed by the 3 p. pl. pronoun "they," appears as ^{I}*Ma-ni-e-el-la-* (Mit. IV 26) for **Maneš̄-la-*. We have seen [65] that stem-ending *-e* changes to *-a-* before the same pronominal element, e. g., *ti-w*[*a*]*-al-la-* Mit. IV 16. The *-e-* of *Mane-lla-* is due, then, to the influence of the suffixed *-š̄* (cf. ^{I}*Ma-ni-eš-ša-a-an* Mit. IV 27), even though the protecting suffix has been assimilated.[26]

The above rule enables us to recognize assimilated *š̄* in some less transparent instances. Thus in ^{d}*Gal-ga-mi-šu-ul* (VIII 61 obv. 8) the agentive case, which is required by the context, is proved by the vowel *-u-* (*-ul/*užl*).[27] The connecting vowel between a consonant and *-l*(*la*) would otherwise have been *-i-*, cf. [85].

It is possible, although by no means certain, that assimilation of the agentive *-š* took place also before *m*. Thus Mâri *i-ša-am-ma* (1. 30, 2. 14, 15) may contain perhaps the agentive form of the independent pronoun "I" *iža-š + ma*.[28] Similarly, the final *m* of *Paḫippini-m* (ibid. 1. 32), *Tešuba-m* (1. 34), *Šimigene-m* (1. 36), *Ušu-m* (2. 18), and *Kibli-m* (2. 20) may have absorbed a preceding *-š*. The meaning of this *-m/ma* is

---

[26] Friedrich (BChG 23) recognizes the possibility of assimilation under the conditions stated above. His alternative that the agentive may have been avoided for syntactic reasons is disproved, however, by the retention of the *-u-* in *ženifu-tta* and *ženifu-lla* as well as in *Galgamiž-ul*.

[27] The significance of *-l* in this instance was first seen by Friedrich, BChG 29.

[28] Cf. JAOS 60 (1940) 267.

open to question. We may have here the subject pronoun of the 3 p. sg. (*me/a*),[29] or perhaps better the particle *-ma* "also, and"; cf. [212]. But our knowledge of the Mâri texts is as yet insufficient to justify a less tentative statement on this point.

76. The positional variation of the Hurrian stops, which was described in another connection in [47-51], represents the assimilatory influence of certain continuants upon the sounds in question. We have seen that stops become voiced when preceded by a vowel, liquid, or nasal.[30] It might seem offhand that what is involved in this process is merely the voicing of normally voiceless phonemes under the influence of any immediately preceding voiced sound. But the change in question is far more complex. For it is an important feature of this process that, on present evidence at least, a doubled stop is not voiced under otherwise identical conditions. The whole problem calls for a further examination.

77. It should be noted first that voiced stops are found also after other medial stops: e. g., *tš̄b-d* (RŠ X 4. 56) and *nb̄dg-d* (Hr. obv. 3), although there is no intervening vowel in either instance, the stems in question being *Teš̄ub* and *Nubadig* respectively.[31] Now the agentive of *Teš̄ub* is formed with *-aš̄* instead of the usual *-uš̄* [75]; cf. XXVII 1 ii 66, 42 rev. 15, 46 i 13 ff.; Mit. I 76, II 65, IV 118; note, furthermore, *Te-šu-ba-am* Mâri 1. 35.[32] It is noteworthy, moreover, that the Akkadianizing orthography furnishes the name ᵈ*Te-eš-šub-'a-dal* (VS VII 72. 10). Since the syllabary does not provide other examples of an initial glottal stop in Hurrian,[33] it is possible that the present writing with ' may have been due to the preceding sound. The behavior of the voiced stops tends to support this possibility. For the use of *-aš̄*

[29] As suggested by Thureau-Dangin, RA 36 p. 8. In that case the process in question would be restricted to a single grammatical category, that of suffixed subjective pronouns. The meaning of *i-ša-am-ma* would on this assumption be "by-me-he."

[30] Not just medially, as is sometimes stated. Mâri *ki-ib-ti-en* (5. 20), e. g., as contrasted with *ḫa-tu-di-en* (5. 19), presents a voiceless dental after wr. *p* (the latter sound apparently a spirant); cf. also [74].

[31] The forms *ḫb̄t-t* RŠ X 4. 56 and *ḫb̄t-d* RŠ XX B 14 are in themselves inconsistent. Moreover, the stem-ending *-t* does not pattern with the Hurrian stops, cf. [51(d)].

[32] For the exceptional ᵈ*Tešub* (= U)*ub-bu-uš* HT 93 ii 9, 10 cf. RA 36 p. 7 n. 3. On the analogy of *Tešub-aš* as we expect *-a-* as a connecting vowel after stem-ending *g* and *d* as well. However, there is as yet no conclusive evidence bearing on this point. Instances like ᵈ*Ḫé-pa-du-uš* XXVII 42 rev. 11, or ᵈ*Ḫé-bat-uš* XXIX 8 iii 47, prove nothing either way because of the character of the final stop in this name (see the preceding note). The curious lapsus ᵈ*Lu-pa-ki-ta* XXVII 13 i 6 (for ᵈ*Nubadig-a*, cf. Br. 566) cannot be used as a safe illustration for any purpose.

[33] For the use of the sign in Nuzi to represent syllable-ending *-ḫ* cf. Berkooz, Lang. Dissert. 23. 41 f.

in place of *-uš*, after *Tešub*, is not inconsistent with the assumption that the *-a-* was induced by a constituent of the voiced stops which was homorganic with this vowel. This would imply that the voiced stops were composite sounds. Such a hypothesis is favored, in turn, by the circumstance that Hurrian does not appear to have tolerated doubled voiced stops, substituting in their stead the corresponding voiceless phonemes; cf. Br. 574 and *a-ta-i-ta* Mâri 5. 5; note also [82]. It is logical, therefore, to postulate that the voiced stops were double sounds to begin with; *Tešub-'adal* would represent in such a case an actual **Tešub'-adal.*

78. There remains the question as to the nature of the assumed component sound inherent in the voiced steps. Theoretically, the choice lies between aspirates (e. g., *bh*) and glottalized stops (e. g., *b'*). Our material is far too scanty for a confident statement, but it seems to favor the latter alternative. For the '-element would best account not only for the voicing of a following stop but also for the *a*-quality of a following connecting vowel.

In the light of the cumulative evidence just adduced we may set up the following tentative scheme:

[p- k- t-] > [-b' -g' -t']; but [*-b'b'- -g'g'- -d'd'-] > [-pp- -kk- -tt-]

It may not be too hazardous to go now one step further. We know that the Hurrian stops patterned differently from the corresponding sounds of Akkadian. But a purely phonetic difference was involved also, in that the main syllabary expressed Hurrian *t*, e. g., by means of signs used since Hammurabi for Akkadian *t* or *d*. In other words, Hurrian *t* may be regarded as approximately intermediate between Akkadian *t* and *d*. If so, the Hurrian stops are in reality voiceless mediae, i. e., [p̥- t̥- k̥-].

For a preliminary discussion of the relations here presented cf. my article in Lang. 16 (1940) 319-40.

79. The situation just discussed helps to explain the method followed by the main syllabary whereby double writing was employed to mark lack of voice. Since doubling of medial stops resulted automatically in loss of voice, double writing could be extended conveniently to indicate voicelessness with other sounds wherever the inherited syllabary lacked the means to signify this distinction. It is no longer surprising, therefore, to find *-šš-* used for *š* or *-ww-* for a phoneme that was apparently [f]. In such cases the principal consideration was the distinction of voice and not of quantity.

The present results have a bearing on the use of double writing to mark lack of voice in Hittite (cf. Sturtevant, HG 74 ff.). Since the influence of the Hurrian syllabary on the Hittite is attested independently [15], and since the employment of double writing to denote voicelessness can be explained on inner-Hurrian grounds, we are justified in concluding that Hittite orthography was indebted to the Hurrians for its method of representing inherited voiceless sounds.

Finally, there is a noteworthy parallel between the process of spirantization in Canaanite and Aramaic and the positional relation of the Hurrian stops. The analogy is strengthened by the circumstance that the non-phonemic alternants of the above Semitic languages revert to their initial values when doubled, as in Hurrian. But the problem of what this correspondence implies cannot be pursued here.[34]

80. The treatment of the verbal formative *-b/m,* which is very common in first elements of onomastic compounds, presents a difficult problem. The suffix is not written uniformly in the syllabic sources and cannot be identified as yet in the alphabetic material. We know from the Akkadianizing syllabary that the consonant in question was voiced; cf. *Ta-di-ba-bu* = *Tad* + *i* + *b* + *abu* (PBS II part II 84. 7); similarly *A-gi-ba-bu* (SMN 3082). That it was a spirant is shown by the graphic interchange with *m*; cf. *Zi-li-pa-dal* (HSS IX 113. 2): *Pu-ut-ti-ma-da-al* (RA 16. 161 rev. 13).

This formative is assimilated regressively, as a rule, to nasals and *k*, but maintained before *t*; e. g., *Ḫažik-kemar* (AASOR 16 34. 46, 42. 40), *Ḫažin--namar* (ibid. 66. 37); but *Ḫažib-tilla* (ibid. 24. 17, 42. 39, etc.). The opposite treatment, however, is also attested; e. g., ^{SAL}*Ḫažib-kanzu* (N 429. 5), ^{SAL}*Elḫib-nuzu* (N 505. 5); as against *Ari-tirm/we* for **Arib-tirm/we.*[35]

A possible explanation of this erratic behavior may lie in the fact that we are dealing here with compounds, where the laws of sound-combination do not seem to have been as rigid as those which governed internal sound-change. In some instances the lack of regularity may be only superficial, being due to the shortcomings of the system of writing. Thus *Taḫib-ženni, Agib-ženni,* and the like would, with the *-b* assimilated, have yielded **Taḫiž-ženi* and **Agiž-ženni* (inasmuch as written *šenni* contains *ž-*; cf. *Pa-i-zé-ni* AASOR 16 95. 21 and RŠ *tgžn* Syria 15. 244 l. 9). In that case, however, there was no convenient way of indicating **-žž-* since *-šš-* would have expressed the voiceless **-šš-*. It is indeed probable that such considerations were responsible for the frequent omission of *-b*[36] without a consequent double writing of the following consonant; cf. [81]. The one thing that is certain about the whole matter is this: when total assimilation took place, it was regressive, unlike the process with the liquids and nasals [66].

81. When the phoneme *ž,* which is found as plural element with possessive suffixes and case-endings [142], was followed by the gen. suff. *-we* or the dat. suff. *-wa,* the labial was lost; e. g., *ši-ni-a-še-*(*na-a-am-ma-ma-an*) Mit. III 40 " (those) of their two," i. e., of the two of them; (*pa-ab-ni*) d i n g i r^{meš}*-ši* (= *enna* + *ži*) VIII 61 rev. 11 " (mountain) of the gods "; *iš-ta-ni-iw-wa-ša* Mit. I. 81, etc. " to us mutually." These forms have to be analyzed as **šin*

[34] See provisionally my remarks in BASOR 74. 5 n. 10.
[35] See Purves, AJSL 57. 182 n. 99.
[36] For which cf. ibid. 176 n. 66.

+ *ya* + *ž* + *we*, **enna* + *ž* + *we*, and **ištan* + *if* + *až* + *wa* respectively.[37] What is less clear is whether the *w* had been elided, or totally assimilated to the preceding *ž*-sound without any trace of that process in the orthography. There is some evidence in favor of the latter alternative.

82. Under analogous conditions the labial is not lost after another labial; instead, doubling takes place, preceded by assimilation when the labials were not identical. Thus "to thy father" is *at-ta-i-ip-pa* Mit. III 52, 58; cf. [53]. Here we find the combination of *-b/w* (poss. suff. of 2 p.) + *wa* resulting in *-ppa*. Similarly, "of thy father" is *attai-ppe-* Mit. III 69; "of thy brother" is *žena-ppe* Mit. I 89. Now *-b/w* is a spirant, as may be seen from a comparison of *še-e-na-pa-an* Mit. I 91 "thy brother" + *an* with *pa-aš-ši-i-it-ḫi-wu-uš* Mit. I 72 "by thy envoy." The combination of two spirants (evidently voiced) yields the written form *-pp-*, a doubled sound (evidently voiceless stop). The important fact is that the end-product is a doubled sound. The same result, following assimilation, is obtained when stem-ending *-b* combines with *w-*; cf. ᵈ*Te-e-eš-šu-u-up-pè* Mit. II 72; ᵈ*Te-eš-šu-up-pí* XXV 44 v 6, XXVII 38 ii 14, 20, etc.; with other suffixes added we get ᵈU*ᵘᵖ-pí-na* XXV 44 v 8, XXVII 14 ii 4; ᵈU*ᵘᵖ-pí-na-aš* XXVII 46 iv 2; ᵈU*ᵘᵖ-pí-na-ša* XXVII 42 obv. 36. In all these occurrences the *-b* of *Tešu/ob* + *w-* yield *-pp-*. That the labial of the case-ending was not lost is shown by its occasional retention in the form ᵈU*ᵘᵇ-wiᵢ-na* VII 58 iii 12; XXVII 1 i 72, 74, 75 as against ᵈU*ᵘᵖ-pí-na* (above).

This assimilation of *w-* is not restricted to instances with a preceding labial. We find it again[38] in ᵈ*Ḫé-bat-te/i* XXVII 1 ii 55, 38 iii 8 and ᵈ*Ḫé-bat-te-na-* XXV 45. 7, XXIX 8 ii 30, alongside the unassimilated forms [ᵈ*Ḫé*]*-bat-wiᵢ* XXVII 4. 5, and with a following *-na* in XXV 44 ii 2, 4, XXVII 4. 4, 8 obv. 16, rev. 1, 4, 5, 7. It follows that the sound was assimilated to more than one kind of preceding consonant, for all the occasional graphic inconsistency in expressing the process. We are justified, therefore, in regarding *-že/i* and *-ža* [81] as the product of *-ž* + *w* + vowel, with the consonant written single only because the double writing might be mistaken for *-š*; cf. [80].

83. The sequence of voiced + voiceless labial spirant results in a doubled voiceless spirant. The combination occurs when the possessive pron. suff. of the 1 p. sg. is followed by the gen. suff. *-we* or the dat. suff. *-wa;* e. g., *še-e-ni-iw-wə-ú-e* (Mit. I 61, II 57, III 21, etc.) "of my father"; *at-ta-iw-wə-ú-a*

[37] The discovery of the function of this *-ž-* before case-endings is due to Goetze, whose article on the subject, scheduled for publication in RHA, I have kindly been allowed to see and use. [See now RHA 39 (1940) 193-204].

[38] So Goetze, cf. the preceding note.

[53] "to my father," *e-e-ni-iw-wə-ú-a* (Mit. III 98) "to my god." The Mit. orthography has evolved here a method of avoiding confusion with the stops by using the digraph *-ww-* for a voiceless labial spirant and adding *-ú-* to mark the doubling before a dissimilar vowel.

84. A different morphologic combination confronts us in the suffix cluster which appears as *-i-uw-wə* and signifies the 1 p. sg. of negated transitive verbs, e. g., *ta-a-nu-ši-uw-wə,* freely "I did not do"; cf. [53 n. 97] and [195]. The component elements are: *-i-* (the stem-vowel with transitive verbs) + **-wa-* (negating element) + suffix referring to the first person.

The nature of the personal suffix in this instance is of special interest. Apart from the present cluster, the first person is indicated by *-a-ú* in verbs and *-iwwə* in nouns (poss. suff.). Since *ta-a-nu-ši-uw-wə* and its analogues are plainly verbal forms, to judge from their syntax which corresponds to that of the un-negated forms, the final *-wwə* has to be compared with *-a-ú*; and yet, the phonetic, or—at least—orthographic correspondence is with -(*i*)*wwə*. It thus becomes evident that *-a-ú* and *-iwwə* are related morphemes which differ phonologically: **-af*: **-ef*. It would follow that the transitive verb employed possessive suffixes: *ta-a-na-ú* (Mit. II 92), i. e., **tan-af* "done by/of me": *še-e-ni-iw-wə* (Mit. I 18, 49, etc.), i. e., **žen-ef* "my brother." Note especially *e-ni-wu-úš* [53] "by my god," where the single *-w-* of the Akkadianizing syllabary of Mâri confirms the conclusion that Mit. *-ww-* represents a single voiceless spirant. This comparison finds support in the analogous relation of the possessive *-i/ya* "his" [146] to the verbal agent-suffix of 3 p. present *-ya* [195]; it is not weakened by the juxtaposition *-v* [145]: *-u/o* [195] in the corresponding suffixes of 2 p.

The cluster *-i-uw-wə* resolves itself, then, into *-i* + **wa* + **af*. The end-product is **-iuf,* in which the vowel of **-wa-* appears to have been lost through syncope with the labial assuming vocalic function, perhaps under accentual influence.

85. When a suffix with an initial consonant is joined to a form ending in *-n,* a secondary vowel will separate the two consonants. That vowel is

(a) *-a-* before the particle *-man*; the preceding *-n* is written double; e. g., *tižann* + *a* + *man* Mit. II 95, III 50; *edi* + *dann* + *a* + *man* Mit. III 46, 83; *Mane* + *nn* + *a* + *man* Mit. II 57, 86, 91, 95, IV 54, 57. Note, however, *annun-man* KBo V 2 ii 23 (cf. *an-nu-u-un* ibid.), which may indicate that the above rule was not followed in Bogh.

(b) *-i-* before the pronominal elements *-tta-* "I," *-lla-* "they," and apparently also the particle *-dan*; the preceding *-n* is not doubled. Cf. *tišan* + *i* + *tta* + *n* Mit. III 87, *wurd* + *en* + *i* + *tta* + *n* ibid. 77; *edi* + *dan*

+ *i* + *lla* + *man* Mit. III 47, *ḫažaž* + *illain* + *i* + *lla* + *n* Mit. IV 23; *su-bi-a-maš-ti-e-ni-dan* Mit. III 88 (i. e., *subiamašt* + *en* + *i* + *dan*).

Another type of secondary vowel seems to confront us in the "connective" *-u-* which is found between a form-ending consonant and the agentive suff. *-š*; cf. [75], and for the pl. *-(na-)šu-uš* see [74].

86. Secondary doubling of *-n* before a suffixed vowel is attested as follows:

(a) Before *a*, when this vowel

(1) constitutes a suffix, e. g., *ti-ša-a-an-na* Mit. III 14, IV 34 (< *tiža* "heart" + *n* + *a* [156]); *šu-u-we-ni-e-en-na* Mit. III 23 (< *šuwe* "of me" + *ne* + *n* + *a*);

(2) begins a suffix, e. g., all occurrences of the particle *-an* [211] when its *a* is written double:[39] cf. *ma-a-an-na-a-an* Mit. I 84; *Ma-ni-en-na-a-an* Mit. I 114, II 7, 111, IV 52; *ti-ši-iw-we-en-na--a-an* Mit. III 75, 85, 89 (< *tižif* "my heart" *-n* + *an*); *ši-ri-en--na-a-an* Mit. III 34 (< *širen* "let [it] accord" *-an*). But when the vowel is written single, the preceding *n* is likewise undoubled; cf. *ma-a-na-an* Mit. I 93; *Ma-ni-e-na-an* Mit. II 13, IV 35; *ta-ri--i-te-na-an* Mit. III 30, *pè-te-eš-ti-e-na-an* ibid. 34; see [88];

(3) is of secondary origin; cf. [85(a)].

(b) Before *u*, e. g., *še-e-ni-iw-ú-e-ni-e-en-nu-uḫ-ḫa ti-ša-a-an-nu-uḫ-ḫa* Mit. II 10 (both words end in *-n* + *uḫḫa*); *ti-ši-iw-wu-ú-un-nu-uḫ-ḫa* Mit. III 86.

(c) Before *i* no doubling occurs; cf. [85(b)].

86a. Of a different type, because it involves the initial consonant of suffixed particles, is the frequent doubling of *n* in *-ne* and *-na* after *-u* or *-a*: cf. *ḫeya-runna* "every" (pl.) [114]; *ši-un-na* XXVII 47 i 10, 48 v 19: *ši-i-e-ni* ibid. 46 i 25, XXIX 8 ii 45, *ši-i-e-na* XXVII 46 iv 8, 18, KBo II 21. 13 [cf. now ZA 46. 95 f.]; similarly, with *-ne,* in *-kkonne,* e. g., *ašḫožikkonne* "sacri-ficer(?)" Goetze, RHA 35. 105 n. 12;[39a] note also KUR *Masrianne-n* Mit. I 10, IV 128 *-we* ibid. II 71.

After *-e* the *n* is normally undoubled [137]. There occur, however, occasional doublets of the type *e-ki-en-ni-in* XXVII 46 i 20: *e-ki-ni-iš* ibid. iv 1; *e-ew-ri-in-ni-iš* ibid. i 21, *ew-[ri-en-]ni*[40] Mit. II 71, 72: *e-wi-ir-ni* Mit. IV

[39] Friedrich, BChG 18, would extend this rule to other consonants, including the stops. But the double writing of *-šš-* in *ᴵGiliyaššān,* which he cites, is due to orthographic and not phonologic considerations; cf. [44].

[39a] Goetze informs me that his reference was not intended as a translation; for this he would suggest "above-mentioned" which may well be right.

[40] For the supplementation cf. Speiser, JAOS 60. 266 n. 5.

127, 129, *e-we$_e$-er-ne* XXVII 38 iv 10 ff. In some instances of this type (e. g., *ewrenne* : *ewerne*) the double *n* appears in the noun as predicate whereas the single form is associated with the noun as attribute. Analogous doubling of radical *n* is found in the onomastic elements *-enni, -ženni* as against *eni, žena* The doubling may thus be syntactic, but the usage seems to lack regularity.

No manifest principle underlies the alternation in *ad-da-ni-bi-en* XXVII 2 ii 4 and *add/ttaniwina* XXV 44 v 9, XXVII 1 i 71, 72 as against *add/ttan-nib/wina-* XXVII 6 i 26, 8 obv. 16, 17, 14 ii 5, 42 rev. 9 (all from *attay* "father").

87. The treatment of *-m* is obscured by morphologic uncertainties. We know, however, that the particle *anam* "thus" [131] Mit. II 96, IV 10, 13 doubles its *-m* before a vowel; cf. *a-nam-ma-a-an* Mit. III 51, *a-nam-mil-la-a-an* ibid. II 56, IV 126, *a-nam-mi-it-ta-ma-an* ibid. III 62, 64. Similarly, the verbal nouns in *-um* double their *-m* before vowels; cf., e. g., *še-e-ḫ̮a-lu-um* XXIX 8 ii 48: *še-ḫ̮a-lu-um-ma-a-al-la* XXVII 46 i 22 (but single *-m-* ibid. 24); note also *id-du-um-mi* Mit. I 93, *wa-aḫ̮-ru-um-me* [*ta-a-d*]*u-ka-a-ru-um-me* ibid. IV 111-2, and cf. the Hurro-Akkadian construction with *-umma epēšu*.[41]

88. The single writing of the vowel in the particle *-an* when a preceding *l* or *n* is written single, and the converse interdependence of double consonant and vowel, have been noted in [22] and [86 (2)]. The regular observance of this interdependence indicates, however, some binding phonologic law. Its precise nature is uncertain, but it is probable that accentual conditions were here the determining factors.

The same law applies also to the phonemes *s̄* and *z̄* when followed by *-an*. On the one hand, we have *še-e-ni-iw-wə-ša-an* Mit. IV 14, 57 and *še-e-na-wə--ša-an* ibid. I 84, instead of *-šš-* for the agentive suffix used intervocalically.[42] On the other hand, we get *u-u-mi-i-ni-iw-wa-aš-ša-a-an* Mit. III 109 "to our lands," and *i-i-ri-i-in-iw-wa-aš-ša-a*[*-an*] ibid. 123 "our aid,"[43] instead of the expected *-š-* which ordinarily marks the plural of possessive pronouns.[44] It appears thus that the phonologic principle involved, whereby the quantity of the vowel in *-an* induced a corresponding treatment of the preceding con-

[41] See Gordon, Orientalia 7. 51 ff. and add Speiser, JAOS 59. 321 n. 86.

[42] The example from Mit. IV 14 is not clear syntactically, although the agentive is probable in this case; it is certain in the two remaining instances.

[43] Cf. JAOS 59. 305 and n. 49. The two instances just cited caused me to regard the sibilant in *-iw-wa-aš* as voiceless; cf. Lang. 16 (1940) 323 f. But the evidence of *iš-ta-ni-iw-wa-ša* Mit. I 81, II 65, 67, etc. shows this pluralizing element to be voiced in this combination just as it is elsewhere.

[44] The first example is in the dative, the other in the nominative.

sonant, outweighed the orthographic principle of marking voice by single writing and voicelessness by double writing [79].

89. When a consonant (especially *-n-* or *-r-*) which follows a contiguous medial consonant is doubled, the resulting cluster is broken up by an anaptyctic vowel which corresponds to the nearest preceding vowel. E. g., *ḫab/wurni* "earth" VII 58 ii 11, XXVII 6 i 13, 42 obv. 34 (cf. also ibid. 6, XXIX 8 ii 48): *ḫawurunni*[45] Mâri 6. 14; XXVII 28 iv 7, 38 ii 10, 15, iv 30, 42 obv. 19, 46 i 19, 22, 28; *pí-iš-ra(-ma-a)* XXVII 38 i 10: *pí-ši-ir-ri* ibid. 14 (< **pišr* + *-ne*); doubtless also *Mi-zi-ir-ri* Mit. I 62, 85, 105 "Egypt" (< **Mizri-ne*) as compared with *Masrianni* Mit. I 10, II 69, 71, etc.; cf. also [108].

90. When a suffix consisting of consonant + *a* occurred at the end of a word, the vowel was subject to loss. Evidence for this process is available especially from Bogh., where the comparative scarcity of *-an*[46] provided the necessary condition for apocopate forms. The evidence is clearest in the case of *-lla*: cf. *Galgamiž* +*ul* [75]; *nu-u-ya-al* XXIX 8 iii 30: *nu-i-wa$_a$-al-la* XXVII 42 rev. 12 (in parallel passages); *ma-a-at-ta-al* XXVII 38 iii 14, 15 (in association with plural forms), and the like. From Mâri we get such forms as *u-wa-al* 1. 1, *u-šu-ul* 1. 2, *ša-a-wu-ul* 3. 16, *mu-ur-ri-il* ibid. 18, but these texts are not sufficiently clear as yet for definite identification of the forms in question.

The directive suffix *-ta* is treated analogously in *aš-te-ni-wa$_a$-ni-id* followed by *e-ti-da* VIII 61 obv. 6; here the usual combination of *edi* + *da* "with regard to" with the dative (*-ni-wa*) is repeated, but an appositional directive suffix (this time *-d*, joined with the aid of the attr. part. *-ne*) is added to the dependent noun in accordance with the Hurrian principle of suffix-duplication;[47] add perhaps also *ú-šu-um-mi-ni-id* VBoT 69 ii 8.

Doubtful instances of apocopate *-ra* [154] are *še-e-li-iš-ti-bur zi-ri-bur* VBoT 69 iii 4.

For *-m* as a probable apocopated form of *-ma* cf. [75] and [212].

91. Haplologic loss of syllables is evidenced by isolated occurrences. Thus ^{URU}*Ša-mu-u-ḫi* XXVII 1 ii 70 obviously represents *Šamu⟨ḫa⟩ḫi*, just as ^{URU}*Ša-mu-u-ḫi-na* ibid. 71 stands for *Šamu⟨ḫa⟩ḫina*.[48] Another good illus-

[45] For the double *n* cf. [86a]. [See now the full list including unpublished occurrences in Brandenstein's account in ZA 46. 86 ff.]

[46] Cf. Friedrich, BChG 21 f.

[47] The so-called "Suffixübertragung," cf. [132, 238]. Whether *ar-pa-aš-du-ud* XXVII iv 12 (preceded by the "prepositional" term *wu$_u$-ri-i-ta*) is another instance of apocopated *-da* is difficult to determine at present.

[48] Noted by Friedrich, Analecta Orientalia 12. 124 n. 3.

tration ^{d}*IŠTAR^{ga}-bi-na-šu-uš* ^{d}*Na-bar-bi-na-šu-uš* XXIX 8 ii 34 "(by the rivers) of Shaushka (and) of Nabarbi," where the gen. suff. *-b/we* is lost after an identical syllable which ends the name of the god. An instance of haplology is also *ša-a-at-ti-la-an* Mit. III 108, and possibly *š*[*a*]-*a*[*t*]-*ti-la* Mâri 6. 13 "we together(?)" for **šatti-dila*(-*n*), cf. [39 n. 61].

92. Metathesis of liquids or *n* and an adjacent consonant is attested frequently in proper names; e. g., *Elḫib-* : *Eḫlib-*, *Nirḫi-* : *Niḫri-*, *Warḫi-* : *Waḫri*, *-šanda* : *-šadna*, cf. Berkooz, Lang. Dissert. 23. 63-4. Note also *Paḫri-* [52] for another writing of the above *Waḫri-*. But the parade example of metathesis is *ewri* "lord," which common-Hurrian form is opposed only by Nuzi *erwi*.[49] Here the choice of this or that phonologic alternant has become characteristic of a dialectal division which separates Eastern Hurrian from other groups which are predominantly western.

92a. Possible evidence of accentual conditions has so far been mentioned in connection with the secondary doubling of consonants [86a, 88]. It remains to be pointed out that the treatment of *-a-* in two common suffixed particles may also be viewed as potential evidence, necessarily circumstantial and by no means conclusive, of underlying stress conditions. The particles in question are *-an* and *-man*. Their vowel is written in Mit. sometimes single and other times double, the alternation corresponding at times to significant changes of meaning [210 ff.]. The inherent probability that the double writing was due to stress, in all likelihood secondary with these "enclitics," will henceforward be indicated in normalized transcription by ` : *-màn* for *-ma-a-an* and *-àn* for *-a-an*.

For the consistent *-lan* with particles, as against normal *-llàn* in other contexts cf. [128].

[49] Cf. Speiser, Mesopotamian Origins 145 n. 90; JAOS 55 (1935) 438. For a proposed Cappadocian parallel cf. *Er-we-* (Oppenheim, RHA 33 [1938] 19); but *ewri* seems also attested in Cappadocia by *Im-ri* (ibid. 18).

IV. MORPHOLOGIC ELEMENTS

93. The available Hurrian material contains for the most part external means for separating the individual words. In the syllabic texts this is made possible by adequate spacing; a notable example of that is the Mitanni letter. In the alphabetic documents special word-dividers are found, as a rule; cf., e. g., RŠ X 4.[1]

94. Linguistic analysis contributes the necessary internal criteria for distinguishing between the underlying stems and the grammatical elements that may be used with them. These elements are placed invariably after the stem, often in lengthy[2] chains which are characterized by a fixed order of composition. Cf., e. g., *a-ru-u-ša-uš-še-ni-e-we* Mit. III 41, where grammatical analysis establishes the following constituents: the verbal stem *ar* "give" + the perfect-participle *ož* + suffix referring to 1 p. sg. *a-ú* (**af*) + nominalizing particle *še* (wr. *-šše-*) + attributive particle *ne* + genitive suffix *we*. Similarly, alphabetic *aržln* RŠ XX B 11 consists of the same verbal stem followed by three suffixes which are indicated here by the consonants *-ž-*, *-l-*, and *-n*.[3] Since the writing marks the above forms as single words, and since the suffixed elements involved are never written alone, we are justified in concluding that these elements were not spoken alone; accordingly, they constitute bound forms. It follows that Hurrian possesses a definite system of morphology.[4]

95. Practical considerations militate, however, against analyzing the facts of Hurrian grammar under the traditional divisions of Morphology and Syntax. Among the many suffixes which a single Hurrian word may accumulate some are derivational and would come under morphology, while others prove to be relational and indicative of syntactic connections. Furthermore, Hurrian employs several groups of "enclitic" elements which clearly belong to the field of syntax. Consequently, the same word would have to be discussed more than once under both heads. Perhaps the strongest argument against this form of divided treatment is the one inherent in our present knowledge

[1] Contrast RŠ X 7, where lack of dividers adds greatly to the difficulty of interpreting the text.

[2] In *aš-ḫu-ši-ku-un-ni-ni-bi-na-aš-ta* XII 44 ii 6 "to those of the sacrificer (?)" as many as ten suffixes can be distinguished, modifying the underlying *ašḫu* : *-ož* + *i* + *kk* + *o* + *nne* + *ne* + *we* + *na* + **ž* + *ta*.

[3] Cf. *a-ru-ši-el-la-a-im* XXVII 8 iii 34 and *a-[ru-ši-]in-na-a-in* XXVII 42 rev. 13.

[4] Cf. L. Bloomfield, Language (1933) 183.

of the subject. Our efforts at a strictly descriptive presentation are complicated at every turn by the need to interpret the material before it can be analyzed grammatically. It is often a question of interpretation whether this or that element is properly of morphologic or syntactic character. For instance, if the *n*-form of the noun is a case-ending, it should not be ignored under morphology; but if it is merely a predicative particle, it is wholly a problem for syntax. Until this and many like questions are settled beyond any doubt, specific listings in the one division as against the other are apt to be prejudicial.

96. In view of these circumstances the arrangement here followed is based on the mechanical principle of distinguishing individual morphemes from complex units. The morphemes include free roots and bound forms, both classes having been combined for the purposes of this discussion under Morphologic Elements. The complex units, whether they constitute a full phrasal word or a sentence, will be surveyed in the next section under the head of Construction. It should be stressed that both these main sections involve questions of morphology as well as syntax. In order to narrow down the semantic range of a number of morphemes hitherto undetermined it will be necessary to examine their respective functions. On the other hand, the order of the individual bound forms within the complex nominal or verbal unit, surveyed in the section on construction, is technically a matter of morphology. The advantage of the present arrangement, which is dictated by the nature of the language and our knowledge of it to date, lies in the fact that we are not concerned with the problem as to which process is morphologic and which is syntactic. What is far more practical, for the time being at least, is that a separate listing of the morphologic elements should help us to understand the means whereby the individual constituents are combined into larger units. The following groupings are intended as a convenient inventory of such basic constituents analytically arranged.

97. The morphologic elements of Hurrian consist, then, of free roots and bound forms, in this case suffixes. For purposes of grammatical organization both types have to be classified into respective parts of speech. Thus far we have been using the conventional terms that are current in Indo-European and Semitic grammars, and have been referring accordingly to nouns, pronouns, verbs, adverbs, and the like. This terminology has been followed as a means of easy reference. It will be retained for the sake of convenience, but subject to the limitations imposed by the internal evidence of Hurrian. This evidence is provided by the distinctive suffixes (as opposed to the non-distinctive root-complements [174 ff.]) with which primary roots and complex stems may combine into full words.

98. Among the suffixes of Hurrian three groups prove distinctive in that each characterizes a separate class of words:

(1) Suffixes indicative of possessive and case relations.

(2) Suffixes which differentiate the supporting root or stem for tense, mood, agent or person, and the like [178].

(3) "Associative" suffixes which are non-morphologic but require the support of some radical element in the sentence,[5] the choice of the specific root depending on the requirements of word-order. These associatives may be conjoined, accordingly, with words of groups (1) and (2), but no other accompaniment is possible in group (3).

It will be seen that from a formal standpoint (1) represents nouns, (2) verbs, and (3) particles. As parts of speech these categories are further individualized by their functions in the sentence. The formal criterion just cited has, however, independent validity in furnishing external indications as to the part of speech involved.[6]

99. These formal differences in the treatment of noun, verb, and particle do not imply a correspondingly sharp semantic differentiation between the three categories. There exist simple means of turning a noun into a verb and a verb into a noun; evidently, therefore, the underlying root-meanings were not always sharply demarcated. Cf., e. g., *arožaf-še-ne-we* [94]; here the finite verbal form *arožaf* (= *ar* + *ož* + *af*) "given-past-by-me" has been turned into a nominal attribute by means of the nominalizing element *-še*, and is provided, consequently, with the nominal suffixes *-ne-we*; examples of this type are numerous. We shall see that the so-called *i*-form of the verb is properly nominal (participial) thanks to the function of the *-i* [170]; this form is capable of employing characteristic nominal suffixes, e. g., *kabožì-ne-b* XXVII 42 rev. 20, *kabožì-b* ibid. 21. Conversely, the noun *turubi* "danger" Mit. III 111[7] appears with a verbal suffix in *du-ru-bi-i-in-nu-uk-ku* Mit. I 17. Even particles, or words which on the analogy of related terms may be regarded as particles, can be made into nouns or verbs; cf., e. g., *kuru* "again" Mit. III 15, 39, etc.; *gu-ru-ú-we* "of the return?" [214] Mit. IV 42; *gu-ru-u-u-*[*ša*] "returned-by-him(?)" Mit. I 45. It follows that the Hurrian

[5] Cf. Sapir, Language (1921) 74 n. 10. In Hurrian we find this type of suffix chiefly among conjunctions and personal pronouns in the subject case; cf., e. g., *billoži-tta-*(*a*)*n* Mit. II 26 "and (*-an*) I (*-tta-*) communicated," where *-tta-* and *-an* are associatives. I use this term (suggested by my colleague Z. S. Harris) in preference to the current "enclitics" because we have no means of knowing that all such elements were atonic; moreover, "enclitic" would be applicable with equal right to other bound forms as well.

[6] For a detailed classification of the suffixes see [132 ff.].

[7] For the meaning and other occurrences cf. Speiser, JAOS 59. 313 f.

root was not at all times inherently noun, verb, or particle; but each of these categories was typified by its ability or inability to take on given grammatical markers, depending on the required function as part of speech which it was to fill in the sentence.

100. The Hurrian noun assumes a number of functions which other languages distribute frequently among separate parts of speech: substantive, adjective, pronoun, numeral, adverb, and even preposition. All of these linguistic forms, including nominalized prepositions, prove to constitute a uniform category in Hurrian, to judge from the fact that they employ identical suffixes to express attributive relations. We have thus, e. g., the same case-endings for adjective and noun in K[UR] *Mi-zi-ir-ri-e-we* KUR *u-u-mi-i-in-ni-e-we* Mit. I 62 "of the Egyptian land" (gen. sg. *-we*) and *u-u-ul-la-a-ša* KUR *u-u-mi--i-in-na-a-ša* Mit. III 73 "to all the lands" (dat. pl. *-ža* < **-ž-wa*); the dat. sg. suff. of the substantive (*-wa*) occurs also with pronoun and preposition in *we-e-wa e-ti-i-wa* ibid. 55 "concerning thee," lit. "to thee, to (the) concern." Similarly, possessive and case-suffixes of the substantive are found in *iš-ta-ni--iw-wa-ša* "we mutually," e. g., ibid. 108 (1 pl. poss. *-ifaž* + loc. *-a*, lit. "in our mutualness"), or "to us mutually," e. g., Mit. I 81 (same poss. suff. + dat. -(*w*)*a*); *ši-ni-a-še-* Mit. III 40 "of their two" (3 pl. poss. *-yaž* + gen. -[*w*]*e*). In subsequent description the conventional terms cited above will be retained to identify the various sub-classes of the Hurrian noun as viewed from our standpoint. For the understanding of Hurrian, however, it is important to note that such subdivisions are not indicated by any morphologic feature apparent to us;[8] there is no proof that they existed in the consciousness of the speaker. All that we can assert is that Hurrian recognizes only nouns as opposed to verbs and particles.

101. The following grouping will distinguish, accordingly, between free roots and bound forms. The free roots will be discussed under three classes: nouns, verbs, and particles. For practical reasons the nouns will be subdivided into substantives (including adjectives), pronouns, and numerals. These subdivisions will simplify the survey of the material, even though they have in Hurrian a syntactic rather than a morphologic standing. But it should be emphasized that the differences between the proposed sub-classes cannot always be drawn sharply; it is difficult to decide at times—since formal criteria are lacking—whether a given nominal root should be cited under this or that heading.

[8] The so-called adjectives in *-ḫe* are merely derivative nouns formed with the aid of a special derivational suffix; their grammatical treatment differs in no way from that of nouns.

The large group which comprises the bound forms will likewise be divided into classes that have reference to function but not necessarily to form.

A. FREE ROOTS

102. The vowels which characterize nominal roots and verbal roots and bases pose the question as to whether they are independent morphemes or an integral part of the root. When present in the noun, they precede any distinctive suffix; e. g., *žarr-a-šiḫe-* "pertaining to kingship" XXVII 42 rev. 15 ff.; with verbs we get forms like *utḫ-a-b, ḫaž-i-b,* and *ur-u-kko.*[9] That some of these vowels may be morphophonemic is indicated by the fact that in verbs *-i-* and *-u-* are used with "transitives while *-a-* is employed with intransitives."[10] We know that analogous uses were possible with the noun; thus *-i* interchanges with *-a* in such forms as *urḫe* "true" (cf. *ur-ḫé-e-en* Mit. II 106) : *urḫa* (ibid.), or *žarri* "king" (XXVII 38 iv 11, 29) : *žarra* (ibid. 19, 21).

Now the morphologic character of the *-a* in *urḫa* is clear: the vowel marks a case-ending, cf. [156]. What is less plain is the interpretation of the final vowel in *urḫe*; and similarly, in *žena* "brother," *ene* "god," or *kuru* "again." For the present it is not advisable, however, to venture a definitive solution of the problem; the question is left open as to whether we should regard all such vowels as morphophonemic or consider some of them as radical.

But the following classification will be simplified if we list the nominal roots with their respective characteristic vowels, wherever possible. For methodological reasons these vowels will be indicated in normalized transcription by suspended letters:[11] e. g., *urḫ^{e}, žen^{a}, kur^{u}.* Forms which have such vowels will be called stems and their vocalic ending will be spoken of as the stem-ending.[12] Where the stem-vowel is zero we may speak of consonant-stems.

As regards verbal roots, practical considerations are against a similar normalized listing. Instead, we shall be able to subsume the available forms under two main functional classes, the transitives and the intransitives, depending in part on the choice of given vowels, although these cannot be regarded as radical; cf. [117].

[9] Cf. JAOS 59. 297 ff.

[10] Ibid.

[11] Following v. Brandenstein (Br. 571 n. 1); he has not set forth, however, his own reasons for this practice.

[12] See already [61 ff.] and [67 n. 14].

1. Nouns

a. Substantives

103. Stems in *-a*.[13] Cf. *el*^{a} "sister" (Mit. III 37); *šal*^{a} "daughter" (Mit. I 47); *žen*^{a} "brother" (*še-e-na-a-an* Mit. II 79; *še-e-na-pa-an* Mit. I 91); *šawal*^{a} "year" (*ša-wə-la-we* RŠ Voc. I 13 and *ša-wa-al-la-ša* Mit. I 79);[14] *tiž*^{a} "heart" (*ti-ša-a-ma-a-an* Mit. IV 32 and *ti-ša-a-dan* Mit. III 92); *pab*^{a} "mountain" [62 n. 3]; also *šey*^{a} "river, water, etc." (Br. 563 n. 2). Here seems to belong *ni-ra-da* Mâri 5. 3, of unknown meaning, with the directive suffix *-da*; perhaps also *wu*$_{u}$*-ga-a-da* VIII 61 rev. 9. A number of geographic names in *-a* are established by the form in *-aḫḫe* [62].

It may be significant that the nouns of this group are confined to primary concepts, such as kinship terms, certain geographic names, and words like "heart" and "mountain." They do not betray any connection with verbal concepts and they fail to include words which are adjectival in meaning.[15]

104. Stems in *-e/i*.[16] This group comprises the great majority of nominal stems. E. g., *ard*^{e} "city" (XXVII 39 rev. 2); *ašt*^{e} "woman" (Mit. III 1; for the *-e* cf. *aš-te-ni-wa*$_{a}$*-ni-id* VIII 61 obv. 6); *awar*^{i} "field" (cf. *a-wə-ri-we* RŠ Voc. IV 25, and for *-wa-* note the forms of the type *a-wa-ar-ri-we*$_{e}$ XXVII 1 ii 12); *en*^{e} "god" [22]; *ež*^{e} "heaven"[17] (XXVII 6 1 13; for the *-e* cf., e. g., *e-e-še-ni* Mit. IV 125); *ewr*^{i} "lord" [92]; *tiw*^{e} "word, thing" (Mit. I 80); *omin*^{i} "land" (ibid. 90). For adjectival concepts cf. *pal*^{i} "false(?)"[18] (*pa-a-*[*li-*]*ma-a-an* Mit. II 106); *tur*^{i} "low" RŠ Voc. IV 5); *urḫ*^{e} "true" (in proper names; cf. also *ur-ḫé-e-en* Mit. II 106).

This stem-vowel is found also with certain pronouns [109 ff.], and the numeral *tumn*^{i} "four" (Mit. II 59).

It should be pointed out that only *-e* can be ascertained for this group. The

[13] In the following examples only one reference is given as a rule, especially when a given word or form is well known. Where the stem-form itself occurs, the actual spelling has not been appended. The citations in parentheses give the form or forms which establish the stem-vowel in other instances, or which indicate the quality of a medial vowel after *w* (e. g., *ša-wa-al-la-ša*: *ša-wə-la-we*).

[14] Cf. JAOS 59. 296 n. 29.

[15] Forms like *šeḫala* "pure," *ḫižma* (for the *-ž-* cf. *ḫižim-* Mit. II 115), etc. do not belong to the nominal class proper. They are intransitive verbal nouns in *-a*, cf. [169].

[16] Although it is not unlikely that the stem-vowel of this group was uniform in quality, orthographic limitations require that both *-e* and *-i* be considered for the time being. In normalized transcription *-e* has been employed when supported by at least one spelling; elsewhere *-i* has been used.

[17] For the meaning cf. Br. 571 n. 1.

[18] Cf. Friedrich, BChG 40.

forms in *-i*, without variant writings with *-e*, are ambiguous in that the orthography does not preclude *e*-quality where such signs as LI, NI, and RI are involved [25]. It is not absolutely certain, therefore, that Hurrian possessed simple nominal stems in *-i*; cf. [105]. In derivative stems, however, based on verbal roots, *-i* is established beyond dispute; cf. [187 n. 232].

105. To this group belong also several known nominalized prepositions [128]. These include *ai-* and *edi/e-* [69]. On their analogy, which extends to syntax and the choice of specific suffixes, we may add *abi-* (e. g., *a-a-bi-ta* XXIX 8 iv 26, 30); *ḫuri-* (*ḫu-u-ri-ta* XXIX 8 iii 38; *ḫu-u-ri-ya-ša* XXVII 42 rev. 19); *paḫi-* (e. g., XXVII 1 ii 4, 44. 4, 9, XXIX 8 iv 11, 25; *pa-a-ḫi-ta* ibid. iii 9, 12, 18; *pa-a-ḫi-i-ta* Mit. I 61; *pa-a-ḫi-ib* XXIX 8 iii 21; *pa-a-ḫi-pa* ibid. ii 36; *pa-a-ḫi-i-wə* Mit. I 60; cf. also *pġd-m* RŠ X 4. 3); *paži-* (e. g., XXIX 8 iv 24; *pa-a-ši-ta* XXVII 42 rev. 17; *pa-a-ši-pa* XXIX 8 iv 18); *wuri-* (e. g., *wu*$_{u}$*-ri-i-ta* XXVII 29 iv 12 and *wə-ri-i-ta* Mit. I 91, III 88!; *wu-ri-iw-wə* ibid. II 94; *wu-ri-a-ša* ibid. III 73). The origin of some of these terms is not clear; thus *ai-* and *edi-* can be used as conjunctions [128], and *wuri-* (and perhaps *paži-*) [19] may be based on the verbal concept "know." But their treatment as nouns in the instances just cited is demonstrated by the suffixes. There remains the question as to the stem-vowel. The use of *-i-* in this connection is inconclusive, since this vowel may represent the pronominal element "his, its" [69]. However, the writing *i-te-pa* [22] shows an *-e* in this particular stem and the substantive *pa-ḫé* Mit. IV 13 indicates the same stem-vowel for the derivative prepositional term. The probability that the remaining forms had the same stem-vowel is thus enhanced.

106. Stems in *-u*. Clear substantival stems in *-u* are rare. From the RŠ Voc. we get *ašḫ*^{u} "high" (IV 5), *uliwər*^{u} "extent" (ibid. 24), and *utḫur*^{u} "side" (ibid. 16). It is uncertain, however, whether the last two are simple stems; their *-r-* may be a derivational element. A nominalized form based on an *u*-stem is apparently *gu-ru-ú-we* (gen.(?) Mit. IV 42). With the plural particle *-na* *u*-stems yield *-unna* (e. g., *a-la-nu-un-na* XXV 42 v 2, 4, 10; *zi-ya-ru-un-na* ibid. 13) in accordance with [86].

For other *u*-stems (in pronouns) see [110]; that this vowel is characteristic of the independent particles may be seen from [127].

107. Diphthong stems. The only clear instances of such stems are *attay* "father" and *allay* "lady"; cf. [68].

[19] Note the verb *wər-* in *wə-ri-e-ta* Mit. III 13, *wə-ri-e-e-ta* ibid. III 15, IV 39, etc. (cf. [214 n. 309]). For *paž-* cf. Nuzi *pa-šu-nu* = Akk. *mûdû* "expert," cf. Gordon, Orientalia 7. 56 f.

108. Consonant stems. Their number does not appear to have been large. Apart from proper names (e. g., [77]), we may note as examples *ḫawur-* "earth" (Thureau-Dangin, RA 36. 23 f.) and *muž-* "exalted," or the like (ibid. 22 f.). Before certain suffixes these stems develop often anaptyctic vowels which correspond to the nearest preceding vowel [89]; cf. also *zu-úr-ki* XXIX 8 ii 41, iv 13 : *zu-ru-un-ki* ibid. ii 42 and *zu-ru-uš-ki* ibid. 44.

b. Pronouns

109. Personal pronouns. Independent personal forms of the first and second persons have been established thus far for the singular only. For the first person Hurrian employs three stems:

iža- (e. g., *i-ša-aš* Mit. III 57) in the agentive;[20]

ište- ([*i*]*š-te-e-en* Mit. II 71) in the subject-case;[21]

šu- (e. g., *šu-u-we* Mit. III 99 "of me") in oblique cases. It is possible that *iža-* and *ište-* contain the same root, but for the present it is advisable to list the two separately.

The second person singular is represented by the single stem *we-*;[22] cf. *we-e-eš-ša-a-an* Mit. III 68 (agentive), *we-e-we* ibid. 58 (genitive), and *we-e-wa* ibid. 55 (dative).[23]

Corresponding plural forms are as yet unknown. A remote possibility for the personal pronoun of the third person is listed in [111]. For the associative personal pronouns cf. [213 ff.].

The identification of *šu-* and *we-* goes back to Messerschmidt, Mitanni-Studien 11 f. and 27.

110. Deictic pronouns. The clearest instance of such a pronoun is *and*^{i} (e. g., *an-ti* Mit. I 57, etc.) "this."[24] Its evident correlate is *ann*^{i} "that"; cf. *an-ni* XXIX 8 iii 59; Mit. II 73, 75, III 121, IV 58; *an-ni-i-in* Mit. III 104; the meaning is apparent from the context in each instance and is confirmed by the two occurrences of *an-nu-dan* (Mit. III 108, 124), which are

[20] Recognized by Friedrich, Analecta Orientalia 12. 133 f.

[21] Cf. Speiser, JAOS 60. 265 ff.

[22] The employment of a single stem for "thou" as against more than one stem for "I" is paralleled in other languages; cf. Friedrich, op. cit. 134, and L. H. Gray, Foundations of Language (1939) 173.

[23] Friedrich, op. cit. 132, finds but one case-form in the written *we-e-wə* of Mit. III 55 and 58 (gen.). But *we-e-wə e-ti-i-wə* (ibid. 55) proves to be an appositive construction in the dative signifying "for thee, for the concern," i. e., "concerning thee"; cf. *at-ta-i-ip-pa* (53) *e-ti-i-ta* (ibid. 52 f.) "for thy father, to his concern," i. e., "concerning thy father"; cf. [235].

[24] A comprehensive treatment of this pronoun is given by Friedrich, RHA 35 (1939) 98 ff.

followed by the anaphoric *šuene-dan*, the whole phrase meaning "because of all this," or "it is because of all this, that . . ." [222].[25]

Perhaps related to *anni*, if not actually identical with it, is the pronoun which occurs in the forms *a-nu-ú-a-ma-a-an* Mit. I 110 (dat.) and *a-nu-ú-ta--ni-il-la* . . ibid. II 69 (directive); neither passage is clear enough, however, for a definite analysis; note, moreover, the single *-n-* in both these occurrences.[26] The corresponding plural is surely to be sought in *a-ni-e-na-a-am--ma-ma-an* Mit. IV 20 "those in particular (*-mmaman*)," preceded by *ti-we* "word(s)." Analogous to *andi* in use is *an-šu-u-a-* Mit. II 69, if we may judge from a single instance.[27]

A pair of correlates paralleling *andi* : *anni* is *agu* : *ak(k)u*; cf. *a-gu-ú-a* Mit. I 81 (dat.) and *a-gu-ú-e* ibid. IV 123 (gen.) "the other of two"; *ag-gu-uš* ibid. I 81 and *ag-gu-uš-ša-a-an* ibid. IV 123 (ag.), *ag-gu-dan* ibid. II 61 (*tan*-form) "the one of two." Except for the last-cited instance, these pronouns are employed in juxtaposition; and *ag-gu-dan* is used in a passage where certain objects (tablets) are enumerated, so that here two "the other of two quantities" is a possible interpretation.

For a different term for "other" cf. [114]. For the pronominal uses of *ma-*, *man(n)-* see [125].

111. A pronominal function seems to inhere in the stem *nuwe*, for which we have the following occurrences: (a) *nu-bi-in* XXVII 38 iv 29; (b) *nu-be-e--ni-na-an* Mit. I 93; the corresponding plural forms are evidently (c) *nu-i--wa$_a$-al-la* XXVII 42 rev. 12 and (d) *nu-u-ya-al* XXIX 8 iii 30, the morphologic identity of the two forms being attested by the parallelism of the passages in question; cf. [27]. Although the context is not altogether clear in any of the above four instances, careful analysis favors the assumption that an anaphoric pronoun is involved. The passages have otherwise nothing in common, the antecedent nouns being respectively (a) "Hittite lord," (b) "Keliya" or "present," and (c, d) "wisdom" (construed as a plural form); but if we take *nuwe* to mean "he, it," or "they" (when followed by *-al[la]*), the difficulty disappears. To be sure, this identification is only provisional. If new material should happen to confirm it, *nuwe* may yet prove to constitute the personal pronoun of the third person.

112. Relative pronouns. We have no evidence for independent relative

[25] For the change of the stem vowel *-i* > *u* cf. [64].

[26] The use of *-ú-* is in accordance with [64]. The stem-vowel was probably *-e*; cf. *anena-* Mit. IV 20. Another instance of this pronoun is perhaps *a-ni-il-l*[*a-a-a*]*n* Mit. I 112.

[27] Both terms are employed with *pis-* "rejoice." Note, however, the *-u-* of *an-šu-u-a-* as against *an-du-ú-a-* Mit. III 89.

pronouns in Hurrian. To form relative clauses Hurrian uses the particle *ya/e-* [130] [28] in combination with *-me/a-* [217] to represent the singular (cf. Friedrich, BChG 25), while the same stem in conjunction with *-lla/e-* [218] indicates the plural (Friedrich, ibid. 29 f.). It may be pointed out in passing that these composite pronominal elements are anticipatory and appositive (Friedrich, loc. cit.); note [130]; e. g., *i-i-al-la-a-ni-i-n* . . . *at-ta-iw-wu-uš* . . . *ti-we-e-na*^{MEŠ} *ta-a-nu-u-ša-a-aš-še-na* Mit. III 55 f. "what-they-indeed(?) . . . -grandfather-my-by . . . things done-past-by-him," i. e., "the things which my grandfather did."

113. Reciprocal relation. This relation is expressed by the stem *ištani-*; it was recognized as far back as Messerschmidt, cf. Mitanni-Studien 37. We do not know, however, whether the stem is simple or composite. What is clear is that it functions like a nominal stem in taking on possessive suffixes and case-endings; cf. [100].

114. Indefinites. The generalizing term for "other" is *ol*^{i} (*u-u-li* Mit. II 79, *u-u-li-ma-a-an* ibid. IV 55, *u-u-li-e-en* ibid. 53); contrast *ak*(*k*)^{u}, which is individualizing "the other of two" [110].

For "every" Hurrian uses the plural form *ḫeyarunna* (e. g., *ḫi-ya-ru-un-na* XXVII 14 iii 4), as has recently been demonstrated by Friedrich, RHA 35 (1939) 93 ff. The stem-vowel induces secondary doubling of the consonant in *-na* in accordance with [86a].

114a. "All" is expressed by means of the stem *šu*^{e}. Since the meaning of this stem has not been recognized so far, and since its uses are varied, a fuller discussion than has been the case with the other stems of this group is in order.

The word is properly a substantive, as may be seen from the instances in which it figures as the subject; cf. *šu-e-e-en an-ti* "this *š.*" Mit. I 57; *šu-e an-ti* ibid. 69, III 4; *an-ti šu-e* ibid. 3.

More frequently this stem appears as an attribute of some pronominal or adjectival element. In such instances it assumes the form *šue* + *ne*. The added element is the attributive particle [136 ff.]. It is noteworthy that *šue-ne* invariably follows the word which it modifies and its concord is only with that word, not with the head-noun of the sentence: ^{I}*Ma-ni-e-el-la-ma-an* (72) *pa-aš-ši-i-it-ḫi-wu-uš wə-ru-u-ša-a-al-la-a-an* (73) *ma-a-na šu-e-ni ti-we-e-e-na ta-a-nu-ša-a-uš-še-na* Mit. I 71 ff., freely,[29] "By Mane, thy envoy, they are

[28] This particle is listed in the present connection in order to make the survey of the pronominal elements of Hurrian more comprehensive.

[29] A strictly literal translation would have to take into account the particles *-man* and *-a-an* and the repeated pronominal enclitic *-lla-*.

known, *m. š.*, the things done by me," i. e., "thy envoy Mane knows the things which I have done — *m. š*"; the untranslated phrase *ma-a-na šu-e-ni* (with singular *-ne*) is independent syntactically from the plural *tiwe-na* which is anticipated by the repeated *-lla-* and resumed by the final suffix of the descriptive verbal noun. Other occurrences of *ma-a-na šu-e-ni* are Mit. I 68 f. (?), 69, II 55 f., III 5, 6; note also *an-du-ú-e-e šu-e-ni-e-e* ibid. III 9; *šuk-kán-ni-ma-a-an šu-e-ni* III 114, 118; *an-nu-dan šu-e-ni-e-dan* III 108 (similarly 124); *ti-i-ḫa-nu-u-lu-ma-a-aš-še-ni šu-e-ni* III 8.

The meaning of *šu*^{e} is bound up with that of the stem which underlies the extended forms *šu-ú-an-na-ma-an* (sg.) and *šu-ú-al-la-ma-an* (pl.). For the latter Messerschmidt suggested "those" (Mitanni-Sprache 21). Friedrich leaves the pair untranslated, but recognizes that the respective suffixes signify number (BChG 4). The invariable use of *-ú-* in these two forms is not necessarily an argument against connecting this stem with *šu*^{e}; cf. [64] for a similar treatment of the vowel of certain pronominal stems before given suffixes. It follows that the ultimate criterion must be the context. If the same basic meaning should be found to suit not only the numerous occurrences of *šu-ú-a-*, but also those of *šu-e* and *šu-e-ni*, the etymological problem might then be considered as settled.

For the understanding of the present pair of forms it is important to point out that both are used after the nouns which they modify and with which they agree in number; in other words, their syntax is the same as that of the established pronominal attributes. The examples (all from Mit.), in reasonably clear contexts, are as follows:

šu-ú-an-na-ma-an:-

KUR *u-u-mi-i-ni-iw-wə š.* I 68, II 17

KUR *u-u-mi-i-ni š.* III 24

ni-ḫa-a-ri-in (28) . . . *pè-te-eš-ti-ten š.* III 27 f.

šu-ú-al-la-ma-an:-

at-ta-a-ar-ti-i-we-na-ma-a-an š. I 88

ti-we-e-na^{MEŠ} *š.*^{MEŠ} I 108; similarly II 80

du-be-na-a-ma-a-an š. II 19 f., 29

i-i-al-li-e-ni[*-i-in*] (21) *tup-pa-ku-u-uš-ḫé-na*^{MEŠ} *š.* II 20 f.

ya-a-la-an . . . [*u-u-u*]*l-la* (83) KUR *u-u-mi-i-in-na š.* II 82 f.

u-u-ul-la-a-an (88) KUR *u-u-mi-i-in-na š.* II 87 f., III 25, 32

u-u-ul-la KUR *u-u-mi-i-in-na š.* II 82 f., 89

KUR *u-u-mi-i-in-na*[*-m*]*a-an* (94) *š.* II 93 f.

wi-i-ra-te-e-na-a-an pa-aš-ši-i-it-ḫé-na^{MEŠ} *š.* III 26

wi-i-ra-te-e-na š. pa-aš-ši-i-it-ḫé-na-a-an š. III 31

i-i-al-li-e-ni-i-in ti-we-e-na^{MEŠ} *š.* IV 30
i-i-al-la-a-ni-i-in KUR *u-u-mi-i-in-na*^{MEŠ} (125) *š.* IV 124 f.

It will be seen from these instances that the noun most frequently found with *š.* is *omini* "land"; [30] next come *tiwe* "word, thing"; *pašithe* "envoy"; (and its companion-term *wirade*), and *dube* "tablet(?)"; *attardi* "father-gift"; *nihari* "dowry," and the unknown term *tuppagošhe* are each mentioned once. Note also that *ominna* is five times described by *olla* "other (pl.)."

The Akkadian letters of Tushratta supply instructive parallel phrases. Here the term *gabbu* "totality, all" is employed frequently with a resumptive possessive suffix followed by the identifying particle *-ma*. Its appositive occurrences are as follows:

mātāti/u gabba/išinā-ma "the countries, all of them" EA 23. 14 f., 29. 134, 135
amāte/u gabbašinā-ma "the words (things), all of them" EA 28. 42, 29. 7, 169
^{LÚ}*mārê šipriya gabbišunūma* "my messengers, all of them" EA 27. 23 f.

[. . .] *gabbišunū-ma* 20. 49 may be translated "[tablets],[31] all of them" on account of the following *kankūtu* "sealed."

In other words, the use of the Akkadian term (with "countries,[32] words, messengers, [tablets?]" parallels exactly the use of *šu(w)allaman*, not only as regards the accompanying nouns but also with reference to word-order and, apparently, also the force of the respective suffixes.[33]

The meaning "all" thus gained suits also *šu*^{e}. As a substantive, with *and*^{i} "this," it yields the sense "this totality, all this." When used attributively, as *šue* + *ne*, the word helps to form adverbs of degree. With *ma-a-na* [125] preceding we get something like "wholly, altogether," and after a negation "at all." After the relative element *ya/e-* the force of *ma-a-na šu-e-ni* appears to be that of an indefinite element.[34] Cf. *ya-a-an . . . m. š.* Mit. III 5, 6 "what . . . altogether," "whatever"; note the parallel passage (with the pronoun in the plural) Mit. II 73 f. in which *m. š.* is omitted, as such adverbs

[30] An additional occurrence cannot be sought in Friedrich's reading (KUR *u-u-mi-i--in-na-ša*) *šu-*[*ú-*]*a-ni-a-ša-a-am-ma-ma-an* Mit. II 96 (Kleinas. Sprachdenkm. 19), since a more probable reading is *šu-zu?-a-ni*—; see now Friedrich, Orientalia 9 (1940) 359.

[31] Or perhaps "[presents]."

[32] It may be observed in passing that *olla(n)* KUR *ominna šu(w)allaman* yields excellent sense: "all the other countries."

[33] Akk. *-ma* would correspond to Hurrian *-man* (short *-a-*), which would then have the force of an emphasizing particle, in some of its uses; cf. [212a].

[34] It can be shown [220] that *-mmaman* is not such an element.

of degree can easily be. Finally, *ti-ši-iw-wa-an ma-a*[*-na*] (56) *šu-e-ni* Mit. II 55 f. may be translated "(and about this I should rejoice very, very much) in my heart, wholly." [35]

115. Other pronominal stems, or stems that may have been employed pronominally, cannot be established on present evidence with a sufficient degree of probability. Some forms, however, are suggestive. This is true especially of the stem *aw*^{e}.[36] It combines with a possessive suffix and a case-ending in *a-we*$_{e}$*-ya-ša* VIII 60 obv. 9 "to/in their . . ." (3 p. pl. poss. + dat. or loc. suff.), but the context is too fragmentary in this instance for a guess about the meaning of the stem. Nevertheless, the suffixes prove its nominal character (in the broad sense of the term). For a possible clue we have to turn to two extended bases: *awenne/a-* (with the same vocalic alternation as in *ya/e-*, *-ma/e-*, and *-lla/e-* [254]), cf. *a-we-en-na-ma-an* Mit. II 78,[37] *a-we-en-na-a--ni-i-in* ibid. IV 24, *a-we-en-ni-e-ni-i-in* ibid. 17; and *aweše-*, cf. *a-we-eš-si-il--la-ma-an* ibid. II 92, *a-we-eš-še-e-ni-in* ibid. III 3; note also *aweš-* in proper names, e. g., ^{SAL}*A-wi-iš-ki-pa* AASOR 16 31. 7, 10 and ^{SAL}*A-wi-iš-na-a-a* ibid. 45. 2. The context in the respective Mit. passages is indecisive, but "anyone" yields good sense for *awenne/a-* in Mit. IV 17, 24.[38] The extension in *-š*(*e*) may impart to the stem an adverbial connotation, the result being perhaps "when, where?" Such an interpretation would be favored by the proper-name compounds with initial *aweš-*, a likely parallel to Akkadian names with *ali/u-* "where?" [39]

[35] Goetze, Lang. 16 (1940) 137 n. 45 equates Hurrian *tižifan mana šuene* Mit. II 55 f. with Akk. *attuya libbi* EA 19. 65. Since he translates *mana šuene* "our own," it is evident that he takes *šu*^{e} as a form of the personal pronoun for "I." But this interpretation fails to apply to other occurrences of *m. š.*, notably, Mit. III 5, 6, where "my own" can scarcely fit both "the Hurrian land" and "the Egyptian land" in a direct statement by Tushratta. In view of the foregoing discussion *šu*^{e} can have nothing in common with *šu-* [109], but is an independent stem for "all."

There are as yet no demonstrable instances of *šu*^{e} in the Bogh. material. We do find *šu-u-i* XXVII 1 ii 13, 14; *šu-u-ni* ibid. 46 i 15 and *šu-ú-ni* ibid. 6 1 20; furthermore, *šu-u-ni-ya* ibid. 46 i 23, 24, 25, 29; *šu-u-ni-ta* ibid. 34 i 15; and *šu-ne-ip-pa* ibid. 46 iv 19. But the passages involved are either too fragmentary or too obscure for the identification of the words just cited, which may indeed represent more than one root.

[36] Attention may be called in this connection to the stem *nuwe-* [111]; *naw*^{e} (Mit. IV 15, *na-wa-a-an* ibid. 7) is as yet obscure.

[37] It is possible, of course, that this particular form contains a secondary *-a-*; cf. [85(a)]. But *awenne-nin* is clearly original and, consequently, the *-a-* of *awenna-nin* cannot be phonologic; note, moreover, the double writing of this vowel (Mit. IV 24).

[38] In JAOS 59. 316 n. 77 I translated *awenne/a-* provisionally as "anyone," while suggesting an adverbial connotation in the case of *aweše-*. These interpretations are still plausible although by no means certain.

[39] Cf. J. J. Stamm, Die Akkadische Namengebung, MVAeG 44 (1939) 285.

c. Numerals

116. The following nominal stems are known to represent Hurrian numerals:[40]

šin "two," Messerschmidt, Mitanni-Sprache 66. The stem-form is furnished by *ši-in* Mit. II 59; *ši-ni* Mit. I 49 is "twice," not "two," to judge from the context, hence apparently with the ending *-ae* > *i* [68].[41] For derived forms with *šin-* cf. Speiser, AASOR 16 p. 133 f.; Friedrich, BChG 34.

kig, perhaps "three," Speiser, op. cit. 133; cf. Friedrich, op. cit. 35 n. 1. [Add now H. Lewy, Orientalia 10. 204 f.]

tumn^{i} "four," Speiser, op. cit. 132; cf. *du-um-ni* Mit. II 59; *du-um-ni-en* ibid. I 45. My interpretation of Nuzi *narkabtu tumnātu* as "four-wheeled chariot" (op. cit. 135) is now confirmed by the Akk. analogue *narkabtu rubūītu*, cf. Lacheman, Nuzi I 538.

šinda (and *šitta*) "seven," Potratz, Das Pferd in der Frühzeit (1938) 208, and Friedrich, Orientalia 9 (1940) 354; ibid. n. 4. [Add now v. Brandenstein, ZA 46. 94 n. 1.]

niž^{i}, probably "nine," Potratz, loc. cit., and Goetze, Lang. 15 (1939) 253.

eman "ten." Speiser, JAOS 59. 320 ff.; cf. Goetze, Lang. 16 (1940) 168.

kiž^{i}, apparently one of the other digits, Oppenheim, AfO 12 (1937) 29 n. 2.

nub^{i} "ten thousand," Lacheman, AASOR 16 127. [Add H. Lewy, Orientalia 10. 222].

Lastly, "one" can be expressed by the bound form *-ne-* [125, 137].

For the general subject of Hurrian numerals cf. Oppenheim OLZ 1937 1-6; Speiser, AASOR 16. 131-5; Friedrich, BChG 33-6; idem, Orientalia 9. 348-60.

2. Verbs

117. Unlike the nouns, where the majority of the roots appear with fixed stem-vowels [102], the verbs lack vocalic endings which might be presumed to form part of the root. They are characterized, however, in a limited number

[40] The first reference in each of the following entries gives the place where the correct value of the given numeral was first demonstrated or, failing that, where the stem was first recognized as a numeral.

[41] According to v. Brandenstein, Orientalia 9. 349 n. 1, the stem proper is *ši-* which is followed by a suffix *-ni*. However, the only such suffix known so far in Hurrian is the attributive particle *-ne* [136 f.], and the loss of its vowel is not paralleled elsewhere; hence *ši-in* would be wholly anomalous on that assumption. Against **šin*^{i} is the circumstance that the *-i* of *ši-ni* Mit. I 49 seems to be morphologic, as indicated above, while the analysis of *ši-ni-a-še-na-* Mit. III 40 is also against the assumption of a stem-ending *-i*; cf. [100]. Further evidence would be needed in favor of a stem for Hurrian "two" other than *šin*. [Cf. now ZA 46. 107-9].

of forms, by fixed connective vowels which we shall call class-markers [185]. Since the choice of the class-marker depends on the grammatical subdivision to which the given stem is felt to belong, the vowels in question may be regarded as morphophonemic.

There is clear evidence of two such distinctive subdivisions which may be designated as transitive and intransitive respectively.[42] The class-markers give us the correct classification automatically, whether we know the root-meaning or not. It is important, therefore, to set forth the conditions under which these markers can be recognized.

118. Transitives and intransitives are juxtaposed by means of distinctive vowels in two groups of forms: (a) before the suffixes *-kk-* and *-wa/e-*; (b) before the element *-ƀ* in onomastic compounds [177]. A few examples will suffice to bring out the difference between these two groups.

119. In group (a) the characteristic vowels are *-i-* with transitives and *-u/o-* with intransitives.[43] These vowels occur not only after simple roots but also after extended bases, whether differentiated for tense or modified by means of other derivational elements; cf. [185].

i-class: *kad-* "communicate" > *kad + ikki* Mit. IV 17, *kad + i + kk + onne* ibid. 2; *wər-* "know" > *wər + i + kk + onne* Mit. III 9; note also the place-name *Ḫaž + i + kkowə* AASOR 16 8.2 < *ḫaž-* "hear" and the occupational term *zil + ik(k) + uḫl-* "witness" [173]. After the perfect-element *-ož-* [181] we get *-i-* in *ḫill + ož + i + kk + onne* Mit. IV 4, 11, *ḫill + ož + i + kk + attàn* Mit. I 52 < *ḫill-* "relate"; *tan + ož + i + kk + attàn* Mit. II 5 < *tan-* "do, make." With the derivational element *-ugar-* [176 (8)] and the perfect *-ož-* we have *tad + ugar + ož + i + kki* Mit. II 79; in conjunction with other elements note *tad + oḫ + ol + i + kkinnàn* ibid. III 4 (both from *tad-* "love"); cf. also *šur-wu-uš-ti-ik-ki-i-in* ibid. II, 103; for the nominalized stem *ašḫ + ož + ikk-* "sacrificer(?)" cf. [94], [181].

The same formation is attested before the negative element *-wa/e-*. E. g., *ul-li-wa-a-en* Mit. III 95;[44] with *-ož-* cf. *tan + ož + i + wa + llanne* Mit.

[42] For Goetze's proposed third class, which is said to indicate "effect" (Lang. 16. 125 ff.) see [170a].

[43] Cf. JAOS 59. 298 ff. The back-vowel proves to have been [u] before *-kk-*, cf. *pu-ud-du-ú-uk-ki-* Mit. III 60; but [o] before *-wa/e-*, cf. *ú-ru-u-wə-en* ibid. 111, 116 (the corresponding *-ú-* from Bogh. is immaterial [28]). Phonologic conditions were apparently responsible for the variation. Note, however, that the back vowel after *-kk-* was [o]; cf. [29] and [186].

[44] These and the following examples are not meant to be exhaustive. A complete list of the forms with *-kk-* would in no way affect the present statement. For instances which seem to be of different origin see below, n. 49.

IV 10; from *ḫaž-* "hear" we have *ḫaž + až + i + wa + en* ibid. 20, 110 and *ḫaž + až + i + wa + llillàn* ibid. 26; *ḫis + uḫ-* "vex" > *ḫis + uḫ + i + wa + en* Mit. III 76, 85, 89, 95; *paš-* "send" > *paš + ar + i + wa + en* Mit. IV 54; after the element *-št-* [183] we find *koz + ošt + i + wa + en* ibid. 40 and *šil + aḫ + ož + ošt + i + wa + en* ibid. 41.

It is as yet uncertain whether this *-i-* occurs with equal regularity before other suffixes applied to transitive bases. For the time being it is best to limit the present statement, and the corresponding one with regard to intransitives, to bases modified by *-kk-* and *-wa/e-*; cf. [185].

120. *-u/o*-class: Examples with *-kk-* are numerous; for *putt + u + kk-* see above, n. 43; cf. also *man-* "be, exist" [125] > *man(n) + u + kk-*;[45] *tupp-* "be strong, ample" > *tupp + u + kk-*;[46] *un-* "arrive"[47] > *un + u + kk-* Mit. IV 3 and *un + ol + ukk-* KBo V 2 ii 26; *ur-* "occur, be present" > *ur + u + kk-*;[48] note also *ir-nu-uk-ku* Mit. III 60 and *ú-bu-uk-ku* XXIX 8 iv 17. With extended bases cf. *i-i-duk-[ku-]un-na-ma-an* Mit. III 84, alongside *i-i-uk-ku-un-na-ma-an* ibid. 94; *u-u[-ul]-lu-ḫi-duk-ku-u-un* ibid 84, perhaps cognate with *ul-lu-ḫu-ug-gu-ú-un* Mit. II 104. From Mâri note *ša-al-ḫu-du-uk-ku* 6. 8 (also ibid. 3, 6, 9; cf. RA 36. 21). From Bogh. cf. *du-un-du-uk-ku* VII 56 i 20; *ú-ru-uk-ku* ibid. 24; *ku-du-uk-ku* XXVII 38 ii 10. From a nominal stem we have *du-ru-bi-i-in-nu-uk-ku* Mit. I 17.[49]

The negative element *-wa/e-* appears with intransitives in *ur-o-wen* (above, n. 43); apparently also in *it-tu-ú-bi-in* VIII 61 obv. 11 < *itt-* "go"; perhaps also in *ap(um?)-pu-bi-in* XXIX 8 iv 20, *gul-du-bi-in* ibid. 19 [200].

121. To turn now to group (b) [118], we shall best restrict ourselves here to onomastic compounds in which the first element serves as the predicate and is marked by the suffix *-b*. It is necessary to stress again the difference between this group and the one just discussed. The suffixes involved in (a) are non-relational class-markers [185]. In (b), on the other hand, the contrasting vowels are participial endings which differ according to voice [168-71, 177]. The two sets of vowels are not comparable.

[45] Cf. JAOS 59. 302 ff.

[46] Ibid. 299.

[47] Cf. Goetze, Lang. 15. 218 ff.

[48] Ibid. 300 f.

[49] The personal name *Ḫa-ni-ku(-ya)* seems to interchange with *Ḫa-nu-qa-a-a*, to judge from AASOR 16 34. 43 as against ibid. 33. 25 (the man being in both instances the father of *Wurdeya*). It is doubtful, however, whether we have here the element under discussion. The name is written consistently with one *-k-* (for other occurrences cf. ibid. p. 150) as compared with *-kk-* of the morpheme involved.

As regards the name *Ḫanakka* (ibid.) there is no evidence that a verbal stem is involved. Quite possibly, we have here a formation with the land-name *Ḫana*. Lastly, Mit. IV 66 contains the form *me-e-na-ak-ki* about which we can say only that it is a derivative of the particle or noun *me-e-na-* ibid. 61, 63.

122. Although a full discussion of the set *-a*, *-i*, *-u* is presented later [168 ff.], a few details may be given here without anticipating unduly the argument which will be developed in its proper place. Most instructive in this connection are compounds with *Un* + *a* + *b* (cf. AASOR 16 p. 166), where the root *un-* "arrive" is followed by *-a-* instead of *-u/o-* as we should expect according to [120]. We know also that *-a* marks the intransitive form as predicate [169]; cf., e. g., *un* + *a* Mit. II 14, *un* + *a* + *n* ibid. III 13, IV 49, *un* + *a* + *l(l)a-* ibid. I 115, III 19. Unlike *-u/o-*, therefore, *-a-* has a definite relational function and is not a class-marker.

This conclusion is confirmed by a further detail of morphology. Some of the verbs employed in onomastic compounds exhibit doublets in *-a* + *b* : *-i* + *b* [177]. This is illustrated by *Ag* + *a* + *b-* : *Ag* + *i* + *b-* (for occurrences cf. AASOR 16 pp. 145 f.). Since *-i-* functions with transitives precisely as *-a-* with intransitives (cf. *Ḫaž-i-b-* ibid. 151, *Tad* + *i* + *b-* ibid. 164, etc.), it follows that *-a* + *b* : *-i* + *b* signalize the same verb as intransitive and transitive respectively. A similar differentiation is apparent in the uncompounded forms of the perfect: *ag* + *ož* + *a* Mit. I 87 (trans.) : *ag* + *ošt* + *a* VII 58 ii 9, 11 (intrans.); cf. [181]. Inasmuch as *ag-* as a transitive is known to mean "direct, grant,"[50] the intr. forms of this root may be rendered "proceed," or the like. The relation would be that of the simple stem to the causative.[51]

The fact that the vowels of group (b) may be used to effect the transfer of verbal stems from one class to the other is thus an added indication of the independence of these vowels from those of group (a).

123. The combination *-u*(+ *b*) is found in proper names with verbs which normally take the form in *-i* + *b*. Cf., e. g., *Ḫaž* + *i* + *b-* (AASOR 16 p. 151, and passim), but *Ḫaž* + *u* + *kelde* N 657. 5; *-(n)naya* AASOR 16 34. 3; *Teḫ* + *i* + *b-* (passim), but *Teḫ* + *u* + *b-ženni* ibid. 1. 53. Here belong also the well-known feminine names *Kel* + *u* + *ḫeba* and *Tad* + *u* + *ḫeba* whose verbal constituents mean "heal" and "love" respectively. I take the verb in these sentence-names with *-u-* and their analogues as forms in a goal-action construction. The forms are free passives, with only the goal indicated but not the agent; cf. [171, 177]. Whereas *Ḫaž* + *i* + *b* + *tilla* means "Hearing (is) Tilla, Tilla hears," *Ḫaž* + *u* + *kelde* represents "Heard (is) good news"; similarly, *Tad* + *u* + *ḫeba* means "Loved (is) Ḫeba(t)," and the like; cf. [171], [177].

124. It follows that the transitives use *-i-* before *-b* in proper names just

[50] Cf. JAOS 59. 298, 310.

[51] For a parallel usage in Urartian cf. Friedrich, Einführung ins Urartäische 5.

as they use the same vowel in forms of group (a); but their free passives are construed with *-u-*. The intransitives, on the other hand, employ *-a-* syntactically, whereas transfer to the "active" class is effected with the aid of *-i-*. The characteristic vowels which may be regarded as invariable, provided that the necessary conditions for their use obtain, are, however, those of group (a). From the standpoint of form, therefore, we may divide the Hurrian verb into two classes: the *i*-class (transitive) and the *u/o*-class (intransitive). This division applies not only to simple stems but also to derivative bases, including denominatives (e. g., *turubinn-u-kko* [120]). A verb may be said to belong to the *i*-class if it is known to use this vowel before *-kk-* or *-wa-*; also, if it occurs normally with agentive suffixes (*-a-ú, -u, -ya*);[52] lastly, if it employs *-u-* for free passives, notably in proper names.[53] The *u/o*-class is signalized by the occurrence of this vowel before *-kk-* or *-we-*; also by the suffix *-a* in the present tense as well as in proper-name compounds.

125. There remains to be discussed the stem *man(n)*- which is difficult to classify for a number of reasons. The orthography is inconsistent in that both *-a-* and *-n-* may be written either single or double. Thus we have *ma-a-an-na-a-an* Mit. I 84, IV 61, as against *ma-a-na-an* ibid. I 93 and *ma-an-na-an* VBot 16 rev. 14; *ma-a-na-at-ta-an* VIII 60 obv. 19 (cf. also rev. 20) alongside *ma-a-an-na-at-ta-ma-an* Mit. II 85, III 63, 65. More troublesome is the fact that certain occurrences of this stem are plainly verbal while others are just as clearly pronominal.[54] Since separate treatment of the respective forms would have distracted attention from the problems at issue, it seemed best to treat this important stem as a unit; the above summary of the verbal classes was, therefore, prerequisite. This does not imply that the pronominal uses of *man(n)*- are secondary. Indeed, the verbal form might with greater probability be viewed as derivative. But a decision on this particular question is not essential to a descriptive account.

[52] This criterion is ambiguous, however, inasmuch as intransitives transferred to the opposite class would presumably employ the agentive suffixes in the present just as they do in the perfect; cf. *ag* + *ož* + *a*: *ag* + *ošt* + *a*. But such changes of class do not appear to have been common. They may have been restricted to verbs of motion and related concepts.

[53] There is no instance of this usage with intransitives, which is fully understandable. Intransitives may be transferred to the active class, but will scarcely require special forms to mark them as passive.

The place of this *-u-* with transitive roots precludes any confusion with the other class. Whether the choice of this vowel was due to its function with intransitives is purely speculative.

[54] The assumption of two independent stems is discouraged by the orthography, which treats both sets of forms alike. Nor is it favored by morphology, in that *manni* betrays its independence by dispensing with the normal intransitive suffix *-a*.

Demonstrably verbal in form and syntax are *ma-a-an-nu-uk-ku* Mit. II 91 and *ma-a-an-nu-uk-kal-la-a-an* ibid. IV 2, both with the element *-kk-* preceded by the intransitive marker *-u/o-* [120]; furthermore, *ma-a-an-nu--l[i-]-e-wa-a-al-la-a-an* ibid. II 122 [192]. Starting from these occurrences it is possible to interpret the various instances of *manni, manni-mmaman, manna-ttaman,* and *manna-llaman* (cf. JAOS 59. 302 ff.) as verbal and to assign to the underlying root the meaning "be, exist," which will be found to suit all the passages involved insofar as they are capable of interpretation (loc. cit.). Of special interest in this connection is the use of *man(n)-* as an auxiliary verb in *mannukkallàn andi unukkalan* Mit. IV 2-3; *manninin tiwe andi unanin* ibid. 13; and *mannadillaman uruḫuštillàn* ibid. 119 (cf. loc. cit. 303); for this use points to a periphrastic function of *man(n)-* which accords well with a verb meaning "to be."

A pronominal value, on the other hand, is apparent in the phrase *ma-a-na šu-e-ni* [114a]; here *mana* occupies a place which elsewhere is taken by the pronoun *andi* "this," cf. Mit. III 9. A similar deictic connotation for *man(n)an* is probable in Mit. I 84, 93. Equally suggestive is *ma-an-šu-u-til--la-a-an* Mit. I 77, which the context brings out as a resumptive pronoun in the agentive plural case followed by the associative *-dillàn*, the whole phrasal word signifying "by these (gods) (< **manžuš-*) we . . .". An analogous pronominal form in the comitative (or instrumental) plural may be *ma-an-šu-ra* Mâri 5. 20. The sense of *ma-a-nu-dan* Mit. IV 64 is uncertain, but a nominal value is indicated by the suffixes in *ma-a-nu-uš* XXVII 46 iv 4 and *ma-a-nu-ra* ibid. i 14, ii 9, although the passages concerned cannot yet be translated. In *ma-a-an-nu-pa-ta-e* Mit. IV 59 we find the same suffix as in *niru-badae* "speedily" ibid. 5, 6, which contains a nominal root. Of doubtful classification are *ma-a-na* XXVII 38 iii 16, *ma-a-nu-ú-un-na* Mit. IV 64 and *ma-a-nu-ú-[u]n-na-a-a[l-la-a-a]n* ibid. III 78.

The foregoing list cannot be concluded without a brief examination of the four occurrences of *ma-a-ni-e-im-ma-ma-an* Mit. III 35, 36, 38 (bis) which cannot be confused with *manni-mmaman* (above) even on formal grounds, on account of the consistent spelling *-ni-i-* as opposed to the present *-ni-e*; cf. [27]. This passage refers to two tablets of dowry and special stress is laid on their enumeration. The concluding *ma-a-ni-e-im-ma-ma-an* (39) *gu-ru tup-pè* (ibid. 38 f.) has to mean "this is the second tablet," literally "this (*ma-*) one (*-ne-*) particular (*-mmama-*) is (*-n*) again (*kuru*) a tablet (*tuppe*)." Accordingly, the first *ma-a-ni-e-im-ma-ma-an* (36) *tup-pè* means "this is one particular tablet." Additional support for this interpretation is furnished by the summing-up phrase *tup-pí-aš* (40) *ši-ni-a-še-na-a-am-ma--ma-an* "their tablets (namely, those of 'my father' and of 'my grandfather'), the ones of the aforementioned (*-mmaman*) two"; note the force of the individualizing particle *-mmama-* [220] throughout this passage.

It follows that we have in *ma* + *ne* + *mmama-* a demonstrative pronoun (*ma-*), the attributive particle *-ne-* used for "one" [137], and the individualizing particle which has a well-defined function with numerals. There remains the question as to the relation of this pronoun to *man(n)-*, which we have seen used as a pronoun and as a verb. We cannot ignore the possibility that *man(n)-*, in both its functions, is morphologically an extension of *ma-*. The use of a pronoun for the verbal copula is, of course, not without parallel.[55] For the time being, however, we have to content ourselves with the statement of the problem without venturing a definitive answer.[56]

3. Particles

126. In accordance with [98], a Hurrian word is regarded as a particle if it is not known to have any bound modifiers and may be combined only with associatives. The criterion is strictly formal. From the point of view of meaning the particles include concepts conventionally classified as adverbs,[57] conjunctions, interjections, and the like. Since they constitute radical elements they will be designated henceforward as independent particles, as opposed to bound particles.

The foregoing definition is subject to two important limitations. While the stems of some particles (e. g., *inu, undu*) are not used for other parts of speech, other stems (e. g., *šukko, kuru*) may be adapted to nominal and verbal constructions; cf. [99]. In other words, certain particles may be nominalized or verbalized by means of appropriate suffixes. They remain, however, as particles so long as they retain a specific stem-form, and it is in that characteristic stem-form that they come under the present classification; cf. *šukko* : *šukkanne*. Where the respective stem-vowels are non-distinctive, accompanying suffixes

[55] For West Semitic, e. g., cf. G. Bergsträsser, Einführung in die semitischen Sprachen (1928) 15. A closer formal parallel, in view of the other ties which link that language to Hurrian, is provided by Urartian. Here we find the verb *manu* "to be" (cf. Friedrich, Caucasica 7. 83 ff.) alongside *ma-ni*, the personal pronoun of the 3 p. (idem, Einführung ins Urartäische 17). It is as yet uncertain whether the basic root of the Urartian pronoun was *ma-* or *mani* (cf. Friedrich, ibid. n. 1); but *ma-* is regarded as the more probable. This correspondence of the Urartian pronoun **ma-*, extended to *mani*, and the verb *manu* with Hurrian pronominal *ma-* and *man(n)-* and verbal *man(n)-*, purely formal though it may be, would reduce considerably the possibility of coincidence. It seems to enhance the likelihood of an underlying etymological connection.

[56] Cf. also JAOS 59. 302 ff.

[57] Most adverbial concepts, however, are expressed in Hurrian by means of a special ending *-ae* [165].

will determine the classification; e. g., *ai-n* is an independent particle, but *ai* + (*i*)*da* a nominalized preposition.

The other limitation concerns the root-form of several particles listed below. In *anam* "thus" the whole word may be the root, but we have no means of proving that the form was not in reality **an* + *am*. Similarly, *tišan* "very" might well contain an inseparable suffix -(*a*)*n*. But it would not be profitable to concern ourselves at present with such speculations. Each independent particle listed below is provisionally regarded as radical.

127. *u*-stems. This group includes

inu "as": probably *i-nu* Mâri 5. 6, 7;[58] with the suffix *-n* note *i-nu-ú-un* Mit. III 3. With pronominal associatives we have 1 p. sg. *i-nu-ud-da* "as I . . ." VIII 61 obv. 3, *i-nu-ú-ut-ta-ni-i-in* Mit. I 74 (and II 60); 3 p. sg. *i-nu-me-e* XXIX 8 iv 8, 16, 27, *i-nu-ú-me-e-ni-i-in* Mit. I 13, 75, II 123, 125, III 97, IV 115, 121; *i-nu-ú-ma-a-ni-i-in* ibid. IV 108; cf. also the variant form *ú-nu-ú-me-e-ni-i-in* ibid. II 66.[59] With the pronoun of the 3 p. pl. we have *i-nu-ul-li-e-ni-i-in* Mit. III 101 (cf. also ibid. II 32).[60]

undu-: The interpretation of this word has varied between a conjunction "when, whereas" (Jensen, ZA 14. 174; Goetze, Lang. 15. 217 n. 12) and an interjection "now then" (Messerschmidt, Mitanni-Studien 54 "und nun," approved by Friedrich BChG 19; Bork, Mitannisprache 35 and passim takes it adverbially (German "also" = "thus"). Each side points to seemingly irrefutable arguments in its own favor. Messerschmidt (loc. cit.) cites several passages which, in his opinion, preclude a conjunction.[61] Goetze (loc. cit.) counters with the fact that *undu* recurs in the sense of "when" in Hurro-Hittite Akkadian. A definitive solution must be sought, however, within Hurrian, and here a conjunction cannot be reconciled with the context of several pertinent passages; the remaining occurrences of *undu-* are ambiguous and depend thus on the interpretation of the disputed instances.

The available forms, all from the Mitanni letter, are as follows: *un-du* II 56, III 61; *un-du-un* IV 35 (bis); *un-du-ma-a-an* II 57, 107, III 2, 11, 21, 35, IV 30. In III 61 *undu* follows the predicate, which is not paralleled with established conjunctions like *inu-*. The whole passage (III 61-3) converted

[58] Cf. Thureau-Dangin, RA 36. 18 f.

[59] For this variation cf. Friedrich, BChG 24 f.

[60] It is possible that *i-nu-ú-ru* XXIX 8 iv 5 is also pertinent, but the form is obscure; cf. [216].

[61] His argument is based, however, on Mit. II 57 f. where the meaning of the term cannot be established conclusively. Messerschmidt erred in associating *undu* with the imperative *agugarašten*, whereas the clause involved ends with *pašitḫe* and the verbal form belongs to the main clause.

into English [62] reads: "And my brother will learn *undu* that those (things) which I sent to my brother in the past I will likewise continue sending to my brother in the future." A subordinating particle is obviously out of place here; we expect an adverb or an interjection. Equally instructive are the nominal sentences in IV 35-6 introduced by *undu-n*; they admit of an interjection, but hardly of a conjunction. If we operate with the semantic range "then—now then," all occurrences of *undu-* in Mit. can be explained without difficulty. Of special interest is the passage II 107-8

un-du-ma-a-an še-e-ni-i[*w-w*]*e-e-en pa-aš-š*[*u-ši* ᴵ*Ma-*]*ni-en-na-a-an š*[*e-e-*] *-ni*[*-iw-wu--u*]*š* (108) *pa-aš-šu-u-u-ša*

The first part of this sentence is clearly a dependent clause. But the nature of this clause is not determined by *undu-màn*. The deciding factor is the *i*-form of the predicate which functions, as we shall see [170], as a participle-gerundive. The above passage has to be translated:

"Now then, my brother having sent a mission, it was Mane that was delegated by my brother."

It is easy to see how *undu-* in conjunction with the *i*-form comes to participate in temporal clauses without itself serving as the respective syntactic marker.[63]

au: This particle is used to introduce declarative sentences in the lengthy mythic-historical passage XXVII 38 iv 8 ff.; e. g., [*a*]*-u* ᴵ*Ma-an-na-mi-iš--du-u-un e-we*$_{e}$*-er-ne* [*šar-ri*] [64] "*au* the lord Manishtushu is/was (*-n*) king.

[62] A literal translation would not affect the argument in the least.

[63] In this association of *undu* with the gerundive clause may lie the explanation of the conjunctive use of the particle in Hurro-Hittite dialects of Akkadian. For "now then, my brother having sent . . ." comes close in meaning to "when my brother sent." Indeed, some such interjection with a temporal force may have been needed in Hurrian itself to impart the sense of "when" to the gerundive phrase. But the conjunctive connotation is inherent in the *i*-form and not the particle.

Incidentally, the use of *undu* in dialectal Akkadian requires further clarification in view of the analogous *šu-un-tu*$_{4}$ N 46. 23.

[64] Ibid. 22. The supplementation [*šar-ra?*] (cf. Friedrich, Kleinas. Sprachdenkm. 35) is not acceptable on syntatic grounds.

The Hurrian form of the above personal name calls for a remark. The medial *-m-* is accounted for if we accept Poebel's etymology *man'iš-tûšu* (cf. JAOS 57. 364 n. 14); *mannamiš-* would go back to **mannawiš* < **manwiš* < *man'iš*. The loss of *-šu*, on the other hand, may be explained on inner-Hurrian grounds. The name would have been treated as **mannamištuš-* whose final *-uš* was viewed as the agentive suffix and hence was omitted in the *n*-form *mannamištu-n*. But the whole matter is far from clear; for a different interpretation of the Akk. name see v. Soden ZA 41. 138 and Stamm, MVAeG 44. 239.

Forrer[65] took the particle in the sense of "lo, behold," and this view is evidently correct.[66]

kuru "again, in return": cf. Mit. III 15, 39, 55, etc. The approximate meaning of this adverbial concept has been known since the beginning of Hurrian studies. The word functions as an independent particle when it is not followed by suffixes. The adverbial connotation helps to explain nominal and verbal uses of the root in the sense of "return" [99].

panu-: cf. *pa-nu-ú-ul-li-e-ni-i-in* Mit. IV 16 which is paralleled by *inu* + *llenin* ibid. III 101 (both are followed by *ewa*-forms [192]).

šukko: cf. *šu-uk-ku* Mit. II 12; *šuk-ku* ibid. III 49, 75, IV 1; with the identifying (restrictive) element *šuk-ku-u-um-ma-ma-an* ibid. III 111. This stem, too, has nominal analogues, which have to be listed at this time inasmuch as the meaning of the root is yet to be established: cf. *šuk-kán-ni* Mit. III 30; *šuk-kán-ni-en* ibid. IV 32; *šuk-kán-ni-ma-a-an* ibid. III 114, 118; *šuk-kán--ni-e-el-la-ma-an* ibid. 54, 56; *šuk-kan-ni-e-wa-an* ibid. II 84 (with the poss. suff. of 2 p.); furthermore, *šu-uk-ku-u-ut-ti* ibid. II 68; *šu-uk-ku-ut-ta-at--ta-am* VIII 61 obv. 12 (and cf. ibid. 13); lastly, with a different stem-vowel, *šug-gu-ú-ud-du-u-ḫa* Mit. III 108 and (with repeated *-u-*) II 70.[67]

The approximate meaning of the independent particle in question is conjectured by Friedrich as "further(more)."[68] This interpretation will stand if it can be harmonized with the nominal cognates of *šukko*. I now assume the underlying connotation to be something like "far, distant, future." This is clear enough in the phrase *šukkanne ežene* Mit. III 30 "the distant heaven." In Mit. III 54, 56 the same term is used of shipments to describe them as "future, subsequent." Ibid. IV 32-3 speaks of *šukkanne-n* (33) *padi tiwene-n* "even by one [125] distant word," i. e., "even remotely."[69] For *šukkuttoḫa tadugaridillàn* Mit. III 108-9 the parallel Akk. passage EA 19. 28 has *nirtana'am(u)* "we shall love each other continuously";[70] the frequentative-durative aspect is not contained in the verb of the corresponding Hurrian phrase, but is indicated by the accompanying adverbial expression *šukkuttoḫa* "far away," i. e., "for ever." In Mit. III 114, 118 *šukkanne-màn*

[65] BoTU 2. 25*.

[66] The complex form *a-ú-un-ni-ma-a-an* Mit. III 121 is not clear.

[67] Little can be done for the present with *šu-uk-ku-a-wə* XXVII 37. 11, *šu-uk-ku-wu-um* ibid. 12, and *šu-uk-ki-ni-* ibid. 35. 5. Friedrich's [*šuk-*]*kán* in Mit. III 89, which goes back to Messerschmidt, is open to serious doubt inasmuch as *šukkanne* alone is established in this formation. I would suggest tentatively [*zu-*]*gán*, for which see [131].

[68] BChG 37.

[69] For an approximate Akk. parallel cf. [*a-d*]*i* 1*en* *a-ma-tu*4 EA 29. 47 "by as much as a single word."

[70] Cf. Poebel, Studies in Akkadian Grammar (1939) 30.

is associated with *šuene* "all" [114a] with the very suitable sense for these passages of "absolutely all."

To return to the independent particle, *šukko* may accordingly be translated "furthermore, moreover," while *šukko-mmaman,* with its restrictive individualizing particle, yields "just the same, nevertheless," which is precisely what the passage (Mit. III 111) requires.[71]

128. *i/e*-stems. This group, too, consists of roots which are attested only as independent particles, alongside other roots which may form the basis of nominal stems with a consequent shift in meaning.

adi- "thus": [72] attested only with the associative *-nin*; cf. *a-ti-i-ni-i-in* Mit. I 16, 90, 94, 95, etc., once with the infixed connective *-ma-* in the sequence *adi* + *nin* . . . *adi* + *ma* + *nin* Mit. IV 119-20 "thus indeed(?) . . . thus, too, indeed(?)." [73]

padi, prob. "up to, as much as" Mit. IV 33, 67, 68, 72. For the apparent correspondence of Hurrian *padi* : Akk. *adi* cf. [127 n. 69].

Here belong also some of the terms which underly the nominalized prepositions [105]. When used as particles, they combine only with associatives such as the subjective pronominal suffixes and the predicative particle *-n.* It is significant that the same roots in combination with morphologic suffixes of the noun may undergo notable shifts in meaning. Thus *edi/e-* as a preposition signifies "sake, regard, concern," e. g., *šu-u-we-ni-e e-ti-iw-wu-ú-e-e* Mit. IV 22 "of me, of my regard," i. e., "regarding me" [69]. But *e-ta-la-an* Mit. IV 45, with the subjective pronominal element -(*l*)*la-* "they," can mean only "why-they + *n*?" [74] Similarly, *ai-* with nominal suffixes yields something like "before, in the presence of" [69]. With the non-morphologic associatives, however, *ai-* functions as an interrogative particle "is it (, that)?," or a conjunction "when, if." Cf. *a-i-i-n* Mit. III 44 f. ("Besides [*ullui*], is it that their tablets of their dowry are comparable [*tuppukko*] to those particular [*-mmaman*] ones of my sister-gift?"); the meaning "if" is apparent ibid. II 53; [75] note also ibid. 86, 90, IV 65, 66, 67, and cf. III 93. With

[71] In JAOS 59. 321 n. 85 I suggested for *šukko* the value "over, above." The modification here proposed is along the same lines, but accords better with the entire evidence and is applicable to the nominal as well as the independent occurrences of the root.

[72] Speiser, JAOS 59. 303.

[73] We have also *a-a-ti* XXVII 34 iv 8, but the context is too fragmentary for analysis.

[74] The whole passage (Mit. IV 45 f.) may be translated: "Now my brother may say, 'Why were they, my envoys, detained by you?' (46) Not at all, they were not detained by me."

[75] Cf. Friedrich, BChG 39 n. 1. But Friedrich confines himself to the exposition of *ai-* alone and is therefore reluctant to associate the particle with the cognate preposition. The parallel instance of *edi/e-* should eliminate all doubt.

the anticipatory pronoun of the 3 p. sg. we have perhaps *a-i-ma-a-ni-i-in* Mit. III 111 ("if it(?) indeed, nevertheless, a difficulty to my brother's country should arise"); also, ibid. IV 9, 54, 59, and perhaps, without the asseverative *-nin*, *a-i-ma* VIII 61 rev. 12, 14. With the pronoun of the 3 p. pl. we get *a-i-la-an* Mit. II 58, 75, IV 20, 26, 128.

This semantic dichotomy in the use of *ai-* and *edi/e-*, in their employment as particles and prepositions respectively, furnishes additional indirect evidence of the independent position of the particle-word in Hurrian grammar. No less significant is the consistent orthography *-la-an* (*-lan*) with the particles as against the normal *-əl-la-a-an* (*-llàn*) in other contexts. For the single writings suggest wholly unstressed syllables [92a] and point thus to accentual shifts as the direct result of the presence of the particles in question.

Finally, we have to list here provisionally the stem *alaže-* which occurs three times in the following passage: (Mit. III 42 f.) *a-la-a-še-me-e-ni-i-in ni-ḫa-a-ri te-a* (43) *a-la-a-še-me-e-ni-i-in ni-i-ri a-la-a-še-me-e-ni-i-in še-e-ni--iw-wu-ú-uz-zi.* Bork (Mitannisprache 105) translates *a.* plausibly as "dass." Another possibility is "whether," and the whole passage may be translated freely "let my brother find out whether the dowry is large, whether it is small,[76] whether it is in conformity with (*-zzi* [160]) my brother." The same form may be restored in Mit. I 55, and the underlying stem may confront us in *a-la-a-ši* XXVII 31 ii 3. Whether the stem is simple or compound cannot be determined at present. The latter alternative appears, however, to be more likely. The final *-že* may be an "adverbial" suffix, as in *ni-i-ri-še* "promptly" Mit. IV 33 < *-žae* (cf. *ni-i-ru-ša-e* Mit. I 55, 58, etc.), cf. [165]; hence *al-la-a-ša-e* XXVII 42 obv. 27 may be a variant of *alaže-*, in which case we would have here in reality a nominal stem.[77]

129. *a*-stems. Here belong

inna-, a particle of uncertain meaning. It is found with the pronoun of the 3 p. sg. as *in-na-ma-a-ni-i-in* Mit II, 6, 14, 16, III 12, 22, 29, and *in-na-me--e-ni-i-in* III 21; with the corresponding 3 p. pl. we have *in-na-al-la-ma-a*[*n*] ibid. IV 129; finally, with *-mmaman* the form is *in-na-a-am-ma-ma-an* ibid. III 110, 116. From the fact that *inna-* is not restricted to any particular type of sentence it may be gathered that it represents an interjection rather than a conjunction. Some such general sense as "behold"[78] may prove suitable,

[76] For this meaning of *niri* cf. *ni-ra-e* RŠ Voc. II 10. I would derive the value "swiftly," which has long been established for *niru-žae* (cf. Messerschmidt, Mitanni-Studien 11), from an underlying "light, slight" and call attention to the range of Sem. *qll.*

[77] For words which are adverbial in meaning but apparently nominal in form cf. *ḫenni* "now" (Messerschmidt, ibid. 34) and *ú-a-du-ra-a-an-ni-* (ibid. 50).

[78] Cf. JAOS 59. 313.

in which case *inna-mmaman* would require a restrictive nuance, perhaps "but see," or the like; cf. *šukko-mmaman* [127].

šuga "along, with": [79] Mit. II 70, IV 52, 53.

uya-, a particle having negative ("no") or adversative ("on the contrary") force; [80] it is found in the combination *u-ya-ma-a-an* Mit. IV 46, 57. It may be significant that in both instances the last syllable of the word which immediately follows is characterized by simplified orthography; this is true not only of *ku-zu-u-ši-iw-wə-la-an* Mit. IV 46 (cf. [128]) but also of *še-e-ni-iw-wə-ša-an* ibid. 57, in spite of the fact that single *-š-* does not indicate the required phoneme; cf. [88].

130. The relative particle *ya/e-* [112] calls for separate listing because its stem-vowel is ambiguous, being subject to the contrastive alternation *-a/e* [115, 254]. The only free occurrence of the stem appears to be *i-e-e* Mit. I 54.[81] With the predicative *-n* we have both *i-i-e-e-en* ibid. II 79 and *ya-a-an* III 5, 6. With subjective pronominal suffixes we find in Mit.: 1 p. sg. *i-ya-at-ta-ma-an* II 5; 3 p. sg. *ya-me-e-ni-i-in!* III 91, *i-i-e-ma-a-ni-i-in* II 101, IV 27, and *i-i-e-me-e-ni*[*-i-i*]*n* II 62; 1 p. pl. *ya-ti-la-a-an* II 74; 3 p. pl. *ya-a-la-an* [82] II 73, 82, 92; *i-i-al-la-a-ni-i-in* I 96, 104, III 55, 57, IV 124; *i-i-al-li-e-ni-i-in* I 98, 111, II 19, 20, III 52, IV 30. The individualizing particle is added in *i-i-a-am-ma-ma-an* IV 18, 24.[83]

Without analogy is the complex *i-i-e-na-a-ma-a-ni-i-in* Mit. IV 21, with its pluralizing particle *-na* followed by *-ma-*; the latter element is attested elsewhere as the pronominal enclitic of the 3 p. sg.,[84] but in this instance we have evidently the connective *-ma-* [212]. Nevertheless, the use of *-na* would still have to be explained in that this suffix accompanies nominal forms and has no place with independent particles. Apparently, *ya/e-* could be nominalized in common with terms like *šukko* [127], *ai-* and *edi/e-* [128]. The resulting compound forms have to be regarded as independent pronouns: *yena-* would mean "what things," unlike the dependent *ya(l)a-n* which requires a resumptive noun. The sg. counterpart of *yena-* is *i-e-ni* XXVII 1 i 75.[85] A possible analogue of these forms is *ya-ra-aš* XXV 42 v 7 (and cf. ibid. 43. 10) which is followed by the prepositional *abi/e-raš*; the meaning of the suffix is unknown, but its nominal character is obvious; cf. [216].

[79] Messerschmidt, Mitanni-Studien 89 f., 131.

[80] Friedrich, BChG 28 and n. 3.

[81] Unless *iya* (see below) is to be included.

[82] Note the single writings in the second syllable and cf. [129].

[83] Perhaps *i-i-im-ma-ma-an* Mit. II 101 is to be added.

[84] This exceptional form is noted by Friedrich, BChG 25.

[85] Cf. also the Nuzi loanword *i-en-nu-ú* noted by Gordon, AJSL 41 (1934) 18.

Uncertain for the present is the classification of *i-ya* XXVII 38 ii 15, 21, iii 1, *i-ya-ma* ibid. ii 17.[86] We may have here an orthographic variant of *ya/e-*, or—perhaps with more likelihood—an independent morpheme whose meaning is close to that of *ya/e-*. At all events, a nominalized function is attested here too by *i-ya-ni-el-* XXVII 29 iv 19. The alphabetic texts seem to employ the same element in the form of *iy* RŠ X 4. 60, *iy-m* ibid. 15.

131. Consonant stems.

anam "thus," used resumptively, often with an antecedent *inu-* "as": e. g., *a-nam* Mit. IV 10, 13 (and cf. ibid. II 96). In XXIX 8 iv 28 we find *a-na-am-mi*, and ibid. 17 *a-na-am-mi-im-ma*. It is doubtful, nevertheless, whether we should posit an *i*-stem alongside one in *-m*. The evidence of Mit. is clearly in favor of a consonant stem. In addition to the free forms just cited note also *a-nam-ma-a-an* III 51. To be sure, *-i-* is found before pronominal suffixes: 1 p. sg. *a-nam-mi-it-ta-ma-an* Mit. III 62, 64 (bis); 1 p. pl. *a-nam--mi-til-la-a-an* ibid. I 76, II 67, IV 122; 3 p. pl. *a-nam-mil-la-a-an/-ma-an* ibid. II 56, III 80, IV 126. But the interposed vowel is secondary, on the analogy of [85(b)]. Accordingly, Bogh. *anammi* is either an instance of the suffixed pronominal element of the 3 p. sg. (*ma/e-*), or perhaps a secondary form influenced by constructions with the pronominal suffixes where the *-i-* was a regular development.

tišan "very" Mit. I 18, 26, 56, etc.; cf. Messerschmidt, Mitanni-Studien 3; note also *ti-iš-ša-a-an* XXI 38 i 59 and cf. Friedrich, Rev. des Ét. I-E. 1. 4.

pè-gán (?) Mit. I 112, IV 107.

zu-gán, cf. Mit. II 11, III 16, IV 67, 68, 72; perhaps also ibid. III 89, cf. [127 n. 67]. The meaning of this particle is uncertain.

B. BOUND FORMS

132. One of the characteristic features of Hurrian is the abundance of bound forms. These elements are placed invariably after the supporting root and are joined to it either directly or through the mediation of other suffixes. One reason for the profusion of bound forms is the presence of "associatives" [98], or non-morphologic elements used in suffixed position. Another reason is the tendency of Hurrian to express by means of suffixes a variety of concepts for which Indo-European or Semitic, e. g., would use independent words; cf. [94]. In this way both the noun and the verb may be built up into lengthy phrasal words. A factor that contributes to the length of Hurrian words is the syntactic peculiarity known as suffix-duplication,[87] whereby the final suffix of the head may be repeated with the attributes [133, 238].

[86] See Friedrich, RHA 35. 96.

[87] More familiar as "Suffixübertragung."

133. Within the suffix-series a definite order is rigidly observed. This will be made evident most effectively in dealing with the various "positions" in the verbal chain [178]. For the present one illustration will suffice to demonstrate some of the functions of these modifiers and thus prepare us for the immediate task of classification. The phrase selected for the purpose exemplifies the nominal series:

DINGIR^{MEŠ}*-na-šu-uš at-ta-an-ni-bi-na-šu-uš šar-ra-aš-ši-ḫi-bi-na-š*[*u-uš*] XXVII 42 rev. 9 yields in normalized transcription

ennaz̄us̄ attannewenaz̄us̄ z̄arras̄eḫewenaz̄us̄

The first word consists of *en*^{e} "god" + pl. attr. part. *-na* + another pl. element used for suffixes, viz., *-z̄-* + connective vowel *-u-* + agent. suff. *s̄*; the whole word means literally "god-ones-pl.-by," i. e., "by the gods." The next word contains the stem *atta*(*y*) "father" + sg. attr. part. *-ne* + gen. suff. *-we* + *-naz̄us̄* and yields "father-one-of-ones-pl.-by." The last word is to be analyzed as *z̄arr*$^{i/a}$ "king" + abstract suff. *-s̄e* + adjectival suff. *-ḫe* + *-wenaz̄us̄* "king-abstr.-adj. suff.-ones-pl.-by." The entire phrase thus represents in English terms "(such and such an act shall be performed) by the gods of the paternal (genius) concerned with kingship." The suffixes of the head (*-naz̄us̄*), which are repeated with the following attributes in accordance with the principle of suffix-duplication, indicate the subject of a clause in goal-action construction (*-s̄*), pluralized (*-z̄-*) and further defined by attributes (*-na-*).[88] The two attributes are in the genitive (*-we*). They are adjectival forms, the first construed with the aid of the sg. part. *-ne*,[89] and the other with the direct adjectival element *-ḫe*. Finally, the latter adjective is based on an abstract noun formed with the aid of *-s̄e* from the concrete concept for "king."

It should be clear from the foregoing example that the Hurrian phrasal word is capable of gathering up a number of varied concepts which can then be recapitulated and linked together with the related members of the sentence. It is also apparent that — where the suffix chain is of sufficient length — the suffixes nearest the radical element have the closest connection with the radical concept, while remove from the root signifies a corresponding increase in relational bearing.[90] Furthermore, we have a special attributive particle which may be differentiated for number (*-ne, -na*). "Case"-endings are in themselves non-distinctive as to number, the same element serving both singular and plural. To mark the plurality of case or possessor a special particle (*-z̄*)

[88] For the uses of *-na* cf. [139 ff.].

[89] This is not the primary function of *-ne*; cf. [86a, 137].

[90] It will be seen later that the syntactic complements designated as "associatives" are placed at the very end of the suffix-chain.

has to be employed. It follows that these relations were expressed in Hurrian by means of elements having a force similar to that of our prepositions. We have thus in Hurrian a language with a technique that was agglutinative to an appreciable degree. The fact that the "case"-endings may be separated from their stems by a series of interposed suffixes points to a similar conclusion.

133a. The above demonstration of some of the varied uses of the Hurrian bound forms may serve to point out the difficulty inherent in an attempt to classify these elements into a comprehensive system. The problem is further complicated by our uncertainty as to the meaning of some of the suffixes and our total ignorance of sundry others. Under these circumstances it will be most expedient to adhere to a formal principle of classification. In accordance with [98] and our analysis of the radical elements, the distinctive suffixes of Hurrian are nominal, verbal, or associative respectively. A division into the above three groups, however, would not exhaust the available material. There is yet another group of bound morphemes whose sole function it is to complement the lexical content of the supporting root. These morphemes occur in nouns as well as verbs. In addition to serving thus as "root-complements" many function also independently as strictly derivational or relational elements and are then specifically nominal or verbal. For the sake of clarity it will be expedient to present the root-complements in a separate section, between the distinctive suffixes of the noun and those of the verb. Accordingly, the bound forms of Hurrian will be listed as follows: (1) Suffixes of the noun; (1/2) Root-complements; (2) Suffixes of the verb; (3) Associative suffixes, capable of combination with the independent particles. The necessary subdivisions will be explained under the individual main headings.

1. Suffixes of the Noun

134. The bound forms which are known to modify nominal roots or to impart to given stems nominal characteristics may be subdivided as follows:

a. Attributional suffixes
b. Possessive suffixes
c. Suffixes which indicate case-relations
d. Adjectival suffixes
e. Suffixes which mark verbal nouns
f. Miscellaneous

a. Attributional Suffixes

135. The term "attributional suffixes" is used here for those elements whose function, or one of whose functions, extends to a series of forms rather than any one particular form. Accordingly, such suffixes may modify the meaning of the noun as a whole or of given modifiers within the nominal complex. Their primary significance will prove to concern number. This group comprises the particles *-ne, -na,* and *-ž* (wr. in the syllabic texts *-š-* between vowels).

-ne

136. The form *-ne,* rather than **-ni,* is assured by such writings as *e-we*$_e$*-er-ne* XXVII 38 iv 10, 13, 19, 20, 22, 26, 28, etc.; *ni-ḫa-a-ar-ri-e-we a-ru-u-ša-uš-še-ni-e-we* Mit. III 41 where the vocalic complement *-e-* with *-r-ri-e* (< **rne* [66c]) and *-ni-e-* indicates the correct quality of the vowel; and many others. The forms with NI are no more than orthographic variants in accordance with [25].

137. In order to determine the meaning of *-ne* we have to examine the principal constructions in which this particle may be used. They are represented by the following types: [91]

1. (a) *ta-še-e-ni-e-we id-du-um-mi* Mit. I 92 f. "present-*ne*-of going-out" (going-out of the present)

(b) K[UR] *Mi-zi-ir-ri-e-we* [66c] KUR *u-u-mi-i-in-ni-e-we al-la-i* Mit. I 62 "Egypt-*ne*-of land-*ne*-of mistress" (mistress of the land of Egypt)

(c) KUR *Ma-a-ás-ri-a-a-an-ni* [92] KUR *u-u-mi-i-ni* Mit. III 7 "Egypt-in [93] -*ne* [94] land" (land of [lit. "in"] Egypt); cf. the parallel phrase *Ḫur-ru-u-ḫé* KUR *u-u-mi-i-ni* ibid. 6 "Hurrian land"

(d) [*e-še*]*-ni-bi-ni-iš al-la-a-iš* VII 56 i 27 "heaven-*ne*-of-*ne*-by mistress--by" (by the mistress of heaven)

In all four instances we have attributive constructions. The attribute, always accompanied by *-ne,* precedes the head. The same word-order is the rule with adjectival concepts marked by the suffix *-ḫe* [158]. Indeed, this word-order and the parallel *Masrianne : Ḫurroḫe* (c) indicate that all of the attributes in the above instance have the function of descriptive adjectives. There is, however, one important exception in form: the attributes in *-ḫe* lack the particle *-ne,* whereas their analogues which are based on genitives and locatives appear with that particle. Evidently, therefore, *-ḫe* alone was sufficient to mark the required relation to the head; in the other examples that

[91] For the sake of clarity the *-ne* will be underlined in the occurrences which follow.

[92] Cf. also ibid. I 10, II 69, 71, III 117, IV 128.

[93] For the locative see [155], and for the absence of contraction in the sequence *-e/i-a* cf. *ḫa-ur-ni-a* Br. 571 n. 1 "on earth."

[94] The doubled *n* is in accordance with [86a].

function devolves on *-ne* (when *-ne* is used with *-ḫe* it merely duplicates the suffix of the head, cf. 238).

This mediative force of *-ne* between case-form attribute and head is further illustrated by (d). Here the particle is found not only before *-be* (< *we*) but also before *-s̄*. Both "case"-endings relate clearly to *allais̄*: the genitive by indicating the syntactic connection with the head and the agentive by restating pleonastically the position of the head in the sentence [133].

Instances similar to (d) appear to have influenced Friedrich in his designating *-ne* as a "suffix-connective."[95] But this formal behavior reflects a special function, since *-ne* is absent in a number of other case-forms; cf., e. g., the above *allai-s̄* or, with the genitive, *tup-pí-ma-a-an ni-ḫa-a-ri-i-we* Mit. III 36, 38 "tablet, that is, of dowry." Thureau-Dangin has committed himself to a more positive interpretation by terming *-ne* the definite article.[96] Once again, however, the explanation fails to account for numerous pertinent occurrences. There is no apparent reason, for instance, why the above *niḫari-we* should be undefined while the examples in (a-d) call for the definite article. A more conclusive objection to this theory will be pointed out in connection with *-na* [140].

2. *tup-pè* (41) *ni-ḫa-a-ar-ri-e-we a-ru-u-ša-uš-še-ni-e-we* Mit. III 40 f. "tablet dowry-*ne*-of given-past-abstr.-by-me-*ne*-of" (the tablet of the dowry that I gave)

Here the two forms which follow the head are in a possessive relation to it, which is indicated by the genitive endings and the placing of the head at the beginning of the phrase. The first genitive is complemented by the second and it is this relation of subordinate head and its attribute that is marked by *-ne* in both nouns.

3. *šu-u-we-ni-e e-ti-iw-wu-ú-e*(*-e*) Mit. IV 18, 22 "me-of-*ne*, regard-mine-of" (regarding me); cf. [69]

Here we have two forms in an appositive relation. The first ends in *-ne* which appears to signify that the phrase is not complete without the word which follows.

4. *X, e-we*$_e$*-er-ne* [KUR] *Lu-ul-lu-e-ne-we*$_e$ XXVII 38 iv 13 f. "X, lord-*ne* land-Lullu-*ne*-of"

X, (30) [*e-we*$_e$*-*]*er-ne ḫa-wu*$_u$*-ru-un-ni* ibid. 29 f. "X, lord-*ne* earth-*ne*"

and contrast

X, ^{URU}*Du-ug-ri-iš-ḫi e-bi-ir-ni* ibid. 14 "X, Tukrishite lord"

In these examples we have phrases consisting of a head and an apposition

[95] Analecta Orientalia 12 (1935) 127.

[96] Syria 12 (1931) 254 ff.; RA 36 (1939) 19.

composed of two nouns in attributive construction. Both the secondary head and its attribute contain *-ne* except when the attribute is a form in *-ḫe* (see above under 1). From the juxtaposition *Tugrišḫe : ḫawurunne* it follows that the latter functions as an adjective.

5. Starting with the above relational uses *-ne* seems to have developed in certain instances the value of a derivational element, perhaps through ellipsis. Thus *ašḫožikkonne* "sacrificer(?)" (cf. [86a] and ibid. n. 39a) may be based on something like "the sacrificing (priest)." By the side of *muž* Mâri 6. 10 ff., and in numerous proper names, we have not only ᵈ*Ḫebat mužne*[97] XXVII 1 ii 37 ff., 3. 19 ff., etc., but also (ᵈ*Ḫebat*) ᵈ*Mužun(ne)*- XXIX 8 iii 32 ff., where the determinative for "god" appears to imply that *-ne* had become part of the stem. Cf. also *ti-iš-ni* RŠ Voc. II 27 (note also similar examples, ibid. IV 9, 19), *pa-ab-ni* Mâri 1. 13, 2. 5 (also in proper names) alongside the common *tižᵃ* "heart" and *pabᵃ* "mountain." In the same way could be explained the frequent *ḫawurne* "earth" (cf. now v. Brandenstein, ZA 46. 87), perhaps originally a reference to some special place.[98] Note also *e-e-še-ni-e-ra*[99] (101) *ḫa!-a-wu-ru-un!-ni-e-ra*[100] Mit. III 100 f. "with heaven and earth."

6. Lastly, we have to note the use of *-ne* in the sense of "one" in *ma-a-ni-e-im-ma-ma-an* Mit. III 35 ff. [125].

To sum up, *-ne* may be used in a variety of constructions. In all but one it has the force of a relational particle. The exception is (5) where this element may be described as a derivational suffix. But all these disparate uses can be traced to a single source if we regard (6) as the starting point. The development of a numerative meaning "one" into a relative particle "one that" is self-evident. As such it can have the force of an article without necessarily implying definition; but the indefinite connotation is nearer to hand than the definite. By relating case-form attributes to their heads *-ne* occupies a prominent place as an attributive particle; cf., e.g., 1 (b): "mistress, one of (the) land, one of Egypt," i. e., "mistress of the Egyptian land, Egypt-land mistress." Attributes thus designated have the full force

[97] For the meaning of *muž* see ibid. 22 f.

[98] [V. Brandenstein, ZA 46 (1940) 87 n. 1 cites in this connection the proper name *Ḫa/ubur*].

[99] The syntactic position of *e-e-še-ni* Mit. IV 125 is obscure and hence also the function of its *-ne*.

[100] [For this reading cf. v. Brandenstein, loc. cit. 85.] See also [64 n. 9]. The double *n* results in this case from the combination **ḫawurne* + *ne-ra* [89] which is confirmed by the analogous *eže-ne-ra*.

and the precise word-order of adjectives. A specialized use of the particle appears in such idioms as *ašḫožikkonne, ḫawurne* (5); here *-ne* coalesces with the underlying stem to the extent that the expanded stem can then take on another *-ne* when the context requires it; e. g., *ašḫožikkonne-ne-wenašta* XII 44 ii 6, *-ne-wena* X 27 iii 9; *ḫawuron-ne-ra* (see above under 5) < **ḫawurne--ne-ra.*[101]

Additional confirmation for this argument is furnished by the plural counterpart of *-ne* which will now be discussed.

-na

138. It is a long-known fact that the plural of Hurrian nouns is indicated by means of *-na* (Friedrich BChG 2 ff.). With *i/e*-stems the suffix appears as *-ena*, occasionally as *-enna* (ibid. 4). With stems in *-a* and *-u* we get *-anna* and *-unna* respectively [86(a)].

139. Thureau-Dangin has expressed the opinion that *-na* is not so much the suffix of the plural as the plural counterpart of *-ne* (RA 36. 19). This view proves to be correct. The necessary evidence may be gathered from these two facts. We know that *-na* may be omitted in certain instances (Friedrich, BChG 6 f.), particularly if the desired concept of plurality is marked elsewhere in the sentence. It follows that Hurrian does not pluralize its nouns directly but expresses the concept by means of a particle which may be dispensed with in special circumstances. That *-na* is indeed a particle is shown also by its use in relating an attribute in the singular to its head in the plural, just as *-ne* is used when both attribute and head are in the singular. In *ᵈIŠTAR^ga-bi-na-šu-uš . . . ši-i-e-na-šu-uš* XXIX 8 ii 30 f. "waters . . . of Shaushka" (in the agent.), e. g., the sg. *Šauška-we* is connected with the duplicated agent. suff. *-žuš* by means of *-na-*, precisely as *-ne-* connects sg. suffixes in [137(1)]. In other words, *-na* patterns like *-ne*. The difference between the two is one of number.

140. It should be pointed out at this time that in the majority of instances *-na* is used absolutely, i. e., not with attributes. In this function it is paralleled, to be sure, by the instances of *-ne* listed in [137 (5)-(6)],[102] but these are comparatively rare. The reason for this disparity in degree will appear

[101] Cf. the preceding note. The stem-ending *-ne* is supported by Akk. *ḫi/uburni* [for which see now v. Brandenstein loc. cit. 87 n. 1].

[102] The examples under (5) may be based on original attributive constructions. Nevertheless, *-ne* comes to be used in such instances in an absolute sense and can be treated as part of the stem.

presently [141]. What is immediately apparent is the fact that *-ne* cannot be the definite article. For the demonstrated parallelism between *-ne* and *-na* would imply that if *-ne* marks determined singulars *-na* must mark determined plurals. We know, however, that the forms in *-na* are normal plurals without regard to definition. The scheme may be exemplified by *tiwe* "word": *tiwena* "words." If *tiwena* is to be interpreted as "the words," we should have the anomalous pattern of plural forms being always determined while the singulars employ the article selectively.

141. This difficulty disappears if we derive the various uses of *-ne* from that of "one" [125] and view *-na* as the corresponding pluralized particle. Accordingly, *tiwe-na* represents "word-ones," the particle having a force similar to that of our anaphoric "ones." The Hurrian plural noun is formed, then, by the suffixing of a differentiated numerative particle to the unchanging stem. The infrequent use of *-ne* for non-attributive purposes as against the common employment of *-na* in that capacity becomes now self-evident. The noun has normally the function of a singular without an appended particle for "one"; but to be marked as plural it requires the particle for "ones." Both particles are employed analogously in attributive constructions.

The pluralizing particle *-ẓ*

142. In addition to *-na*, which is used to pluralize stems, Hurrian employs a special particle to mark bound forms as plural. This particle appears as *-š-* in the syllabic texts. For possible alphabetic occurrences (wr. *ẓ*) cf. [154].

Within the nominal complex[103] *-ẓ-* combines with the suffixes which represent possessive pronouns and case-endings. To mark these forms as plural the particle is added to the respective singulars. It is placed after the pronominal elements, with *-a-* serving as the connective vowel, but before the case-endings; e. g., ^{d}*e-en-ni-iw-wa-a-še-e-en* Mit. II 77 "of our gods + *n*," i. e., **enna* "gods" (< *en*^{e}*-na* [66a]) + *if* [53] + *aẓ* + *e* (< *we* [81]) + *n* [203 ff.]; similarly, *ši-ni-a-še-* Mit. III 40 "of their two" [81]. In both these instances the particle occurs between a possessive suffix and the gen. ending. A common instance with an intervening possessive is *enna-ẓuṣ̌* (i. e., *enna* + *ẓ* + ^{u}*ṣ̌*) "by (the) gods," cf., e. g., XXVII 42 rev. 9, 18, XXIX 8 iii 37, Mit. I 78, II 52, IV 117. A literal translation of this form would yield "god-ones-pl.-by," i. e., "gods-pl.-by." The pleonastic indication of the plural is only apparent. The

[103] In the verbal complex we have a pluralizing element *-ẓa* [198] which can scarcely be separated from the present particle. We shall have reason to see also a possible relationship between the possessive suffixes of the noun and the agentive suffixes of the transitive verb.

force of the complex word is rather "gods, by several," with radical element and agentive suffix treated as semantically independent units. The technique of such constructions is plainly agglutinative [133].

For the pluralized possessive suffixes cf. my note in JAOS 59. 315 n. 70. The mistaken ascription of voicelessness to the sibilant in *-iw-wa-aš* has been rectified in [88 n. 43]. For the pluralizing function of *ž* with case-endings, which has been pointed out by Goetze, see [81 n. 37].

b. Possessive Suffixes

143. The suffixes which indicate possessive pronouns form the following paradigm:

	Singular	Plural
1 p.	*-if*	*-ifaž*
2 p.	*-v*	
3 p.	*-i/ya-, -di*	*-i(y)až*

144. 1 person. The stem-ending is lost before the vowel of this suffix. For the pronunciation of the labial cf. [53]. In Mit. the orthography is regularly *-iw-wə*: cf. *še-e-ni-iw-wə* I 18, 49, 65, etc. "my brother" < *žen*^{a}; *pa-aš-ši-i-it-ḫi-iw-wə* I 114, IV 36, 40, 45, 51 "my envoy" < *pašitḫ*^{e}. Mâri writes *-w-*: *e-ni-wu-úš* (with agent. suff.) 6. 10 ff. "by my god" [53]. In Bogh. we lack as yet absolutely clear examples; but *e-ir-bi-ri-ib-bi* XXIX 8 ii 37, *i-te-ib-bu-ú-ta* ibid. 38 "for my sake(?)," *ni-ḫi-ni-ḫi-ip-pi* ibid. 39, and *ḫa-a-ḫi-ip-pí-na-ma* ibid. iii 26 may perhaps prove pertinent.[104] RŠ X 4. 3 reads *in atynpš*, and ibid. 5 *in atynpd*. The context suggests strongly "god, my father," with agent. suff. in the first instance and a dir. suff. in the other.[105]

[104] *at-ta-ni-ip-pal* XXVII 25. 10 appears to be an instance of the poss. suff. of 2 p. in the gen., on account of the following *pu-u-ri-bu-ta-al*; hence "of thy father(s), they(?)" [However, *at-ta-ib-bi-na-a-ša* cited by v. Brandenstein, ZA 46. 114 may refer to 1 p.]

[105] The *-n-* of these forms is obscure as is the corresponding *-(n)ni-* of similar syllabic forms [cf. ZA 46. 114]. It may represent an extension of the stem in accordance with [137 (5)]; in the alphabetic instances just cited it cannot be a mere attributive element before the gen. suff. [137 (1)], since that suffix would be expressed in RŠ by *-b*. Since the attached case-endings are in the sg. it is improbable that we have here the pl. element *-na*.

At any rate, with possessive suffixes there arises the question of the difference between, say, "my god" and "my gods." We would expect the former to be **enif* and the latter **ennif*; indeed we actually find ^{d}*e-en-ni-iw-wa-a-še-e-e-en* Mit. II 77 where a possessive (1 p. pl.) is attached to a form with double *n* in a context which clearly refers to "gods." But we have also *e-e-ni-iw-wa-šu-uš* ibid. 76 and *ew-ri-iw-wa-šu-uš at-ta-iw-wa-šu-uš* ibid. IV 118 in all of which demonstrable plurals fail to be marked by the expected particle. The omission of the particle has to be interpreted in accordance with

145. 2 person. The suffix is attached to the stem-ending. For the pronunciation of the labial cf. [53]. The orthography in Mit. is not uniform, both *-b/p* and *-w* being employed. Cf. *ša-a-la-pa-an* "thy daughter + *an*" I 51, IV 93 (= *šala-v-an*); *še-e-na-pa-an* I 91 "thy brother + *an*"; but *pa-aš-ši-i--it-ḫi-wu-uš* I 72 "by thy envoy" (= *pašitḫe-w-*^{u}*š*); *ti-wi-i-wa-an* II 84 "to thy word + *an*." Bogh. writes *-b/p*: e. g., *ḫa-zi-iz-*[*z*]*i-bal* XXVII 42 rev. 12, *ḫa-wu*$_{u}$*-ši-bal* ibid. 14, *ḫu-ub-ri-pa-a-al* ibid. 24; all three forms consist of a radical element in *-i* + poss. suff. of 2 p. sg. + *al* "they." For other instances of this suffix see, e. g., [212 n. 295].

146. 3 person. This relation is expressed by two different forms: (a) *-i/ya-*; (b) *-di*. For (a) cf. [69]; Bogh. furnishes, among other possible instances, at least one likely example in *ti-i-ši-ya-an* XXVII 34 iv 11. (b) is known so far only from the RŠ Voc.; cf. <*ut-ḫu-*>*ri-di* ibid. IV 16 "its side," alongside *ut-ḫu-ru* = Sum. á ibid. 15; <*ša-wə-*>*nu-di* ibid. 20, alongside *ša-wə-ni* = d a "proximity" ibid. 19; note also <*tižni/u*> [106] *-di* ibid. II 28 "his/its heart" and the forms in *-di-e* ibid. I 3 11, II 29 where the final *-e* corresponds to Sum. šè (Akk. *ana*) "for, into." [107]

It is a reasonable assumption that *-i/ya-* and *-di* expressed different shades of meaning, but we have no means of ascertaining where that difference lay.

147. Plural forms are obtained from the singulars by the addition of the particle *-ž* preceded by the connective vowel *-a-* [142]. Thus far we have only instances of the 1 p. and 3 p., the latter with *-i/ya* but not *-di*; e. g.,

[139]. There remains to be considered the possibility that "our gods" would be rendered by **enifena*, with the particle following the possessive. To this there is a valid syntactic objection. We know from forms in *-šena* [164], and the like, that *-na* in that position marks the attribute and not the head. Provisionally, therefore, we may posit *-na* before the possessive suffixes as a means of expressing plurality of the radical element in non-attributive constructions. The assumed tentative scheme with *at(t)ay* as the radical element is, then, as follows:

**at(ta)if* "my father"	**at(t)an(n)if* "my fathers"
**at(t)aifaž* "our father"	**at(t)tan(n)ifaž* "our fathers"
**at(t)aifena* "(things pertaining to) my father"	**at(t)an(n)ifena* "(things pertaining to) my fathers"
**at(t)aifažena* "(things pertaining to) our father"	**at(t)an(n)ifažena* "(things pertaining to) our fathers"

The hypothetical character of these reconstructions cannot be stressed too strongly.

[106] Friedrich, Kleinas. Sprachdenkmäler 152 n. 1, reads *ti-iš-di* for the MIN-*di* of the text. The objection to this is the voiced stop of the suffix [12a], which would be anomalous after *ž*; cf. [74]. For the retention of *-ne* cf. the preceding example; the change of its vowel to *u* before the dental may be in accordance with [153].

[107] This vowel may represent the stative *-a* [156].

iš-ta-ni-iw-wa-š(a) [100] (in) our mutualness"; *tup-pí-aš* Mit. III 39, 45 "their tablet(s)."[108] In the majority of pertinent instances case-endings follow the pluralized possessive elements; cf. **ištan-if-až-wa*[109] (above).

c. The So-called Case-endings

148. The relations which inflecting languages usually express by case-forms are marked in Hurrian by a number of special suffixes. These endings follow the possessives and to that extent they are less intimately connected with their radical element. Moreover, they may be used pleonastically in the process of suffix-duplication [238] which is a further instance of comparatively loose association with the given nominal stem. It follows that these suffixes are not fused with their stems and the question arises, therefore, whether they are in reality flexional elements. From a formal standpoint at least they have the characteristics of particles rather than case-endings. But it would be premature to attempt a definitive solution of the problem at this time. The term "case"-endings has been retained in this study, with the important reservation that it refers both to conventionally recognized functions and a given set of morphemes. The case-relations listed below are distinguished, accordingly, through the combined evidence of syntax and morphology.[110]

(1) Subject-case ("nominative")
(2) Agentive; marks the actor in goal-action constructions involving a logical object
(3) Genitive
(4) Dative
(5) Directive
(6) Comitative
(7) Locative (possibly identical with the dative)
(8) "Stative"

This list cannot be regarded as exhaustive in view of the nature of our sources. We can eliminate, however, some forms which might appear to be pertinent at first glance. Such forms are those in *-dan* [222] and *-ae* [165 ff.]; the former ending proves to be an associative in that it occurs with nouns, verbs, and particles; the suffix *-ae*, on the other hand, indicates a special class of verbal nouns.

[108] For the problem of indicating plurality of the radical concept cf. [144 n. 105].

[109] The *š* is posited on the analogy of [74].

[110] The whole section belongs properly in the next chapter. It is included here so as to make the survey of the common bound forms as complete as possible.

149. Subject-case: zero suffix. This case is characterized by the absence of a special suffix, being represented by the bare stem-form. It is often followed by *-n*, but this element is non-morphologic and has no direct bearing on the case-relation; cf. [203]. It is still customary to regard the stem-form, with or without *-n*, as the "accusative" or "object-case." The following facts will show that such a view is no longer tenable.

The stem-form marks the subject in (a) nominal sentences and (b) with intransitives; e. g.:

(a) *un-du-u-un* [I]*Ma-ni-e-na-an še-e-ni-iw-wu-ú-e pa-aš-ši-i-it-ḫi* Mit. IV 35 "now-then [127] + *n* Mane-*n-an* brother-my-of (is) envoy"[111]

(b) *un-du-ma-a-an in-na-me-e-ni-i-in še-e-ni-iw-wu-ú-e aš-ti ú-ni-e-et-ta* ibid. III 21 "now-then-*màn* behold(?)-she-indeed(?), my-brother's wife arrive-will"

i-nu-me-e uš-ḫu-ni ši-ḫa-a-la XXIX 8 iv 27 "as it the silver (is) clean"[112]

In (a) we have a nominal sentence whose subject is followed by two associatives (*-n-an*). In (b) are cited two clauses which contain intransitive predicates. The subject of the first is the stem-form *aš̄ti* preceded by two independent particles, each with an associative; the other clause has as its subject *ušḫune*, apparently an extended stem in *-ne* [137 (5)]; note that this clause lacks any associative containing *-n*.

So far we have had clear subjects represented by the stem-form. Incidentally, we have seen that a suffixed *-n* may be attached to the subject or to some other element at the beginning of the sentence; but there are sentences without this *-n*. The stem alone thus emerges as the subject-case.

(c) In sentences which contain a transitive verb together with its logical subject and object, the subject is marked by the suffix *-š̄* and the object is placed in the stem-form; e. g.:

še-e-ni-iw-wu-uš-ša-a-an aš-ti ša-a-ru-u-ša Mit. III 1. Freely translated, this sentence means "my brother[113] requested a wife." From a grammatical standpoint, however, *aš̄ti* in the present instance is identical with the occurrence of the same form in (b); in other words, it should represent the same "case." There is abundant independent evidence to show that this is indeed true [233]. In constructions of this type the verb indicates a goal-action relation and the *š̄*-case, which is restricted to these constructions, introduces

[111] The associatives, which have been left untranslated, will be discussed below; cf. [202 ff.].

[112] Cf. Goetze, RHA 35 (1939) 107.

[113] The sentence-connective *-àn* (for the transcription cf. [92a]) cannot be translated adequately in this and many similar instances; cf. Friedrich, BChG 16.

the agent. Accordingly, the logical object becomes the grammatical subject. Any literal translation is likely to be too definite in that it would impose upon Hurrian the limitations of an unrelated language. The closest that we can come, however, to the character of the original is by rendering it "brother-my-by-and wife requested-past-by-him."

The three uses of the stem-form just cited comprise the great majority of the available occurrences. Most of the remaining instances lend themselves to analogous interpretations. Thus RŠ Voc. introduces lexical entries without any case-ending; e. g.:

(d) *ti-iš-ni* "heart" ibid. II 27; *e-la-mi* "oath" III 28 In other words, the stem-form serves as the "nominative" proper. No less significant are the examples of the type

(e) *am-ma-ti-iw-wu-ú-e-e-en ša-a-la at-ta-iw-wu-ú-e e*[-*e*]-*la* (38) *ma-a-ni--e-im-ma-ma-an tup-pè* Mit. III 37 f. "(as for) my grandfather's daughter, my sister, (38) this (is) one tablet in particular" [125] Here the stem-forms *šala* and *ela* function as "absolute cases" or "nominatives absolute."[114]

It follows from the foregoing that the stem-form is used to express the subject. The current interpretation of this form as the "'object-case" or "accusative" goes back to the earliest stage of Hurrian studies[115] and proceeds from an analysis of type (c). This analysis has to be revised in accordance with the progress in our understanding of the Hurrian verb. At any rate, the occurrences of the form in (c) cannot be separated from those in the remaining groups where it clearly represents the subject. The designation "subject-case" is accordingly the only one which can be justified on the basis of the various characteristic sentence-types in which this form is capable of analysis.[116]

[114] The one occurrence of the stem-form which cannot offhand be taken as the subject is [. . .]*-a-an ša-a-la-pa-an* (*aš-ti-iw-wu-ú-un-na a-ri*) Mit. I 51; cf. Goetze. Lang. 16 (1940) 131 f. The difficulty is due primarily to our present inability to analyze the construction involving the 2 p. imperative, for which there is only one other example in the gloss *zu-zi-la-ma-an* EA 170. 11 Akk. *ù pa-ni-šu-nu ṣa-bat* "so get ahead of them (?)," cf. [197]. All the other instances which Goetze (ibid. 135 f.) would regard as analogous in their employment of the stem-form require different interpretations of the accompanying predicates; cf. [205].

[115] See Friedrich, op. cit. 7 n. 1.

[116] Theoretically, the subject-case need not correspond to the traditional "nominative"; it might conceivably dovetail with the "accusative." The real question is whether the stem-form introduces the subject or the object. If we incline with Goetze to the latter alternative (leaving aside for the moment the interpretation of the *i*-form with verbal roots), we are forced into such tangential renderings of the above types (a) and (b) as are implied by Goetze's statement (Lang. 16. 137): "This means that the

The plural does not call for a special discussion since the pluralizing particle *-na* [138 ff.] cannot alter the underlying case-relations.

Friedrich (BChG 9 f.) was the first to stress the incidental character of *-n* with the case-form just discussed. Accordingly, he proposed the term "stem-case," while adhering to the earlier opinion that the case in question denotes the accusative. A notable advance in the analysis of the *-n* is due to Goetze (JAOS 60. 217 ff.) who demonstrated that where this element is not with its noun it is present, nevertheless, elsewhere in the sentence. But *-n* is to Goetze the mark of the sg. object and *-la* the corresponding pl. element [see now id. RHA 39. 202 ff.]. Goetze's interpretation is bound up with his analysis of the *i*-form in the verb (Lang. 16. 125 ff.); contrast [170a]. For the use of *-n* see [203 ff.].

150. Agentive: *-s̄*. For the term [117] see JAOS 59. 308. The suffix is written *-š* in the syllabic texts, *-šš-* with a vowel following [44]. The alphabetic counterpart is *-s̄*; e. g., *ts̄b-s̄* [44], *kmrb-n-s̄* RŠ X 4. 8. After consonants the connective vowel is *-u-*, cf. [77].

The plural form is *-z̄us̄*, cf. Friedrich, BChG 10 ff. It consists of the pluralizing particle *-z̄-* [142], the connective *-u-* and the agentive element *-s̄*. Cf., with *a*-stem: *ᴵGe-li-i-aš* Mit. IV 27; *e/i*-stems: *e-ni-iš* Mâri 1. 32 "god-by," *aš-ti-iš* Mit. III 7, *aš-ti-ni-iš* Mâri 4. 25 "wife-by"; *u*-stem *ag-gu-uš* Mit. I 81 "the-other-by"; consonant-stem: *ᵈGal-ga-mi-šu-ul* (with assimilation of the agent. suff. to *-l*) VIII 61 obv. 8 [75]. Pl.: *e-e-en-na-šu-uš* Mit. I 78 [142]; with 1 p. possessive *ew-ri-iw-wa-šu-uš* ibid. IV 118, lit. "lord(s)-my-pl.-by, by our lord(s)."

In addition to these normal forms which typify a great number of instances there are isolated examples from Bogh. which exhibit irregularities. The most transparent of these is *e-en-na-aš a-da-an-nu-uš* XXV 42 v 6; since this phrase is preceded by an enumeration of gods, all with the agent. suff., we should expect here **ennaz̄us̄ at(t)annaz̄us̄* "by the parental gods." More obscure is a series of forms in XXVII 46; here the clear agentives *ᵈUᵘᵇ-aš e-ew-ri-eš* i 30 "by Teshub (the) lord" are paralleled by *əḫ-li-ya-na-aš šu-ub-ri-ya-na-aš* i 19, [. .]*-na-ša-aš šu-ub-ri-na-ša-aš* ibid. 30, and [*əḫ?*]*-li?-li-ya-aš šu-ub-ri-ya-aš* ibid. 31 (cf. now Goetze, RHA 39. 198 n. 32). No less perplexing are *ya-ra-aš a-a-bi-ra-aš* (preceded by agentives) XXV 42 v 7, and cf. ibid. 43. 10; note also *a-a-bi-ri-eš* XXVII 10 iv 26. The stems involved seem to be the relative particle *ya-* and the prepositional element *abi-* [130], but the suffixes are difficult to interpret especially because of the interposed *-ra/e-*. It may be doubted altogether whether the agentive is involved in the majority of the foregoing instances; cf. [216].

From the standpoint of syntax it may be remarked at this time that the

Hurrian language instead of 'he comes' actually says 'there is coming on his part.'" Actually, the cumulative evidence of Hurrian syntax fails to confirm the existence of a grammatical object altogether.

[117] I have chosen it in preference of the "ergative" of the Caucasic grammars in order not to imply a definite parallelism before it has been demonstrated beyond all doubt.

agentive is used, so far as can be seen at present, only in constructions involving transitives accompanied by both logical subject and object; cf. [149(c)]. It then represents the agent while the goal is put in the subject-case in accordance with the goal-action character of such sentences. Except for these tripartite constructions the Hurrian sentence is of the actor-action type, as will be shown below. The subject-case and not the agentive is employed in utterances of the type

(a) Teshub is king
(b) Teshub has come
(c) Teshub guides
(d) Teshub is loved

But the Hurrian would not use the phrase "Teshub has given a son." Instead, he would employ

(e) Teshub-by (was) son granted-by-him

The agentive occurs only in type (e). For actual examples see [205, 246 f.].

151. Genitive: *-we*. The orthography of the labial varies sufficiently to cause difficulty. In Mit. it is normally *we*; cf. URU*Ni-i-nu-a-a-we* III 98 "of Nineveh"; *šu-u-we-ni-e* (*šu* + *we* + *ne*) ibid. IV 18, 22 "of me" (the *e*-quality of the vowel of the ambiguous sign PI as used here is indicated, e. g., by such genitives as *e-ti-iw-wu-ú-e-* which follow the above *šuwene* and are appositive to it). Several pronouns, however, have their genitives expressed by *-ú-e*, e. g., *a-gu-ú-e* IV 123; cf. [64]. The same writing indicates the gen. suff. after 1 p. possessive, e. g., *še-e-ni-iw-wu-ú-e* I 61, II 57, etc., cf. [83]. After stem-ending *-ƀ* and the 2 p. possessive *-v* the gen. suff. appears as *-ƀ/pe*, cf. d*Te-e-eš-šu-u-up-pè* II 72, *še-e-na-a-ap-pè* I 89 "of thy brother" [82]. After 3 p. possessive in certain forms the suffix is *-ye*, e. g., *e-ti-i-e-e* IV 19, 28 [69]. The usual form in Bogh. is *-ƀi*, e. g., *šar-ri-ni-ƀi* XXVII 46 i 24 "of (the) king"; but we find also *-we* (e. g., d*IŠTAR-we*$_e$ ibid. 1 ii 16) and *-wi* (e. g., d*Ku-mar-ƀi-ni-wi*$_i$ ibid. 19). RŠ Voc. has *-wə* (e. g., *ša-li-ni-wə* IV 22 "of (the) house"), and so has Mâri (e. g., *ka-nu-me-ni-wə* 1. 4).

All these variant forms appear to point to [v]. The sole objection to thus normalizing the labial[118] is the consistent orthography of Mit. with *-w-*. Elsewhere Mit. signalizes [v] by alternating *ƀ* and *w*, e. g., in the 2 p. possessive [145]. It has seemed advisable, therefore, to set up provisionally the form *-we* pending more conclusive evidence.

The plural is *-že* <*-ž-we* [81]. Cf. Mit. d*e-en-ni-iw-wa-a-še-e-en* II 77 "of our gods + *n*," *ši-ni-a-še-na-* III 40 "of their two." Bogh. has *-še* and

[118] As is done, e. g., by Thureau-Dangin, Syria 12. 257.

-ši; cf., e. g., DINGIR^{MEŠ}*-na-a-še* KBo II 21. 11, but the same form with *-ši* XXVII 42 obv. 14 "of (the) gods"; cf. RHA 39. 201 ff.

152. Dative: *-wa.* The writing of the labial shows the same variations as in the case of *-we.* In Mit. the orthography is ambiguous in that the sign PI is used without vowel-complement for *-wa* as well as *-we* and we have to rely on the context to distinguish between the two cases. Thus *we-e-wə e-ti-i-wə* III 55 cannot be gen. because the sentence speaks of "(things done by my grandfather) for thee, for thy regard," i. e., "regarding thee." With 2 p. possessive we get *at-ta-i-ip-pa* III 58 "for thy father." With certain pronouns [64] and 1 p. possessive the suffix is written *-ú-a,* cf. *a-gu-ú-a* I 81 "for the other"; *še-e-ni-iw-wu-ú-a* I 102, 107, III 14, 20, 62, 112 "for my brother." Bogh. favors *-pa,* e. g., *i-ti-pa pa-a-ḫi-pa* XXIX 8 ii 36.

Syntactically, it is of interest that the directive *edi-*(*i*)*-da* is preceded by the dative of the noun thus defined by the prepositional form; e. g., *a-gu-ú-a e-ti-i-ta* Mit. I 81 f. "for the other, to his regard (regarding the other)." Accordingly, we have to vocalize *ta-še-e-ni-e-wa̱ e-ti-i-ta* ibid. 104 "regarding the present," *at-ta-i-i-wa̱ e-ti-i-ta* ibid. 106 "regarding his father," etc.; cf. [235].

The plural is *-ža* <**-ž-wa* [81]; cf. DINGIR^{MEŠ}*-na-a-ša* (30) *tar-šu-wa-an--na-a-ša a-a-bi-ta* XXIX 8 iv 29 f. "(prepositional element) gods (and) men," *abi-da* being construed here with the dat. pl. just as *edi*(*i*)*-da* (above) is with the dat. sg.

For the possible identity of the dative and the locative see below [155].

153. Directive: *-t/da.* That this form expresses direction towards or to a given point was recognized by Messerschmidt, Mitanni-Studien 7. This function is seen best from *ú-ú-na-a-al-la-a-an še-e-ni-iw-wə-ta* Mit. I 115 "so that (*-àn*) they get to my brother," and *id-du-u-uš-ta-ma-a-an* (12) *še-e-ni-iw-wə-ta* ibid. III 11 f. "and she has gone to my brother." [119] For a series of pertinent forms from Bogh. cf. XXVII 34 (e. g., ^{d}*Na-ra-ta-an* i 9, *Ši-mi-*[*g*]*e-ni-ta-an* 13; *tar-šu-wa-an-ni-ta* ibid. iv 18, and many others). The postvocalic form is *-da*; cf. *Ku-ma-ar-wi-ni-da-al* Mâri 5. 4 "Kumarwe-to-they" (also ibid. 3), where the Akkadianizing orthography [12a] reflects a voiced stop. RŠ writes accordingly *-d* (Br. 573). The main syllabary writes mostly *-ta,* rarely *-da* (e. g., *e-ti-da* VIII 61 obv. 6). After consonants we find [t]; cf. *a-ta-i-ta* Mâri 5. 5 (= *at*(*t*)*ay-ta* [33, 51] and see the plural forms below. The connective vowel after consonants is *-ú-,* cf. ^{I}*Ma-ni-e-ta pa*[*-aš-š*]*i-i-it-ḫi-wu-ú-ta* Mit. I 53 "to Mane, to thy envoy" (**pašitḫe* + *v* + *u* + *da*). We may, there-

[119] For the meaning of these two verbs cf. Goetze, Lang. 15 (1939) 215 ff.

fore, transliterate safely *še-e-ni-iw-wu-ta* and the like; cf. also *i-te-ib-bu-ú-ta* XXIX 8 ii 38 [144].

The plural is *-š-ta* (<*-ž-da) [74]. Cf. RŠ *ḫdn-š-t ḫdlr-š-*[*t*] (Br. 573); *e-še-en-na-aš-ta-an* XXVII 34 i 11 "and to the heavens," *du-ú-ḫu-na-aš-ta e-en-na*[*-aš*]*-ta-an* ibid. 9, *aš-ḫu-ši-ku-un-ni-ni-bi-na-aš-ta* XII 44 ii 6 "to those of the sacrificer(?)."

The directive is commonly employed with the nominalized prepositions [105], which is easily understood if we assume a term like "before" to be in reality something like "to the face." For a possible connection with the associative *-t/dan* see [222].

154. Comitative: *-ra*. For the term see Bork, Mitannisprache 48. The interpretation of this form as the "with"-case proves to be correct, but several uses of it have to be distinguished:

(a) *it-ta-in-na-a-an pa-aš-ši-i-it-ḫi-iw-wə-ra* Mit. IV 53 "let him go with my envoy"

ᴵMa-ni-e-ra-la-an ú-na-aš-še-na ibid. II 116 "they, the ones arrived with Mane," i. e., "the things which Mane brought"

a-nam-mi-it-ta-ma-an še-e-ni-iw-wə-ra ur-ḫu-ub-du-ši-li-wa ibid. III 64 "and thus with my brother I would keep faith" [120]

The above citations contain three clear instances of the comitative proper.

(b) *e-e-še-ni-e-ra* (101) *ḫa!-a-wu-ru-un!-ni-e-ra* ibid. III 100 f.,[121] lit. "with heaven and earth." It is plain, however, from the context that the wealth of the Egyptian ruler is said here to be as extensive as heaven and earth. Thus "with" is used in the derived sense of "like," and this use is carried over into the Akkadian letters of Tushratta, where *itti šamê ù erṣeti* (EA 29. 59) is used in a comparison.

(c) ÍD^MEŠ^*-na* ḪUR.SAG^MEŠ^*-šu-ra* (= **šiyena pabannažura*) VII 58 iii 15, obviously "rivers and mountains." Thus *-ra* may function as a plain conjunction.[122] Incidentally, this phrase gives us the plural form *-žu-ra*, with a connective vowel after the pluralizing particle instead of the *-ž-* which we find with the other case-endings. Another instance of this plural form is [. . .]*-ti-iw-wə-ra ta-a-ta-uš-še-na-šu-ra* Mit. I 71.[123] The alphabetic texts

[120] For a suggestion as to the connective vowel with the 1 p. possessive see Lang. 16 (1940) 325 n. 26.

[121] For the reading cf. [64 n. 9].

[122] For parallel developments attention may be called to Sumerian - b i. d a "with it, and"; for NW Caucasic cf. G. Dumézil, Études Comparatives sur les Langues Caucasiennes du Nord-Ouest (1932) 64.

[123] The context is fragmentary. Unless *-ti-iw-we-ra* is a contracted form of **tiwefura* this cannot be a complete word.

contribute *trḫnẑr* RŠ X 4. 57 and *aštḫnẑr* ibid. 58 "with the male ones, with the female ones." [124]

155. Locative: *-(*y*)*a*. Although there are numerous instances in which a locative is clearly required by the context, our material admits of doubt as to the means of indicating this case. Generally, Hurrian is assumed to combine its dative and locative in one form.[125] This view may be right. In the plural the dative *-ẑa* (<**-ẑ-wa*) would be identical phonetically with a posited locative **-ẑ-a*. What slight reason there may be for separating the two forms is provided by a few occurrences of the singular. The starting point is *e-bar-ni ḫa-!-ur-ni-ya* (cited in Br. 571 n. 1) "lord on earth." Since a suffixed *-wa* is not known otherwise to change in this position to *-ya* (cf. *Ši-du-ur-ri-wa$_a$ aš-te-ni-w*[*a* . .] VIII 61 obv. 4 "for the woman Shiduri"; *aš-te-ni-wa$_a$-ni-id* ibid. 6), we are justified in assuming **-a*, or perhaps **-ya*. Note also KUR *Ma-a-ás-ri-a-a-an-ni* "one in Egypt" [137 (1c)]. As against this there is the phrase ^{URU}*Ni-nu-wa-a-wa$_a$* ^{d}*IŠTAR-an* XXXI 3 rev. 5. The context is fragmentary, but the place-name appears, nevertheless, to be in the locative. Unless the *-w-* of the suffix is secondary (like the first), the locative could be expressed at times by *-wa* in common with the dative. In these circumstances a satisfactory solution is as yet impossible. It seems safer, however, to keep the two case-relations apart for the time being with the reservation that a formal identity of the two is by no means unlikely.

At all events, the context enables us not infrequently to distinguish the locative-relation from the dative. The clearest examples happen to be in the plural. Thus *ti-ši-a-ša-an* Mit. I 78 is plainly "in their hearts" (= **tiẑ^a + ya + ẑ + w/a + n*); *ša-wa-al-la-ša* ibid. 79 is necessarily "in the years." [126] Similarly, *iš-ta-ni-a-ša* ibid. III 110 (also II 70, IV 129) has to be rendered "in their mutualness, they mutually." Cf. also [*e*]*-še-na-ša* Br. loc. cit. "in the heavens," and add <*ut-ḫu-ri*>*-ya-ša* RŠ Voc. IV 17, evidently "at their side." For the singular we have *ti-ši-iw-wa-an* Mit. II 55 [207], IV 111 [127] "in my heart."

[124] [v. Brandenstein, ZA 46. 104, speaks of *-ra* as the element of the collective plural, but there is nothing in the instances which he cites to support this assertion. His reference to Friedrich, BChG 6 is irrelevant since the *-ra* discussed there represents the particle *-na* with the *-n-* assimilated to the *r* of the radical element.]

[125] Cf. Thureau-Dangin, Syria 12. 257. Bork, Mitannisprache 22 f., equated with the locative not only the dative but also the genitive (in spite of its *-we*); in function, Bork held, "the locative could express all conceivable case-relations."

[126] Cf. JAOS 59. 296 n. 29. In citing several instance of *-ša* from Nuzi I listed them in that note under the locative but failed to realize that the suffix is composite and includes the pluralizing particle *-ẑ-*; cf. [142].

[127] For this passage cf. JAOS 59. 300 n. 41.

156. "Stative": *-a* cf. [207]. The inclusion of this form with the present group is provisional and the term is advisedly indefinite. There is nothing vague, however, about the prominence of the form in the language. The main question is whether its *-a* acts more distinctly as a particle than is true of the preceding "case"-endings. For unlike those, the present suffix appears to function also as an element forming intransitive participles [169]. At any rate, we do find it with nominal roots as a relational marker. To that extent it belongs with the above group.

First we have to justify the individual listing of the suffix as distinct from that of the locative. The evidence is phonologic. Whereas the locative ending is added to the stem-vowel (*ḫawurne-ya*), the ending of the stative is attached to the nearest consonant and any intervening stem-vowel is elided; e. g., *ur-ḫa* Mit. II 106 <*urḫ*^{e}; *pa-a-la* ibid. <*pal*$^{i/e}$; *ta-a-ti-a-a-aš-ša* III 92 <**tadiya-še.*

Functionally, the form conveys the idea that something is or has been placed in a given state. It is used hence frequently for the adverbial attribute and the circumstancial adverbial clause. E. g.: *ur-ḫé-e-en pa-a-la gu-li-a-a-ma pa-a*[*-li-*]*ma-a-an ur-ḫa g*[*u-l*]*i-a-a*[*-m*]*a* Mit. II 106 "what is true as questionable he will not declare, and what is questionable as true he will not declare"; [128] *^{I}Im-mu-u-ri-aš-ša-a-an za!-lam-ši ta-a-nu-u-ša ḫi-ya-ru-uḫ-ḫa na-ak-ka-aš-ša* ibid. III 106 "By Immuriya a statue was made, of chased gold"; [129] *Uš-ḫu-ne e-we*$_{e}$*-er-ne šar-ra uš-ta-e* XXVII 38 iv 19 "U. (the) lord was made(?) king" [102].

This function accounts for the use of the ending with adjectival forms in *-ḫe* and participial forms in *-še.* Cf. *e-e-ma-na-a-am-ḫa ta-a-nu-ša-ú* Mit. IV 32 "(these) tenfold (were) carried out by me," alongside the denominative verbal form *e-e-ma-na-a-mu-ša-ú* ibid. III 54, 57; [130] note also *a-ru-u-ma-a-aš--šu-ḫi-ḫa* ibid. 13, *a-ru-u-ši-im-bu-ú-uš-ḫa* ibid. 16. For *-ša,* note, e. g., *^{I}Ge-li-i-an ^{I}Ma-ni-en-na-a-an ḫa-šu-u-ša-ú it-ta-aš-*[*š*]*a* ibid. II 7 "Keliya and Mane (were) heard by me as having gone," i. e., "I heard that K. and M. had left." In this way the forms in *-ša* comes to express the equivalent of the "that"-clause.

Finally, an important use of the stative is with the noun-complex in which the predicative *-n* is employed internally [207]. A good example is *še-e-ni-iw-wu-ú--ul-la-a-an ti-ša-a-an-na* (108) *ú-ú-ri-a-a-aš-še-na* Mit. I 107 f. "brother-my--by-they-and, in-accordance-with-what-is-the-heart, the-ones-desired-by-him," i. e., "the things heartily desired by my brother." The Akk. equivalent of *tišanna* (*<*tiš*^{a} + *n*(*n*) + *a*) in the Tushratta letters is *ša libbišu* EA 20. 75,

[128] Cf. Friedrich, BChG 40.

[129] For this meaning of *nak-* note already Messerschmidt, Mitanni-Studien 14.

[130] Speiser, JAOS 59. 320 f.

29. 154. This usage is wide-spread. Cf. *aš-ti-in-na* Mit. III 104 "as wife," lit. "as (one who) is a wife"; *aš-ti-iw-wu-ú-un-na* ibid. I 51 "as my wife"; *še-e-ni-iw-wu-ú-e-ni-e-en-na ti-ša-a-an-na* ibid. III 14 "in accordance with what is my brother's heart." A further extension of the above phrase by means of the adjectival *-ḫe* occurs in *še-e-ni-iw-wu-ú-e-ni-e-en-nu-uḫ-ḫa ti-ša-a-an--nu-uḫ-ḫa* ibid. II 10 "in accordance with what is the fraternal heart of my brother." The first word consists of **z̄en*^{a} "brother" + 1 p. sg. possessive *-if* + gen. *-we* + attr. part. *-ne* + pred. part. *-n* + connective vowel *-u-* + adject. suff. *-ḫe* + stative *-a*; the whole is employed as an attribute of *tiz̄annuḫḫa* with the customary suffix-duplication.[131]

With this stative *-a* I would compare the *-e* of the RŠ Voc. which combines with the 3 p. possessive to form *-di-e* [146], Sum. -b i. š è (corresponding to Akk. *ana x-šu*). By the side of <*ti-iš-ni/u-*>*di* [146 n. 106] ibid. II 28 "his (her, its) heart" we have MIN-*di-e* 29 "as/into his heart." Since there is otherwise no evidence for a particle *-e* and since the force of this suffix accords perfectly with the above *-a*, we may equate the two. That the difference between them may be one of orthography rather than quality is indicated by the variation *a/i* within the RŠ Voc. itself; cf. *te-ša-ḫi* III 9 : *te-ši-ḫi* ibid. 11.

157. To sum up, the suffixes which mark the case-relations of Hurrian are as follows:

	Singular	Plural
Subject-case	. . .	*-az̄*
Agentive	*-s̄*	*-z̄us̄*
Genitive	*-we*	*-z̄e*
Dative	*-wa*	*-z̄a*
Directive	*-da*	*-s̄ta*
Comitative	*-ra*	*-z̄ura*
Locative	*-(*y*)*a*	*-*z̄a*
"Stative"	*-a*	*-*z̄a*

All these suffixes follow other morphologic elements but precede the associatives, which are non-morphologic. The one exception to this rule is in the construction of the stative which may use the predicative *-n* internally.

d. Adjectival Suffixes

158. *-ḫe* and *-ḫḫe.* It has already been demonstrated that these two forms differ phonetically [56 ff.]; for alongside syllabic *Ḫal-pa-a-ḫi, Ḫa-al-pa-ḫi*

[131] The above translation of the phrase is periphrastic since we cannot otherwise indicate in English the adjective of "my brother's."

[58 n. 109], with one *-ḫ-*, we have alphabetic *ḫlb-ġ*, whereas syllabic *turuḫḫe* "male" and *as̄tuḫḫe* "female" [57] correspond to RŠ *trḫ*(*n*) and *as̄tḫ*(*n*) respectively [59]. The single *-ḫ* of the main syllabary reflects thus the voiced velar spirant as against the voiceless which is written *-ḫḫ-*. At the same time there is scarcely an appreciable difference in meaning between these two forms, so far as we can tell.[132] If both forms represent one and the same morpheme we fail to understand the reason for the established phonetic variation; if, on the other hand, they differed in connotation the nature of that difference is wholly a matter for speculation. For the present, therefore, the two forms have been grouped together as a single morpheme, although they may have to be separated in the future.

For the *-e* cf. [56]. A preceding stem-ending *-i/e* is changed to *-u-*, e. g., *Ḫatti* : *Ḫattoḫe* [61], but *-a* remains, e. g., *Ḫalbaḫe* [62].

The meaning of the suffix has been discussed by Friedrich, Analecta Orientalia 12 (1935) 122 ff. For its function as a descriptive attribute, which precedes its head, cf. *Ḫurroḫe* KUR *omini* "Hurrian land" [137 (1)]; a parallel construction is with the gen. preceded by *-ne-*, cf. *ez̄enewe-nes̄ allai-s̄* "by the heavenly mistress" [ibid.]. From among the numerous other instances of this parallelism note the two forms in apposition in XXVII 1 ii 27-29, 46-47, etc.

The suffix is used frequently in conjunction with the "root-complements," for which see [175].

159. *-ne*. Apart from the combination of *-ne* + *we* to mark attributive relation, as has just been indicated, this particle is used in certain instances independently, thus acquiring the force of an adjectival suffix; cf. [137 (5)]. Such uses are rare, however, confined apparently to a few elliptical expressions. Wider use is attested for *-anne*, *-inne*, and *-unne*, all of which seem to represent an extension of *-ne* under conditions which cannot as yet be specified; cf. provisionally [89]. The adjectival force of these elements is evident from a series of terms used to describe horses in AASOR 16. 98-100; e. g., *zi-ir-ra-ma-an-nu*, *am-qa-ma-an-nu*, *ba-ab-ru-un-nu*.[133] Less clear is the precise function of *-inne* in the denominative *du-ru-bi-in-i-nu-uk-ku* Mit. I 17 alongside *turubi* "need, danger,"[134] or in Nuzi *urbarinni* "butcher"[135] from **urb-ar-* "slaughter."[136] For *-unne* cf. the agent nouns of the type *as̆ḫoz̄ikkonne*

[132] A possible solution, suggested with all due reserve, is offered in [57]. It is too uncertain, however, for adoption in the present listing.

[133] The final *-u* is to be ascribed to Akkadian influence.

[134] Cf. Speiser, JAOS 59. 313.

[135] Cf. Gordon, Orientalia 7. 54.

[136] For the extension with *-ar-* cf. [176 (3)]. The root alone appears in the Nuzi phrase *urbumma epēšu*, cf. Gordon, loc. cit.; Friedrich, BChG 60. I normalize here *b* for *p* on account of the preceding *r*.

[137 (5)], and for *-anne* we may plausibly adduce *taršuwanne* "man."[137] If these suffixes were found only with verbal roots they could be classed with the elements which form verbal nouns. As it is, their function appears to have been more general; see also below, n. 138, and cf. [221].

160. *-zi.* On the basis of *še-e-ni-iw-wu-ú-uz-zi* Mit. III 43 Bork set up a special case-form, the "equative of quality" (Mitannisprache 47) and translated the above word "worthy of my brother." Now that this suffix has come up in a number of other occurrences it can be seen that Bork's classification was premature. The element is adjectival with the range of "pertaining to, appropriate to," or the like. A good example of its force is *aš-du-uz-zi* AASOR 16 p. 134, which I first took to mean "good" (ibid.). However, it is obviously an analogue of *aštuḫḫe* "female." The thing described by *aštuzzi* is a garment (loc. cit.), and the adjective means evidently "feminine"; the juxtaposition *-uḫḫe: -uzzi* is significant for our present purposes. Another instance is *ur-uḫ-zi* RŠ Voc. II 21 "stable, just," a derivative of *urḫe* "true, firm." But the suffix finds its widest application with personal names where it may be preceded by *-a-*, *-i-*, or *-u-*; cf. the well-known *Agizzi* of Qatna (EA 52-55, 57), and for the numerous names from Nuzi see L. Oppenheim, WZKM 44 (1936) 206. Here the adjunctive force of the suffix is self-evident.[138]

e. Suffixes Employed with Verbal Nouns

161. The suffixes grouped under this head are not homogeneous in the sense that all are used to form participles and infinitives. A historical inquiry might show, e. g., that *-še* started out with the noun as an abstract element, whereas *-ae* could be traced to permansive forms with certain verbs; *-um* was the infinitive proper, capable of appearing in the subject-case as *-ummi* and in the stative as *-umma*; finally, *-i* and *-a* were the marks of the agent-noun with transitives and intransitives respectively. All these interpretations would be consistent with what we can learn about Hurrian from the scanty material at our disposal. Indeed, the brief discussion which follows will support these identifications. Our primary objective, however, is a logical descriptive arrangement; from this standpoint the elements here discussed, whatever their origin, are employed chiefly with verbal forms used attributively, or else

[137] For the meaning cf. v. Brandenstein, in Friedrich, BChG 8 n. 1. Since the Hurrian primary roots are predominantly monosyllabic we may regard the present word as a complex form.

[138] The same may be said of the names in *-nne* listed ibid. 195 (except those in *-enni* which may include the element *-ene* "god"). This correspondence in function confirms the broader grammatical relationship between this element [159] and *-zi*.

as predicates in nominal sentences. To that extent we may group all these forms together as verbal nouns. It will be recalled that the boundary between noun and verb in Hurrian is not sharply marked [99]; the demarcation is for the most part not inherent and has to be indicated by the respective bound forms. We shall see presently that a complex verbal form signifying "I gave" (lit. "given-in-the-past-by-me") can be turned into an attribute by means of the suffix *-še* whereupon it is free to take on any relational suffix of the noun.

-še

162. Descriptively this suffix occupies an intermediate position between the adjectival elements cited above and the verbal modifiers which follow. It occurs with simple nominal stems to form abstracts, but when used with verbs it fails to affect the syntax of the underlying element; transitives involving goal and agent are still construed with the agentive [164].

The voicelessness of the consonants is assured by the consistent *-šš-* in Mit. between vowels and the scarcely less regular double writing in the other sources of the main syllabary such as Bogh. or Nuzi [44].[139] This careful orthography helps to avoid confusion between such forms as, e. g., *ú-ú-ri-a-a-aš-še-na* Mit. I 108 "the ones desired by him" (<*uriya* + *še* + *na*) and *ši-ni-a-še-na-* ibid. III 40 "the ones of their two" (<*šin* + *ya* + *ž* + *ᵉna*).

163. With nouns there are numerous instances of the abstract force of the suffix. Cf. Nuzi *erwiše* "feudal service" alongside *erwi* "lord,"[140] and note Bogh. *e-ew-ri-iš-ši-ḫi-* "pertaining to lordship" XXVII 42 rev. 5, 6, 25; *dam-g/qar-ši* = Akk. *tamkarrûtu* "commercial traffic" AASOR 16 pp. 122 f., and note *dam-qar-ra-aš-ši* XXVII 1 ii 23; *šar-ra-aš-ši* ibid. 3, (also 42 rev. 8 ff.) "kingship"; after a consonant the suffix is written *-še/i*, as in the above *dam-g/qar-ši* and evidently also in *za-lam-ši* "statue" (<Akk. *ṣalmu*) Mit. III 77 ff.[141]

164. The commonest use of *-še* (pl. *-še* + *na*), however, consists in nominalizing complex verbal forms. Cf. *aš-ti-in še-e-ni-iw-wu-ú-e* (34) *a-ru-u-ša-ú še-e-ni-iw-wu-ú-e-ni-e-en ti-ša-a-an-na ši-ra-aš-še* Mit. IV 33 f. "(the) wife of my brother was[142] given by me, pleasing (*šiirase*) in accordance with my brother's heart."[143] Here the *še*-form marks an appositive complement of the

[139] Cf. also Lang. 16 (1940) 323 f.

[140] Cf. P. Koschaker, SBer. sächs. Ak. Wiss. 1928 p. 15 and Speiser, AASOR 10 (1930) 14 n. 28.

[141] Note also v. Brandenstein, Orientalia 8 (1939) 85 n. 28.

[142] The verbal copula is expressed by the pred. part. *-n* [206].

[143] Cf. [156].

subject (*aš̄ti-n*). The suffix cannot indicate the object, as was formerly supposed,[144] because *šir-a* is an intransitive form.[145] Nor can it be regarded as a relative particle ("*who pleases") because it is not construed as a relational element, in that it can be followed by the attributive *-ne*, *-na* and case-endings (see below). It comes closest to acting as a participle, but such a designation would be too limiting with intransitives and primary nouns. We shall do best by describing the suffix as a derivational element capable of transforming complex verbal forms into unified nominal stems.

Let us take, e. g., *tup-pè* (41) *ni-ḫa-a-ar-ri-e-we a-ru-u-ša-uš-še-ni-e-we* Mit. IV 40 f. [99, 137 (2)]. The verbal form *a-ru-u-ša-ú* (see above) "given-past--by-me" has been transformed into a descriptive attribute by means of *-s̄e*. As such it is treated exactly like the preceding noun *niḫ̮ari*, both being supplied with *-ne-we*, this in spite of the agent-suffix with the verb (*ar-*) which is differentiated for tense (*-oz̄-*). Another instructive instance is *i-i-al--li-e-ni-in še-e-ni-iw-wu-ú-uš du-be*[*-na-a-ma-a-an*] (20) *šu-ú-al-la-ma-an ge-pa-a-nu-u-ša-a-aš-še-na* Mit. II 19 f. "what-they-indeed brother-my-by tablets(?)-*màn* all-they sent-by-him-*s̄e-na*," i. e., "all such tablets as my brother sent." Here the transitive verb with goal (*du-be-*) continues to construe with the agentive ("by my brother"), although the form is no longer the predicate but merely an attribute of the grammatical subject. This ability to retain their normal syntax is characteristic of all *s̄e*-forms. In ^{I}*Ma-ni-e-ra-la-an ú-na-aš-še-na* Mit. II 116 "Mane-with-they the-arrived-ones," i. e., "the (things) brought by Mane" we have the comitative [154]. The dative occurs, e. g., in *še-e-ni-iw-wu-ú-a-al-la-a-an* (18) *ge-pa-a-nu-ša-a-uš-še-na ge-pa-nu--ša-a-ul-la-ma-an* Mit. III 17 f., freely "the (things) sent by me to my brother were sent by me"; the force of the *s̄e*-form is here that of a gerundive: "that which was to be sent, I sent." Finally, a verb referring to l. p. pl. is nominalized in the instance of *ú-ú-ra-ú-ša-aš-še-na-ma-a-an ti-we-e*^{MEŠ} Mit. I 80 "the things desired by us."[146]

-ae

165. Although this suffix occurs frequently in Mit., Bogh., and the RŠ Voc., its interpretation is exceedingly difficult. On the basis of Mit. *ni-i-ru-ša-e* I 55, 58, 70, 82, IV 38 "swiftly" and *te-u-u-na-e* II 49, 55, etc. "much" it was concluded as long ago as the turn of the century that this element forms adverbs.[147] In the RŠ Voc., however, *-ae* and its variants *-ai* and *-e/i* (cf. [69] for the analogous process *ae* > *ai* > *i*) appears to form adjectives: *ni-ra-e*

[144] Cf. Messerschmidt, Mitanni-Studien 36; Bork, Mitannisprache 62.

[145] Cf. JAOS 59. 307.

[146] For the suffix *-a-ú-ša* see [198].

[147] Messerschmidt, Mitanni-Studien 11; P. Jensen ZA 14 (1899) 177.

II 20 "slight," *pa-ḫi-ri-e* 22 "good," *tu-bu-e* 23 "strong," *ki-ra-i* ibid. IV 28 "long."[148] It would thus seem that *-ae* should be classified with *-ḫe* and *-zi*[149] as an adjectival suffix which in certain instances could be used also for adverbs. In partial support of such an attempt would be the circumstance, which is yet to be brought out (cf. [175]), that *-ae* has in common with *-ḫe* the ability to interpose root-complements between itself and the radical element. But there are arguments against this classification. The Hittite passage *ma-a-an I-NA* UD II^{KAM}*-ma* VII *ú-i-da-a-ar pí-an-zi nu* [...] (10) *me-ma-i* XXVII 23 ii 9 f. "When on the second day, however, they give seven waters, he speaks [...]" is followed by the Hurrian passage *ši-i-na-a-i ši-in-ta-ta-a-i ši-ya-a-i* ibid. 9. Since *šin-*, *šind-*, and *šiya-* signify "two," "seven,"[150] and "water"[151] respectively, the Hurrian is in some way a translation of the Hittite. In that case the repeated *-ai* would recall the suffix-duplication which we have encountered with case-endings [132-3]. Similar repetition of this suffix is found also in other passages, notably XXVII 42 rev. 20 ff., XXXI 8 iii 8 ff. The question is justified, therefore, whether the suffix is not after all a case-element, say, "adverbiative."

Cf. Goetze, RHA 39. 196 and n. 21 for the tentatively assumed "adverbialis."

166. The answer has to be in the negative on account of yet another use of the element *-ae*. For in addition to representing adjectives and adverbs this suffix occurs also with verbal roots, and some of the forms thus treated show a construction which can be recognized as verbal. First we have to note *ú-ša-e* RŠ Voc. II 25. In the corresponding passage from the Series ḪAR.*ra: ḫubullu* II we get Sumerian g á l . l a, Akk. *i-ba-šu-ú* "existing" (subjnc.); cf. Thureau-Dangin, Syria 12. 239; evidently, therefore, the Hurrian form corresponds to a participle (loc. cit. 246, ad II 25). An analogous form, perhaps related etymologically, is *uš-ta-e* XXVII 38 iv 19, with which we may compare the intr. form *uš-ta-a-an* Mit. IV 91. Most important, however, is the fact that words in *-ae* may be construed with the agentive; cf. *a-u* ᵈ*Ḫi-i-dam e-we$_e$-er-ne* (21) [*wu*]*ú!*[152] *-ut-ti-la-a-e* ᵈ*Ku-mar-we$_e$-ne-eš šar-ra* XXVII 38 iv 20 f., which suggests the translation "lo, [127] Ḫidam, the lord, was set

[148] Note also Thureau-Dangin's comment, Syria 12. 246.

[149] Indeed, listed with the above forms in *-ae* is *ur-uḫ-zi* "true, firm" (RŠ Voc. II 21).

[150] For these numerals see [116].

[151] For the meaning of this noun cf. Br. 563 n. 2. [Add now also ZA 46. 95 f. Incidentally, v. Brandenstein cites ibid. 94 the Hurro-Hittite passage quoted above, but he does so in an entirely different connection and indicates at the same time his perplexity as to the nature of the grammatical forms involved.]

[152] This supplementation appears preferable, to judge from the copy, to [*l*]*u-*, for which see Kleinas. Sprachdenkm. 35.

up(?) by Kumarwe as king." At any rate, the verbal forms in *-ae* act like those in *-še* when the sentence includes a logical object. Another example of this construction is *tup-pu-pa-a-ta-a-al-la-ma-an i-i-in ew-ri-en-na-šu-uš pal--du-pa-te* Mit. III 48. Here the grammatical subject is expressed by *-lla-* "they" and the logical subject by the agentive meaning "by the lords." The predicate can be sought only in *tuppubada-* which can scarcely be other than a form in *-ae* whose *-e* was changed to *-a-* in accordance with [65]; cf. the concluding form in *-bade*. I would translate "whether (*i-i-in* for *ai* + *n*) they were treated generously [153] by the lords, in reality." [154] It is clear that in the sentence forms in *-ae* could, in given circumstances, serve as the equivalent of finite forms referring to 3 p. in passive construction.

167. The adjectival-adverbial and the verbal connotations of *-ae* can best be brought into harmony by positing an underlying gerundial value. Specifically, the suffix seems to have the force of "becoming something, made into something," not unlike the Akkadian permansive. This would account with ease for adjectives like *ki-ra-i* "long" ("become, rendered long"), [155] or adverbs like *te-u-u-na-e* "much" ("being great"). Finally, gerundial forms can be used in Hurrian in common with participles proper to function as gerundives; this has already been indicated [164], and will be stressed again later [251]. Accordingly, the Hurrian parallel to the Hittite passage cited in [165] may provisionally be translated "there being on the second (day) seven waters, . . ."

Additional examples of terms in *-ae* will be listed under "root-complements" [175].

[153] For the meaning of *tupp-* see JAOS 59. 299.

[154] For *pald-* "authentic" cf. Friedrich, BChG 40.

[155] A different form based on the radical element *kir-* is *ge-ra-aš-še-* (*n*[*a-ša-til?-l*]*a-a-an ša-wa-al-la-ša*) Mit. I 79, which manifestly means "long-(in-we-and years-in)," i. e., "through long years we . . ."; cf. JAOS 59. 296 n. 29. The significance of the doublets *kirae/i* and *kerаše* is twofold. They furnish independent confirmation of the grammatical parallel between *-ae* and *-še* and consequently also of the participial character of *-ae*. Moreover, these doublets illustrate some of the means whereby adjectival concepts could be expressed. Since Hurrian does not recognize the adjective as an independent part of speech [100], such roundabout constructions are easy to understand.

The supplementation given above is demanded by the syntax. Friedrich, Kleinas. Sprachdenkm. 12 reproduces (with reservations) the earlier *ge-ra-aš-še-n*[*a-a-al-l*]*a-a-an*; cf. Messerschmidt, Mitanni-Studien 34, Bork, Mitannisprache 88. But the loc. pl. suff. of the head (*-ža*) must be anticipated with the attribute; moreover, the associative pronoun cannot refer to "in-the-years," hence *-lla-* "they" is out of the question. On the other hand "we" not only accords with the syntactic requirements but is supported also by the five previous instances in the same context (ibid. 76 f.).

The participial endings *-a, -i, -u*

168. There are several significant points of difference between the forms which contain one of the above endings and those which end in *-ae* or *-še*. The latter are nominalized constructions which function principally as attributes. They may be construed with the agentive. The use of *-ae* and *-še* extends to non-verbal elements where it marks adjectives, adverbs, and abstract nouns. On the other hand, the forms in *-a*, *-i*, and *-u* still show a direct relation to the underlying verbal root. They function principally as predicates and are construed invariably with the subject-case. The sentences which contain these forms are equational and show no syntactic difference from the nominal sentences proper. The combined evidence leads to the conclusion that the forms in question are participial. As such they have to be treated together with the other nominal forms.

Morphologically, *-a*, *-i*, and *-u* will be shown to express distinctions of voice. Since *-a* is all but restricted to intransitives it may be regarded as the marker of the middle participle. Similarly, *-i* may be viewed as the ending of active participles in that it characterizes transitive verbs. It should be stressed, however, that the classes "transitive" and "intransitive" do not coincide completely with the form-groups "active" and "middle" respectively. A given verb is inherently transitive and member of the *i*-class [119], or intransitive and hence member of the *u/o*-class [120]. The further differentiation according to voice is secondary and morphologic. This is immediately apparent from the fact that intransitives, which have *-u/o-* as class-marker, employ *-a* in the forms under discussion. Furthermore, the same verbal root, e. g. *ag-*, may appear either with *-a-* or with *-i-*, as it does in the onomastic constructions beginning with *ag-a-b-* and *ag-i-b-*. Here the agent-noun is marked as middle or active respectively, whereas the class of the underlying root is not capable of variation.

The morphologic form in *-u* is more difficult to interpret because the material at our disposal is comparatively scanty and virtually limited to onomastic compounds. It is clear, at all events, that this ending is used with transitives and is thus grammatically in contrast with the form in *-i*. What evidence there is favors the conclusion that *-u* marks passive forms alongside the active ones in *-i*. But the evidence is not conclusive and there is room for other interpretations.

All three endings are prominent in onomastic elements, particularly in combination with *-b*; for this construction see [171]. For the present we shall restrict ourselves to the material which shows the above three endings unobscured by additional elements.

169. *-a.* This suffix is characteristic of the verbs which constitute the *u/o*-class, i. e., intransitives [120]. Cf. *ú-ú-nu-uk-ka-la-an* Mit. IV 3 "they come to pass (*un* + *u-*), but *ú-ú-na* ibid. II 14 "(he) is coming." The final *-a* indicates that the action involved affects the actor. It is thus the mark of the middle voice; contrast the force of *-i* and *-u* [168] and below.

The evidence concerning the nature of the *a*-forms has to be sought in the type of sentence in which these forms occur. The following illustrations are typical:

(a) *a-ti-i-ni-i-in* ᴵ*Ma-ni-e-na-an še-e-ni-iw-wu-ú-*[*e*] (14) *pa-aš-ši-i-it-ḫi ú-ú-na* Mit. II 13 f. "so-indeed Mane-*n-an* brother-mine-of envoy (is) coming"

(b) *ú-ú-na-a-al-la-a-an še-e-ni-iw-wu-ta* ibid. I 115 "coming-they-and brother-my-to," i. e., "and they come to my brother"

(c) *a-ti-i-ni-i-in ma-a-an-na-at-ta-ma-an* ibid. II 85, III 63, 65

(d) [*m*]*a-a-an-na-til-la-ma-an* ibid. IV 119

(e) *i-nu-me-e uš-ḫu-ni ši-ḫa-a-la ḫi-iš-ma* . . . XXIX 8 iv 27[156] "as-it, (the) silver(?), (is) pure, firm(?) . . ."[157]

In (a) the *a*-form is predicate of a noun in the subject-case and is thus the equivalent of 3 p. sg.[158] In (e) the subject is marked by the associative pronoun of the same person. The subject of (b) is the corresponding pronoun of 3 p. pl. In (c) we have an analogous construction with the pronoun of 1 p. sg. (*-tta-*); the predicate includes *mann* + *a* [125]. The analysis of the form is simplified by the circumstance that the clause involves only one other word, the particle-complex *adi* + *nin*, cf. (a); subject and predicate are confined, therefore, within *mann* + *a* + *tta* + *man*.[159] Finally, (d) has the same predicate as (c), viz., *mann* + *a-*, but the subject is this time the associative pronoun of 1 p. pl. It follows that the *a*-form is constant with all persons.[160] The underlying stem may be differentiated for tense, e. g., *un* + *ett* + *a* Mit. III 12!, 21 "will be coming" [182], but this does not affect the characteristic final vowel.

The foregoing examples point to the conclusion that *-a* introduces a participial form. This is indicated in the first place by the impersonal character

[156] Similarly ibid. 8.

[157] Cf. Goetze, RHA 35 (1939) 104 ff.

[158] The suffixes left untranslated contain a reference to the verbal copula [206].

[159] Cf. JAOS 59. 302 ff.

[160] The second person is not represented because the associative pronoun for that person remains to be identified. However, the first and third persons, both singular and plural, are construed with the *a*-form so that it is logical to assume the same construction for the second person as well.

of the form; contrast the transitive forms that are differentiated for agent [194]. With the *a*-form the person is indicated by the subject of the sentence. Moreover, the *a*-form is not predicative in itself; in order that it may function as a predicate there is need in the sentence of a special predicative marker, such as *-n* [206] or an associative pronoun.[161]

The above conclusion is confirmed by the complete parallelism between sentences involving the *a*-form and the nominal sentence. We need refer only to *un-du-u-un* [I]*Ma-ni-e-na-an še-e-ni-iw-wu-ú-e pa-aš-ši-i-it-ḫi* Mit. IV 35 "now-then-*n* Mane-*n-an* (is) brother-my-of envoy." The correspondence with the above type (a) is obvious. Both sentences are introduced by a particle. In both the subject is precisely the same: Mane-*n-an*. But instead of the nominal predicate in the present instance ("(is) envoy"), the other example substitutes an *a*-form, while "envoy" becomes an apposition to the subject. It is thus clear that *un-a* functions exactly like the noun *pašitḫe* of (a). Syntactically the *a*-form is a noun. Grammatically it must be taken as a participle "coming, arriving." Both sentence-types are equational, the predicate of the one being specifically a noun and of the other a participle.

It was indicated above [168] that the forms in *-a* are virtually limited to intransitives. It was stressed, furthermore, that the concept "intransitive" is inherent in the given root and may be signified by the absolute class-marker *-u/o-* (which is not to be confused with the participial ending *-u* [171]). As against this marker, *-a* is an incidental element specifying the connection between the underlying verbal root and the subject. Accordingly, the distinction involved is one of voice. The *a*-form can refer only to the middle voice.

170. *-i*. For the *i*-quality cf. [187 n. 232]. The use of the *i*-form offers a complete syntactic parallel with that of the *a*-form. Both show the actor-action construction. Neither form is personal; like the form in *-a* the *i*-form may be used for any person, singular or plural. This correspondence in function is sufficient to establish the form in *-i* as participial. Added support for this analysis will be found in the fact that the *i*-form may be used with the attr. part. *-ne* and the 2 p. poss. *-b*, which are distinctive nominal endings [134 ff.].

With primary stems, which mark the present tense, the *i*-form is confined to transitives, i. e., verbs of the *i*-class [119]. With past stems, however, which are formed with the suffix *-ož-* [181], *-i* is found to characterize both transitives and intransitives. The reason for this irregularity is not far to seek. Theoretically, the past participle of intransitives should end in *-*ož-a*,

[161] These pronouns are used with or without *-n*. They were apparently predicative without the attached particle; cf. example (e) above.

on the analogy of the present in *-a* and the future in *-ett-a*. But *-ož-a* (wr. *-u-ša*) is the regular and exceedingly common ending of 3 p. sg. trans. in the perfect tense. It appears, therefore, that the perfect participle of intransitives was modeled after the transitives to avoid confusion with the finite form.

The foregoing statements are illustrated by the following citations:

(a) *ú-nu-ú-me-e-ni-i-in za-al-bu-u-*[. . . . .] (67) *ta-a-du-ka-a-ri* Mit. II 66 f. "as-he[162] -indeed . . . . . (is) loving"

(b) *ša-a-at-ti-la-an* . . . . . (109) *ta-a-du-ka-a-ri-i-til-la-a-an* ibid. III 108 f. "together-we-so . . . . . (are) loving-we," i. e., "we love each other"

(c) *pa-aš-ši-na-an*[163] *še-e-ni-iw-wə* (113) *šu-ú-ú-ta* ibid. III 112 f. "sending-*n-an* brother-my me-to"

(d) [. . . .] *ḫé-en-ni-e-en še-e-ni-iw-wə pa-aš-šu-ši*[164] ibid. I 65 "now-*n* brother-my sending-past," i. e., "now my brother having been the sender"

(e) *pa-aš-še-ti-i-dan* (117) *še-e-ni-i*[*w-wu-t*]*a* ibid. III 116 f. "sending--fut.-for brother-my-to," i. e., "will send for it to my brother"[165]

(f) *pí-sa-an-du-ši-i-it-ta-a-an* ibid. IV 9 "rejoicing-past-I-and," i. e., "and I rejoiced"

(g) *ka-bu-u-ši-ni-ib* XXVII 42 rev. 20; *ka-bu-ši-ib* ibid. 21

In (a) the subject is the associative pronoun of 3 p. sg., the predicate the trans. root *tad-* "love" extended by means of the root-complement *-ugar-* [176 (8)] and employed in the *i*-form. The same extended stem appears in (b),

[162] Or "she, it."

[163] The inverted word-order in this instance and in (e) is due to the nature of the subordinate clauses involved; cf. JAOS 59. 313 f. and [253].

[164] The missing introductory word was probably [*un-du-ma-a-an*]; cf. Goetze, Lang. 16 (1940) 129 and see above [127].

[165] Goetze, loc. cit. 130 and n. 22, takes the sign *-d/tan* of the predicate as representing the pronoun *-tta-* + *-n*. He anticipates the objection that the consonant of the pronoun should be written double but rejects it on the ground that "the first person is absolutely necessary." This is surely begging the question. Nor does it help much to add that "the passage includes one of the rare occurrences of the sign *-tan*." Mit. contains well over a score of instances of this sign (I 48, II 9, 11 [two times], 49, 61 [three times], 84, III 16, 46, 50, 69, 81, 87, 88, 90, 92, 108 [two times], IV 64, 115, 116). What is more, wherever this sign is used in final position it stands for the particle *-dan* [222]. On the other hand, there is no other demonstrable instance of the pron. *-tta-* with the consonant written single. Finally, *-dan* is construed with such verbs as *pal-* "ask" (III 46), *šar-* "request" (ibid. 90 f.), *anzannoḫ-* "beg" (ibid. 50) [222], so that is natural also with "send (for)." That the first person is necessary in the passage under discussion is true enough. But we can scarcely assert that Hurrian had no other way of referring to this person save by employing *-tta-*. It seems far more appropriate to interpret written *-tta-* and *-dan* in the sense in which each is safely attested elsewhere.

this time with the pron. of 1 p. pl. In (c) we have the *i*-form of the trans. verb *paš-* "send" in a sentence in which "my brother" is the subject. The same subject and predicate appear also in (d) except that the perfect stem of the verb is used in that instance. In (e) the underlying root of the predicate is once again *paš-*, this time in the future stem. The form ends in the associative particle *-dan* "for, about" [222].[166] The subject, which from the context should be the 1 p. sg., is not expressed in this particular clause, but is implied by the preceding *šu-u-u-wə* "of me" and *-iw-wə* "mine"; a break towards the beginning of line 116 unfortunately adds obscurity to the syntax of the utterance as a whole. In (f) we find the *i*-form with the past stem of the intr. root *pis-* "rejoice" extended by the root-complement *-and-* "about." The subject is the associative *-tta-* "I." Finally, (g) furnishes two examples of the *i*-form with a past stem followed by the poss. *-b* "thine"; the first of these examples contains also the attr. *-ne*. These suffixes bring the nominal character of the *i*-form into sharp relief. Although the meaning of the underlying root *kab-* is as yet unknown, the use of the past element *-ož-* is sufficient to establish the two forms in question as verbal nouns.[167]

170a. A different interpretation of the *i*-form has been given by Goetze in his article on "The Hurrian Verbal System" Lang. 16 (1940) 125-40. Goetze sees in this form a third main type of the Hurrian verb (III), alongside the active (I, our *i*-class; e. g., *tad* + *ya* 3 p. sg.), and the middle (II, our *u/o*-class [120]; e. g., *un* + *a*); cf. op. cit. 129, 140. This third type is said to indicate "the effect of an action of undefined origin upon a person or thing" (p. 140).

Goetze's position cannot be reconciled with the complete evidence with regard to the case-system of Hurrian. We should have to view the *š*-case as marking the subject, contrary to the argument presented in [150]. Furthermore, the stem-case [149], with or without *-n*,[168] would have to be looked upon as "much closer to our accusative than to anything else" (p. 136). The transitive verb would be translatable only as an active (p. 140), in spite of the full weight of the evidence detailed in [246].[169]

All of these premises are interdependent. Each can be refuted on grounds

[166] See the preceding note.

[167] Any attempt to see in the written *-ši* of these forms the abstract suffix *-še* [163] would be ruled out by the single writing of the consonant. The sequence *-u-ši* can indicate only *-oži*. Now *-ož-* is abundantly established as the particle of the perfect tense [181]; it lacks the slightest evidence of any other use. The residual *-i* has ample parallels among the instances just cited.

[168] For the problem of the *n*-form see [203 ff.].

[169] I. e., when the sentence includes both agent and goal.

which do not involve the *i*-form. But even if these points are granted provisionally, Goetze's interpretation of his verb-type III will remain precarious. We have seen that the Hurrian verb shows a sharp dichotomy which is reflected by two distinctive formal classes [119-20]. Each class has its own favorite sentence-type, the *i*-class construing with the agentive and the *u/o*-class with the subject-case. To establish a third class we should first have to show that the verbs assigned to it cannot be transferred without adequate reason [170] to either of the previously recognized classes. This cannot be done with Goetze's type III. Cf.

un-du-ma-a-an še-e-ni-i[*w-w*]*e-e-n pa-aš-š*[*u-ši* [171] ^I^*Ma-*]*ni-en-na-a-an š*[*e--e-*]*ni*[*-iw-wu-u*]*š* (108) *pa-aš-šu-u-u-ša* Mit. II 107 f. In the first clause of this utterance we find the verb *paš-* in the *i*-form, construed with the "*n*-case," whereas the next clause has the same verb with the normal ending of the transitives, and is construed with the *š*-case. Thus the same verb would appear in two consecutive clauses as member of types III and I respectively. For just as *ta-a-a-nu-u-ša* (fr. *tan-* "do") Mit. I 85 configurates with the present tense-form *ta-a-ni-a* ibid. III 81, both being used with nouns in the *š*-case, so must *pa-aš-šu-u-u-ša,* when found with the same case (above), configurate with a form **pa-aš-ši-a.* Both verbs are transitive and both show the characteristic construction of one and the same class. It follows, therefore, that *pa-aš-šu-ši* cannot reflect another distinctive class but must represent some particular morphologic variant of the type found in *pa-aš-šu-u-u-ša.* This variant is best identified as a participial form, as we have seen. The assumption of a third independent type, by the side of the transitives and intransitives of Hurrian, is not borne out.

In conclusion, it should be indicated that two known forms which end in *-i* present difficulties. One is the concluding word of the incompletely preserved sentence [. . . . . .]*-a-an ša-a-la-pa-an aš-ti-iw-wu-ú-un-na a-ri* Mit. I 51,[172] and the other is the Hurrian gloss *zu-zi-la-ma-an* in the Akkadian letter EA 170. 11.[173] Although neither context is clear it is probable that we have here imperatives of 2 p. sg. [193 (i)]. But it is far from certain that these forms end in the same morpheme which characterizes the participle just discussed; cf. [196]. For the unrelated termination in *-ili/e* and *-ikki* see ibid.

[170] With verbs of motion, e. g., Hurrian uses both transitive and intransitive constructions [168]. The former have then the value of causatives, for instance, "come": "bring," or the like.

[171] The restoration is supported by Mit. I 65 and is accepted by Goetze, loc. cit. 129 n. 16.

[172] Cf. ibid. 31 f., and note [149 n. 114].

[173] Cf. Friedrich, BChG 22.

171. *-u.* The evidence for this element is less conclusive than that for *-a* and *-i.* It is attested definitely in onomastic compounds only, the syntax of which remains to be clarified. Moreover, it cannot as yet be asserted with confidence that a form like *Tadu-Ḫeba* does not stand in reality for **Tadu-b-Ḫeba.* However, such extensions in *-b* would not in themselves affect the morphology of the underlying stem. And while our analysis cannot be definitive under present circumstances, it will be aided by the fact that the *u*-form is formally parallel to the other two, although it is contrasted with them as far as meaning is concerned. For the extensions in *-b* cf. [177].

The available material is illustrated by two types of compounds: (a) SAL*Ḫaž-u*[174] *-kelde* N 557. 5, 28, *Ag-u-ženi* AASOR 16 26. 17, 71. 38, where the *u*-form is followed by a common noun; and (b) SAL*Tad-u-Ḫeba* XXVII 23 iii 2 ff., 24 i 6, Mit. III 103, IV 67, 89, EA 27, 4, etc., SAL*Kel-u-Ḫeba* EA 17. 5, where the *u*-form is followed by the name of a deity. In each instance the underlying verbal root is transitive.[175] Now there is a trans. form of the type **ḫaž* + *u* representing the 2 p. sg. But such forms have to be construed with an agentive, which is not the case in the instances under discussion. Moreover, the second element of the onomastic compounds, usually in the stem-form, represents the subject-case in such names as *Erwi-žarri* "The lord is king"; accordingly the stem-form must contain the subject and not the object in the present set of examples as well. Finally, the verbal elements in the types *Un-a-b-Tešub* "Teshub arrives" and *Zil-i-b-Tilla* "Tilla witnesses" are in themselves impersonal; it would follow that the analogous (SAL)*Tad-u-Ḫeba* or, with the additional *-b-*, *Teḫ-u-b-ženni* (AASOR 16 1. 45) also lack the personal suffix.

The examples under (a) cannot be rendered, therefore, "Thou hearest good news" and "Thou guidest the brother" respectively because the nouns involved represent the subject. But the construction cannot be active. Something like "The brother guides" has to be sought in the very common type *Ag-i-b-ženni* (e. g., AASOR 16 45. 13, 96. 21), i. e., with the *i*-form. Besides "Good news hears" would not make sense. The only solution is to regard the *u*-form as passive, specifically, as a passive participle, comparable to the forms

[174] The quality of this *-u-* is ambiguous inasmuch as Mit., which alone could decide the issue, does not provide us with a double writing of the vowel in this form-type. A complementary *ú* or *u* would have settled the point. On the other hand, the corresponding class-marker is attested as *-o*, at least in open syllables (before *-wa/e-*) in *ú-ru-u-we-en* Mit. III 111, 116.

[175] The parallel expressions *pa-aḫ-ru-ma pu-u-ri* XXVII 42 rev. 26 and *pa-aḫ-ra pu-u-ri* XXIX 8 iii 54, both involving *waḫr-* "good," are obscure in meaning and syntax, so that it is doubtful whether *pa-aḫ-ru-ma* has anything to do with our *u*-form.

in *-a* and *-i*. We thus get (a) "Good news (is) heard" and "The brother (is) guided";[176] (b) "Hebat is loved" and "Hebat is satisfied."[177]

It is worth noting that the names with the *u*-form are known to be for the most part feminine. This is true of three out of the four instances cited above. Cf. also SAL*Puḫuya* N 113. 4 ff., 440. 3, 5, 501. 5, 23, 638. 4 ff.; SAL*Puḫu-men(n)i* H IX 144. 3, RA 23 76. 10, TCL IX 1. 26 f.; contrast *Puḫi-ženni* N passim. There is not a single instance of a masculine name with *Puḫu-*[178] or of a feminine name with *Puḫi-*. Note also SAL*Tulbu-nnaya* AASOR 16 15-45, but *Tulbiya* N 253. 32, 339. 18, etc., *Tulbi-ženni* N 80. 5, 248. 18, etc. Nevertheless, the *u*-form must not be interpreted as a grammatical reference to the feminine gender, which Hurrian does not recognize. This is immediately clear from the above masculine name *Agu-ženi* and its analogues with *-u-*. All that we are entitled to conclude from these examples is that the *u*-form was favored with feminine names without being restricted to them any more than the *i*-form was limited to masculine names. It is not our province to speculate about the reasons for these preferences, if such they were indeed.

Infinitive

172. Hurrian forms an action-noun with the aid of the suffix *-umme/i*. This is illustrated by

[*še-*]*e-ni-iw-wu-ra-a-ma-a-an ti-ši!-iw-wa-an*[179] [*t*]*e-u-u-na-e tiš-ša-an wa-aḫ--ru-um-me* (112) [*ta-a-d*]*u-ka-a-ru-um-me ú-ú-*[*r*]*a-ú* Mit. IV 111 f. "And with my brother in my heart goodness and affection are desired[180] very much." The intransitive stem *waḫr-* is well known in the sense "(to be) good" and *tadugar-* is equally clear in its meaning "love, show affection,"[181] being an extended stem of the common *tad-* "love." The sentence is perfectly clear syntactically. It includes a trans. verb, with the agent indicated by the suffix of 1 p. sg. (*-a-ú*) and the goal expressed by the two forms in *-umme*. This ending represents, accordingly, the subject-case of the infinitive. Another instance of this form is found in *ta-še-e-ni-e-wə* (93) *id-du-um-mi* ibid. I 92 f.

[176] This *Ag-u-* is not to be confused with the initial element in *Ak-ku-le-(en-)ni* AASOR 16. 146, where the double *k* points to a different root.

[177] The juxtaposition of *kelde* "well-being, good news," and trans. *kel-* indicates an underlying meaning "please, satisfy," or the like.

[178] The apparent exception *Pu-ḫu-ub-bi* N 192. 32 should be read *Te!-ḫu-ub-bi* according to P. M. Purves.

[179] For this reading cf. JAOS 59. 300 n. 41. For an approximate equivalent of this phrase in Tushratta's Akk. cf. EA 17. 51.

[180] For the idiom "hold in the heart, desire" see ibid. 299 f.

[181] Cf. [170 (a)-(b)].

"present-*ne*-of departure," i. e., "the going-out of the present." [182] The syntax is the same as in the preceding instance.

This suffix apparently lends itself also to use with nominal stems, probably to form abstracts.[183] Thus *ta-šu-um-mi* XXIX 8 iv 6 is shown to be based on *taže* "present" by the occurrence of *ta-še-ni* ibid. 3. Similarly, ⌈*ḫu-u-*⌉*um--nu-um-mi* ibid. 7 points back to *ḫu-u-um-ni* ibid. 3, of unknown meaning. For other possible occurrences of the same suffix cf. XII 44 ii 11-13, XXV 42 V 11, XXVII 34 i 5; perhaps also, with *-ne* added, *ši-u/ú-um-mi-ni* XXVII 23 ii 7-8, *ú-wu(?)-mi-ni-wə* Mâri 1. 3, *ka-nu-me-ni-wə* ibid. 4; note also *x-bu-mi* RŠ Voc. II 35 and possibly *mi-zi-mi* ibid. 34 for Sum. z i. g a which is elsewhere rendered by Akk. abstract nouns.[184]

In another case-form the action-noun seems to confront us in the hybrid Hurro-Akkadian phrase *x-umma epēšu*; for examples cf. Gordon, Orientalia 7. 51 ff. and for a criticism of Gordon's interpretation see JAOS 59. 321 n. 86.[185] Since this phrase means either "to become something" (e. g., *ewurumma epēšu* Gadd 51. 9, N 513. 7, H V 67. 15 "to become secondary heir"; cf. JAOS 55 [1935] 436 f.) or "to be made into something," the form in *-a* accords well with our "stative" case [156].

Finally, there remain to be noted a few occurrences of the suffix *-um*; cf. *a-ku-um* XXIX 8 iv 3, *še-e-ḫa-lu-um* ibid. ii 48; also in masculine names ending in -*a*-RI, e. g., *Kelum-* H IX 114. 20, *Melkum-* N 253. 25, *Šurkum-* N 207. 16.[186] Whether these forms are infinitives which stand in the same relation to those in *-ummi* as we get in *anam : anammi* [131], or whether they represent an independent morphologic type we are not in a position to decide at present.

f. Miscellaneous

173. *-t/d-*.[187] This element followed by a stem-vowel is found in a few instances to convert verbal roots into nouns. Cf. *kel* + *di/e* "well-being": *ge-e-el-ti* Mit. IV 43, *ge-el-ti-wə* ibid. 44, *-ge-el-te* N 657. 28, from *kel-* "please, satisfy" [171 n. 177]; *ardi* "gift" in the compounds *at-ta-(a-)ar-ti-* "bridal gift" (for the father) Mit. I 8, 88, III 50, 87, etc., *e-e-la-ar-ti-* "sistership-

[182] See also ibid. II 98 in obscure context.

[183] Cf. the use of *-še* [163].

[184] Cf. Syria 12. 239.

[185] The objection which I expressed in that note to Bork's interpretation of the form has not been borne out.

[186] Contrast *Te-ḫu-um-še-en-ni* H V 58. 19 where *-um* may well stand for *-ub* before a consonant. It is not impossible, however, that the same change occurred before a vowel. In that case we should have no instances of original *-um* in personal names.

[187] For this positional variation cf. [76].

-gift" ibid. III 44, from *ar-* "give"; here may perhaps be included *pí-ša-ša-te, pí-šu-šu-te* RŠ Voc. III 16, 22 "built" cf. [176 (12)]. Note also *pal-ta-a-la-an* Mit. IV 23, *pa-al-ta-a-la-an* ibid. 29 "and they (are) authentic," perhaps from *pal-* "judge(?)." [188]

-uḫli. This element, which is known primarily from the Nuzi material, is used to form agent-nouns designating officials and occupational terms. Cf. *ḫalz-uḫl-* Gordon, Orientalia 7. 57; *ma(n)zad-uḫl-* "constable" ibid. 59; *zilik-uḫl-* "witness" ibid. 60, and Speiser, Lang. (1938) 308 f. It may be doubted whether this morpheme is a bound form proper. The common onomastic element *eḫ(e)l-, eḫli-* suggests the possibility that we have here a radical element meaning something like "oversee"; in that case the above examples would represent in reality compounds.

-ḫuri. This element, too, is used in occupational terms and it may be likewise a radical element. It occurs in *a-mu-mi-iḫ-ḫu-ri* AASOR 16 62. 27 "representative(?)," cf. ibid. 111; and in *pè-ni-ḫu-ru(m)* N 49. 36 "surveyor," cf. Gordon, op. cit. 55.

1/2. Root-complements

174. The nature of these bound morphemes was indicated in [133]. They complement the lexical content of the supporting root and are used in this sense with nouns as well as verbs. They differ from the suffixes proper in that they never express independent grammatical relations. A root augmented by a complement has the semantic value of a compound.

The increment in meaning which the complements may impart is varied. Although the value of a number of the elements involved is still obscure, some light is shed by the more transparent instances. Thus with the nouns, specifically adjectives and adverbs, the root-complements may express comparison or emphasis; e.g., *nir-ae* "lightly," *nir-ož* [189] *-ae* "very promptly"; *tea* "great," *te-on-ae* "much," *te-ol-ae* "exceedingly much." With verbs emphasis is also expressed in this way, e.g., *ḫaž-* "hear," *ḫaž-až-* "hear

[188] By the side of the trans. *pal-* "ask" there is also an intr. homophone which is represented by *pal-la-in* Mit. IV 64 and *pal-la-i-šal-la-ma-an* ibid. 65. Furthermore, the above *pal-d-allan* "authentic-they-and" contrasts with *pa-a[-li-]ma-a-an, pa-a-la* Mit. II 106 "false" or the like (cf. Messerschmidt, Mitanni-Studien 82, Friedrich, BChG 40 n. 2). We have thus evidence for at least a formal differentiation of *pal-*. I would connect *pald-* with the intr. form and adduce further such onomastic compounds as *Pal-tešub* (e.g., AASOR 16 75. 35) and the like. In all of these uses the meaning "judge" appears to be appropriate; "authentic" could well go back to "judged, considered."

[189] For the nature of this *-o-* see below, [175 n. 193].

attentively." [190] For the most part, however, the complements have here the value of our preverbs, e. g., *paš-* "send," *paš-ar-* "send along"; *pis-* "rejoice," *pis-and-* "rejoice about (something)."

With adverbial forms in *-ae* several root-complements may be used at the same time, *nir-ub-ad-ae* (an analogue of *nir-ož-ae*); *tad-ar-až-k-ae* (with *ž* > *š*; from *tad-* "love").

The elements which are employed as root-complements seem to be cognate, in some instances at least, with given regular grammatical suffixes of the noun or the verb. They differ, however, from the latter not only in function and distribution (being used both with nouns and verbs), but also in position: as a rule, the complements cannot be separated from the root by other morphologic elements. Their independent listing is therefore amply justified.

175. Root-complements with nominal forms. These elements are used normally with adjectival forms in *-ḫe* [158] and "adverbial" forms in *-ae* [191] [165 ff.]. This specialization helps to narrow down the semantic range of the group as a whole. It is apparent that at least some of the complements served to express gradation of the underlying root-meaning, and this conclusion is supported by actual occurrences (see below). But our material does not admit of a precise evaluation of the individual elements.

In the following alphabetic list of complements the illustrations are based on translatable roots, wherever possible.

(1) *-k/g-*: (a) With *-ḫe*, *a-zu-uz-ik-ḫi* XXVII 34 iv 16; (b) with *-ae*, *ta-a-ta-ra-aš-ka-e* Mit. III 51, 107 <*tad-* "love."

(2) *-l-*: (a) No clear instance; [192] (b) *pa-ša-la-a-e* XXIX 8 iii 14 (followed by *pa-ša-a-e pa-a-ša-na-e*); *te-u-u-la-e* Mit. IV 130, alongside *te-u-u-na-e* ibid. II 49, 55, 62, etc. "much," *te-a* ibid. III 42, 69, 94, IV 118.

(3) *-n-*: (a) No clear instance; (b) *paž-an-ae*, *te-on-* [193] *-ae*, see above. The combined evidence of (2) and (3) favors the assumption that in *-ae*, *-n-ae*, *-l-ae* we have the basic, comparative, and superlative grades respectively,

[190] The added *-až* is not due to the iteration of the stem *ḫaž* as supposed by Friedrich, BChG 36 n. 2, 37. There is so far no evidence for iterated stems in Hurrian. Moreover, *ž*-complements are well attested [175 (6)].

[191] For the variants *-a-i* and *-e/i* cf. [69].

[192] A possible instance is Nuzi *ḫa-wa-al-ḫi* Orientalia 7. 57 (the meaning "grove" proposed by Gordon, ibid., is questionable).

[193] The vowels which accompany the root-complements vary considerably. It appears, however, that *-a-* is normally a connective, whereas *-o-* (note *te-u-u-na-e*) is morphologic. In *ni-i-ru-ša-e*, *ni-ir-ša-e*, *ni-i-ri-še* (see below) the vowel seems again secondary; when present it probably had *o*-quality, to judge from *-bi-ir-du-u-uš-ḫe* EA 22 iv 29. On the other hand, *pa-aš-ši-i-it-ḫi* (see below) indicates a primary vowel by its double *-i-*.

or a Hurrian approximation to such grades. The collocation of all three forms under (2) is instructive. The basic or simple grade is to be seen, of course, in the uncomplemented stem. As to the choice between *-l-* and *-n-*, we have to be guided by *te-on-ae : te-ol-ae*. The latter occurs but once, in the last sentence of Mit., where a reference to "exceedingly great" love would be entirely in accord with the tone of the letter. The rather common *te-on-ae*, on the other hand, could well mean something like "more than ordinarily, a great deal."[194] In this connection, some significance may attach also to the fact that *-l-* rather than *-n-* is found in onomastic compounds with *-en(n)i* "god" [177]. In cases like *Urḫa-l-enni* SMN 652 or *Kiba-l-enni* N 79. 2, RA 23 18. 2 the superlatives "most true" and "most firm(?)" are more suitable than comparatives when referring to a deity.

(4) *-p/b-*: (a) Perhaps the name *Piža(i)ž*[195]*-ab-ḫe* Br. 563 n. 1; (b) *ene* "god" > *e-ne-pa-a-i* XXVII 42 rev. 20, 21; ^{d}*IŠTAR*^{ga}*-pa-a-i* XXIX 8 ii 50; cf. also *i-ši-ni-eš i-ši-pa-a-i pu-ul-li-iš pu-li-ti-pa-a-e* ibid. iii 19 (also 9-10). Although this complement is amply attested, there is little to suggest its approximate meaning. The stems with which it may be used include divine names (*Šauška*) and *ene* "god." I would suggest provisionally an asseverative connotation, something like "truly, verily."

It is worthy of note that *-bae* is found occasionally with extended stems rather than basic roots; cf. *ul-lu-ḫu-ši-pa-a-e* XXIX 8 iii 20, *ki-el-di-ni-pa-a-e* ibid. 23. But the attr. *-ne* of the latter shows that the *-b-* stands in such cases for 2 p. poss. + *-ae*. Note the poss. form *pa-a-ḫi-ib* ibid. 21 in the same context.

(5) *-r-*: (a) Perhaps *e-la-mi-ir-ḫé-na* XXVII 38 iii 15, cf. *e-la-mi* "oath" RŠ Voc. III 28; (b) *ḫa-(a-)ša-(a-)ra-a-e/i* also (*-ri*) XXVII 42 passim, XXIX 8 iii 21, 23, 39 = *ḫžr* RŠ X 4 1 ff. <*ḫaž-* "hear"; *ta-a-ta-a-ri*[196] XXVII 42 obv. 29 <*tad-* "love," cf. *ta-a-ta-a-e* which immediately precedes; also in conjunction with other complements, e. g., *tad-ar-až-k-ae* (1). The latter instance points to a reciprocal meaning for the complete form but we do not know which of the three complements involved is responsible for it.

(6) *-ž-*: (a) *aš-ta-aš-ḫi ta-ḫa-a-aš-ḫi* XXVII i ii 15; *ap-pí-eš-ḫi* ibid. 42 obv. 33; among the many names of objects may be noted *pè/til-ku-uš-ḫi* Gadd 66. 19, N 7. 55; *wa-ra-du-uš-ḫu*[197] H V 72. 13 (a type of building), and

[194] Both forms are used with *tišan* "very" and this adverb may even be repeated for emphasis. If the above interpretation of these root-complements is correct, *tišan* was used pleonastically. It might be argued that *te + on + ae tišan* is difficult to explain if *te + ol + ae* was itself a superlative. But such uses need reflect no more than stylistic variation.

[195] That the initial labial was apparently a voiceless spirant is indicated in [49].

[196] For the final *-i* cf. n. 191.

[197] The interpretation of this word which I gave in AASOR 13 (1933) 49 f. was incorrect.

from the Amarna material *aš-ki-ru-uš-ḫu* EA 18 rev. 4, 25 ii 1, iii 27 ff., *a-ú-a-ta-a-mu-lu-uš-ḫe* ibid. iv 29, and the like. (b) *ni-i-ru-ša-e* Mit. I 55, 58, 70, 82, IV 38, *ni-ir-ša-e* ibid. IV 66 and *ni-i-ri-še* [198] ibid. 43 "promptly"; DINGIR.MEŠ^{na}-*ša-a-i* XXVII 23 iii 5; *tar-šu-wa-na-ša-a-e* [199] XXIX 8 iii 16. Except for "promptly," the above examples and their numerous uncited analogues permit an interpretation of *-z̄-* as an element which imparts the idea of plurality or collectiveness. If this should prove correct, a comparison with the pluralizing particle *-z̄-* [142] would be difficult to avoid. The complement in *nir* + *oz̄* + *ae* would then have the function of imparting emphasis. But no such decision as to etymology is called for or advisable at present.

(7) *-t/d-*: (a) Here belong the agent-nouns *pas̄* + *id/t* + *ḫe* Mit. I 55, 59, 72, etc. "envoy" and *šu-a-na-at-ḫu* AASOR 16 7. 2 (p. 72), perhaps "messenger"; note, however, *šu-ra-at-ḫu* ibid. p. 121 and *ta-ku-la-at-ḫu* Orientalia 7. 55, where the class-meaning corresponds to that of (6a); see, however, Lacheman, Nuzi I 539 for *lā atḫu* in Akk. context. (b) *i-te-e-ta-i* XXIX 8 ii 43 <*ede/i-* [105]; *ši-in-ta-ta-i* XXVII 23 ii 10 <*šinda-* "seven"; *we$_e$-ú-ta-i* ibid. 25. 11.

Root-complements in nominal forms which do not end in *-ḫe* or *-ae* are rare. Cf. *zu-ru-un-ki* XXIX 8 ii 42 and *zu-ru-uš-ki* ibid. 44, alongside *zu-úr-ki* ibid. 41. The identification of the elements here interposed with the above (3) and (6) respectively is probable. Note also *ti-wi-i-li-na* Mit. IV 6, clearly <*tiwe* "word, thing," where the additional *-il-* is perhaps to be compared with (2).

Mention has already been made that more than one complement may be used in a single form. Cf. *e-na-ra-a-ša-e* XXIX 8 iii 12 and *ḫu-u-ta-an-na-ra-ša-i* ibid. 13 (*-r-* + *-z̄-*). It is particularly in such combinations that our division into nominal and verbal forms, made solely for the purpose of facilitating the survey, proves inadequate. For a complement-chain followed by a nominal ending may be attached to a verbal root, or a verbal form with root-complements may be based on a nominal root; cf. [99]. For other combinations note, e. g., *tad-ar-az̄-k-ae* (1), which contains *-r-* + *-z̄-* + *-k-*; [*na-*]*-na-ti-la-a-e mi-lu--la-ti-la-a-e* XXVII 38 iv 15 (*-d-* + *-l-*), cf. [*na-*]*na-a-i* ibid. 27. Instances which involve (4) + (7) are common; cf. *ma-a-an-nu-pa-a-ta-e* Mit. IV 59; *ni-i-ru-pa-a-ta-e* ibid. 5, 6; *pal-du-pa-a-te* ibid. III 48; from Bogh. note *pa-aḫ-ru-pa-a-ti* XXIX 8 ii 40; *aš-ku-pa-a-te-ni-ta* XXVII 34 iv 24 and *ša-a-ḫa-pa-ti-ni-ta* ibid. 21 (both with the case-form *-ne* + *da*); *ša-aš-šu-pa-a-ti*

[198] Cf. n. 193.

[199] This *-z̄ae* (with the consonant wr. single before vowels) should not be confused with the *-šae* (wr. *-ššae*) of such forms as *ša-ta-an-ni-iš-ša-e* XXIX 8 iii 11, where *-ae* is joined to a form in *-še* [162 ff.]. The latter, but with a different ending, confronts us again in *ki-e-bu-la-a-eš-ša* ibid. 12 and *še-e-ḫa-lu-la-eš-ša* ibid. iv 23, all in the same text.

ibid. 6 i 17. Finally, the sequence *-pažḫ-* is found with stems in *-(a)m* [176 (10)] in *šu-ra-am-ba-áš-ḫi-* AASOR 16 54. 16, *te-ḫa-am-pa-aš-[ḫi-]* ibid. 35. 4, 9 and *šuḫarampašḫa* Lacheman, Nuzi I 533 (syllabic division not given); note, furthermore, *a-lu-um-pa-az-ḫi-* XXVII 24 iv 3 (suggested by Goetze); cf. also [183a].

Some of the above elements (*-p/ba-t/da-*, *-ža-*) might be equated with the corresponding case-forms. But no satisfactory meaning could be assigned to such forms; there would remain others which have no connection with cases; and the parallel instances with verbs would have to be explained independently.

176. Root-complements with verbal forms. It was indicated in [174] that these elements characterize verbs as well as nouns. This was confirmed indirectly in the preceding section in connection with the forms in *-ae*. Since this suffix is used primarily to form verbal nouns, it follows that the pertinent instances comprised a number of verbal roots, although the complete forms had to be regarded technically as nouns. The following list will emphasize primarily verbal forms. It will include complements which we have met already with nominal forms, but will present also additional elements not yet encountered.

First, however, an explanation is in order as to how the verbal complements can be recognized. In this respect the evidence of position proves decisive. The various elements which may enter into the composition of a given verbal form are each joined in a fixed order. The root-complements are placed immediately after the radical element (position 1). Next come the tense-markers (position 2) and following these we have a category of bound forms which we shall classify simply under "position 3." Where there is but one element in the place allowed theoretically for positions 1-3, and independent evidence is lacking, some ambiguity as to proper classification is inevitable. For the most part, however, the criterion of position is conclusive. E. g., the *-ill-* of *ka-til-li-ta* and the *-ol-* of *ti-i-ḫa-nu-u-ul-li-e-et-ta* (see below under 9) are root-complements because they precede known tense-markers. Hence *ú-nu-u-lu-uk-ka-ma-an* KBo V 2 ii 26 (*un* + *ol* + *ukk-*) proves to contain the same complement even though it is followed by *-ukk-* (cf. [186]) without an intervening tense-element. The same classification is valid also in forms like *ge-pa-a-nu-lu-u-uš-ta-a-aš-še-na* Mit. III 59 and *ti-i-ḫa-nu-u-ul-li-e-et-ta* ibid. 22. There remains the question whether a given verbal form can include several root-complements. We have just seen that complement-chains are tolerated in nouns and so the same ability may be assumed in the case of the verb. Accordingly, the identical *-an-* in the last two forms would suggest that we have here a bound form, hence another complement. These examples indicate the method at our disposal as well as the difficulties involved and the necessarily tentative character of some of the results attained.

(1) *-an-*: For *ge-pa-a-nu-* and *ti-i-ḫa-nu-* see above; perhaps to be compared with [175 (3)].

(2) *-and-*: *pí-sa-an-du-ši-i-it-ta-a-an* Mit. IV 9 "and I was happy about (it)," *pí-sa-an-ti-iš-ten-na-a-an* ibid. 44 "so that I may be happy about (my brother's well-being)," alongside *an-du-ú-a-at-ta-a*[*-an*] (55) .... *pí-su--uš-te-e-wa* ibid. II 54 f. We thus have here plainly the common *pis-* "rejoice" + the deictic pronoun *andi* [110]; cf. Friedrich, RHA 35. 101 for a cautious statement.[200] The complement may be compared in this instance with our preverbs.

(3) *-ar-*: For verbal stems with this complement which end in *-ae* see [175 (5)]; here we may add the verbal form *pa-aš-ša-ri-i-wa-a-en* Mit. IV 54 "let him not send along"; note also *ḫa-a-ša-ri-in-na* VIII 61 obv. 2, from the common *ḫaž-* "hear" already cited with the nominal group. The same complement is thus safely established with nominal and verbal forms alike.[201]

(4) *-p/b-* and *-t/d-*: These two elements cannot be separated from [175 (4), (7)]. They occur together in the verbal form *ur-ḫu-ub-ti-in* Mit. IV 112 "let him keep faith," obviously cognate with *urḫe* "true"; cf. also *a-nam--mi-it-ta-ma-an še-e-ni-iw-wu-ra ur-ḫu-ub-du-ši-li-wa* ibid. III 64 "and thus I with my brother shall keep faith." We may add, furthermore, *tup-pu-pa-a--ta-a-al-la-ma-an* ibid. 48 (<*tupp-*), which construes with the agentive, although it probably contains a form in *-ae*; cf. [166].

For individual occurrences note *na-aḫ-ḫa-ab* and *na-aḫ-ḫu-ud* Br. 571 n. 1, both with the same verb of unknown meaning. The respective syllabics *-a-* and *-u-* can scarcely be dissociated from the corresponding participial endings discussed in [168 ff.]. The correspondence is made complete by the inclusion of *pa-ši-ib* Mâri 1. 3, 2. 9 and *ḫi-ri-ib* ibid. 1. 4, 2. 11. Since forms of this type are especially common in onomastic compounds, which are discussed in the next section, the question of their meaning need not be taken up here.

[200] See also Goetze, Lang. 16. 127 n. 13. The objection that *an-du-ú-a-* Mit. II 54 actually corresponds to *ge-el-ti-i-wə* (Goetze, ibid.) is irrelevant. All that these occurrences show is that (1) *pis-* may be used with an oblique case; (2) that case is employed pleonastically when *and-* is joined to the root. This use is entirely in accord with the marked tendency of Hurrian to duplicate attributive elements. Note also the analogous *ù am-mi-ti dan-neš ḫa-da-a-ku* EA 19. 54 "and I rejoice greatly over it," where the demonstrative pronoun in the gen. construes with the verb "rejoice" without the expected preposition. This is, then, another of the numerous Hurrianisms in Tushratta's Akkadian.

[201] A further occurrence of the suffix is in *ur-pa-ri-in-ni* "butcher" alongside *ur-pu--um-ma epēšu* "flay," cf. Orientalia 7. 54.

(5) *-aẑ-*: *ḫaẑ-aẑ-* <*ḫaẑ* "hear," cf. Mit. IV 20, 23, 26, 29, 110, and from Bogh. XXVII 42 rev. 12, XXIX 8 iii 30; evidently an emphasizing element.

The elements which follow appear to be verbal complements on positional grounds, as explained above. Their exact function remains to be established. It may be felt by some that these particular suffixes should be listed together with those which I have grouped under "position 6" [186]. But the formal evidence of position is once again the determining factor.

(6) *-o/uḫ-*: The presence of this morpheme is indicated by *an-za-an-ni* Mit. II 66: *an-za-an-nu-u-ḫu-ša-a-ú* ibid. III 50, 51 (also I 18, IV 129), with a stem-meaning "beg," or the like;[202] note also *ta-duḫ-ḫu-li-ik-ki-in-na-a-an*[203] ibid. III 4, if it is derived from *tad-* "love." Similarly, the repeated *ul-lu--ḫu-ug-gu-ú-un* of Mit. II 104 (perh. "different") may be compared to *ul-li-wa-a-en* ibid. III 95. There is thus good reason to look for the same morpheme in *ḫi-su-ú-ḫi-wa-a-en* Mit. III 76, 85, 89, 95, etc., from the stem for "vex," or in the as yet obscure *u-u-lu-u-ḫ-* ibid. II 11, III 16, IV 60. From Bogh. we may adduce as possible analogues *še-el-lu-ḫu-ul-la* VIII 61 rev. 10 and *ta-ku-ḫu-u-la* VBoT 14. 7. At any rate, the existence of an element *-o/uḫ-* seems safely established. I have no suggestion to offer as to its force.

(7) *-aḫ*: Perhaps a morphologic variant of the above; cf. *ma-az-za-ḫa-a-at--ta-a-an* Mit. II 8, *ši-la-a-ḫu-uš-ḫa* ibid. IV 66, *ši-la-a-ḫu-šu-uš-ti-wa-a-en* ibid. 41.

(8) *-ugar-*: This element[204] is familiar from two well-known stems, *ag-ugar-* "dispatch" (<*ag-* intr. "proceed," trans. "guide, lead") and *tad-ugar-* "love, show affection" (<*tad-* "love"). It occurs also in several other stems. Cf. *a-gu-ka-ra-aš-ti-en* Mit. II 58, 86, *a-ku-qa-ru-um-ma* N 297. 37, 636. 15;[205] *ta-a-tu-ka-a-ri* Mit. II 67, IV 130 (also, with other forms, I 9, 19, II 79, etc.), *ta-du-ga-ra-a-e* XXIX 8 iii 16, *da-a-du-ga-ra-a-i* ibid. 7. Note also *pí-id-du--ka-a-ra* Mit. III 110 (also I 21) "prosper(?)";[206] *pu-ku-ka-ri-id-du-li-e-eš* XXVII 42 rev. 16. With nominal forms we have *aš-du-ka-a-ri-iw-wa-ša* Mit. II 76 and *pu-u-ru-uš-du-ga-ri-ša* XXVII 46 i 22. From Nuzi we get further *at-ta-mu-qa-ru-um-ma* N 101. 3 and *pu-ḫu-qa-ri/a* H IX 35. 9, N 646. 5.[207]

[202] Cf. Messerschmidt, Mitanni-Studien 23.

[203] The double writing of *-ḫ-* appears to be irregular; cf. [57 n. 104].

[204] It is quite possible that this suffix is of composite origin.

[205] Cf. J. Lewy, RÉS 1938 68 n. 8 and Goetze, Lang. 16. 122 n. 32. See now also H. Lewy, Orientalia 10 (1941) 209 n. 4. The meaning "return" obtained by J. Lewy, loc. cit. from Nuzi would accord with an underlying "lead back," in which case *-ugar* would have, at least in some instances, the value "back, in return."

[206] For an attempted etymology see Goetze, loc. cit. n. 33.

[207] Cf. ibid. n. 34. This term may well underlie Hittite *puḫugari* "expiatory?"; for occurrences cf. Götze-Pedersen, Muršilis Sprachlähmung 27, 64.

Goetze has recently suggested (Lang. 16. 132 f.) that -ugar- may have a resultative force; stems containing this morpheme are compared with Akk. factitives and causatives. But the form *pitt-ugar-a* (above) weakens this interpretation in that its *-a* marks an intransitive. At all events, -ugar- fails to alter the underlying verb-type. Neither is it clear in what significant way *tad-* differs from *tad + ugar-*. The morpheme in question seems to do no more than introduce an extension of meaning. It is thus an apparent root-complement whose exact value is yet to be ascertained.[208]

(9) -l-: In classifying this suffix it is important to bear in mind that -l-, with various accompanying vowels, occurs in several positions and forms part therefore of more than one element (cf. the introductory remarks in this section). Thus it seems to mark aspect + agent in *ḫa-ši-i-i-li* Mit. IV 43 [189], but aspect alone in *ur-ḫu-ub-du-ši-li-wa* ibid. III 64; in the latter instance the suffix follows the tense-element *-oz̄-*, hence it and its numerous analogues cannot be grouped with the root-complements. But in *ka-til-li-ta* Mit. IV 21 and *ti-i-ḫa-nu-u-ul-li-e-et-ta* ibid. III 22 we find *-il(l)-* and *-ol-* respectively before tense-markers, which constitutes positional evidence for root-complements. Indirect evidence to the same effect is provided by the onomastic compounds which involve -l- [175 (3)] and [177]. For if *-b* in *Aga-b-* is a complement, then the *-l* in *Urḫa-l-* belongs to the same category.

Cf. (a) *kad-ill-ed-a* (above), and similarly ibid. II 50, 102, IV 109; *ḫa-ša-a-ši-il-li-i-il-la-a-an* ibid. 29 (<*ḫaz̄ + az̄ + ill + ili + lla + àn) "heard + attentively (-az̄-) + root-compl. + by-me-will (-ili-?) + they (-lla-) + and." i. e., "I will give them the most careful attention "; *ta-a-ni-il-li-e--ta-a-al-la-a-an* ibid. I 109; cf. also [182]. (b) In addition to the three forms cited at the beginning of this section, cf.: *ge-pa-a-nu-ul-ul!-li-e-wa-a-at-ta-a-an* Mit. III 63; [209] *ḫi-su-ú-ḫul-li-e-et-ta-a-an* Mit. IV 10; *ta-duḫ-ḫu-li-ik-in-na-a-an* ibid. III 4; evidently also *ḫu-ub-lu-lu-uš-te-la-an* ibid. II 22, [..]-*na-a-ku--lu-uš-te-la-an* ibid. 24. From Bogh. note *pu-du-ú-li-ma-aš-ši-na-ma* XXVII 46 i 25 (also 29); *še-e-ḫa-du-li-ma-aš-ši-na-ma* ibid. 26, 30; perhaps also *še-lu-u-li-tu* XXVII 38 i 8, 9 and *ḫu-u-lu-li-tu* ibid. 8, 9. From Nuzi cf. *za-ḫu-lu-um-ma* Orientalia 7. 60, alongside *za-ḫu-um-ma* ibid. Whether *-il(l)-* and *-ol-* were morphophonemic variants or two distinct morphemes cannot be

---

[208] Suggested identifications of this morpheme with Sanskrit *kr* " do," which still come up, can hardly be sound. Hurrian may well have borrowed from Indo-European some individual elements. But the same cannot apply to a morphologic element of widely established use. Moreover, the factitive function of -ugar- is far from proved.

[209] The second -ul- is due probably to dittography; cf. Friedrich, Kleinas. Sprachdenkm. 23.

decided at present. The increment in meaning appears to have been one of emphasis.

(10) *-m-*: This element, too, is found with several accompanying vowels and may figure, in reality, in more than one morpheme. There is, however, no evidence that any of these forms was something other than a root-complement.

From *eman* "ten" (cf. JAOS 59. 320 ff.) we get *e-e-ma-na-mu-ša-ú* Mit. III 54, 57, obviously *eman* + *am* + *ož-*, i. e., (A) + (1) + (2) [178]. Another instance is *ir-ka-a-mu-u-ša-ma-a-an* ibid. I 92. Before *-št-* [183] we have what is apparently the same morpheme in *šu-ra-a-maš-ti-en* Mit. IV 42, 51 "let him hasten" (Friedrich, BChG 15 n. 1) and perhaps in *su-bi-a-(a-)maš-ti-en* ibid. III 72 (also 88) "let him increase(?)" (JAOS 59. 320).

In *ú-ru-u-muš-te-e-wa-a-dan* Mit. II 9, alongside *ú-ru-u-mu* ibid. IV 47, the positional evidence is the same as above. Although the meaning of these two forms is as yet obscure and the underlying root uncertain (**urom-* being a possibility), there is independent evidence for a morpheme *-mu/o*. Cf. [..]*-šu-u-u-li-u-u-mu* Mit. II 23; *pa-li-u-mu-u-li-i-in* ibid. IV 97 (99); *ti-lu-u-lu-mu* XXVII 29 iv 8, and perhaps *wi*$_i$*-na-mu* ibid. 7.

Before *-še* *m*-forms are especially common. Cf. *a-ru-u-ma-a-aš-šu-ḫi-ḫa* Mit. III 13; *pa-li-a-ma-a-aš-še-* ibid. 46; *ti-i-ḫa-nu-u-lu-ma-aš-še-ni* ibid. III 8. From Bogh. note, e. g., *ḫa-a-šu-ma-a-aš-ši-* XXVII 42 rev. 11; *pu-du-ma-a-aš-ši-* ibid. 10 (contrast *pu-du-ši-* ibid. 11); *pu-du-ú-li-ma-aš-ši-* ibid. 46 i 25, 29; *ku-li-ma-a-aš-ši-* ibid. 19; *še-e-ḫa-du-li-ma-aš-ši-* ibid. 26, 29, 30. Cf. also *šin* + *am-* JAOS 59. 321 "second, duplicate, etc." Here may perhaps belong the nominal(?) forms *wə-ri-i-ma-in* Mit. IV 122 and *a-lu-ma-a-in* VIII 61 obv. 1, 9, *a-lu-ma-a-i* ibid. rev. 7 (with *-ai-*?). Some of the above examples suggest a factitive function for this *-ma-*. If this should prove correct, there would still be the problem whether that signification was primary.

(11) *-(u)ppa-*: Cf. *ka-tup-pa-a-ni-i-in* Mit. IV 14 and *ta-a-nu-up-pa-e-* *-t*[*i..*] ibid. II 114. The classification of this and the following suffixes is doubtful.

(12) *-t/d-*: Cf. [*na-*]*na-ti-la-a-e* *mi-lu-la-ti-la-a-e* XXVII 38 iv 15; *na-na-a-tum* *mi-lu-la-a-du* ibid. 17; [*na-*]*na-a-du-un-na* ibid. 18, alongside [*na-*]*na-a-i* ibid. 27. Perhaps also *še-e-ḫa-du-li-ma-aš-si-* (10); *i-su-di-iš* Mâri 5. 6 : *i-si* ibid. 1; *al-lu-lu-da-i*[*š*] ibid. 7 : *al-lu-li-e* ibid. 2. Note, furthermore, *ḫi-ši-im-du-a-ú-ú-un* Mit. II 115 (alongside *ḫi-iš-ma-aš-ši-* ibid.); *i-li-im-du-um-ma* AASOR 16 42. 18 and p. 96. Perhaps also *pí-ša-ša-te* RŠ Voc. III 16, *pí-šu-šu-te* ibid. 22, provided that the second *-š-* stands for the root-complement *-ž-* (5) and not for the perfect-element *-ož-*; but cf. [173].

(13) *-tt-*: Cf. *ge-ra-at-tu-u-li-iš* XXVII 42 rev. 14, alongside *ki-ru-li-eš*

XXIX 8 iii 28; *pu-ku-ka-ri-id-du-li-e-eš* XXVII 42 rev. 16; perhaps also *zu-ge-et-ta-al-la-a-an* Mit. IV 71, cf. *zu-ku-u-u-un* ibid. 69. Another nominal analogue is *šukku/o-tt-* VIII 61 obv. 12, 13, Mit. II 68, 70, III 108.

177. Onomastic compounds with infixed elements. This designation refers to personal names of the type *Agi-b-ženni* as opposed to *Ḫažu-kelde*. The added morpheme always refers to the first word of the compound, never to the second. For Hurrian does not use prefixed morphemes; furthermore, we have occasional uncompounded forms like *na-aḫ-ḫa-ab* or *pa-ši-ib* [176 (4)]. The question is to determine the meaning of this *-b* and its analogues when employed in proper names.

Two facts have to be pointed out at the outset. First, the vowel preceding the suffix may be *-i-* (as above), *-a-* (type *Una-b-Tešub*), or *-u-* (type *Teḫu-b-ženni*). Second, the suffix is *-b* in the vast majority of instances; but we find also *-l* (type *Urḫa-l-enni*) and *-š* [210] (type *Eni-š*-tae*). There is also the possibility that *-n* and *-r* were similarly employed; at best, however, these would be isolated occurrences.[211]

Our inquiry must proceed from the compounds in which no bound form is used: *Erwi-žarri* "The lord is king" and *Ḫažu-kelde* "Heard is good news" [171]. The presumption is that the names with suffixes constitute the same sentence-type. Moreover, the several suffixes in question should belong to the same category inasmuch as they appear in strictly parallel forms.

The only established morpheme *-b* which might be adduced here is the possessive pronoun of 2 p. But no known possessive pronouns are expressed by *-l* or *-š*, not to mention *-n* and *-r*.

One proposed solution was to regard *-b* as a "desiderative" element.[212] There is, however, no evidence for such a formative in the entire Hurrian material.[213] Besides, the assumption is not borne out by the uncompounded forms in *-b* which have recently been found in the Mâri texts.[214] The effort has also been made to connect *-b* in some way with the masculine names and

[210] The phonetic character of this *-š* will be taken up presently. We shall see that the sound was *ž* etymologically, which would become, however, *š* before *t* [74]. For present purposes I shall write **Eni-ž-tae* in order to bring out the original nature of the morpheme involved (*ž*). For *Še-ri-iš-a*-RI, which belongs here, but has been interpreted by Friedrich, BChG 13, as an instance of the *š*-case, cf. [241].

[211] See provisionally the remarks of L. Oppenheim, AfO 12. 37 ff. For a full account reference must be made to the forthcoming publication of Purves-MacRae.

[212] See A. Gustavs, OLZ 1912 350 f. and Mitt. Altor. Ges. 10 (1937) 56 f.; cf. Oppenheim, loc. cit.

[213] Comparison with the element *-ewa* [192] is precluded at the outset by the fact that it has two vowels which are essential and unvarying.

[214] Cf. Thureau-Dangin, RA 36. 8.

to assign an *m*-suffix to names of women.[215] There are, however, masculine names with written *-m* as well as feminine names with *-b*; the variation is a phonologic one [216] and thus the alleged independent *-m* in onomastic compounds is eliminated.

To return to the original question, the vowels which precede the suffixes involved can be accounted for without much further discussion. All recur in the onomastic compounds which are formed without suffixes, where they have been identified as distinctive participial endings [168 ff.]. Accordingly, the addition of suffixes to the first elements of the compounds supplemented in some fashion the meaning conveyed by the underlying participial forms.[217] This increment in meaning, however, did not carry with it any change in the sentence-type of the names; for compounds containing identical radical elements may add the bound forms or may not. In other words, the suffixes added to the meaning of the phrase without modifying the relation of the component elements; they served as root-complements.

In the light of these remarks it can hardly be a matter of coincidence that all the known suffixes of the first elements in onomastic compounds have independently been established as root-complements with nominal and verbal forms alike. In [175-6] we find not only *-b* and *-l* but also *-n* and *-r*. In both sections there occurs also *-ž* which can now be used to remove the phonetic ambiguity from the written *-š* of the names: we may, therefore, safely write **Eni-ž-tae* in normalized transcription; cf. n. 210.

The meaning of the complements involved, so far as known, proves suitable throughout with the names under survey. For *-l* we have deduced the value of a superlative [175 (3)]; *Urḫa-l-enni* would represent "Most true is the god," on the analogy of *te-ol-ae* "exceedingly great." In the case of *-ž* the indications point to "much" [175 (6)]; hence "X (agent-noun or epithet)-much is A." [218] The suggested values of *-n* and *-r* would fit equally well in an onomastic context. Finally, the suffix *-b*, which is more common by far in names than all the others combined, appears to have had an asseverative connotation [175 (4)]; "Arriving-verily is Teshub" would be an excellent example of the type as a whole.

In conclusion, attention should be called to the fact that the suffixes may

[215] Oppenheim, loc. cit.

[216] See Purves, AJSL 57. 176 n. 66.

[217] This is not to say that all the underlying forms need be participial. They have to be agent-nouns (which are represented by participles) or epithets (which may be nouns of the *e/i*-class).

[218] The meaning of *eni* in **Eni-ž-tae* (cf. also *Ini-b-žarri* N 501. 28) is uncertain. Against identification with *ene* "god" is the normal Nuzi writing with double *n* and the variation *e/i*.

interchange in otherwise identical initial elements.[219] Cf., e. g., *Ḫai-b-z̄arri* N 47. 19 : **Ḫai-z̄-Tešub* N 158. 9; **Tambu-z̄-til* N 14. 16 : *Tambu-b!-z̄enni* N 280. 5 (as collated by Purves). It can readily be seen that the alternation of "truly" : "much" was a natural one and that it did little to modify the significance of the phrase as a whole. Incidentally, such alternations contribute a compelling argument in favor of viewing the onomastic suffixes as interrelated. Their classification as root-complements can alone fulfill that requirement.

2. Suffixes of the Verb

178. As indicated in [176], the various elements which may enter into the composition of a given verbal form are placed in a fixed order. The respective positions are as follows.

(A) Root
- (1) Root-complements, of which more than one may be used in the same form
- (2) Tense-markers
- (3) The element *-št-*
- (4) The element *-id(o)-*
- (5) Class-markers
- (6) The "state"-determinatives *-kk-* and *-wa/e-*
- (7) Indication of voice
- (8) "Aspect"-determinatives
- (9) "Mood"-determinatives
- (10) Agent-suffixes
- (11) Other modifiers

(B) Associatives

The morphemes under (A) and (B) are discussed as separate groups. Those listed under (1)-(11) are all suffixes which occur in verbal forms or are employed with verbal nouns. It is immediately apparent that no single form can include all the positions just mentioned. Some of the verbal nouns necessarily lack agent-suffixes (10), and the same is true of all intransitive forms. In other words, syntactic requirements and the sharp division of the verb into two classes [119-20] combine to limit the number of entries in any given form. But the order of elements is not affected by these conditions.

[219] Noted by Oppenheim, loc. cit. But the author fails to draw from these examples the necessary conclusion that the interchange of suffixes presupposes relationship in function. If *-b* and *-m* referred to gender, then the remaining suffixes must have been parallel markers. This in turn would imply more than two genders or analogous categories, although the Hurrian texts do not show any such distinction. Cf. note 216 for the refutation of the basic premise.

Incidentally, the criterion of order may serve as a guide to the range of meaning which a given position was meant to represent, since position and function prove to be interconnected. The elements which as yet are doubtful as to their relative order are therefore altogether problematic as to function.

(1) Root-complements

179. For a discussion of these elements with verbal roots see [176-7].

(2) Tense-markers

180. This group comprises (a) *-ož-* and *-ošt-* [219] and (b) *-ed-* and *-ett-*. Of these, *-ož-* and *-ed-* have long been known as tense-elements, whereas *-ošt-* and *-ett-* have yet to be interpreted. For the place of the tense-markers after the root-complements cf., e. g., *pis-and-ož-* [176 (2)]; *kad-ill-ed-* ibid. (9); *ša-a-ri-il-li-it-ta* Mit. IV 116.

181. *-ož-* and *-ošt-*. The former shows an invariable *-š-* in the syllabic texts, *-ž-* in RŠ [45]. When the preceding vowel is written double in Mit. the sign U is always used, which points to *o* [30 f.]. E. g., *a-ru-u-ša-ú* Mit. III 11; *pa-aš-šu-u-u-ša* ibid. II 108. As for *-ošt-*, the *-o-* is attested by *id-du-u-uš-ta-* Mit III 2, 11, *ú-ú-nu-u-uš-ta-* ibid. II 110, but the first consonant is necessarily *š* (before *t*), even though it may have been *ž* originally [74].

Whenever *-ož-* is used in finite forms and the context is clear a reference to the past is unmistakable. On this there is general agreeemnt.[220] Friedrich, BChG 37, calls the form "preterit." But in view of the nominal forms with *-ož-*, such as the occupational term *ašḫ* + *ož* + *ikk* + *onne*, where the idea of something completed in the past can scarcely have played a major part, I would regard "perfect" as less committal than "preterit."

The question must now be raised whether *-ož-* was employed freely with transitives and intransitives alike. In the great majority of its occurrences the element is known to be used with transitives. This is true of all the instances with agent-suffixes of 1 and 2 pp. [194].[221] But the sequence *-ož* + *a* is not restricted to 3 p. of the transitives. We get not only *ar* + *ož* + *a* Mit. I 46 (root-meaning "give"), *kad* + *ož* + *a* ibid. 96 ("communicate"), *tan* + *ož* + *a* ibid. 85, III 106 ("do, make"), etc., but also *un* + *ož* + *a* Mit. I 86 and *waḫr* + *ož* + *a* ibid. 60 from the known intransitives *un-* "come" and *waḫr-* "good" respectively.

[219] Not to be confused with the element *-št-* listed under position 3; cf. [183].

[220] Messerschmidt, Mitanni-Studien 109, simply has "uš-a er hat gethan - -." Bork, Mitannisprache 51 regards the form as "perfect," although on p. 48 he lists it under "preterit."

[221] For examples cf. Friedrich, BChG 37.

What prevents us from regarding *-ož-* as the sole marker of the perfect is the use of *-ošt* + *a* to express the same tense, this time without reference to agent, in attested intransitives. Cf. *pí-su-uš-ta* Mit. II 62 "was happy" (with 1 p. sg.); *id-du-u-uš-ta-ma-a-an* ibid. III 2, 11 "departed" (3 p. sg.); *ú-ú-nu-u-uš-ta-ma-a-an* ibid. II 110 "arrived" (3 p. sg.); perhaps also *a-a-ad-du-u-uš-ta-* ibid. IV 8; *ḫu-šu-uš-ta* XXVII 38 i 13. We get thus the doublets *un* + *ož* + *a* : *un* + *ošt* + *a* and this is paralleled by *ag* + *ož* + *a* Mit. I 87 : *ag* + *ošt* + *a* VII 58 ii 9, 11. It is tempting to view *-ošt-* as the perfect-element of intransitives and its *-a* as the impersonal ending identical with that of the pres. *un* + *a* [169], unrelated to the finite suffix of 3 p. in *ar* + *ož* + *a* and the like. Accordingly, *-ož* + *a* with intr. roots would have a factitive connotation: *ag* + *ož* + *a* "was-made-by-him-to-proceed, granted--was-by-him," *un* + *ož* + *a* "brought-was-by-him."

But this simple solution cannot pass unchallenged. Against it speaks the fact that *-ošt* + *a* may be construed with the agentive case; cf. *e-e-ni-iw--wa-šu-uš u[š-]t[a-a-]-nu-u[-u]š-ta* Mit. II 76; *ši-du-ri-ya-aš ḫu-u-uš-ta* XXVII 42 obv. 23. It follows that the suffix may characterize also finite transitive forms. Similarly, the agent-noun *na-aḫ-ḫu-uš-ti* (Br. 571 n. 1), paralleled by *na-aḫ-ḫa-ab* (ibid.), configurates with *na-aḫ-ḫu-(u-)uš-a* XXVII 38 i 14, 15. The corresponding form in *-ož* + *i* is obviously the perfect participle; cf. *ar* + *ož* + *i* Mit. II 87; *paš* + *ož* + *i* ibid. 50, 65, II 107; *tad* + *ugar* + *ož* + *i-* ibid. I 9, II 79; and the like. A satisfactory way out of the difficulty does not seem to present itself just now. It may have to be sought along lines analogous to *-ed-* : *-ett-* (below).

182. *-ed-* and *-ett-*. The difference is marked phonetically by single writing of the consonant in the case of *-ed-* and double writing in that of *-ett-*. What is more important, there is a corresponding difference in usage: *-ed-* is used to mark the future in finite transitive forms [222] and in the active participle *pa-aš-še-ti-i-dan* Mit. III 116; [223] *-ett-a* occurs with intransitives and with those transitives which show non-finite construction (without logical object).[224]

For intransitive forms cf. *ú-ni-e-et-ta* Mit. III 21 (also ibid. 12!) "will arrive"; apparently also *pè-te-eš-te-e-et-ta* ibid. 29; *ti-i-ḫa-nu-u-ul-li-e-et-ta* ibid. 22, *u-u-lu-u-ḫé-et-ta* ibid. IV 60. With transitives in actor-action construction we have the same form in *gu-li-e-et-ta* Mit. IV 60 (preceded by

[222] This tense was identified by Messerschmidt, Mitanni-Studien 112 f.; cf. Friedrich, BChG 38. Bork, Mitannisprache 56 f., saw in *-ed-* a marker of the inchoative stem; he has since called it a marker of "future 1," cf. AfO 8 (1933) 311.

[223] Cf. [170 n. 165].

[224] Cf. my preliminary statement in Lang. 16. 331, where the importance of Mit. orthography is duly stressed. For Bork's "future 2" cf. loc. cit.

ol + *oḫ* + *ett* + *a*); *ka-til-li-e-et-ta-* ibid. 109; *ša-a-ri-il-li-it-ta* ibid. 116. All three forms have parallels in *-ed* + *a* accompanied by agentives: [I]*Ge-li-i-aš* [I]*Ma-ni-eš-ša-a-an gu-li-e-ta* Mit. IV 27; [I]*Ma-ni-eš* [I]*Ge-<li->ya-al-la-a-an ka-til-li-ta* ibid. 21; *ag-gu-uš-ša-a-an* . . . . (124) . . . *ša-a-ri-il-li-e-ta* ibid. 123 f.

On present evidence there is nothing to contradict the assumption that *-ed-* marks the future with transitive roots, regardless of whether the form is finite or participial. On the other hand, *-ett-a* signifies the same tense in middle forms and is used for that reason both with intransitives as well as transitives in non-finite construction.

(3) *-št-*

183. For the position of this element cf. *ši-la-a-ḫu-šu-uš-ti-wa-a-en* Mit. IV 41; the analysis of this form cannot but isolate *-ož* + *u/ošt-*, the first of these suffixes being necessarily the perfect-element, however uncertain the meaning.[225] The listing before *-id(o)-* (position 4) is indicated by *ta-a-ta-aš-ti-te-en* Mit. I 78 (**tad* + *ašt* + *id(o)* + *en*); *pí-ši-iš-ti-di-en* Mâri 5. 17.

The argument against identifying this suffix with the tense-element *-ošt-* [181] is as follows: The preceding vowel may be in the present instance *-a-*, *-e/i-*, or *-o-*.[226] The tense-marker is attested only in the perfect, whereas the element under discussion occurs with modal suffixes and may refer to the future. Added to this is the positional factor just cited. Thus we have to separate the perfect *pí-su-uš-ta* Mit. II 62 [181] from the modal form *pí-su-uš-te-e-wa* ibid. 55 which is correlated with the future *ge-pa-a-ni-e-ta* ibid. 54. This pair alone would suffice to bring out the functional difference between the two *št*-forms involved.

Concerning the meaning of the element under discussion opinions have varied. Messerschmidt, Mitanni-Studien 16, favored the causative, at least for *-ašt-*, on the basis of *ta-a-ta-aš-ti-te-en* Mit. I 78, and Friedrich, BChG 10, evidently concurs since he translates this form by "mögen . . . zur Liebe veranlassen." Bork, Mitannisprache 51, argues for the future tense. Neither view can be upheld. We have just seen that a tense-element cannot be involved here; see also Bork's more recent identification of the element as "iterative," AfO 8. 311. The assumption of a causative may satisfy some occurrences but will not suit others. Before we proceed with the problem of meaning it is in order to list the pertinent instances with *-št-* which are likely to represent verbal forms.

(a) *-ašt-*: *a-gu-ka-ra-aš-ti-en* Mit. II 58, 86 "let him send back"; *su-bi-a-a-*

[225] The root-complement *-ž-* should have *-a-* before it [176 (5)]. The form as a whole is a negated form of command. The supplementary *-ož-* may have here the same ("perfective?") force as in *ašḫ* + *ož* + *ikk* + *onne* [181].

[226] For this vowel-quality cf. the following note.

-maš-ti-en ibid. III 72, (88) "let him increase(?)"; *šu-ra-a-maš-ti-en* ibid. IV 42, 51 "let him hasten"; *ta-a-na-aš-ti-en* ibid. I 82, III 75, 78 "let him do"; *ta-a-na-aš-ta-ú* ibid. I 44 (context lost); *ta-a-na-aš-du-en* ibid. IV 15 (ending obscure); *ta-a-ta-aš-ti-te-en* ibid. I 78 (below); *ut-ta-aš-ti-te-en* III 80 (same suffix as above; context lost; "let them . . ."). Outside Mit. there are only doubtful instances; cf. *ar-pa-aš-du-ud* XXVII 29 iv 12; *a-a-aš-ḫa-aš-du-um* ibid. 36. 4; *ḫa-ša-aš-du* ibid. 42 obv. 38; *ḫa-za-aš-ta-ri* Mâri 3. 18, 19.

Most of the above occurrences represent imperatives or optatives [193]. There is one finite form with the agent of 1 p. sg. (*-a-ú*). The rest is unintelligible. The translatable forms could, to be sure, be regarded as causatives. But there is nothing that actually requires such an interpretation; for the element *-m-* which occurs in two of the forms see [176 (10)], where a possible factitive connotation has been suggested for this complement. The basis of the causative interpretation is *tad* + *ašt* + *iden* Mit. I 78 (cf. Messerschmidt, Mitanni-Studien 16). Actually, however, it is here in particular that such a rendering would be out of place: "the gods shall cause us to love." Whom are Tushratta and Nimmuria to be made to love? If it is "one another," then *-ašt-* should be a reciprocal element. If we leave this element untranslated we get literally "loved-x-by-them-shall-be," i. e., the gods shall love us (*-til[l]a-*, which is used five times in this one sentence to indicate the goal of the one verbal form in question). If we provisionally posit for *-ašt-* an intensifying function the syntax will remain undisturbed. That function is fully as suitable in the remaining occurrences as is the causative.

(b) *-e/ išt-*: *pí-sa-an-ti-iš-ten-na-a-an* Mit. IV 44 "and (I) shall rejoice"; *pè-te-eš-te-el-la-a-an* ibid. II 26, *pè-te-eš-ti-ten* III 28 (34), *pè-te-eš-te-e-et-ta* ibid. 29, and *pè-te-eš-ta-iš* ibid. IV 50; *pí-ši-iš-ti-di-en* Mâri 5. 17 (alongside *pí-ši-di-en* ibid. 16); from Bogh. *šu-li-li-iš-du* and [.]*-le-e-eš-du* XXVII 29 iv 13, and perhaps *ki-ri-iš-du-un-na* XII 12 v 14. In this whole group only one underlying root is definitely known. This is *pis-*, which in the form cited does not lend itself to an interpretation as a causative in that no goal is mentioned with it.

(c) *-ošt-*: *ge-pa-a-nu-lu-u-uš-ta-a-aš-se-na*[227] Mit. III 59 "the ones sent + *-ol* + *ošt-*"; *ku-zu!-uš-ti-wa-a-en* ibid. IV 40 "let him not detain"; *ḫu-ub-lu-lu-uš-te-la-an* Mit. II 23 and [. . .]*-na-a-ku-lu-uš-te-la-an* ibid. 24; *pí-su-uš-te-e-wa* Mit. II 55 and [*p*]*í-su-uš-ta-iš* ibid. I 80; *pu-ug-lu-uš-ti-en* ibid. III 25; *ši-la-a-ḫu-šu-uš-ti-wa-a-en* ibid. IV 41; *šur-wu-uš-ti-ik-ki-i-in* ibid. II 103; *ú-ru-u-mu-uš-te-e-wa-a-dan* ibid. II 9.[228] The above remarks concerning *pis* + *and* + *išt-* (b) apply also to *pis* + *ošt-*.

[227] This form with its orthographic U establishes the *o*-quality of the vowel in question.

[228] In this connection the following forms present a problem: *wa-aḫ-ru-uš-til-la-a-an*

Summing up, the element *-ošt-* is not capable as yet of a satisfactory interpretation although it occurs in a considerable number of pertinent forms. In many of these it cannot be viewed as a causative suffix. It is found frequently in forms having an imperative or optative force. Most likely it was an intensifying marker, but it is not certain whether this signification would apply to the action, the subject or object ("extensive" meaning something like "severally"), or perhaps to any one of these, depending on the given circumstances. In function it seems to be close to the root-complements, but cannot be grouped with them on account of its position in the suffix-chain.

183a. Of doubtful classification is the element *-imbu-*. Its place is after the tense-marker, cf. *a-ru-u-ši-im-bu-ú-uš-ḫa* Mit. III 16 and *ša-a-ru-ši-im--bu-ú-*[*uš-šu?* [229]]*-uḫ-ḫa* ibid. 86 (IV 108), hence position 3 is the lowest possible in the suffix-chain. But we have no conclusive evidence against listing this element in position 8 or 9. Furthermore, two of the roots here included (*ar-* and *al-*) take the root-complement *-m-* [176 (10)], and the noun possesses a complement-group *-amba-* [175 end]. Although the positional criterion prevents us from classifying *-imbu-* as a verbal complement, all the forms in question have nominal terminations with underlying verbal roots; it is thus a question whether the suffix is verbal at all.

Other examples are: *ú-ri-im-bu-ú-uš-šu-uḫ-ḫa-ma-a-an* (96) *na-ḫu-ul-li-im--bu-ú-uš-šu-ḫa* Mit. III 95 f.; *ta-a-du-ka-a-ri-im-bu-ú-uš-še-ni-e-ra-a-an* ibid. IV 96.

(4) *-id*(*o*)-

184. For the position of this element after *-št-* cf. *tad* + *ašt* + *iden* [183(a)]; the form *na-ak-ki-du-u-we-en* Mit. II 52 "let them not dispose" indicates a place before the negative element *-wa/e-* (position 6); it suggests at the same time that the full suffix was *-ido-* (note the writing with U).

The element has long been regarded as marking the plural (Jensen, ZA 14. 176; Messerschmidt, Mitanni-Studien 16; Friedrich, BChG 36). Indeed, the subject of transitive forms with *-id*(*o*)- is clearly plural in the instances just cited; the same is true of (*e-e-en-na-šu-uš*) *na-ak-ki-te-en* Mit. IV 117 "let them dispose." In [*a-nam-*]*mil-la-ma-an ut-ta-aš-ti-te-en* ibid. III 80 "and thus they shall . . ." we have apparently an intransitive form with a

Mit. IV 113, *še-eḫ-ru-uš-til-la-a-an* ibid. 119, and similarly *u-ru-uḫ-ḫi-iš-til-la-a-an kàr--kut-tiš-ti-la-a-an* ibid., 120. Since the associative pronoun in each of these forms is *-til*(*l*)*a-* (1 p. pl.), and not *-l*(*l*)*a-* (3 p. pl.), the preceding element cannot be *-o/išt-* unless haplology (of *-t-* + connective *-i-*) is assumed; cf. [91] for such a loss of *-ti-*. Otherwise the above forms must have contained an original *-ž-* [223], which seems less probable.

[229] The supplementation is favored by IV 108.

plural subject (*-lla-* indicates actor-action construction). Nevertheless, there are good reasons for doubting whether *-id(o)-* was specifically a plural element.

We have seen earlier that the negative element is placed elsewhere after the agent-suffix [84]. It will be shown later that an element used to pluralize the suffixes of the agent is placed as far down as position 11 [198]. As a pluralizing suffix *-id(o)-* would thus be considerably out of position. There is yet another and perhaps more significant objection. Agent-suffixes are restricted to transitives construed with the goal of action. But the above *utt* + *ašt* + *iden* seems to be intransitive, and other plainly intr. forms with *-iden* will be adduced presently. Finally, *-id(o)-* is not confined to predicative forms; in *i-i-duk-[ku-]un-na-ma-an* Mit. III 84 : *i-i-uk-ku-un-na-ma-an* ibid. 94, and perhaps *u-u-[ul-]lu-ḫi-duk-ku-u-un* ibid. 84 : *ul-lu-ḫu-ug-gu-ú-un* ibid. II 104 the element can have nothing to do with agent or number.

The possibility of intr. forms with *-id(o)-* is enhanced by *it-ti-ten* Mit. III 22 "may (she) go." That this word is to be analyzed as *itt* + *id* + *en* is demonstrated by *pè-te-eš-ti-ten* ibid. 28 (with sg. subject) : *pè-te-eš-ti-e-na-an* ibid. 34. In other words, *ped* + *ešt* + *en* is capable of expressing much the same meaning as *ped* + *ešt* + *id* + *en* (since both have an optative connotation in their respective contexts). We get thus an independent morpheme *-id-* which may be used with sg. forms in actor-action construction. Furthermore, the suffixes in *itt* + *id* + *en* and *nakk* + *id* + *en* are phonologically identical; in both instances we may have therefore the same element *-id(o)-*.[230]

Other examples of *-iden* in forms which are construed with the subject-case and are in themselves neutral as to number are: *ti-i-ḫa-ni-(i-)ten-* Mit. III 24 (sg.), ibid. 27 (pl.); *ta-ri-i-ten-* ibid. 30; *pí-ši-di-in* Mâri 5. 16, *pí-ši-iš-ti-di-en* ibid. 17 *pí-sa-an-ti-iš-ten-* Mit. IV 44. In *ki-ib-ti-en* Mâri 5. 20 and *wu-ur-te-ni-it-ta-a-an* Mit. III 74 [214] the *-i-* seems to have been lost; in *ḫa-tu-di-en* Mâri 5. 19 *-u-* appears with the same element.

So far *-id(o)-* has been found in conjunction with "optative" elements when the forms involved served as predicates. There are, however, also some non-optative forms with what is apparently the same element. Unfortunately, all occur in fragmentary or unintelligible contexts. Only *pa-al-ti-tu* VBoT 69 ii 6 is accompanied by a pl. noun (*enna-*); the same or a similar construction may be presumed for *na-ak-ki-tu* ibid. 7 and perhaps *ḫa-i-tu-ug* XXVII 38 ii 13 (preceded by *-el* [for **-eš-la?*]. With loss of the final *o* owing to a following *-a-* we have *id-ki-ta-an-nim* XXIX 8 ii 29, 35 (with agentive pl.); cf. *id-ki/u-* Br. 559 n. 3. But there is little to guide us in the

230 Cf. my provisional statement in JAOS 59. 318 f., which is now to be corrected in accordance with the present analysis.

case of *še-lu-u-li-tu* XXVII 38 i 8, 9, *ḫu-u-lu-li-tu* ibid. 8, 9, and *ḫu-u-me-iš-ti-du* ibid. 42 obv. 13. Whether *ki-bi-du* ibid., *du-ú-i-du* ibid. 24 ff., *pa-a-ḫi-du-ú* VIII 61 obv. 5 and *a-ša-aš-te-du-u-ú* ibid. 7 are pertinent forms is not quite clear.

To sum up, we are led to the tentative conclusion that *-id*(*o*)- was not a relational suffix but rather an element which was used principally in association with "optative" endings applied to transitive as well as intransitive stems. This collocation appears to bespeak some intensifying function. With transitives construed with plural nouns in the agentive, *-id*(*o*)- may have come to reflect in the optative the plural of the agent. It is wholly a matter for speculation whether such incidental specialization resulted in the emergence of this morpheme as a pluralizing element with transitives in general.[231] At any rate, we cannot overlook those forms which correlate with the subject-case without regard to number; neither can we ignore the derivational character of *-id*(*o*)- in *i-i-duk-*[*ku-*]*un-* and *u-u-*[*ul-*]*lu-ḫi-duk-ku-u-un* (above).

(5) Class-markers

185. Before *-kk-* and *-wa/e-* (position 6) the transitives employ *-i-* [119] and the intransitives *-u/o-* [120]. The only exception appears in the sequence *-ido* + *wa-*; cf. *nakk* + *ido* + *wa* + *en* [184], where it is explained automatically by phonologic conditions, the transitive marker *-i-* having contracted with the preceding vowel. Otherwise the distribution of *-i-* and *-u/o-* respectively is so regular and well-attested as to preclude any possibility of being explained away. If we should say instead that it is better to posit simply *-ikk-* and *-iwa/e-* with transitives, and *-u/okk-*, *-owa/e-* with intransitives, the final result would remain the same since the morphophonemic alternation would still confront us.

It may be significant that the class-markers are placed after root-complements, tense-markers, *-št-*, and *-id*(*o*)-. This shows that positions 1-4 had a more intimate connection with the underlying root than was true of the subsequent positions. On formal grounds alone we are justified in regarding the elements listed under 1-4 as derivational. The remainder would have, accordingly, more of a relational character, transcending the direct connotation of the stem as such. The following discussion tends to bear out this premise.

[231] The Urartian suffix *-itu* which marks 3 p. pl. trans. (cf. Friedrich, Einf. ins Urart. 5 f.) may be adduced by some as an argument in favor of the relational force of Hurrian *-id*(*o*)-. If the two were cognate (which is possible, though by no means established), there is still no evidence that the Urartian suffix in question appears in its original sense. But comparisons and deductions of this kind would be premature under present circumstances.

(6) *-kk-* and *-wa/e-*

186. For the position of these two elements immediately after the class-markers see [119-20]. There is no instance of any other suffix ever being interposed between these two positions. If further evidence were needed, one could adduce *za-li-ik-ku-li* XXVII 38 ii 17. Although the meaning of the form is unknown, the positional analysis of its component elements, excepting the final vowel, admits of no doubt: *zal* + *i* + *kk* + *ol* + *i*, i. e., (*A*) + (5) + (6) + (8) + (9?), cf. [178].

The meaning of *-wa/e-* has long been known. The element is used to negate (cf. Messerschmidt, Mitanni-Studien 29, Bork, Mitannisprache 50) certain "optative" forms (Friedrich, BChG 37). With transitive stems and class-marker we get thus *-i* + *wa-* [119], *-o* + *we-* only after *-id*(*o*)- [184]. The corresponding sequence with intransitives is *-o* + *we* [120]. It should be stressed that the transitives with *-wa-* have their subject in the agentive; e. g., *enna* + *žuš nakk* + *ido* + *wen* Mit. II 52 "may the gods not dispose."

Concerning *-kk-* there is no similar agreement. Messerschmidt (op. cit. 113 f.) was inclined to see in *-kku* and *-kki* an indication of 1 p. sg. Bork (op. cit. 54 ff.) countered with the valid objection that the same person could not well be expressed with the aid of varying vowels. Bork accepted the identification of *-kk-o* (so!, in accordance with [29] as a reference to the first person), but ascribed the personal element to the vowel only; *-kk-* was to him the element of the "intensive."

In the light of the material now available *-kk-* proves to mark "state" and the vowel which follows, if it is final, may indicate person. But the state cannot be the "intensive," and neither can *-o* refer to 1 p. sg.

Since numerous occurrences of the element *-kk-* have already been cited [119-20] it remains now to single out only such instances as may lead to an understanding of its function. In *inu* + *me* . . . . . . (17) . . . *ub* + *u* + *kk* + *o anammi* + *mma* XXIX 8 iv 16 f. we have coordinate equational clauses "As-it . . . . is-x, so," the rest being immaterial for present purposes. The first clause begins with a particle containing the associative pronoun of 3 p. sg. It follows that the predicate refers to the same person. Since the verb is an intransitive (class-marker *-u-*), the construction must be of the actor-action type. Furthermore, the tense is the present, which is evident from the lack of differentiating tense-markers. The final *-o* is correlated with 3 p. sg.; it is not clear, however, from the above passage whether this vowel could mark that person independently, without an antecedent pronoun or a noun in the subject-case. It is noteworthy that in parallel passages we read *inu* + *me* . . . *šeḫal-a* ibid. 8, 27. Presumably, therefore, the form without *-kk-* would in the above instance have been *inu* + *me* - **ub* + *a*.

Other forms in *-kk-o* which correlate with sg. nouns in the subject-case are: (*[I]Mane + nnaman*) *mann + u + kk + o* Mit. II 91; (*ženifennàn*) (46) . . . . . . *ur + u + kk + o* ibid. III 45 f. (cf. also ibid. II 95, III 123, 124; VII 56 i 24 is in a fragmentary passage).

But *-kk + o* may refer also to plurals in the subject-case. Cf. *tupp + iaž tupp + u + kk-o* Mit. III 45; *-llàn . . . irn + u + kk + o* ibid. 60. Before an associative pronoun (of 3 p. pl.) the *-o* changes, however, to *-a-*: *mann + u-kkallàn* (3) . . . *un + u + kk + alan* Mit. IV 2-3, cf. *un + allàn* ibid. I 115. It would appear that *-o* was used to mark the *kk*-form as impersonal, at least with intransitives. The possibility that the same was true of transitives as well is inherent in forms like the place-name *Ḫaž + i + kk + owə* and perhaps in the combination *-ikkonne* (see below).

A different function has to be assumed, however, for the vowel in *-kk + i*. In *tiwallàn . . . ženifuda kadikki* Mit. IV 16 f., lit. "word-they-and . . . brother-my-to communicated + *kki* (i. e., "I-?-communicate words to my brother") the *-i* must refer to 1 p. sg., just as it will be shown to do in *-il + i/e* [196]. The same construction is evident in *tadugarožikki* Mit. II 79, but the passage in question is not sufficiently clear. On the other hand, the medial *-i-* after *-kk-* in *šur-wu-uš-ti-ik-ki-i-in* ibid. 103 and *ta-duḫ-ḫu-li-ik--ki-in-na-a-an* ibid. III 4 is something else, perhaps the vowel of the element *-i/en*.

Goetze (Lang. 16. 128) finds an original *-a* after *-kk-* in *ḫi-il-lu-ši-ik-kat-ta-a-an* Mit. I 52 and *ú-ú-nu-uk-ka-la-an* ibid. IV 3. A better instance would have been *ma-a-an-nu--ùk-ka-ti-la-an* ibid. III 17, where the syllable in question was never closed (unlike *-kkalan* < **-kkallàn*). However, this *-a-* must be regarded as secondary. This is independently attested before the associative pronouns *-tta-* and *-lla*, cf. [65]; the ending *-adilan* is an analogous instance. There is thus no satisfactory evidence for an original and morphologically significant *-kka*.

As regards the function of *-kk-* we lack conclusive information. In equational clauses (*inu + me . . . ub + u + kk + o* XXIX 8 iv 16 f.; *adi + nin . . . irn + u + kk + o* Mit. III 59 f.) a durative or iterative connotation is likely. A similar sense of the incomplete is probable in Mit. IV 2 ff., 11, 17, where the context refers to future eventualities. Neither is it inconsistent with Mit. II 90 f. and III 44 f., two passages introduced by *ai + n* "whether, if" [128]. At all events, the semantic range of *-kk-* was apparently quite broad. Provisionally, I would seek it in the sphere of the "iterative-durative." This would suit admirably the nominal forms of the type *ul-lu-ḫu-ug-gu-* and *i-i-duk-ku-* [120]; the sense would be "being something lasting or repeated."

The foregoing suggestion has to be checked, however, on the basis of those forms in which *-kk-* appears in conjunction with the perfect-element *-ož-*

[119]. These forms are restricted to active bases (regardless of the root-class) in accordance with [181]. In *ya + tta + man tan + ož + i + kk + attàn* Mit. II 5 the context is damaged and we cannot tell whether "that which I was doing" would fit or not. The same constructon comes up in *ḫill + ož + i + kk + attàn* ibid. I 52 (<*ḫill-* "relate"), but this passage is even more poorly preserved; perhaps "I talked at length." An agent-noun from the latter base is *ḫill + ož + i + kk + onne* Mit. IV 4, 11. This compares with the occupational term *ašḫ + ož + i + kk + onne* "sacrificer(?)" [94] and [181], where a perfective element is quite in order; cf. also *am-mu-ši-ik-ku-un-ne* XXVII 38 iii 20 and *i-šu-ú-ḫu!-ši-ik-ku-u-un-na* Mit. IV 92. With all due reservations I would propose for the complex *-ožikkonne* the meaning "one who has performed a certain act repeatedly."

In the suffix-chain of the verb position 6 is thus found to express negation with forms of command and, in addition, a state of repetitiveness or permanency. For purposes of ready reference we may view the negated "optative" also as a "state" of the Hurrian verb. If the positional criterion is at all valid, the two forms signified related concepts as viewed by the Hurrians.

(7) Indication of voice

187. The problem of voice in the Hurrian verb was raised in [168 ff.] in connection with participial forms. It was indicated there that transitives may form an active (*-i*) or a passive (*-u*) participle, whereas intransitives use a middle participle in *-a*. But transitives and intransitives alike form a perfect participle in *-ož + i*; e. g., *anzann(n) + oḫ + ož + i* Mit. I 18 "having sought," but *pis + and + ož + i + ttàn* ibid. IV 9 "I was happy about (it)." The question now arises as to the position in the suffix-chain which these and other voice-markers occupy.

So far we have had evidence for a position somewhere after the tense-markers (cf. also *paš + ed + i + dan* Mit. III 116). It remains to determine how far that may be. Now the forms in *-u + kk + o* just discussed have been found to be impersonal; in other words, they are noun-predicates. Since the nominalizing element involved can be only the final *-o*, this vowel proves to be a participial marker. In *ur + ukk + o* and its analogues the root involved is intransitive. But we have found also agent-nouns from transitive bases formed with the class-marker *-i-*,[232] e. g., *ašḫ + ož + i + kk + onne*. With *-ne* attested as an adjectival suffix [159], the part following *-kk-* has to be analyzed as *-o + nne*. We see thus that *-o* was a participial ending with

[232] For the *i*-quality of this element cf. the spellings *ma-a-an-ni-i-im-ma-ma-an* Mit. I 16, III 5, 10, 100; *pí-sa-an-du-ši-i-it-ta-a-an* Mit. ibid. 9; *pa-aš-še-ti-i-dan* ibid. III 116.

certain transitive forms. Accordingly, some participial elements were placed after position 6. For the sake of consistency, and in the absence of any evidence to the contrary, we shall assign to position 7 all the elements which are known to form participles.

As regards the meaning of the above *-o*, it comes close to that assigned to *-a* [169], except that the former is not restricted to intransitives. I would identify *-o* provisionally as the mark of the medio-passive participle. An independent example of this form, not associated with *-kk-* seems to be *pí-su-u-u-ni-i-n* Mit. III 4 (*pis* + *o* + *nin*).

At this time it may be in order to distinguish the several *u/o*-elements which have been discussed so far. The class-marker was phonetically [u], except before *-wa/e-* [119 n. 43]. The present element, on the other hand, is established as [o]. Furthermore, there is a functional difference between the two. The class-marker characterizes only intransitive forms and has no syntactic value, whereas the participial element in question imparts a special meaning to both transitives and intransitives. Finally, the positional treatment differs in the two instances.

Less clear-cut is the contrast between the *-u* in, say, *Ḫaž-u-kelde* [171] and the final vowel of *ur* + *ukk* + *o* or *pis* + *o*(+ *nin*). The two may have been differentiated phonetically, as is suggested by the above normalized writings and the evidence behind them. Moreover, we have yet to find an intransitive form of the type *ḫaž* + *u*. But in view of their related participial functions *-u* and *-o* cannot be separated definitely pending more conclusive evidence. In case of their ultimate identity the assumption would be justified that both *-a* [169] and *-u* [171] were represented by *-o* in a number of derived stems.

The problem of voice arises also in connection with the contrasted pairs of elements which will be taken up presently. We shall see that *-i/el- : u/ol-* and *-i/en- : u/on-* differ as to the underlying action-type; it is tempting, and by no means unwarranted, to regard the *-i/e-* of such instances as the mark of the active and the corresponding *-u/o-* as indicating the medio-passive. But this would carry our analysis to unpractical lengths.

(8) "Aspect"-determinatives

188. As has just been indicated, we have to place in this position the pairs *-i/el- : -u/ol-*, *-i/en- : u/on-*, and perhaps *-i/er- : -u/or-*. Within each pair the vowels appear to be contrasted morphophonemically. The contrast involved was probably one of action-type. The ascription of aspectual function to this group of elements is more or less arbitrary. It does not imply any similarity to the aspect of the Slavic languages, but is intended only to distinguish the above morphemes from the "state"-determinatives (position 6) and the "mood"-determinatives which will be described under position 9.

For the place of the present group in the suffix-chain cf. the form *ḫa-ša-a-ši-wa-al-li-i-il-la-a-an* Mit. IV 26. Its analysis is *ḫaž-* (*A*) + *-až-* (1) + *-i-* (5) + *-wa-* (6) + **-il-* (8) + *-i/e* (9) + *-llàn* (B), cf. [178]. The form may be translated freely "and I will not listen to them." [233] We see from this that **-il-* is placed after the negative (position 6). Although it may contain an indication of voice, the added *-l-* would place it after position 7.

189. *-l-*. For the meaning of this element we may juxtapose the types (a) *ḫaž-il-e* and (b) *ḫaž-u/ol-ež*.

(a) The key passage is *še-e-ni-iw-wu-ú-e-ma-a-an ge-e-el-ti ni-i-ri-še ḫa-ši-i-i-li* (45) *pí-sa-an-ti-iš-ten-na-a-an tiš-ša-an še-e-ni-iw-wu-ú-e-ni-e-we ge-el-ti-i-we* Mit. IV 44 f., freely "and my brother's well-being let me hear about promptly so that I may rejoice concerning my brother's well-being." [234] Similarly, *ḫa-ša-a-ši-il-li-i-il-la-a-an* ibid. IV 29 and *ḫa-ša-a-ši-wa-al-li-i-il-la-a-an* [188]. With the change of **-r* + *ile*>*-rre* [66] we have *ta-a-du-ka-a-ar-ri-e* [235] Mit. II 85 and, with *-ewa* following, *ur-ḫu-ub-du-ši-li-wa* ibid. III 64 and *ta-a-du-ka-a-ar-ri-e-wa* ibid. 65, IV 123. For *kul-li* <**kul-ili* cf. Friedrich, BChG 36 f.

In all these occurrences the 1 p. sg. is involved. That is due, however, to the accompanying *-i/e* [196]. For if *-a-* is substituted instead the form will be found to refer to 3 p. Cf. (pl. subject + a number of agentives +) *a-ru-ši-el-la-a-im* XXIX 8 iii 34; *ḫu-u-ši-el-la-an-ti-in* ibid. 38; *ni-wu*$_u$*-ši-el-la-an-ti-in* ibid. 42; *ša-ku-ši-el-la-an-ti-in* ibid. 46, 50; *ul-lu-ḫu-ši-el-la-a-in* ibid. iv 13. That this *-ella-* can have no connection with the pronoun of 3 p. pl. is made clear by the parallel passage in XXVII 42 rev. 13 ff. where forms in *-enna-* are substituted although the plural subjects are retained; the elements involved are therefore parallel verbal suffixes and not pronominal associatives; cf. [190].

For other examples in obscure contexts cf. *da-pa-aš-ti-li* VIII 60 obv. 15, *na-aḫ-ḫi-li* ibid. 16; *wu*$_u$*-ri-li* ibid. rev. 14; perhaps also *a-za-al-ti-li* XXXI 3 rev. 4 (note *a-za-al-ta* Mit. IV 67). With *-ež* we get *ḫa-a-ša-ši-li-e-eš* XXIX 8 iii 30 (also XXVII 42 rev. 12) and *maš-ti-li-e-eš* ibid. 35. The form *ḫa-u-li-il-la-an-tu* XXVII 38 ii 19, iii 1 parallels the above occurrences ending in *-an-ti*.

Friedrich is undecided as to whether the form in *-ili/e* marks 1 p. sg. of the "voluntative" or the "optative." [236] We have seen, however, that the

[233] Cf. Friedrich, BChG 37.

[234] Cf. Friedrich, BChG 44 n. 4 and see [214].

[235] Cf. JAOS 59. 307 f. n. 56. This form suggests that the wr. LI of the element before us represents [le]. But this is true only in form-final; before *-ll-* the vowel was *-i-* (cf. the examples given above).

[236] BChG 36.

personal marker was not an integral part of the "aspectual" element involved. In evaluating the aspect itself Friedrich was doubtless on the right track. We have here a form which may be termed "voluntative," "cohortative," or the like. It is necessary to add that the same element is found also with perfect stems thus paralleling the perfect formations with *-kk-* [186]. In the foregoing instances the meaning is probably "may/let X have done something." Significant for the interpretation of the element is its use in forms construed with the agentive, as well as its absence from known intransitives. For the syntax of the forms involving the first person cf. [196].

(b) For *-ol-* there are numerous examples. The type *ḫaz̄* + *ol* + *ez̄* (RŠ *ḫz̄lz̄*) is illustrated by Br. 559 n. 3 and Goetze, RHA 35 (1935) nn. 15 ff. Note, furthermore, *a-na-u-li-e-eš* XXIX 8 iii 34; *ḫi-in-zu-ru-la-a-eš* ibid. 36: *ḫi-in-zu-u-ri-li-e-eš* XXVII 42 rev. 18; *u-uš-šu-li-e-eš* ibid. 24. Apart from this type we have to note, on the analogy of *ur-ḫu-ub-du-ši-li-wa* (above), the Mit. forms *ma-a-an-nu-li-e-wa-a-* II 122, *tup-pu-li-e-wa* III 100, and *ú-ru--li-e-wa-* ibid. 115, all three from known intransitives. We may now add *tup-pu-la-in* Mit. III 26, and hence also *ka-šu-u-ul-la-in* ibid. IV 114. The latter instance points to *-ol-* (similar spellings in Bogh. are inconclusive), and this normalized form has therefore been adopted. From Bogh. note *a-šu-la-in* XXIX 8 iv 12. In view of the above instances we must list also *ur-du-li-e-wa* Mit. II 53 (class and meaning unknown); *ḫi-il-lu-li-e-wa* ibid. III 102, IV 24, 45 (<*ḫill-* "talk" or the like, but the root is not attested with agent-suffixes); and *ka-tu-li-en* HT 93 ii 6 (perh. <*kad-* "communicate"). Finally, with *-i/e* note *ma-a-tu-u-li* XXVII 38 ii 15 and *za-li-ik-ku-li* ibid. 17; perhaps also *al-lu-li-e* Mâri 5. 2 and *uš-šu-li-e* XXIX 8 iii 51 (if not a slip for *us̄* + *ol* + *ez̄*; see above).

The general meaning of the type *ḫaz̄-ol-ez̄* was discovered by Goetze, loc. cit. 103 ff.[237] The "imperative" force ascribed to this form as a whole is undoubtedly correct. But its restriction to 3 p. sg.[238] is not borne out; cf. *ḫa-zi-iz-zi-bal šal-ḫu-u-li-eš* XXVII 42 rev. 12 and *ḫa-wu*$_u$*-ši-bal ge-ra-at--tu-u-li-iš* ibid. 14, where the *-al* indicates plural subjects. Goetze contends that this imperative is wholly dependent on the final *-ai/i/ez̄*[239] for which see, however, [223].

There remains the problem as to the difference between *-i/el-* and *-ol-*. A review of the forms with *-ol-* will show a predominance of intransitives (*man-*, *tupp-*, *ur-* [in the sense "be present, occur"]) and such adjectival terms as *kir-* "long" and *šeḫl-* "pure." We expect therefore to see in *-ol-* an element characteristic of intransitives. This is refuted, however, by *ḫaz̄-ol-ez̄*

[237] Cf. also Friedrich, WZKM 47 (1939) 212 ff.

[238] Loc. cit. 107.

[239] Cf. Lang. 16. 134 n. 36.

which contains the common and plainly transitive root *ḫaž-* "hear"; the form cannot mean "let X hear" and has to be interpreted as "let X be heard." The contrast between *-i/el-* and *-ol-* was thus not one of verbal class (position 5) but rather of voice. The forms with *-ol-* prove to be medio-passive.[240]

190. *-n-*. This element, too, is attested in two forms: (a) *-i/en-*; (b) *-u/on-*.

(a) All but one of the roots found in XXIX 8 iii 34 ff. with *-ella-* and correlated with plural subjects and agentives (see above) have *-i/enna-* in the parallel passage XXVII 42 rev. 13 ff.: *a[-ru-ši]-in-na-a-in* 13, *[ḫu-u]-ši-in-na-an-ti* 19, *ni-bu-u-ši-in-na-a-in* 22, and *u-ul-[lu?-]ḫu-ši-in-na-a-in* 15; add also *pu-du-ši-in-na-a-i* 11.[241] Since these forms are also correlated with plurals, *-i/enna-* cannot be a singular-marker.

(b) Mit. contributes two intransitive forms with *-u/on-* which clearly show imperative or cohortative force: *pí-su-un-ni-en* I 79 "may/let X be happy" I 79 (subject "we") and *wa-aḫ-ru-un-ni-en* ibid. 81 "may/let (the years) be good." Once again reference to plurals is certain.

The instances under (b) show that *-u/on-* represents the same action-type as *-ol-*; those under (a) are active forms, precisely as the examples with *-i/el-*. The formal and syntactic parallelism is thus complete. There remains the problem of meaning. The available evidence is insufficient to disclose an appreciable shade of difference between the two pairs involved. The possible suspicion that we are confronted by a mere phonetic variation (*l/n*) is rendered extremely unlikely by the Mit. occurrences, since such confusion in that source would be without precedent. We are thus compelled to conclude that the aspect marked by *n*-morphemes was within the range of the imperative. Beyond that we cannot venture as yet.

191. *-r-*. The connection of this element with the two preceding pairs is

[240] I am uncertain about the translation of *ḫaž-až-il-ez*, cf. above under (a). "Let X hear" is suggested by the use of *-il-* but the context does not make clear whether such a rendering would fit.

For the homophonous root-complement cf. [176 (9)]. In most instances position, construction, and context serve to prevent confusion between the two.

[241] The form *aržln* RŠ XX B 7, 11, 15 may perhaps be compared with *a-ru-ši-el-la-a-im* XXIX 8 iii 34, especially in view of the final *-n* in the parallel *a[-ru-ši-]in-na-a-in* (above) and the general correspondence of the Bogh. passages just cited with this particular RŠ document and the longer and well-preserved text RŠ X 4. The latter contains a number of paragraphs which conclude with verbs in *-žnnk* (e. g., *aržnnk* ibid. 28) just as the clearly marked paragraphs in XXVII 42 rev. 12-13, 14-15, and 17-19 conclude with verbs in *-i/ennain* or *-i/ennandi*. The only element that remains to be accounted for is the final *-k* in RŠ X 4; cf. [200].

For forms in *-anni* and *-inna* which seem to be independent of the above group see [221].

altogether doubtful. We find it several times in the difficult text XXVII 38 iv, and it seems to have other doubtful witnesses. The present tentative listing is due to the occurrence of *-ir-* alongside *-ur-*, and also to the remote possibility that the sense of the latter may be medio-passive.

(a) *a-ri-ir-e* XXVII 38 iv 25.

(b) *ḫa-mu-úr-e* ibid. 9; [*wu*]*ú!-uš-tu-ur-e*[242] ibid. 12; *ta-ḫa-wuú-úr-e* ibid. 27. Note also *šu-ú-ur-e* ibid. ii 21, which is in parallel context with *ma-a-tu-u-li* ibid. 15 and *za-li-ik-ku-li* ibid. 17.

The medio-passive connotation is hinted by the juxtaposition of *šar-ra uš-ta-e* ibid. iv 19 (note the *a*-case) and *šar-ri* . . . (12) [*wu*]*ú-uš-tu-ur-e* ibid. 11 f. (with subject-case). If the former means something like "became king" then the latter should yield "was . . -ed king." Note also the parallelism of *-ur-* with *-ol-* (above). However, much more evidence is needed before this hypothesis could be considered plausible.[243]

(9) "Mood"-determinatives

192. The suffix *-ewa*. The position of this element is established by forms of the type *man(n)* + *ol* + *ewa-* [189 (b)]; it is placed after the "aspect"-marker.

Both vowels of *-ewa* are attested as constant by occasional full spellings. For *-e-* cf. *ú-ru-li-e-wə-* Mit. III 115 (from an intr. root); without the interposed *-ol-* note *wə-še-e-wə* ibid. 112, which is shown to contain an intr. root by the form *wə-ša-i-na-an* ibid. 33.[244] With trans. stems cf. *ta-a-du-ka-a-ar--ri-e-wə* ibid. 65. For the final *-a* note the double writings in open syllables: *u-u-lu-u-ḫé-e-wa-a-ti-la-an* Mit. II 11 and *ú-ru-u-muš-te-e-wa-a-dan* ibid. 9. Accordingly, we are justified in transcribing also the uncomplemented *-wə* of this element as *-wa*; e. g., *ur* + *ol* + *ewa-* (above).[245]

Forms in *-ewa* are in themselves neutral as to number and person. The necessary reference to the actor is derived from the subject or indicated by an associative pronoun. E. g., *še-e-ni-iw-we-en-na-a-an ḫi-il-lu-li-e-wa* Mit. IV 45 (3 p. sg.); *ge-pa-a-nu-ul*[[*-ul*]][246] *-li-e-wa-a-at-ta-a-an* ibid. III 63

[242] Friedrich, Kleinas. Sprachdenkm. 35 (following Forrer) reads [*l*]*u-uš-tu-ur-e*.

[243] In view of *i-ya-a-ri* XXVII 42 obv. 17 [216] (cf. *i-ya* ibid. 38 ii 15, 21 and *i-ya-ma* ibid. 17) it is unlikely that *ir-ḫa-a-ri* ibid. 22 and *za-a-az-za-ri* ibid. 25 have any connection with *-ir-*: *-ur-*. Note also *ku-ni-ya-ri* XII 12 vi 4, XXVII 10 v 12.

[244] For *-ain* with intrans. forms cf. [193 (g)]. The sense of *wəž-* cannot be far from "happen" (cf. JAOS 59. 313), "take place"; it suits both passages.

[245] Cf. Bork, Mitannisprache 53.

[246] This element cannot be the "cohortative" *-ol-* [189] because of the double *-ll-*; contrast *tup-pu-li-e-wa* and its analogues (below). It is this fact that prevents us from

(1 p. sg.); *u-u-lu-ḫé-e-wa-a-ti-la-an* ibid. II 11 (1 p. pl.). As far as syntax is concerned *-ewa* is analogous to the forms in *-a*, *-i*, *-u* [168 ff.] and *-ae* [167].

All investigators concur in suspecting *-ewa* of some modal function. Messerschmidt (Mitanni-Studien 113) simply appends "(Modus?)" to the list of pertinent forms from Mit. Bork (Mitannisprache 53) speaks of the "desiderative," but fails to give any proof; the only two forms which he cites are incorrectly analyzed. In JAOS 59. 315 ff. I indicated the likelihood that *-ewa* represents a conditional or potential mood by rendering Mit. IV 45 (see above) "My brother may say," etc. The same suggestion was advanced independently by Goetze (Lang. 16. 129 n. 15).

The available occurrences of *-ewa*, all from Mit., may be classified as follows:

With the root alone: *wə-še-e-wa* III 112; *i-i-iš-ḫe-e-wa* IV 16

With the root-complement *-oḫ-*: *oloḫ-ewadilan* (above); note the corresponding form without *-ewa*: *oloḫadilan* III 16

Wtih the root-complement *-ol*: *kebanoll-ewattàn* [247] (above)

With the "intensifying" element *-ošt-* [183]: *pí-su-uš-te-e-wa* II 55, (64); *ú-ru-u-muš-te-e-wa-a-dan* II 9

With "cohortative" *-il-* [189]:[248] *ka-ti-li-e-wa* IV 18; *ta-a-du-ka-a-ar-ri-e-wa* III 65, IV 123 (*-rre-/*-rile-*); *ur-ḫu-ub-du-ši-li-wa* III 64

With "cohortative" *-ol-*: *ḫi-il-lu-li-e-wa* (III 102), IV 24, 45; *ma-a-an-nu-li-e-wa-a-al-la-a-an* II 122; *tup-pu-li-e-wa* III 100; *ú-ru-li-e-wa-ma-a-ni-i-in* III 115; *ur-du-li-e-wa* II 53

The "conditional" force of *-ewa* is self-evident after *a-i-i-in* (II 53) and *a-i-ma-a-ni-i-in* (the same particle emphasized, III 111 f. [211]); note that *-manin* is suffixed also to *urolewa-* (ibid. 115). *kadilewa* IV 18 and *ḫillolewa* ibid. 25 occur in clauses introduced by the pronoun *awenne/a* "anyone(?)" [115]; the two passages deal with contingent events. It is significant that *ewa*-forms are employed in II 55, (64), III 63, 100 in clauses which are subordinated to future forms. The only time that an *ewa*-form is not introduced by a particle or placed in a dependent clause is IV 45; and here the rendering "My brother may ask" is favored by the context. The interpretation of the form as modal is in no way invalidated by the frequent association of that form with the "cohortative" *-i/ol-*; the meaning of such occurrences can be approximated by means of our "would, should, might." To allow for

regarding the first *-ul-* of the text as a root-complement and the second as the mark of the "aspect." See above, n. 209. The root-complement is established independently in the form *ge-pa-a-nu-lu-u-uš-ta-a-aš-še-na* Mit. III 59.

[247] Cf. the preceding note.

[248] In JAOS 59. 309 I failed to make clear the independent character of the *l*-form as associated with *-ewa*.

this variety of related connotations I propose to classify *-ewa* as an element marking the "conjunctive" mood.

193. Indication of command. It was pointed out in [189] that the ending *-olež* marks the forms concerned as some type of imperative. The *-ol-* contained therein has in itself "cohortative" force. But suitable though this element may be in expressions of command, it is by no means restricted to them. Closely related to *-ol-* and its (active) analogue *-i/el-* is the "aspect"-determinative *-n-* (in medial position), cf. [190].

We know also that command may be indicated without the aid of the above *-l-* or *-n-*. It follows that these aspectual markers were not essential constituents in imperative forms, certainly not in all of them. Before we attempt to determine what actually marked a given form as one of command it is in order to list the types which are known or may be assumed to have that force.

(a) *ḫaž* + *il* + *i/e* "let me hear" [189] (1 p. sg.)

(b) *-ella(i)-*: cf. *a-ru-ši-el-la-a-im* (ibid.; subject in the agentive)

(c) *ḫaž-olež* "let be heard" (ibid.; sg. or pl.); note the variants in *-olaež*, e. g., *ḫi-in-zu-ru-la-a-eš* XXIX 8 iii 36, *ta-ku-la-a-eš* ibid. iv 30

(d) *-inna(i)-*: e. g., *a[-ru-ši]-in-na-a-in* [190]; corresponds to (b); note *pu-du-ši-in-na-a-i* (ibid.) without *-n*

(e) *pis* + *u/onn* + *en* "let be happy" [190] (attested as impersonal pl.); corresponds in part to (c)

(f) *ḫaž*(+ *i*) + *en* Mit. I 113, II 13, III 49 "let (him) hear." This is the normal form for 3 p. sg., primarily with transitives, in which case the goal is in the subject-case and the actor in the agentive; cf. *a-ri-en* Mit. III 96, 97; *na-ak-ki-en* ibid. IV 42, 51; *pa-aš-ši-en* ibid. 52, 54, 57. For intransitives of this type cf. *ši-ri-en-na-a-an* Mit. III 34 and the various intr. forms in *-iden* [184].

The corresponding negated form is of the type *ḫažaž* + *iwa* + *en* "let (him) not hear" [119]. For the plural cf. *nakk* + *id* + *en* [184], negated pl. *nakk* + *id* + *owen* (ibid.).

(g) *itt* + *ai* + *n* Mit. IV 53 "let (him) go." That this form is favored in actor-action constructions may be seen from the instances in *-ol* + *ai* + *n* [189]; *pal-la-in* Mit. IV 64 appears to be analogous. But goal-action construction is certain in *pal-la-a-en* Mit. IV 56.[249]

(h) *itt* + *ai* + *žallàn* Mit. IV 52 "let (them) go." This is the plural counterpart of (g). Another clear instance is *pal-la-i-šal-la-ma-an* ibid. 65. Here are evidently to be included the two RŠ forms (*ša-ḫa-la*)*-ša-*[*la*] Voc.

[249] Cf. [173 n. 188].

II 32 = Sum. i n . d a d a g . e . m e š "they shall purify"[250] and accordingly (*ki-ba*)-*ša-la* ibid. I 32 = Sum. [i n . g a r . e . m e š] "they shall establish."[251]

(i) *a-ri* Mit. I 51 "give"; *zu-zi-la-ma-an* EA 170. 11 (Akk. *ù pa-ni-šu-nu ṣa-bat* "then get ahead of them(?)").[252] These two forms appear to be imperatives of the 2 p. sg., but in neither instance is the context clear.

These nine types differ from one another in a number of ways. It is neither certain nor likely that all had exactly the same force, even if we discount the conjoined morphemes that may be interposed between the root and the final suffix (e. g., *-l-*, *-n-*). But all imply some form of command. Friedrich refers to type (f) as "optative" (BChG 36) and Goetze calls (c) "imperative" (RHA 35. 107). In the preceding discussion I had occasion to refer to both these terms. To allow, however, for individual shadings which may be brought out in the future I suggest "jussive" as a common designation for all the types concerned. This term will be employed henceforward.

More important than the question of terminology is the difference in construction which sets apart (a) and (i) from the rest. Whereas (b)–(h) are impersonal, in that the actor is indicated only by the subject of the sentence, (a) includes a reference to 1 p. (sg.) and (i) seems to be similarly restricted to 2 p. (sg.). These agent-markers will be discussed under the next heading. For the present we are left with forms which may be characterized by final *-n*, as in (d)–(f), or *-ž* (c). However, neither element is a primary component of jussive forms. This is particularly clear from *itt* + *ai* + *n* (g) : *itt* + *ai* + *žallàn*,[253] *kiba* + *žala* (h); cf. also *pudož* + *inn* + *ai* (d). As for *-ž*, it will be shown that this suffix is used also with forms which cannot possibly be jussive [223].

The one element which is shared by the majority of the impersonal jussive forms is *-ae/i-*. We find it in (b), (c), (d), (g), and (h). For (f) it is made probable as a variant of *-e-* by the transitive form *pall-ae-n*, which I have

[250] Cf. Goetze, RHA 35. 106 n. 15; his translation "they purified" needs a comment. The corresponding Akk. form would be *ub-ba-bu*; cf. Thureau-Dangin, Syria 12. 239, and see the next note.

[251] For the Akk. equivalent *i-šak-k*[*a-nu*] in a recently published fragment of the ḪAR . r a = *ḫubullu* texts see Landsberger, AfO 12. 135 line 77. Landsberger's identification of the above Hurrian entry with Akk. *išakkan* (loc. cit. line 76, and p. 136) cannot be right. The Hurrian entries merely translate i n . g a r (ibid. 75) and i n . g a r . e . m e š (77) but not i n . g a r . e (76). The suffix *-la* has nothing to do with "future (or durative)" but is here and in Voc. II 32 the associative pronoun of 3 p. pl. Incidentally, the wr. *-šu* of *ša-ḫa-la-šu* ibid. 31 and *ki-ba-šu* ibid. I 31 represents the consonant of the perfect-element *-ož-* and is thus unrelated to the element *-ža-* [198] of the respective succeeding lines.

[252] Cf. Friedrich, BChG 22 and see [149 n. 114].

[253] The final *-an* of this particular form represents the connective particle [211].

listed in (g) for purely orthographic reasons. It would thus appear that *-ae/i-* was an original and apparently significant component of many jussive forms, while the added suffixes seem to have been incidental.

The position of this *-ae/i-* (>*e, i* ?) is established as (9) by its correspondence to that of *-ewa*; cf., e. g., *tupp* + *ol* + *ewa* Mit. III 100 : *tupp* + *ol* + *ai* + *n* ibid. 26. Hurrian evidently placed its "conjunctive" and its "jussives" in a single category, which may be plausibly identified with "mood."

There remains the question as to the possible relationship of the *-ae/i-* just isolated to the homophonous suffix which was previously assigned to the "gerund" [165-7]. The occasional use of the latter with the agentive [166] would tend to lend color to such an assumption; conversely, the jussive *ḫi-in-zu-ru-la-a-eš* XXIX 8 iii 36 from the nominal form *ḫi-in-zu-ri-* (e. g., ibid. iv 34), or the use of *ki-ra-i* RŠ Voc. IV 28 by the side of *ki-ru-li-e-eš* XXIX 8 iii 28 lead to the same result. That the wide range of the Hurrian gerund was not inconsistent with the use of this form as jussive goes without saying. When thus used, however, the form was generally provided with additional elements in accordance with the syntactic requirements of the phrase.[254]

(10) Agent-suffixes

194. The sharp division between transitives and intransitives, reference to which has been made frequently in the preceding sections [177 ff.], finds perhaps its clearest expression in the contrasting sentence-types in which the respective verbs are used. The sentence in which the predicate is formed from an intransitive is equational. The verbal element involved is participial and hence impersonal [169]. Reference to the actor is possible only by means of associative pronouns which are non-morphologic elements in included position [213 ff.]; e. g., *un* + *a* + *llàn* Mit. I 115 "coming-they-and," or more freely "and/so they come."

This subjective construction characterizes also other participles, including those from transitive roots; cf. the forms in *-i* and *-u* [170 f.], the derivative participle with *-kk-* [186], and the conjunctive in *-ewa* [192]. But a sentence thus construed cannot include both actor and goal of action.

Where goal and source of action are involved at the same time we are confronted with transitive forms which are not employed as noun-predicates. The goal is then expressed by the subject-case and the source of action, if independently stated, by the agentive [150]. An indication of the agent must be

[254] This is best exemplified by *-n* which is so common in jussive forms; its interpretation as an associative [196] leaves little room for doubt.

included with the predicate. This reference is accomplished by means of pronominal elements which agree with the agentive. They are, accordingly, agent-suffixes. To go a step further, the essentially possessive character of these suffixes is virtually assured by the juxtaposition of *-if*, *-v*, *-i/ya* with nouns: *-a/eg*, *-u/o*, *-ya* with verbs [84] and [195].

The following illustrations will show the difference in the pronouns used in actor-action sentences on the one hand, and goal-source-action sentences on the other:

(a) *ḫi-il-lu-ši-i-it*[*-ta-*]*a-an* (19) ^I^*Ma-ni-e-ta* Mit. II 18 f. "talk-past-I-and Mane-to," i. e., "and I talked to Mane"

(b) *a-nam-mil-la-a-an un-du še-e-ni-iw-wu-ta gu-lu-ša-ú* ibid. 56 "thus--they-and then brother-my-to tell-past-by-me," i. e., "and these (things) then I told my brother"

In (a) 1 p. sg. is expressed by *-tta-* and no goal is involved. In (b) the same person is marked by written *-a-ú* and the goal is indicated by the associative *-lla-* attached to the introductory particle. When the subject-marker of (a) is attached to the verbal root of (b) the bearing of the sentence is changed completely; e. g., *gu-lu-u-ša-a-at-ta-a-an* Mit. IV 5 "I was told by him." The associative pronoun now marks the goal, not the actor; the source of action is indicated by the added *-a-* which refers to 3 p. sg. The analysis of the latter form is (A) + (2) + (10) + (B^2 [*-tta-* + *-àn*]); in (b) the associative which marks the subject is attached to the first word of the sentence.

It follows that agent-suffixes cannot be used with intransitives; where this is done the form in question is factitive. "I arrive" would be **un* + *a* + *tta-*; **ú-na-ú* "I am brought," or the like; cf. ^I^*Ma-ni-e-ra-la-an ú-na-aš-še-na* Mit. II 116 "those (things) brought along by Mane." This instance shows that agent-suffixes can be used also with finite forms nominalized by *-še* [164]. Finally, the gerund in *-ae* [166] may construe with the agentive, in which case the former has the value of an agent-suffix of 3 p.

In surveying the available agent-suffixes we shall find them differentiated not only for person but also according to the type of form which they are employed to modify. One set of these suffixes is used with the indicative (which Hurrian does not mark by special elements); another set is employed with jussives. A few remaining suffixes are as yet difficult to classify.

195. Agent-suffixes with indicative forms. These elements are found with the present, perfect, and future. The first person is the same in all three; the second is attested definitely in the perfect, and may be presumed to have been the same also in the present and future, for which no examples happen to be available. For the third person we have *-ya* or *ia* in the present, but *-a* in the perfect and future. All three elements were correctly related to their respective persons in the early days of Hurrian studies; cf., e. g., Messerschmidt, Mitanni-Studien 109 ff. and Bork, Mitanni-Sprache 48 f. But the view that they functioned as subjective pronominal endings is no longer tenable.

It is important to note that we do not have a separate set of suffixes for the plural. In all likelihood the plural was indicated by the addition of a special particle to the given singular element [198], just as was done to pluralize the case-endings and the possessive suffixes with the noun [142].

(a) 1 p. Present: *ta-a-na-ú* Mit. II 92 "done-by-me" (or "doing-my") freely "I do";[255] *ta-a-ta-ú* ibid. I 75 "I love." Perfect: *a-ru-u-ša-ú* Mit. III 11, IV 34 "I gave"; *ḫa-šu-u-ša-ú* ibid. II 7 "I heard." Future: *ka-te-e-ta-ú* Mit. III 99 "I shall communicate."

When negated, this person results in forms which are written with *-i-uw-wə* [53]. In the present we have the complex *ú-ú-ri-uw-wu-un-na-a-an* Mit. IV 56 "so/then I do not want him";[256] the perfect yields *ḫi-su-ú-ḫu-ši-uw-wə* ibid. 33 "I did not vex, annoy"; *ku-zu-u-ši-uw-wə-la-an* ibid. 46 "I did not detain them"; and *ta-a-nu-ši-uw-wə* ibid. II 113. The negated force of these forms, which was discovered by Messerschmidt (Mitanni-Studien 85), is not open to doubt. As for the person involved, only the last-cited instance is dubious on account of its fragmentary context. In the three remaining examples the 1 p. is plainly involved. Moreover, there are independent phonologic grounds for seeing in this complex a fusion of the negative element *-wa-* [186] and the ending of 1 p.; cf. [84].[257]

We have to note here also two Bogh. forms as possible analogues: *ka-ti-i-ú* VIII 61 obv. 10 and *pa-a-li-uš-še-ni-w*[*ə*] ibid. 3. The context is indecisive and does not preclude the 2 p.[258] There is, however, no evidence of a diphthong in 2 p., whereas the alternative interpretation involves only the contrast Bogh. *-i-ú* : Mit. *-a-ú*. The nominalized form in *-še* is well known in Mit.; cf. *a-ru-u-ša-uš-še-ni-e-we* III 41 "of the one given (in the past) by me."

Finally, there is the problem of the phonetic character of the ending *-a-ú* (and possibly *-i-ú*). It was pointed out in [35] that postvocalic *-ú-* may

[255] To avoid the awkwardness of the passive forms in English I shall use the free translation in the following instances, except for one example (b) where the active would call for a relative sentence and thus give a false picture of the form as a whole. But it cannot be stressed too strongly that this is merely a concession to English usage.

[256] Cf. JAOS 59. 300.

[257] In favor of interpreting these forms as referring to 1 p. is the statement of Friedrich, BChG 37. The dissenting view of Goetze, Lang. 16. 135 f. n. 44, is bound up with his position concerning the *i*-form; cf. [170a].

[258] As translated by Ungnad, Kulturfragen 4/5 p. 27; Friedrich, BChG 38 n. 1, is inclined to view *ka-ti-i-ú* as 1 p.

represent both [w] and [f]. Since the digraph *-ww-* stands for a voiceless labial spirant [53] and the combination *-ww-* + *-ú-* gives us the same spirant doubled [83], it would appear that *-ú-* was used for single [f] or [w̥]. Accordingly, I normalize the suffix tentatively as *-af*, although *-aw* (or *-aw̥*) cannot be disregarded entirely. The form *a-ru-u-ša-ú-ú-un* Mit. III 2 (and others like it) would thus represent *ar* + *ož* + *af* + *un*.[259]

(b) 2 p. Cf. the perfect forms *ge-pa-a-nu-u-šu-u-uš-še* Mit. III 69 "sent by thee in the past"; *ku-zu-u-šu* ibid. IV 45 "thou hast detained." The former would seem to indicate that the suffix in question was *-o*. As against this we have *tap-pu-šu-ú* Mit. IV 104, which is preceded by *it-ti-i-wa-an*, apparently with the 2 p. possessive; note also *ki-i-bu-šu-ú-uš-ši* ibid. IV 38. These two examples plainly show [u], but it is altogether doubtful whether they contain the suffix under discussion. Nevertheless, the quality of the agent-suffix of 2 p. cannot be established with confidence.

(c) 3 p. Present: e.g., *ta-a-ni-a* Mit. III 81 "he does"; *ta-a-ti-a* ibid. I 74 "he loves"; *ka-ti-ya* VIII 61 rev. 7 "he communicates." Perfect: *ge-pa-a-nu-u-ša* Mit. III 107 "he sent"; *ka-du-u-ša* ibid. I 96 "he communicated"; *ta-a-a-nu-u-ša* ibid. 85 "he did." Future: *ge-pa-a-ni-e-ta* Mit. II 54 "he will send"; *ka-til-li-ta* ibid. IV 21 "he will communicate"; *ša-a-ri-il-li-e-ta* ibid. 124 "he will demand."

196. Agent-suffixes in jussive forms. Here again all three persons appear to be represented, the third more abundantly than the other two. It is noteworthy that the elements to be discussed are entirely different from the corresponding morphemes just cited. There was thus an external distinction between indicative and modal forms as far as reference to the agent was concerned.

1 p. For the ending *-i/e* see [189], and for the combination *-ili* cf. Messerschmidt, Mitanni-Studien 83 and especially Friedrich, BChG 36 f. That this person should be associated intimately with the cohortative is not surprising. Command to oneself is emphasized in a similar manner in other languages.[260]

[259] If we are right in our phonetic analysis of the agent-suffix of 1 p. as *-af* (Bogh. *-if*), comparison with the possessive *-if* of 1 p. [144] appears to be indicated. In partial support of this I would cite the identical orthography *-əw-wə* which in Mit. serves both the possessive and the negated agent-suffix of 1 p. [84]. An analogous connection in 2 p. is not impossible in view of the *-u/o* in the verbal form and the wr. *-w/b* in the nominal. Finally, the 3 p. is *-y/ia* in the present (see above) and *-i/ya* with nouns [146]. Since the agent-suffixes identify the originator of a given action attributively ("done by X") and not subjectively ("X does"), there is no functional discrepancy between the respective suffixes of agent and possessor.

[260] Cf., e. g., the special "cohortative" with 1 p. in Hebrew, Bergsträsser, Hebräische Grammatik, Verbum 45 ff.

The pertinent occurrences with *-il-* have been cited in [189]. The final *-e* is suggested by *ta-a-du-ka-a-ar-ri-e* Mit. II 85. This would point to a phonetic distinction between the jussive form in question and the *i*-form of the participle (cf. *pí-sa-an-du-ši-i-it-ta-a-an* Mit. IV 9, *pa-aš-še-ti-i-dan* ibid. III 116), so that one form could not be mistaken for the other in speech; e. g., the participle *ḫill* + *i* Mit. I 84, 93) <*ḫill-* would contrast with the jussive **kulle* ibid. II 12, III 49, IV 1 <**kul* + *il* + *e*. At all events, the jussives in question are all clear in their reference to 1 p. in Mit., where alone the context is capable of analysis. Note especially *ḫa-ša-a-ši-il-li-i-il-la-a-an* (**ḫažaž* + *il* + *i* + *llàn*) Mit. IV 29 "they will not be heeded by me," in a sentence where 1 p. is essential but not otherwise indicated.

The same jussive suffix occurs also with the element *-kk-* in *ka-ti-ik-ki* Mit. IV 17, where 1 p. is beyond doubt, and apparently also *ta-a-du-ka-a-ru-ši-ik-ki* ibid. II 79, in obscure context; cf. [186]. The former may be translated "I shall keep on telling"; the latter "I shall have shown affection." From Bogh. we have *a-ru-ú-ši-ik-ki* VBoT 59 ii 12, where 1 p. is rendered likely by the preceding *šu-u-ta*, apparently "to me."

2 p. Cf. [193 (i)]. The two pertinent occurrences (*a-ri* Mit. I 51 and *zu-zi-la-ma-an* EA 170. 11) unfortunately lack the support of completely intelligible contexts. Nevertheless, *zu-zi-* is glossed by an Akk. imperative of 2 p. and has to be interpreted accordingly, with Bork (OLZ 1932. 377) and Friedrich (BChG 22); *a-ri* would be an analogous instance (contrary to Goetze, Lang. 16. 131 n. 28).

How the participle **ar-i* could be distinguished from such an imperative is hard to tell. A relevant form in an intact passage might solve the problem.

3 p. This person is indicated in the sg. of transitives by *-en* joined to stems in *-i*; e. g., *a-ri-en, na-ak-ki-en* [193 (f)]. The same suffix appears with plurals but the underlying stem ends this time in *-id(o)*; see ibid. and [184]. We know, however, that *-en* and *-n* were used also with intransitive jussives of 3 p.; cf. [193 (e), (g)]. Moreover, forms which appear to be jussive and construe with 3 p. are found with *-m, -andi,* and *-andin* [189-90] as distinct from *-en*. Apparently, therefore, there was no special agent-suffix for 3 p. jussive, the appended elements being probably emphasizing associatives rather than independent agent-markers.

197. Other agent-suffixes. The ending *-i-a-a-ma* has been assigned by Friedrich (BChG 38 ff.) to 3 p. of the negated future. E. g., [I]*Ma-ni-en še-e-ni-iw-wu-uš pa-aš-ši-a-a-ma* Mit. IV 55 "Mane by my brother will not be sent"; similarly, *gu-li-a-a-ma* ibid. II 106, IV 21, 27 <*kul* "say." Reference to 3 p. and construction with the agentive are clear in this form (cf. also *ir-nu-u-ḫu-ši-a-a-ma* Mit. III, 67, 70); but its formal analysis (one morpheme or more?) is in doubt.

In *ge-lu-u-šu-a* Mit. I 89 and *ni-i-nu-šu-ú-a* ibid. IV 7 (the latter with an accompanying agentive) we have a suffix which appears to refer to 3 p. Goetze, JAOS 60. 222 takes it as negated 3 p. of the indicative. In both instances, however, the context is obscure. The same is true of *ta-a-na-aš-du-en* Mit. IV 15, also with an agentive.

Agreement with plural agentives is apparent in *pa-pa-na-šu-uš a-du-da* Mâri 5. 8 and *ši-we-na-šu-úš nu-du-un-da* ibid. 9. The meaning and analysis of the predicates remain to be determined.

(11) Other modifiers

198. Indication of the plural. In *ú-ú-ra-ú-ša-aš-še-na-a-ma-a-an ti-we-e-e*^{MEŠ} Mit. I 80 the first form consists of the verbal root *ur* "desire" + agent-suffix of 1 p. *-af* + *ža*, followed by the nominalizing *-še*, the attributive pl. element *-na*, and the associative *-màn*; the whole form is in agreement with the next form "words, things." If it were not for the interposed *-ža-* the whole phrase might be rendered "the things desired by me." But the added element cannot be ignored. Now the subject of the sentence which immediately precedes is *-til(l)-a* "we," which is stated no less than five times. The same subject is plainly wanted with the transitive form before us; it could be referred to only by means of an agent-suffix. We do find such a suffix in the spelling *-a-ú*, which in all its other numerous occurrences signifies 1 p. sg. It follows that the required plural is indicated by the *-ža*, evidently a pluralizing element.[261] The whole form may now be translated "those desired by us."

The same suffix is to be sought in the four instances of intr. jussives 3 p. pl. cited in [193 (h)]; e. g., *itt-ai-ža-llàn* Mit. IV 52 "let them go."[262] Although the associative *-lla-* "they" which follows is pleonastic, such double marking of the plural is known also from the noun; cf. *enna-žuš* [150]. It will scarcely be hazardous to connect the above *-ža-* with the pluralizing *-ž-* which is amply attested in nominal forms [142].

199. The element *-š* (which may stand for *-ž* or *-š*) of such forms as *pí-su-uš-ta-iš* Mit. I 80 or *i-su-di-iš* Mâri 5. 6 will be listed with the associatives [223]. To take it as a marker of 3 p. sg. imperative with Goetze (Lang. 16. 134 n. 36) is inadvisable on account of the dependence of the above Mâri form upon *inu* "as" (loc. cit.). Note, moreover, the nominal form *e-ti-iš* Mit. III 122.

261 So already Messerschmidt, Mitanni-Studien 36.

262 Cf. JAOS 59. 294.

200. Two other suffixes found with verbal forms appear to be associatives because the same suffixes seem to be used with nouns as well. One is *-ki* in <*ḫi-li*>*-šu-ki* RŠ Voc. I 16; it is a gloss to the Sum. form meaning "he did not speak" and is preceded by *ḫi-li-šu* ibid. 15 "he spoke." This element has been compared (Br. 569), perhaps rightly, with the *-k* of the alphabetic forms *arẑnnk* RŠ X 4. 28, and the like; cf. [190 n. 241]. There are also forms in *-ki* from Bogh.; cf. *zu-úr-ki* XXIX 8 ii 41 and also iv 13, 20; *zu-ru-un-ki* ibid. ii 42, *zu-ru-uš-ki* ibid. 44; *i-ku-du-ud-ki ku-la-mu-du-ud-ki* ibid. 43, and similarly ibid. iv 14-15, 22; *ḫa-bal-ki* ibid. 13, 20!; *la-a-bi-eš-ki* XXVII 42 obv. 33. In view of the fact that these words are not intelligible it would be rash to assert that they all include the same final morpheme; but the inherent probability of such an assumption cannot be disregarded. Now *zur-ki* and its cognates with *-n-* and *-š-* point to a nominal construction. If this is true, it is possible that the suffix was used both with verbs and nouns. With all due reservations I suggest for *-ki* the value "un-, non-."

The other suffix is *-lam*, which is even more problematic than *-ki*. It too occurs in RŠ and in Bogh.: *e-di-la-lam* Voc. II 29, 30 (verb); *ki-ra-ri-in-ni-lam* XXIX 8 iii 27 (alongside the nominal form *ki-ra-ri-in-na* ibid. 26); *še-ḫa-lu--la-am ka-aš-lu-la-am* ibid. 53 (cf. *še-ḫa-la-a ga-aš-la* ibid. iv 8); *šu-wə-ni-lam* ibid. iv 14 and *šu-ú-wə-nu-u-la-am* ibid. 17. All that we can say about this form is that it occurs in XXIX 8 iv 14-22 in a context which includes forms in *-ki* and two possible negated jussives *gul-du-bi-in ap-pu-bi-in* (ibid. 19-20), cf. [120]. I suggest provisionally the meaning "without"; cf. [212].[263]

201. Since the nominalizing element *-še* may be placed after an agent-suffix (cf. [164]) its proper place in the suffix-chain must be position 11. But the various nominal elements which may follow *-še* have manifestly no connection with the verb. The subsequent treatment of a form in *-še* is like that of any simple nominal root.

4. Associatives

202. As was pointed out in [98], the associatives are non-morphologic elements that are not to be confused with other bound forms, whether derivational or relational. They differ from the free particles chiefly in that they require the support of a radical element, much as do the enclitics of Indo-

[263] The RŠ Voc. fails to help us in this instance; I 28 seems to equate *-la-* with Sum. n u "not." But the Sum. column is damaged in lines 29-30 which cite Hurrian *-lam*. Furthermore, the preserved Sum. [. . .]n i g . g a (29) finds no counterpart in the corresponding fragment published by Landsberger in AfO 12. 135. The same fragment lists i n . g a r . r a which may have been the reading of RŠ Voc. II 30. We have seen, however, [193 n. 251] that in line 32 the Hurrian scribe skipped an entry in the original so that this particular part of the Vocabulary is not reliable.

European. Our reason for avoiding the term "enclitic" in the present instance is based on the marked tendency of Hurrian to employ more than one associative in the same word; it is unlikely that in these circumstances all the elements in question were atonic.

The choice of the supporting form depends on the requirements of word-order. That form may belong to any one of the three attested parts of speech, namely, noun, verb, or particle. A suffix which is known to occur with more than one of these is automatically to be classified as an associative; connection with free particles alone leads to the same result inasmuch as such particles cannot take morphologic suffixes. In a given suffix-chain the associatives are placed after bound modifiers of the noun or verb.[264]

For purposes of classification the associatives may be arranged into: (a) the particle *-n*; (b) syntactic connectives; (c) subjective pronominal suffixes; (d) deictic elements; and (e) miscellaneous.

(a) The Particle *-n*

203. This element has been linked generally to that case-form which is customarily regarded as "accusative" or "object-case," but should be interpreted instead as the "subject-case" [149]. But Friedrich (BChG 9) is inclined to regard this *-n* as incidental to the actual case involved,[265] on the ground that the "accusative" lacks this ending in the majority of instances. Goetze has shown, however, (JAOS 60. 217 ff.) that when *-n* is not used with its noun it is found elsewhere in the same sentence. While admitting that the element in question and its plural counterpart *-la* differ from other case-endings in the looseness of their contact with their respective nouns, he assigns to them, nevertheless, the function of object-markers, i. e., case-endings (ibid. 223).

The argument from form alone would be enough to refute Goetze's interpretation. If we ignore for the moment the subject-case, as the one under dispute, there are seven other cases in Hurrian [148 ff.]. In none of these can the case-ending be omitted from its noun and substituted with another word in the sentence. If the elements which characterize these seven forms are case-endings, it follows that *-n* and *-la* must be something else, especially in view of the positional rigidity of the morphologic elements in Hurrian. Furthermore, *-la* is attested as the pl. subject of intransitives [218]; but

[264] The one exception to this statement would be the use of *-n(n)* in the "stative" forms in *-a*, cf. [156], provided that this medial element has been linked correctly with the particle *-n*. However, the forms in question are properly phrase-words, in which *-n(n)-* may have come to be used medially as a result of secondary developments.

[265] Followed by Speiser, BASOR 74 (1935) 6; JAOS 59. 291, 307.

none of the ascertained case-endings is used with verbs in this or any other capacity.[266] It is plain, therefore, that neither *-n* nor *-la* can be regarded as distinctive nominal suffixes of any kind. Their free combination with any part of speech marks them automatically as associatives. The problem is to define their function. For the time being we are concerned with the use of the element *-n*.

204. Before we survey the internal evidence, however, there is one further detail of form that may prove significant. Owing to its comparative freedom from morphologic restrictions *-n* may be found attached to established case-endings. E. g., with gen. sg.: *at-ta-iw-wu-ú-e-en ša-a-la* Mit. III 35 "father--my-of-*n* daughter"; *am-ma-ti*[267] *-iw-wu-ú-e-e-en ša-a-la* ibid. 37; *ša-a-li-iw--wu-ú-e-en* ibid. 76; *še-e-ni-iw-wu-ú-e-en* Mit. II 118, III 11; with gen. pl. *^{d}e-en-ni-iw-wa-a-še-e-en* Mit. II 77.[268] Furthermore, the same element is joined to verbal forms. E. g., with transitives: *a-ru-u-ša-ú-ú-un* Mit. III 2; *ḫa-šu-u-ša-ú-(ú-)un* ibid. IV 9, 92, *ḫa-šu-u-ša-un-na-a-an* ibid. 6; *ḫi-il-li-in* Mâri 6. 10, 11, *ḫi-il-lu-ši-i-in* Mit. IV 4; *ḫi-ši-im-du-a-ú-ú-un* ibid. II 115; *ḫi-i-šu-ša-a-un-na-a-an* ibid. IV 106; *pa-aš-ši-na-an* ibid. III 112; *ú-ú-ri-iw-wu--un-na-a-an* ibid. IV 56. With intransitives: *ú-na-a-an* Mit. III 13, *ši-ra-a-an* ibid. 14; *ú-ru-uk-k[u-u-u]n* ibid. II 95, *ú-ru-uk-ku-un-na-ma-an* ibid. III 124. It is difficult to see how the same form could be marked as genitive and be provided at the same time with an accusative ending, without an intervening *-ne-* to relate it to its head. If such an un-Hurrian combination should be admitted for the moment, for the sake of the argument, the force of *-n* would be that of an objective pronoun rather than a case-element. This interpretation becomes imperative when we consider the forms in *-n* attached to transitive verbs. But the same ending is found also with intransitives, as we have seen. An attempt to explain accusative pronominal suffixes with intransitives is apt to raise more problems than it would solve.[269]

205. More positive light on the function of *-n* is to be gained from an examination of the various sentence-types in which the element occurs. One example will be cited for each characteristic occurrence.[270]

[266] Unless, of course, the verb is nominalized by *-še*.

[267] Meaning "grandfather."

[268] I have not listed here possible *n*-forms after cases in *-a* (dative, locative), such as *ti-ši-iw-wa-an* Mit. II 55 [125], to avoid the objection that the final element may in reality be the connective *-an* [211]. The above instances with the genitive are sufficient for the purpose and they cannot be questioned.

[269] Thus Goetze is compelled to asume "that the Hurrian language instead of 'he comes' actually says 'there is coming on his part'" (Lang. 16. 137). Even if this should be so, we are no longer dealing with a case-element but with a pronoun.

[270] The appended translations have to be literal and come as close to the original as

(1) *aš-ti-i-in še-e-ni-iw-wu-ú-e* (34) *a-ru-u-ša-ú* Mit. IV 33 f. "wife-*n* brother-my-of given-past-by-me"

(2) *un-du-ma-a-an še-e-ni-iw-wu-ú-e-en aš-ti a-ru-u-ša-ú* Mit. III 11 "now--then-and [271] brother-my-of-*n* wife given-past-by-me"

(3) *še-e-ni-iw-wu-uš-ša-a-an aš-ti ša-a-ru-u-ša* ibid. III 1 "brother-my-by--and wife requested-past-by-him"

(4) *a-ti-i-ni-i-in ta-še-e-en id-du-u-uš-ta* Mit. I 90 "thus-indeed(?) present-*n* gone (past tense)"

(5) *un-du-ma-a-an še-e-ni-iw-we-e-en pa-aš-š[u-ši]* Mit. II 107 "now-then--and brother-my-*n* having-sent"; cf. [170a]

(6) *un-du-u-un* I*Ma-ni-e-na-an še-e-ni-iw-wu-ú-e pa-aš-ši-i-it-ḫi* Mit. IV 35 "now-then Mane-*n*-and brother-my-of-envoy"

(7) *un-du-ma-a-an a-ru-u-ša-ú-ú-un* Mit. III 2 "now-then-and given-past--by me-*n*"

(8) *še-e-ni-iw-wu-uš-ša-a-an wə-ri-e-ta a-ru-u-ma-a-aš-šu-ḫi!-ḫa ú-na-a-an* ibid. 13 "brother-my-by-and known-future-by-him gift-laden(??) arriving-*n*"

These eight types will be contrasted with

(9) *i-nu-me-e uš-ḫu-ni ši-ḫa-a-la* XXIX 8 iv 27 "as-it silver clean"

(10) *un-du-ma-a-an in-na-me-e-ni-i-in še-e-ni-iw-wu-ú-e aš-ti ú-ni-e-et-ta* Mit. III 21 "now-then-and behold(?)-she-indeed(?) brother-my-of wife arriving-future"

Type (1) shows *-n* with the subject which is the first word in the sentence; the predicate is a transitive form with agent-suffix. In type (2) we have the same sentence-type except that the subject constitutes the third word; here the *-n* is attached to the preceding genitive. It is to Goetze that we owe the demonstration of the movable nature of *-n*, depending on word-order [203]. From (3) it may be inferred that when the first noun, which would normally take *-n*, carries the connective *-àn* (wr. *a-a-an*) the expected particle is omitted; the same principle is apparent in (8), where the first two words represent an analogous clause. An actor-action sentence with an intransitive as predicate is cited in (4); the first word is a particle followed by the associative *-nin*; [272] the next word is the subject which ends in *-n*. In (5) we have a similar sentence

our analysis permits. No doubt, the renderings are far more rigid and committal than the originals ever were to the speakers. This might be avoided in part in a free translation. But that would be begging the question so long as the morpheme under discussion remains to be determined. It has been left untranslated for the time being, which adds considerably to the awkwardness of the translation.

[271] This does not imply that I take *-màn* (here translated "and") as a single morpheme. I accept Goetze's view that this form was composite, but cannot follow him throughout in the identification of the second component; cf. [212a].

[272] Goetze analyzes *-nin* as *-ni* + *n*, but the evidence fails to bear this out; cf. [220a].

save for a noun-predicate in *-i* [170] instead of the above *a*-form. The subject, again in second position, takes *-n*. The first word is a particle followed by *-màn*. A third example of an equational sentence-type is given in (6); the predicate is this time a noun. The element *-n* is used twice: with the introductory particle and with the subject, a personal name which supports, in addition, the connective *-an*. In view of the fact that the three sentences cited in (4)-(6) are syntactically parallel it is probable that (4) and (5) conceal a second *-n*, on the analogy of (6). Since the place of that *-n* would be with the first word of the sentence, and since in both instances the first word ends in an associative with final *-n*, it appears that the independent morpheme *-n* was omitted here just as it was in (3) under similar conditions.[273] A different position is given the same element in (7); it is attached to the predicate, a transitive form with agent-suffix. It is important, however, to note that this clause lacks a noun, the subject (*aš-ti*) carrying over implicitly from the preceding clause.[274] A similar situation confronts us in (8) where *-n* is attached to the predicate, this time an intransitive form. The implicit subject (again *aš-ti*) is stated five clauses back.[275] Finally, (9) is an example of an actor-action sentence which dispenses with the use of *-n*; the actor is introduced by the associative pronoun of 3 p. *-me* which stands in apposition to a noun in the subject case. In view of this instance, type (10) might be viewed as analogous. For here too the subject is anticipated by *-me-* and the predicate is an *a*-form. To be sure, the first two words have independent *n*-endings which could take the place of the morpheme *-n* as is the case in (4) and (5). But they need not have been involved in this double duty any more than was the *-màn* of (2).[276]

Type (9) calls for one additional remark. It is our only example from Bogh., all the remaining ones being from Mit. It should be emphasized that such regularity as can be observed in the use of *-n* obtains only in Mit. The

[273] The important observation that the types listed above as (4)–(6) employ two *n*-suffixes is again due to Goetze (Lang. 16. 136 f.). But the matter needs further study. According to Goetze's analysis of *-màn* as *-ma* + *n* (JAOS 60. 219) type two would have two *n*-suffixes, although in his own opinion it should not have more than one (Lang. 16. 136 under form III).

[274] This sizeable group (for other instances cf. [204] under verbs + *n*) was overlooked by Goetze in his treatment of the *n*-form.

[275] The whole sentence consists of six clauses all of which share the subject *aš-ti*. The same rule is in force when the subject follows the verb thus inverting the normal order: *pa-aš-ši-na-an še-e-ni-iw-wə* Mit. III 112; *pa-aš-še-ti-i-dan* (117) *še-e-ni-iw-wə* ibid. 116 f.

[276] In other words, the connectives which are written *-a(-a)-an* and *-ma(-a)-an* and the element *-nin* may take the place of the morpheme *-n*, apparently because all end in the consonant *-n*. Their mere presence, however, does not imply automatically that the morpheme *-n* is to be understood.

other Hurrian sources are not consistent in this respect [209]. Consequently, our inquiry can refer only to Mit. usage until the remaining material has been adduced for comparison. The probability exists that the employment of *-n* as reflected in the above types (1)-(8) is a special dialectal development.

To sum up, the morpheme *-n* confronts us in all the principal sentence-types of Mit., namely: with transitives construed with goal and agent (including also jussive forms, cf. [193]); in actor-action constructions where the predicate is a participial form; in nominal sentences proper; and lastly, in sentences whose subject is carried over implicitly from a preceding clause, unless it follows the verb in inverted clauses, the *-n* being then placed after the verb. The question may also be posed whether the use of the pronoun *-me* (which in Mit. alternates with *-ma-* [277]) cancels the expected *-n*; and if so, whether the same holds true of the other associative pronouns.[278]

206. We are now prepared to inquire into the function of the morpheme *-n* in Mit. where it is found in all the characteristic sentence-types. It can be seen at a glance that the prevailing construction is equational. This is immediately apparent in the nominal type (6) and in the participial types (4)-(5), (8) [-(10)]. It is no less true, however, of the sentences employing transitive predicates with agent-suffixes. For these suffixes mark the actor as instrument or possessor [195 n. 259]. The forms in question are thus in themselves attributive rather than predicative. What is lacking, therefore, in the various sentence-types of Mit., so far as the respective elements have been analyzed and translated, is an indication of the verbal copula. Now all of these sentences involve the morpheme *-n*, whether actually present or replaced by an associative in *-n*. The completeness of this circumstantial testimony surely justifies the assumption that the morpheme *-n* has the force of a verbal copula.

[277] For the variation *-me-* : *-ma-* in Mit. see [217]. It is interesting that the other occurrences of *-me* in Bogh. (XXIX 8 iv 16, 27) also figure in *n*-less sentences. In Mit. the situation is ambiguous in that the clear occurrences of this pronoun (when combined with *inu-* "as," cf. Friedrich, BChG 24 f.) are all followed by *-nin*; but the sentences concerned do not contain an independent *-n*. Now *-me/ma-* may combine also with other particles (ibid. 25), again with *-nin* following. In three of these instances there are independent *n*-forms in the given sentence; two with *inna-manin* (Mit. II 6 f.) and one with *ai-manin* (Mit. IV 55). But in all three *-n* is employed with personal names, which follow independent rules with regard to *-n* as we shall see [209].

[278] Viz., *-tta-* "I," *-til(l)a-* "we," and *-l(l)a-* "they." Unfortunately, all are followed in Mit. by associatives which end in the consonant *-n*. We are not in a position to determine with confidence how many such occurrences imply the morpheme *-n*. Bogh. *i-nu-ud-da* VIII 61 obv. 3 is in a fragmentary context with no *-n* present in the extant part; but the evidence of Bogh. is inconclusive for our present purposes, as has just been pointed out.

Let us first review the eight typical sentences of Mit. as listed above, through the medium of freer translations, substituting the copula (in italics) for the previously untranslated *-n*.

(1) My brother's wife *has been* given by me
(2) Now than my brother's wife *has been* given by me
(3) A wife *was* requested by my brother
(4) And so the present *has* gone
(5) Now that my brother *has* sent a mission [279]
(6) Now then *it is* Mane *who is* my brother's envoy
(7) Now then (the wife) *has been* given
(8) It will *be* discovered by my brother that (the wife) *has* come laden with gifts (??)

The respective subjects and predicates are now linked together. Even the repeated *-n* of (6) is consistent with this interpretation. The same locution is suitable in (4)-(5) as well, if the repeated *-n* may be regarded there as a certainty. Throughout we find this morpheme to mediate between subject and predicate linking the one with the other into a unified utterance. In short, *-n* functions as a predicative particle.

207. This interpretation can now be checked in a series of marginal instances: where *-n* has caused difficulty hitherto; where the need of a predicative particle is not immediately apparent but the alternative assumption of a connective *-an* would be altogether gratuitous; and finally, where the element is used medially in forms ending in the "stative" *-a*.

Mit. IV 32 f. reads: *ti-ša-a-ma-a-an še-e-ni-iw-wu-ú-e šuk-kán-ni-en* (33) *pa-ti ti-we-e-ni-en ḫi-su-ú-ḫu-ši-uw-wə.* Goetze (Lang. 16. 135) translates "there was no anger in the heart with regard to my brother's . . . word." The sense would be "in [my] heart"; in that case, however, we should expect the possessive suffix *-iw-wə*, cf. Mit. II 55, III 75, 85, 86, 89, 95, IV 111. When *tiž(a)-* is not used with a possessive it refers invariably to the accompanying noun; in the present instance we can have only "and the heart of my brother." Even more troublesome is the repeated *-n* (with *šukkanne-* and *tiwene-*). Goetze is compelled to analyze the latter form as *tiwe-nin* and to explain the unparalleled orthography with *-e-* (as against the otherwise invariable *-ni-i-in* [220a]) as due to the vowel of *tiwe-* (JAOS 60. 219 n. 11). In reality, the particle *-ne* is essential in this form in order to relate it to the attribute *šukkanne-* [137]. We cannot but translate "I did not vex my brother's heart even by what is a distant word"; cf. [127].

Another case in point is the conjunction *a-i-i-in* "whether, if" [128].

[279] Cf. [127] and [170a].

The underlying meaning is apparently "is it that . . . ?" without reference to subject; contrast *a-i-ma-a-ni-i-in* and *a-i-la-an* (Friedrich, BChG 39 n. 1) with associative pronouns which refer respectively to 3 p. sg. and pl.

In Mit. II 57 (and analogously IV 111) *ti-ši-iw-wa-an* cannot, from the context, contain the connective *-an*. The form constitutes an independent circumstantial clause. It must mean "in what is my heart." A series of *n*-forms confronts us in the difficult passage Mit. II 104 f.: *ul-lu-ḫu-ug-gu-ú-un še-e-ni-iw-wu-ú-an t[i-w]i[-i-y]a-[an]* [280] *ul-lu-ḫu-ug-gu[-ú-u]n* (105) *šu-u-wa-an ti-wi-iw-wa-an gu-li-a-a[-ma-a]-an*. For the verbal form, a negated future 3 p. sg. [197], cf. Friedrich, BChG 38 ff. It ends in *-n*, as do also the other six words of this sentence. The verb might be suspected of ending in a connective. However, the agent (*ᴵMa-ni-eš*) is implied from a preceding clause, hence this *-n* should be judged as an instance of type (7), cf. [205]. The two occurrences of *ul-lu-ḫu-ug-gu-ú-un*, in parallel clauses, have each an *-n* that is clearly predicative. The rest consist of dative forms in *-n*, the case being evidently the one with which the goal in question construes. I would translate: "A different [281] (thing) from (dat.) what is my brother's word, a different (thing) from what is my word, he will not say." Thus the same explanation consistently applied accounts for every occurrence of *-n* in a sentence which uses this particle with each single word.

The use of the same morpheme in forms which end in the "stative" *-a* has already been discussed [156]. It was pointed out that *tiža-n(n)-a* Mit. I 107 may very likely correspond with Akk. *ša/kī libbišu* "according to his heart," here and similarly in Mit. III 14, IV 34 "in accordance (*-a*) with what is (*-n[n]-*) the heart (of my brother)." There are other examples of this construction [156]. The use of the particle before non-associative elements may be ascribed to the special composite character of this particular form.

Finally, there are passages in the Akkadian letters of Tushratta which sound like translations from Hurrian in their suggestion of an underlying *-n* in the value of "it is that . ." The clearest instance is EA 19. 27 f.: *an-nu-ú šu-ú šu-ur-ru-um-ma ša i-na be-ri-ni ša it-ti a-ḫa-meš ša ni-ir-ta-na-'a-a-mu*

280 The supplementation is based on the contrast *še-e-ni-iw-wu-ú-e-ni-e a-a-i-e-e* (3 p. possessive) : *šu-u-we-ni-e e-ti-iw-wu-ú-e* (1 p.); cf. [69]. With the 1 p. clearly stated in the second clause, the first clause requires the suffixed pronoun of 3 p. with the head-noun. Friedrich (Kleinas. Sprachdenkm. 19) reads *t[i-w]i-[-i-]t[an]*, which can scarcely be justified from the standpoint of context. What is more, the extant traces are just as suitable for *-[y]a-* as they are for *-t[an]*, and there is enough room in the text for an added *-[an]*.

281 The supporting root in *ul-lu-ḫu-ug-gu-ú-un* is in all probability *oli* "other"; cf. also *ul-li-wa-a-en* Mit. III 95 "let him not alter," to judge from the sequel "my heart let him not vex."

"it is this, plainly,[282] that between us, that jointly, that we continually maintain mutual affection." This passage is just as unidiomatic in Akkadian as is its translation into English, chiefly because of its thrice-used *ša* "that"; but in Hurrian *n*-forms would be entirely in order in these respective positions. While nothing can be proved from such departures from normal style, they are useful as incidental illustrations of linguistic usage established on ample internal evidence.

208. It should not be assumed, however, that the predicative particle *-n* must be connected with a morpheme meaning "to be" just because it may serve as the verbal copula. For such a step there is not the slightest evidence. On the contrary, present indications point to an underlying pronominal value. Thus the ending of *itt-ai-n* "let him go" [193] appears to refer in some way to 3 p sg. In the agent-suffix *-en* of the jussives [ibid.] we again find reference to the same person, the plural being marked here by the independent morpheme *-ido-*. The *-en* of the intransitives [ibid.] is in itself indecisive since such form are impersonal, the actor being stated only with the subject. Another suggestion to the same effect is inherent in the contrast *šu(w)a-nn-aman* "it-all" : *šu(w)a-lla-man* "they-all" [114a].[283] If the comparison of the predicative particle with the pronominal element just suggested is a valid one, the semantic development of such a pronoun into a copula would have striking parallels elsewhere. Cf., e. g., the Aramaic phrase which means literally "we they His servants," for "we are his servants"; or in Hebrew "Thou He the God," for "Thou art the God." [284]

A pronominal origin of the particle *-n* would explain also the curious fact, pointed out by Friedrich (BChG 25), that Hurrian *-me-/-ma-* "he, she, it" cannot be attached to verbs, unlike the other suffixed personal pronouns. If *-n*, which is frequently attached to verbs, was itself pronominal in origin and syntactic function, there was no need in that position for another pronoun of 3 p. The cumulative evidence, slight as it is, seems thus to favor the assumption that the morpheme *-n* was ultimately identical with a pronominal (deictic?) element which is still recognizable in that capacity in a small number of occurrences.

209. As against the regularity in the use of *-n* in Mit., to which source we have restricted ourselves temporarily, there is, however, the evidence of the

[282] In Nuzi *šurrumma* has the value of "promptly, forthwith." In the present passage an asseverative expression is required with somewhat different emphasis. For the term cf. Oppenheim, Orientalia 7 (1938) 378; J. Lewy's equation of *šurrumma* with *širumma* (RES 1938. 69) is incorrect, cf. JAOS 59. 295 n. 25.

[283] Cf. Friedrich, BChG 4 f.

[284] See JAOS 56 (1936) 30 f.

remaining Hurrian sources which does not yield a uniform picture. Whether this is due to a difference in contents and consequent disparity in style (cf. Friedrich, BChG 14), dialectal specialization in Mit., or to other causes not now apparent, we are unable to say at present. It is certain, at any rate, that sentences which would require *-n* in Mit. are found elsewhere without that particle. Thus, e. g., there is not a single *n*-form in the first eleven lines of the perfectly preserved text Mâri 5, or in the first nine lines of Mâri 1 which happen to be intact. On the other hand, we find *al-la-a-e-en* ibid. 16 and *Ša-ú-úš-a-an* ibid. 17, in uncertain context. The archaic text XXVII 38 iv, which deals with historic-mythological kings, yields results that are equally unsatisfactory. In one marked paragraph (lines 8-12) all subjects are in the *n*-form; in another (lines 19-21) no *n*-form appears. The same apparent lack of regularity confronts us in XXVII 1 ii 36 ff., in connection with proper names. In the marked paragraph 41-45 *-n* is used in ᵈ*Iš-ḫa-ra-an* (43), but not with any other name of deity, although there is no evident contextual or phonetic difference that might account for the disparity. But in 46-47, and similarly in 48-50, the subjects are in the *n*-form while the dependent adjectives and genitives are *n*-less.[285] In these circumstances no decision can be reached and it would be futile, therefore, to multiply examples. Quite likely, the religious text from Mâri and Bogh. reflect earlier grammatical conditions than does the secular Mitanni letter. If this is true, the assumed specialization of a pronominal element into a predicative particle was a comparatively late development.[286]

(b) Syntactic Connectives

210. This term refers to associative elements which are used to connect words or clauses, as contrasted with vowel-connectives which are purely phonologic and secondary [85]. The syntactic connectives are *-àn/an* and *-ma-*; the two together yield *-màn/man*.

The normalized transcription with *-à-* which I have followed in accordance with the principle stated in [92a] is meant solely as an arbitrary indication of full writings, as in *-a-an, -ma-a-an*. The alternative resort to *-ā-*, which is favored by Friedrich (BChG 14 ff.), does not appear justified in view of the serious doubts which attend the problem of vowel-quantity in Hurrian [22].

[285] The published god-texts from Nuzi (AASOR 16 46-50) include ᵈ*Ištar ir-wi-in* ibid. 48. 18 and ᵈ*A-zu-[i-iḫ-ḫé* ᵈ*]Za-ar-wa-an* ibid. The latter instance parallels the *n*-forms in XXVII 1 ii 46-47 in that an attribute precedes. This use corresponds to that of the attributive particle *-ne* rather than that of the *n*-form in Mit.

[286] [V. Brandenstein, ZA 46. 91 n. 1, speaks of a serial particle *-n* without giving his reasons. It is clear, however, that in Mit. *-n* is not to be confused with the connective *-an*.]

It is probable, but by no means certain, that double writings of the vowel in the above forms were meant to express a particular form of stress. Until more evidence can be adduced, however, the diacritic mark employed here in instances which call for normalized transcription is to be regarded as no more than an indication of full spellings.

211. The connective *-àn/an.* This particle has been fully discussed by Friedrich (loc. cit.). His views may be summarized as follows: *-àn* is found to connect (1) nouns, e. g., *ᴵGe-li-i-an ᴵMa-ni-en-na-a-an* Mit. II 7 " Keliya and Mane " (both nouns in the *n*-form); (2) verbs, e. g., *ḫa-šu-u-ša!-ú-ú-un pí-sa-an-du-ši-i-it-ta-a-an* Mit. IV 9 " I heard and was happy "; (3) whole clauses, e. g., *ᴵGe-li-i-a-aš-ša-a-an pa-aš-ši-i-it-ḫi<-iw>-wu-uš ti-we an-ti gu-lu-u-u-ša* [287] Mit. I 83 " And Keliya, my envoy, has told this word." It may be added that *-àn* is used frequently to introduce paragraphs as it does in the foregoing instance.

Two further important observations are made by Friedrich (ibid. 16 f.). One is that this connective may be used to introduce subordinate clauses, in which case it has the value of our " so, that, then," and the like. I would add in this connection a citation from Mit. III 111 ff.: *a-i-ma-a-ni-i-in šuk-ku-u-um-ma-ma-an du-ru-be* (112) [*še*]*-e-ni-iw-wu-ú-a* KUR *u-u-mi-i-ni-i-ta wə-še-wa pa-aš-ši-na-an* [288] *še-e-ni-iw-wə* (113) *šu-ú-ú-ta* [289] " if, nevertheless, a danger to my brother's country should arise, so that (*-an*) my brother sends to me." The other point concerns the frequent use in Hurro-Akkadian texts of the Akk. conjunction *ù* " and " with values that correspond to those of Hurrian *-àn* but are not idiomatic in Akkadian. There is no need to cite fresh instances of this wide-spread usage.

Where the vowel of this connective is written double there is no difficulty in distinguishing the morpheme in question from the particle *-n.* It is different, however, when a given word ends in plain *-an.* Unquestionably, *-an* can represent the predicative particle when joined to a form in *-a*; cf., e. g., [207]. An analogous instance is *šuk-kán-ni-e-wa-an ti-wi-i-wa-an e-ti-i-dan* Mit. II 84 " because of thy *š.* word "; here the repeated connective would be entirely out of place, whereas the predicative particle is in order; since the first two words are datives (governed by *edi-*) and thus end in *-a,* the added *-n* must appear

[287] The spelling of the verb with double *-u-* is based on Friedrich's collation, Kleinas. Sprachdenkm. 12 n. 1. Curiously enough, Friedrich himself reverts to the spelling with triple *-u-* in BChG 15, perhaps through an oversight.

[288] The instance of *paš-še-ti-i-dan* ibid. 116 is not analogous because a parenthetic clause precedes.

[289] For an earlier analysis of the whole passage cf. JAOS 59. 313 ff. For *šukko-mmaman* see now [127].

as *-an*. On the other hand, the connective is assured in ^I^*Ge-li-ya-na-an* Mit. IV 36, 37 and ^I^*Ar-te-e-eš-šu-pa-na-an* ibid. 36, not only because the predicative element is already expressed by the first *-n* (*Keliya* + *n-*) but also on account of the double writings in the parallel ^I^*A-sa-a-li-in-na-a-an* ibid. 36, 37; the full spelling surely marks *-àn*. Accordingly, *pa-aš-ši-na-an* Mit. III 112 yields *paš* + *i* + *n* + *an*, the last element being the connective and not the predicative particle with secondary *-a-*. But there is little to guide us in the case of *a-i-la-an* Mit. II 58, 75, IV 20, 26, 128 and *e-ta-la-an* ibid. IV 45 where both the *-a-* and the preceding *-l-* of the pronoun are marked by the orthography as simple sounds [128]. One might adduce *a-i-i-in* [207] as presumptive evidence in favor of *-n*; but conclusive proof is lacking.

Outside Mit. *-àn/-an* is relatively rare; cf. Friedrich, BChG 21; in a number of instances it is difficult to decide between the connective and *-n*. In general, a definite syntactic pattern is apparent with regard to the connective only in Mit., just as it is evident in the same source in the use of the predicative particle [209].

212. The connective *-ma-*. In JAOS 60. 220 Goetze has advanced the assumption that Mit. *-man* is a composite form and that the connective force generally ascribed to it belongs in reality to *-ma*, the final consonant representing an independent morpheme. Although Goetze has not backed up his thesis with direct evidence, resting it merely on his analysis of the form *-man* (for which see [212a]), the statement concerning *-ma* is correct.[290] The available evidence is abundant.

For Mit. the significant passage is IV 119 f.: *a-ti-i-ni-i-in ma-a-an-na-til-la--ma-an u-ru-uḫ-ḫi-iš-til-la-a-an* (120) *kàr-kut-tiš-ti-la-a-an a-ti-i-ma-ni-i-in k*[*ar?-*]*ra-a-ti-la-an*, etc. It is not necessary to attempt a translation of the whole passage. Its grammatical analysis will suffice. Apart from the two particles *adi-* we have here four actor-action forms with *-dil*(*l*)*a-* "we" as the subject in each instance. The scheme is "*adi-nin* we are x, x, *adi-ma-nin* we are x." Since *adi-nin* may be rendered "thus-indeed(?), *adi-ma-nin* cannot be far from "thus, too, indeed(?)" [128]. The identification of this *-ma-* with the pronominal element *-me-/-ma-* [217] is precluded by the emphatically announced "we."

Another case in point is *i-i-e-na-ma-a-ni-in* Mit. IV 21. The combination of the pl. *-na* with a sg. pronoun *-ma* would be wholly without parallel, the more so since a resumptive *-lla-* "they (are)" follows. The troublesome *-ma-* (which Friedrich, BChG 25, had to label as exceptional) can only be the connective for "and, but."

[290] That Goetze is aware, however, of the independent evidence is shown by his reference in RHA 35. 106 n. 17.

However, two instances of this kind could not be accepted as valid proof. But there are many others, chiefly from Bogh. First let us compare *i-nu-me-e uš-ḫu-ni še-ḫa-la ga-aš-la ta-a-ki* XXIX 8 iv 8 "As it, the silver (is) clean, pure(?),[291] firm,"[292] with *i-nu-me-e uš-ḫu-ni ši-ḫa-a-la ḫi-iš-ma ta-ki-ma ki-ra-ši-ma* ibid. 27 f. "As it, the silver, (is) clean, bright(?), firm(?)-*ma*, lasting-*ma*."[293] In the first sentence the epithets are connected asyndetically. In the other, the last two words[294] are followed by -*ma*, which cannot but be a connective "and, also," or the like. Accordingly, *a-na-am-mi-im-ma* ibid. 17 will mean "so, too," which is precisely what the context requires. One other passage from the same text may be cited because it is significant for its apparent pattern, although the individual words are obscure: *pa-a-e-ni-ib šu-ra-ag-ga-an-na ki-ra-ri-in-na* (26) *te-bi-e-na ki-ra-ri-in-na ḫa-a-ḫi-ip-pí-na-ma* (27) *ki-ra-ri-in-ni-lam* ibid. iii 25 ff. "for thy p.[295] the *š*. (are) *k*., the *t*. (are) *k*., and/but my *ḫ*. (are) not/without(?) [200] *k*." If the scheme here suggested is correct, -*ma* could well carry the nuance of "but."

Of the numerous other occurrences of -*ma* only few can be cited here. Cf. *a-ru-wa-al-la-e-na* XXVII 38 i 16: *a-ru-wa-al-la-e-na-ma* ibid. 17 (in the concluding line of the paragraph); *i-ya* ibid. ii 15, 21, iii 1: *i-ya-ma* ibid. ii 17; *ḫa-wu$_u$-ru-u-un-ni* ibid. 46 i 19: *ḫa-wu$_u$-ru-un-ni-ma* ibid. 28; *pu-du-ú-li-ma-aš-ši-na-ša* ibid. 29: *pu-du-ú-li-ma-aš-ši-na-ma* ibid. 25; from Mâri note *i-ša-am-ma* 1. 30, 2. 14. The particle *i-ya*, *i-ya-ma* cited above (cf. [130]) may be paralleled by *iy*, *iy* + *m* RŠ X 4. 60, 15 [ibid.]. If so, a number of other RŠ forms in -*m* (cf. Br. 572) may be pertinent. Furthermore, the particle *a-i-ma* VIII 61 rev. 12, 14 is also a probable analogue. But Mit. *a-i-ma-a-ni-i-in* III 111, IV 9, 54, 59 is ambiguous in that its -*ma*- may represent a pronoun (cf. Friedrich, BChG 39 n. 1). This is less likely in Bogh. where the only attested pronominal form of this type is -*me-e* [217]. Finally, the negating element -*yama* [197] may well contain a final -*ma*. How a connective "and, also, but" came to be associated with particles like *ai*- is a matter for speculation alone. A possible analogue with -*an* might be sought in *a-i-la-an* and *e-ta-la-an* [211].

Bogh. furnishes also evidence for a particle -*m*. Once again examples are numerous, though few are at all suggestive. Cf. *a-ru-ši-el-la-a-im* XXIX 8 iii

[291] See Goetze, RHA 35. 106.

[292] Ibid. n. 18.

[293] This word is clearly to be connected with *kirai* "long"; cf. JAOS 59. 296 n. 29.

[294] The -*ma* of *ḫi-iš-ma*, however, is not pertinent since -*m*- is here part of the stem; cf. [176 (12)] and the personal names with *Ḫižm*-; the meaning "bright" is guessed from the parallelism with *kažl*-.

[295] The meaning of *pae*- has to be approximated on the basis of the parallel *i-ti-ib* ibid. ii 29, 31, 35, iii 34 "for thy sake," or the like; *pa-a-ḫi-ib* ibid. iii 21 "in thy direction, for thy advantage(?)"; the final -*b* is surely the poss. suff. 2 p.

34: *a[-ru-ši]-in-na-a-in* XXVII 42 rev. 13; *id-ki-ta-an-nim* XXIX 8 ii 29, 31, 35 (i. e., **idk* + *id(o)* + *anni* + *m*), in association with *ši-nim* ibid. 30, 34 (also *ši-ni-im* Mâri 1. 18; *šnm* RŠ X 4. 16, 46, 59, 62); *a-ba-ri-im nu-ri-i[m]* XXIX 8 iv 2: *nu-u-ri-ḫi-ni a-pa-ar-ri* ibid. 4; note also *šu-uk-ku-ut-ta-at-ta-am* VIII 61 obv. 12: *[šu-u]k-ku-ut-ta-at-ta* ibid. 13, and cf. *aš-ti-im* ibid. 14. Perhaps the most significant pair is *an-ti-na-mu-uš-ša-am* VII 58 ii 9 (in association with other forms in *-m* and *-ma*): *šar-ru-mu-uš-ša-an* ibid. 10. For unless the above endings are due to phonetic interchange (for which evidence is lacking), or to a slip of the scribe, we have here presumptive evidence for the equation *-m* = *-an* "and," which would be followed necessarily by the further equation *-m* = *-ma*.

The element *-m* is found also in Mâri. In addition to *ši-ni-im* (above) cf. *Pa-ḫi-ip-pí-ni-im* 1. 32, *Te-šu-ba-am* 1. 34, *Ši-mi-ge-e-ni-im* 1. 36, *Ú-šu-um* 2. 18, and *Ki-ib-li-im* 2. 20.[296] It is worthy of notice that in the enumeration of gods which is given in 1. 31 ff. the first name (*É-a*) is without suffix while the remaining three end in *-m*. It is difficult to escape the conclusion that this use of *-m* proves it to be a connective. Since there is nothing in the Bogh. material to oppose such a conclusion, the identification of *-m* with *-ma* should now be valid for both Bogh. and Mâri, inasmuch as the evidence from one tends to confirm the other. Consequently, *-m* may be regarded as an apocopate variant of *-ma*.[297]

One final observation is now in order. Mit. employs the connective *-àn/-an* very frequently, whereas the use of *-ma* is limited there to a few possible occurrences. The converse distribution is apparent in Bogh. and Mâri, where *-ma/-m* predominate. Preference for the given connective seems thus to reflect dialectal specialization.

212a. The form *-màn/-man*. The limited use of the connective *-ma* in Mit. is true, however, only in so far as it serves as word-final. There can now be no doubt about Goetze's assertion (JAOS 60. 220) that Mit. *-ma-a-an* and *-ma-an* consist of *-ma* followed by another morpheme. It is the identity of this latter element that still remains to be decided.

Friedrich (BChG 18 ff.) sees in the form with full spelling of the vowel a phonologic variant of *-àn*, thus accepting the view of Messerschmidt (Mitanni-Studien 54; cf. also Bork, Mitannisprache 25 f.); according to this view *-m-* is used to avoid the hiatus which would be caused by adding *-àn* to a form ending in a vowel other than *-a*. There are, however, instances of wr. *-ma-a-an* after *-a*, e. g., *du-be-na-a-ma-a-an* Mit. II 29, and the like (BChG 18 n. 3). Friedrich would solve the difficulty by positing *-man* "but" (ibid. 20), which

[296] Cf. [75].

[297] For other suffixes with apocopated *-a* cf. [90].

may be written also *-ma-a-an*; the full writing of the vowel after a form in *-a* would thus represent the morpheme for "but" and not "and."

This involved explanation is no longer necessary. Alongside *-àn/an* Mit. (and to a much lesser extent Bogh.; see ibid. 21) used also *-ma* + *àn/an*. The full writing of the vowel was in accordance with the practice obtaining for the latter element and did not in itself imply the meaning "and" as against "but." We have seen [212] that both meanings could be expressed by *-ma* alone; it follows that the composite *-màn/-man* had the same range. As far as Mit. usage is concerned *-màn* was a free variant of *-àn* when a dissimilar vowel preceded; while thus favored by phonologic conditions, the form was not in itself secondary since its *-m-* represents an independent morpheme. Where a contrastive value was required, such as "but, however, that is," or the like, *-màn* or *-man* would naturally be used; note especially *tup-pí-ma-a-an ni-ḫa-a-ri-i-we* Mit. III 36, 38 "tablet, that is, of dowry."

There still remains the problem whether *-man* (wr. *-ma-an*) could result from the combination *-ma* + the predicative *-n*. Goetze (loc. cit.) would extend this particular combination to *-màn* and *-man* in general. But this is surely going too far. We have seen that *-màn* can be used where no predicative particle is required [205 (2) and n. 273]; similar instances could be added. Possible combinations with *-n* should be looked for only in the form *-ma-an*. Even this form is just as ambiguous, however, in this respect as is the uncompounded *-an* [211].

A safe instance of *-ma* + *an* is found in the common *šu(w)anna-man* "it-all" and *šu(w)alla-man* "they-all" [114a]. The vowel of the final element is always written single and, moreover, the position of these forms at the end of the sentence speaks against a connective. Finally, the Akk. equivalent of the plural form is *gabbišunū-ma, gabba/išinā-ma* [ibid.], i. e., an independent appositive clause. It is reasonable, therefore, to interpret *šu(w)anna-man* as "being all of it" and *šu(w)alla-man* as "being all of them." The identifying particle *-ma* of the Akk. forms is not without interest. It suggests a similar force for the *-ma-* in the corresponding Hurrian form. What is all the more striking is the fact that Akk. *-ma* is also used at times as a connective. But this extensive parallelism in function should not be taken as an indication of ultimate etymological identity. Although the respective Hurrian and Akkadian particles were homophones, their many-sided correspondence is doubtless due to no more than a very remarkable coincidence.

(c) Subjective Pronominal Suffixes

213. The elements which comprise this group have recently received exhaustive treatment at the hand of Friedrich (BChG 22 ff.), following the very suggestive remarks by Bork (AfO 8. 310).[298] In view of Friedrich's treatment a few additional occurrences will suffice to round out the discussion. As regards the syntactic interpretation of the forms, however, an important change will have to be made. According to Bork (loc. cit.) they are objective suffixes which may also serve the dative; at the same time a subjective use is possible, so that *-tta-* may mean "mir, mich, ich." Friedrich obtains the same results for the 3 p. pl., in that *-lla/e-* is interpreted "eos, eas, ea" in the great majority of instances, but as the marker of nominal predicates (hence in the subject-case), or even a mere plural ending, in others (BChG 30-32). This alleged syntactic diversity is not borne out by the facts. It would be in marked contrast to the established relational uniformity which characterizes all the other groups of forms, especially that which indicates case-relations. More significant is the fact that such occurrences of the associatives in question as are at all translatable refer consistently to the subject-case alone [194]. This situation obtains regardless of the nature of the supporting root: noun, particle, or verb; in the case of the latter it is demonstrable with transitives and intransitives alike. Note, moreover, that the marker of 3 p. sg. [217] is never joined to verbs, where it would normally be expected if it served indeed as object-suffix. Pertinent illustrations will be given with each individual suffix.

Another important feature of the elements under discussion is their evident predicative character. Thus **ene-na* > *enna* "god-ones, gods" (with the attributive pl. ending *-na*) contrasts with *eni-llàn*, lit. "god-they-(are)," i. e., "the gods (are)," cf. [218]. This inherent function of the subjective pronominal suffixes is given added emphasis in Mit. where they are always followed by *-(a)n* (unless replaced by *-àn, -man, -nin* [205]), often in contexts that do not seem to justify the use of a connective.

214. *-tta-* "I." The two key passages, both cited by Friedrich, are:

(a) *i-n[u-ú-]ut-ta-a-ni-i-in ḫé-en-ni še-e-ni-iw-wu-uš ta-a-ti-ya* Mit. I 74, freely "As my brother now loves me"

(b) *an-du-ú-a-at-ta-a[-an] te-u-u-na-e tiš-ša-an tiš-ša-an pí-su-uš-te-e-wa* Mit. II 54 f. "so that I should rejoice over it very very much"

In (a) *-tta-* is construed with the agentive and a transitive verb followed by the agent-suffix of 1 p. In (b) we have actor-action construction as required in clauses with *-ewa* [192]. The function of *-tta-* as subject-case in (b) is self-evident.[299] In (a), however, the assumed objective character of the

[298] While the discovery of the pronominal values of *-tta-* and *-me-* is due to Bork, it was left to Friedrich to lend it authority by a thorough investigation of the pertinent material. It is to Friedrich that we owe also the demonstration that *-t/dil(l)a-* is another member of this group.

[299] Goetze (Lang. 16. 132) cites Lat. *taedet me* for the analogous use of the accusative

pronoun is due to viewing the verb as active and the *š*-form of the accompanying noun as nominative. Not to rely for the moment on the argument concerning the agentive case [150], let us examine another pair of instances:

(c) *ḫi-ya-ru-uḫ-ḫa-a-at-ta-a-an te-u-u-na še-e-ni-iw-wu-uš ge-pa-a-nu-en* Mit. III 73 f., in Friedrich's translation [300] "and much gold let my brother send to me"

(d) *ḫi-il-lu-ši-i-it*[*-ta-*]*a*[*-a*]*n* [I]*Ma-ni-e-ta* Mit. II 18 f., for which Goetze proposes two alternative translations: "there was an instruction of mine to Mane," [301] or "an instruction was given by me to Mane" [302]

If these translations reflect at all the syntactic relations of the original, *-tta-* has the value of a dative in (c) and of a genitive or instrumental in in (d). It cannot be emphasized too strongly that the problem is not translational alone. The question is whether *-tta-* can express the indirect object (c), the possessive (d), the subject (b), and the direct object (a) without any formal modification on its own part. It does not matter by what name we designate the respective relations. The question is whether these relations were at all distinguished in Hurrian when applied to the pronouns in question. We know that they were strictly differentiated with the noun.

Since the various case-relations are not interchangeable in the noun, where they are marked by individual suffixes, and since the actor-action sentence cited under (b) yields the subject-case for *-tta-*, it is necessary to inquire whether that case fits the other three sentences as well. The results follow:

(a) "As-I-indeed(?) now brother-my-by (am) loved-by-him"

(b) "about-it-I-and much very very rejoice-should"

(c) "gold-I-and much brother-my-by sent-shall-be," i. e., "May I be sent much gold by my brother"

(d) "having-told-I Mane-to," or "I have told to Mane"

The answer is plain. By assigning the same function to *-tta-* in the several sentence-types cited we obtain a pattern that is consistent throughout. The suffix represents the subject in actor-action sentences. When goal and agent occur with transitive verbs, the same suffix marks the goal. It becomes now apparent why *-tta-* is the only method whereby Hurrian marks the first person with intransitives, whereas the transitives have a wholly unrelated agent-marker for the same person [195 (a)]. Cf. *man*(*n*) + *atta-* VIII 60 obv. 19 (and rev. 20); Mit. I 56!, II 85, III 63, 65 "I am" [125], and especially

with affective verbs; *-tta-* would be an instance of the same general type. However, there is nothing comparable in the case of *ḫill-ož-i-ttàn* (below d) and its analogues.

[300] Op. cit. 22. Cf. also [222] for an approximately similar context (Mit. III 87), but with *-tta-* joined to the adverb *tišan*.

[301] Lang. 16. 135. [302] Ibid. n. 42.

ḫa-šu-u-ša!-ú-ú-un pisand + ož + i + ttàn Mit. IV 9 "it was heard by me and I rejoiced about (it)," where the difference between agentive and subjective constructions is witnessed in two consecutive forms. Since the Hurrian sentence announces its subject as early as possible [244], *-tta-*, being an associative, is attached as a rule to the first word of the given clause, whatever that word may be: particle, as in *inu + tta + nin* (above, a),[303] *anammi-tta-man* Mit. III 62, 64 "thus-I-and;[304] noun, as in *še-e-ni-iw-wu-ú-ut-ta-a-an ši-la-a-ḫu-šu-uš-ti-wa-a-en* Mit. IV 41 "by my brother (**ženifuš-ttān* [75]) may I not be refused(?)," and similarly, Mit. II 50, III 71. In common with *-tilla-* and *-lla/e-* we may have *-tta-* at the beginning of the clause and then repeated as the subject of an impersonal verbal form; e. g., *a-nam-mi-it-ta-ma-an še-e-ni-iw-wu-ú-a ge-pa-a-nu-ul*[[*-ul*]]*-li-e-wa-at-ta-a-an* Mit. III 62 f. "and thus to my brother I shall (continue) sending." When not anticipated in this manner, *-tta-* follows the impersonal form as the sole subject of the clause; cf. *pisand + ož + i + tta-* (above), which approximates our included construction: "having-rejoiced-I," i. e., "I-rejoiced." It is perhaps this approach to "conjugation" that is responsible for placing the pronoun after a transitive verb with agent-suffix, even though that verb observes the normal order and does not open a clause; e. g., *ni-i-ru-pa-a-ta-e gu-lu-u-ša-a-at-ta-a-an* Mit. IV 5 "promptly told-by-him-I," i. e., 'promptly he told me."

One occurrence of *-tta-* appears to contradict the above statement that this form invariably indicates the subject-case. It occurs in a lengthy passage (Mit. IV 41-4) which has to be quoted at length: *pa-aš-ši-i-it-ḫi-iw-wə-la-an* (42) *še-e-ni-iw-wu-uš šu-ra-a-maš-ti-en na-ak-ki-en ti-wa-a-at-ta-a-an gu-ru-ú-wə* (43) *še-e-ni-iw-wu-ú-e-ma-a-an ge-e-el-ti ni-i-ri-še ḫa-ši-i-li* (44) *pí-sa-an-ti-iš-ten-na-a-an tiš-ša-an še-e-ni-iw-wu-ú-e-ni-e-we ge-el-ti-i-we.* Before this passage is analyzed it is well to cite its close Akkadian parallel (EA 17 47-50) which has been pointed out by Friedrich, BChG 23 n. 1: *aḫi-ya ḫa-mu-ut-ta li-me-eš-šir-šu-nu-ma te-e-ma ḫa-mu-ut-ta li-te-ru-nim-ma ki-me-e šul-ma-an-šu ša aḫi-ya e-še-im-me-ma ù a-ḫa-ad-du* "let my brother dispatch them (the envoys) promptly so that they bring word to me in order that I may hear about my brother's good health and rejoice."

To return now to the Hurrian passage, Friedrich's version of it is as follows: "And my messengers let my brother hasten and send away, and the word of ⟨*kuru*⟩ to me, as well as my brother's well-being let me hear soon so that I rejoice about my brother's well-being very much."[305] If this interpretation of the clause *tiwa-ttàn kuruwə* is right then *-tta-* does represent in this instance the indirect object. However, in parallel phrases the suffixed pronoun indicates the goal only; cf. *ti-wa-a-al-la-a-an šur-we še-e-ni-iw-wu-ú-ta ka-ti-ik-ki* ibid. 16 f. "word-they *š.* my-brother-to telling-repeatedly-

---

[303] Bogh. *i-nu-ud-da* occurs unfortunately in a broken context.

[304] For *n*-forms added to the pronouns under review cf. [213], final paragraph, and see Goetze, Lang. 16. 130 n. 23.

[305] BChG 15 + 23.

-by-me," or "I shall keep on telling *š*.-words to my brother" [196]; similarly, *ti-we-e-ma-a-an šuk-ku še-e-ni-iw-wu-ta kul-li* Mit. IV 1 "Let me, furthermore, tell a word [306] to my brother," and *ḫa-ša-a-ši-il-li-i-il-la-a-an* ibid. 29 "they will not be heeded by me" [196]. In the present instance, then, we expect *tiwa-llàn* [307] or *tiwe-màn*, not *tiwa-ttàn*. The sentence as a whole causes trouble in other respects, too. In line 43 *-màn* as a word-connective (with Friedrich) would be without parallel, for elsewhere such connectives join the respective nouns directly; but *tiw-* and *keldi* are separated from one another by two other words. In these circumstances we have to regard *-màn* as a sentence-connective and *tiwa-ttàn kuruwə* as a separate clause. This gives us a complete parallel with the Akkadian passage: "so that they bring word to me" followed by "in order that (Hurrian *-màn*) I may hear (Hur. *ḫaž-il-i/e*)." How *tiwa-ttàn kuruwə* comes to tally with Akk. *ṭêma . . . litêrūnimma* is hard to tell. A verbal form *kuruwə* would be wholly without analogy, hence *tiwa-ttàn* should somehow express the predicate. Was *tiwe* [308] *kuruwe* an action-form meaning "to hear in return"? In that case the clause would signify "that I hear in return," *-tta-* being its subject. But guesses of this kind are of little benefit.

Incidentally, the verb-sequence *ḫa-ši-i-i-li pí-sa-an-ti-iš-ten-na-a-an* also causes difficulty. When a transitive form is followed immediately by an intransitive or participial construction, the latter marks the first person by means of *-tta-*; cf. *ḫa-šu-u-ša!-ú-ú-un pi-sa-an-du-ši-i-it-ta-a-an* "I heard and rejoiced" (see above) and *še-e-ni-iw-wu-uš ge-pa-a-nu-en* (above c) *wu-ur-te-ni-it-ta-a-an* Mit. III 74 "let my brother send so that I should be pleased(?)." [309] Accordingly, we expect **pisand-ešt-en-ittàn*.[310]

I have deemed this lengthy digression necessary because this is the only passage in which a suffixed pronoun raises syntactic problems in an otherwise intelligible context. Our analysis has not led to any positive results. It has shown, however, that by any other interpretation *-tta-* would still be problematic. It is clear, at any rate, that this particular instance cannot be used as yet to back any deductions whatsoever.

215. *-t/dil(l)a-* "we." The voiceless form of the initial sound can be posited only after certain other consonants [76]. Nearly all the clear instances of this suffix are postvocalic; the form is then *-dil(l)a-*, the dental appearing invariably in single writing. Occurrences after a consonant are cited in [183 n. 228]. For the variation *-ll-/-l-* see [22, 92a, 128].

The meaning of this associative was discovered by Friedrich, BChG 32 f.

[306] Or "word-it" if *-ma-* represents the pronoun of 3 p. sg., cf. [217].

[307] For the analysis of this form cf. [218 n. 321].

[308] For the change of *-e* > *-a-* before *-tta-* see [65].

[309] A. Gustavs (AfO 8 [1932] 131 f.) would connect this stem with Bogh. *wur-* and the onomastic element *Wur-*. However, *wu*$_u$*-ri-li* VIII 60 rev. 14 betrays a transitive root; its probable connection lies with Mit. *wər-* "know." On the other hand, the *-t/den-* of *wur* + *den* + *i* + *ttàn* (with sg. subject) points to an intransitive [184]. The attributive *-ne* which underlies Gustavs' rendering "das versprochene" is out of the question on morphologic grounds (the form would have to be **wurra-še-ne-*). Bork (ibid. 310) manages to find in *wurdeni-* the word for "iron" without worrying in the least about the resulting anomaly in word-order.

[310] For the connective vowel *-i-* which is abundantly attested in identical position cf. [85].

As regards its syntactic function, the argument developed in connection with *-tta-* applies with equal force to the present pronoun and to the other pronouns of this group. A few examples will suffice to indicate the usage.

(a) As goal of transitives with agent-suffix: *a-nam-mi-til-la-a-an* [^{d}*T*]*e-e-eš-šu-pa-aš* ^{d}*Ša-uš-kaš* ^{d}*A-ma-a-nu-ú-ti-la-an* (77) ^{d}*Ši-mi-i-ge-ni-e-ti-la-an* ^{d}*E-a-a-šar-ri-ni-e-ti-la-an ma-an-šu-u-til-la-a-an* (78) DINGIR^{MEŠ} *e-e-en-na*[-*š*]*u-uš ti-ši-a-ša-an tiš-ša-an tiš-ša-an ta-a-ta-aš-ti-te-en* Mit. I 76 ff. "so-we--and Teshub-by Shaushka-by Amon-by-we Shimige-by-we Ea-sharri-by-we [311] these-by-we [312] gods-by hearts-their-in [313] very very loved-much [314] -several-by--shall-(be)"; or in other words, "(As now my brother loves me, and as I myself now love my brother,) so let Teshub, Shaushka, Amon, Shimige, and Easharri, (all) these gods love us both very much in their hearts."

(b) As subject in actor-action sentences: Note first *ge-ra-aš-še-n*[*a-ša-til-l*]*a-a-an ša-wa-al-la-ša pí-su-un-ni-en* ibid. 79 "we shall rejoice through the long years." [315] For other examples in undamaged context cf.: *ša-a-at-ti-la--an* [316] ... *iš-ta-ni-iw-wa-ša* ... (109) *ta-a-du-ka-a-ri-i-til-la-a-an* Mit. III 108 f. "We together . . . shall show affection . . . to each other"; add also *u-u-lu--u-ḫé-wa-a-ti-la-an* . . . *e-e-ši-iw-wa-a-aš-tan a-a-wa-ad-du-dan* Mit. II 11, as compared with *u-u-lu-u-ḫa-a-ti-la-an* . . . *e-ši-iw-wa-a-aš-tan* (17) *ma-a-an--nu-uk-ka-ti-la-an a-a-wa-duḫ-ḫa* Mit. III 16 f. These two passages cannot be translated in full because two of the words involved are still obscure. But the scheme is clear in both instances: "we do something (*oloḫ-*) for our (*-fašton*) heavens for some purpose (*awattu-dan*, which alternates with 'so that we are constantly [*mannukka-dilan*] in a state [*-uḫḫa*] of *awattu-*')." Note also the alternation of modal (*-ewa*) and non-modal forms which serve as predicates to *-dila-*.

In view of *-tta-* "I": *-t/dil(l)a-* "we": *-lla-* "they" (see below) it would be tempting to regard *-t/dil(l)a-* as *-tta-* (with zero-vowel) + *-lla-*, on the analogy of *tiwe-* "word": *tiwalla-* "words" [214] < "word-they (-are)." However, such a hypothesis would have to be rejected. The conclusive argument against it is the unvarying *-tt-* in the sg. pronoun as against the single *-t-* of the plural in identical position (after vowels). If the contrast was due

[311] The *-ne* of the last two forms imparts to the names an adjectival force which cannot be analyzed.

[312] See [125].

[313] For *-i(y)až-* "their" cf. [143]. For the predicative *-n* (lit. "in what is their heart") cf. [207].

[314] For the "extensive" force of *-št-* see [183]; for the *-id(o)-* which follows cf. [184, 196].

[315] The supplementation is explained in [167 n. 155].

[316] For the haplologic loss of *-di-* in **šatti-dilan* cf. [91].

to secondary developments we have no means of tracing them. At all events, we should expect the pluralizing morpheme to be *-na* or *-ž* rather than *-lla-*, which is a syntactic and not a morphologic element (see below [218]).

216. Indication of 2 p. No associative pronouns for 2 p. have yet been identified. This is not surprising, in view of the fact that *-tta-*, *-me/a-* and *-t/dil(l)a-* have been established only in recent years, on the basis of Mit. evidence. There is little likelihood of finding the corresponding element for 2 p. in the same source. In his letter Tushratta addresses his son-in-law almost invariably (save for the rare use of the independent *we-* "thou" [109]) in the third person: "My brother does/is so-and-so." With Mit. thus virtually eliminated, the necessary evidence would have to come from the remaining sources, fragmentary and obscure as they are. So far there is nothing that would justify so much as a plausible guess.

On the basis of the incomplete form [. . . *š*]*a-ú-?-ni-il-l*[*a-a-a*]*n* Mit. I 112 (which he reads [*pa*]*r* + *uš* + *a* + *u* + [*n*]*ni* + *ll* + *an*), Bork obtained a suffix *-nni* "to thee," which he then proceeded to find in a number of forms (now known to be agent-nouns [186] in *-nne*); cf. Mitannisprache 64 f. These findings were accepted by Gustavs who translated, e. g., *wu-ur-ra-an-ni* Mit. III 4 "er verspricht dir" (AfO 8 132).[317] While we know next to nothing about *-anni* and similar elements, which may or may not be analogous, it is certain that in *ta-a-nu-ši-wa-al-la-a-an-ni* Mit. IV 10 the second person is not expressed; this would seem to take care also of the other occurrences; cf. [221].

The particle *inu-* "as," which is found with known subjective pronouns (*-tta-* Mit. I 74, II 60; *-me-* ibid. I 13, 75, etc.; *-lle-* ibid. III 101), occurs once in the form *i-nu-ú-ru* in XXIX 8 iv 5. Unfortunately, the context is unintelligible and there is no way of determining whether the suffix in question is pronominal and, consequently, fills the vacant spot in the paradigm. The relative particle *ya/e-*, which also combines with subjective pronouns (*i-ya-at-ta-ma-an ta-a-nu-ši-ik-kat-ta-a-an* Mit. II 5 "that which I have been doing"; with *-me-* Mit. II 62, III 91; with *-lla/e-* Mit. I 96, 98, 104, etc.), is accompanied by *-ri* in *i-ya-a-ri* XXVII 42 obv. 17 and *-ra-* in *ya-ra-aš a-a-bi-ra-aš* XXV 42 v 7; cf. ibid. 43. 10 and XXVII v 26; cf. [150]. The comitative case cannot be involved here because its pl. form is *-žu* + *ra* [154] and not *-ra/ež*. For the present it would be gratuitous to hazard the guess that *-ru/i* means "thou" and **ra/ež* "ye." The two may not be related and neither has more than a semblance of analogic support for being regarded as a pronoun.

217. *-me-/-ma-* "he, she, it." The normal form is *-me-*; cf. *i-nu-ú-me-e-ni-i-in* Mit. I 13, 75, II 123, 125, III 97, IV 115, 121; *ú-nu-ú-me-e-ni-i-in*

[317] Bork, op. cit. 101 renders this form "Du mit Silber(?)."

II 66; from Bogh. add *i-nu-me-e* XXIX 8 iv 8, 16, 27. With the relative particle *ya/e-* [130] we get *ya-me-e-ni-i-in* [[-*in*]] Mit. III 91, *i-i-e-me-e--ni-i-in* ibid. II 62. There is also *in-na-me-e-ni-i-in* ibid. III 21. As for *-ma-*, we have the problem of distinguishing between the connective [212] and its possible pronominal homophone. It has been shown [ibid.] that *a-ti-i-ma--ni-i-in* Mit. IV 120 can contain only the connective *-ma-*; the same applies to *i-i-e-na-a-ma-a-ni-i-in* ibid. 21, where the pl. *-na* and an assumed sg. pronoun *-ma-* could hardly be tolerated side by side.[318] We must be suspicious, therefore, of the forms with *-ma-* even where an anticipatory pronoun of 3 p. would be in order.[319]

This does not mean, however, that we may dispense altogether with *-ma-* as a variant of *-me*. Apart from the fact that the same variation is attested in *ya/e-*, *-lla/e-* and *awenna/e-*,[320] the parallelism of *in-na-me-e-ni-i-in* Mit. III 21 and *in-na-ma-a-ni-i-in* ibid. 22 (and hence also ibid. 12) cannot be ignored. But many individual instances are bound to remain ambiguous.

The syntactic function of *-me/a-* can be seen from the following selected illustrations.

With transitives in goal-agent-action sentences:

[*i-*]*nu-ú-me-e-ni-i-in ḫé-en-ni še-e-ni-iw-wə i-ša-aš ta-a-ta-ú* Mit. I 75 "as-he--indeed(?) -(is) now brother-my me-by loved-by-me," or "as I myself now love by brother"; *i-i-e-me-e-ni-*[*i-i*]*n* (63) *še-e-ni-iw-wu-uš ge-pa-a-ni-e-ta-* ibid. II 62 f. "what-it-indeed(?) brother-my-by sent-future-by-him"

In actor-action sentences: *in-na-me-e-ni-i-in še-e-ni-iw-wu-ú-e aš-ti ú-ni-e--et-ta* Mit. III 21 "behold(?)-she-indeed(?) wife coming-future"; *i-nu-me-e uš-ḫu-ni ši-ḫa-a-la* XXIX 8 iv 27 "As-it the silver (is) pure"

218. *-l(l)a/e-* "they." For the vocalic alternation cf., e. g., *i-i-al-la-a-ni-i-in* Mit. I 96, 104, III 55, 57, IV 124: *i-i-al-li-e-ni-i-in* ibid. I 98, 111, II 19, 20, III 52, IV 30, and *a-a-el-li-e-ni-i-in* ibid. II 28. For the variation *-ll-/-l-* cf., e. g., *ur-ḫal-la-a-an pal-ta-a-la-an* Mit. IV 23, (29); [. . . .]*-na-a-ku-lu-uš--te-la-an pè-te-iš-te-el-la-a-an* ibid. II 24; cf. Friedrich, BChG 27 and see [88]. Bogh. shows a strong tendency toward apocopate forms [90]; cf. *nu-u-ya-al* XXIX 8 iii 30: *nu-i-wa-al-la* XXVII 42 rev. 12, which coordinates with *ḫa-zi-iz-zi-bal* ibid.

Friedrich's exhaustive treatment of this element (op. cit. 26-32) contains all the essential information. The only point that needs to be modified pertains to syntax; instead of seeing here a suffix which is ambiguous as regards case-relations we have in reality the pronominal associative of 3 p. pl. which refers

[318] Cf. [212].
[319] See also Friedrich's cautious statement on the subject (BChG 25).
[320] Cf. [115].

only to the subject; cf. [213, 214]. Nor is *-lla/e-* a mere plural ending under given conditions (op. cit. 30). That function is reserved for *-na* [138 ff.]. When the two are used together, *-lla/e-* is plainly predicative whereas *-na* is attributive. Cf., e. g., *i-i-e-na-a-ma-a-ni-i-in* ^{I}*Ma-ni-eš!* ^{I}*Ge-<li->ya-al-la-a-an ka-til-li-ta* Mit. IV 21 "and (*-ma-*) such (things) as (*yena*) will (*-ed-*) indeed(?) be (*-lla-*) told by Mane and Keliya." In other words, *-na* refers to the implied subject (*tiwe-*), while *-lla-* is not only the anaphoric substitute for it but also the link between it and the predicate. Or conversely: *i-i-al-la-a--ni-i-in gu-ru at-ta-iw-wu-uš we-e-wa e-ti-i-wa ti-we-e-na*^{MEŠ} *ta-a-nu-ú-ša-a-aš--še-na* Mit. III 55 f. "again, the things (*tiwena*) that were indeed(?) done by him (*yallanin tañoža-*), namely those done (*-šena*) by my father, for thy sake." Here, too, *-na* refers to the subject, which is this time stated explicitly (*tiwena*); *-lla-* mediates between that subject (for which it serves also as an anaphoric substitute) and its predicate. We know that the attributive plural element may be omitted (cf. Friedrich, BChG 6), especially when it is stated or implied elsewhere in the sentence; e. g., *ú-ú-ra-ú-ša-aš-še-na-ma-a-an ti-we-e-e*^{MEŠ} Mit. I 80. It is in this light that we have to view the omission of *-na* when *-lla*/e- is present in

(a) Goal-agent-action sentences; e. g.,

še-e-ni-iw-wu-ú-ul-la-a-an pa-aš-ši-i-it-ḫi-iw-wə šu-ra-a-maš-ti-en na-ak-ki-en Mit. IV 51 (and similarly, ibid. 41 f.) "Brother-my-by-they(-be) envoy-my speeded dismissed," i. e., "let my brother promptly send back my envoys"

(b) Actor-action sentences; e. g.,

DINGIR^{MEŠ} *e-e-ni-il-la-a-an še-e-ni-iw-wu-ú-e-na pal-la-i-šal-la-ma-an* ibid. 65 "and the gods who are (*-lla-*) those (*-na*) of my brother shall judge(?)"; [321] or the common *šu(w)a-lla-man* "that is, all of them" [114a].

With *-na* stated with the subject (*yena-ma-nin*) the nominal predicate has *-l(l)a-* in *ur-ḫal-la-a-an pal-ta-a-la-an* Mit. IV 23 "they are true and

[321] Goetze, JAOS 60. 222 f., regards *eni-lla-* (which Friedrich cites as an example of *-lla-* serving as a mere plural suffix, cf. BChG 31) as the product of **eni-na-la*. But **eni/e-na* alone yields *enna* [66]. One cannot see how this phonemic *-nn-* would be simplified and the vowel of the singular restored while the form itself remained plural. Furthermore, how is one to account for the difference between *enilla-* and *tiwalla-* or *urḫalla-*, which Goetze notes but leaves unexplained? Plainly, the situation is the other way around. In *tiwalla-* and *urḫalla-* we have forms in which the change *-e*>*-a-* is backed by independent phonologic evidence (e. g., before *-tt-* where the condition posited by Goetze does not obtain; cf. [65]). Hence *enilla-* must owe the retention of its *-i-* to other causes. The reason is obviously to be seen in the need of avoiding confusion with *-na*; the form required by phonologic process would have been **ena-lla-* and thus subject to mistaken comparison with **enna-la*.

authentic."[322] But in the parallel instance (ibid. 27-29) *-na* is omitted (*ye-ma-nin*).

It cannot be said, therefore, that *-lla/e-* is more or less equivalent to *-na* in relative sentences or in other contexts. From what we have seen, the attributive particle may be omitted if the corresponding associative is present. The conclusion is justified also that *-na-* and *-lla/e-* are not used together with the same root; cf. *eni-lla-* (above), *e-e-ni-iw-wa-al-la-a-an* Mit. IV 64 (note the single *n* in both instances and contrast ᵈ*e-en-ni-iw-wa-a-še-e-en* Mit. II 77 [142]), and *ti-wa-a-al-la-a-an* ibid. 16.[323] This is in itself a striking indication of the independent syntactic character of such pronominal associatives. They were not interchangeable with the morphologic elements that marked person or number, and the two types were not tolerated together in the same form unless each construed with a different element in the sentence.

(d) Deictic Elements

219. Under this head may be grouped several elements which seem to have the value of emphasizing, restrictive, or asseverative particles. They are associatives in that they may occur with nouns, independent particles, or verbs; furthermore, they are placed either at the very end of the given form or, at any rate, after the known morphologic suffixes. The elements involved include: *-mmaman*, *-nin*, and the group *-a/unni*, *-andi/u*, *-inna*.

220. The particle *-mmaman*. The doubled initial *-m-* is probably phonologic. If the isolated *ma-a-an-ni-i-im-ma-ma* Mit. III 5 can be trusted, the *-n* of all the remaining examples was an added element. The particle is possibly composite (**mma* + *ma-?*). The wide distribution of the particle may be judged from the following selected occurrences, all from Mit.[324]

(a) With substantives: ᵈ*Ši-mi-i-ge-ni-e-wə-ni-e-im-ma-ma-an* I 94; *e-e-la--ar-ti-iw-wu-ú-e-na-a-še-im-ma-ma-an* III 44

(b) With pronoun: *a-ni-e-na-a-am-ma-ma-an* IV 20; with pronoun and suffixed numeral "one": *ma-a-ni-e-im-ma-ma-an* III 35, 36, 38; cf. [125]

(c) With independent numeral: *ši-ni-a-še-na-a-am-ma-ma-an* III 40

(d) With verbs: *ka-til-li-e-ta-*[*a-*(*am*)]*-ma-ma-an* II 102, IV 109; *ge-pa--a-ni-e-ta-a-am-ma-ma-an* II 63; *ma-a-an-ni-i-im-ma-ma-an* I 16, III 5, 10, 100

[322] The single *l* in *paldalan* as opposed to the *ll* of *urḫallàn* receives the same treatment before the connective that we have seen also in the case of *-t/dil(l)a-* [215] and numerous forms in *-n* [86]; cf. my remarks in Lang. 16. 336 f. Goetze's skepticism with regard to *paltalan* (loc. cit. 323 n. 30) proves thus unnecessary.

[323] See above, n. 321.

[324] I have excluded uncertain passages as well as combinations with unknown or doubtful stems.

(e) With particles: *i-i-a-am-ma-ma-ma-an* IV 18, *šuk-ku-u-um-ma-ma-an* III 111; perhaps also *i-i-im-ma-ma-an* II 98, 101, *i-i-um-mi-im-ma-an* ibid. 99

According to Messerschmidt (Mitanni-Studien 55) *-mmaman* is a generalizing element. Friedrich finds its value obscure in most instances; he agrees with Messerschmidt, however, to the extent that he accepts the indefinite connotation where pronouns are involved (BChG 21). As against this view we have to cite certain occurrences in which *-mmaman* has quite the opposite value: that of an identifying or isolating element.

This is immediately apparent in (c). Having listed two specific tablets as those of his sister and aunt, Tushratta continues (Mit. III 39 f.): "So let my brother read(?) their tablets, of-the-two-of-them-*mmaman*." Here the particle can mean only "the afore-mentioned," or "specifically." In the same passage (35 ff.) each tablet is introduced by *ma* + *ne* + *mmaman* (b) "this one specifically, in particular." Finally, in line 44 (see under a) Tushratta again uses *-mmaman* in a reference to the two tablets which he had mentioned before; cf. [128].

Dependence on the foregoing context is evident also in the other occurrence under (a) as well as with *manni-* (d), which is always preceded by *adi* + *nin* "thus." Nor does the combination of the relative particle *ya/e-* with *-mmaman* necessarily result in an indefinite. The generalizing connotation is inherent in *ya/e-* by itself. With *-mmaman* added there is an increment in meaning which has to be sought in a different direction. The combination *ye* + *me* + *nin* . . . *keban* + *ed* + *a-mmaman* II 62 f. (cf. above under [d]) is well represented by something like "what given (or 'special, particular') thing he will send," etc. In IV 20 (*anena-mman*) it is precisely "those particular (words)" and not "any words" that the context requires. As for *ya-* *-mmaman* (e), this form serves as an attribute to *tiwe šurwə* (IV 17) which is mentioned once before in the preceding line; hence here something like "as just stated." With *šukko-mmaman*, "just the same" is the sense that the context obviously requires [127]. Other occurrences of the particle come up in obscure passages that make closer analysis hazardous. They can scarcely deviate, however, from the examples already discussed.

To sum up, *-mmaman* is used in enumerations for the purpose of specific identification. Elsewhere, too, it is used to refer to particular things or actions. It is, therefore, a restrictive rather than a generalizing element.

220a. The particle *-nin*. The orthography is consistently *-ni-i-in*, which plainly marks *i*-quality. The single possible exception is *nu-be-e-ni-na-an* Mit. I 93, assuming that this form contains the particle in question; if so, the single writing would merely represent the primary value of the sign NI, without indicating in any way a reading **ne*. Goetze (JAOS 60. 219) rightly stresses the established vocalic quality, although he would adduce *ti-we-e-ni-e-en* Mit. IV 32 as an instance of exceptional spelling (ibid. n. 11); but this form cannot contain the particle under review; cf. [207]. Nor is there any valid evidence in favor of analyzing *-nin* as *-ni* + *n*. In any case, we have here a form that can have no relation to the attributive particle *-ne* [136 f.].

Of the several combinations (all attested in Mit.) in which *-nin* may figure the commonest by far is with pronominal elements. Cf. *inu-tta-nin* I 74, II 60; *inu-lle-nin* III 101. Especially frequent is its use with *-me/ma-*; cf. [217]. Note also *awenne/a-nin* IV 17, 24; *aweše-nin* III 3, and cf. [115]; for *nu-be-e-ni-na-an* see above and cf. [111]. The particle *adi-* "thus" is invariably associated with *-nin*, once with the interposed connective *-ma-*; cf. [128]. Another particle with *-nin* is *a-i-ma-a-ni-i-in* III 111, IV 9, 54, 59. Finally, verbal forms that end in *-nin* are illustrated by *ma-a-an-ni-i-ni-in* . . . . . *ú-na-a-ni-i-in* IV 13, *ka-tup-pa-a-ni-i-in* ibid. 14, and *ú-ru-li-e-wa-ma-a-ni-in* III 115.

The exact force of *-nin* is difficult to determine. The frequent association with pronouns suggests a deictic element. A specific demonstrative connotation is not favored by the verbal forms just cited, so that we are obliged to look for something of a more general nature. In JAOS 59. 303 I suggested the equation with Akk. *lû* "verily, indeed," a particle that is very common in the Akkadian letters of Tushratta. This comparison still appears plausible; but other possibilities cannot be ruled out as yet.

221. In *a-i-ma-a-ni-i-in* (10) *še-e-ni-iw-wu-uš a-nam ta-a-nu-ši-wa-al-la-a-an-ni* Mit. IV 9 f. "if-indeed(?) my brother had not done these things" the agentive noun compels us to analyze the verbal form as **tan* + *ož* + *a* + *i* + *wa* + *lla-* + *nni* "done-past-by-him-classmarker-not-they-*nni*."[325] It follows that *-lla-* represents the goal and *-nni* must be, therefore, another associative which has no positional standing in the verbal complex as such. Accordingly, we have to view in the same way *a-ku-u-ša-a-an-ni* Mit. II 60 and *wu-ur-ra-an-ni* ibid. III 3. This enables us to include also *id-ki-ta-an-nim* XXIX 8 ii 29, 31, 35 (which construes with a plural agentive (in *-nažuš*); it yields *idk* + *id* + *anni* + *m*, the last morpheme being apparently the connective *-m*. Now *-id-* is known from jussive plural forms, e.g., *nakk* + *id* + *en* [184, 193 (f)]. It is altogether likely that the present form has a similar force; for other verbs in the same text are characterized by the cohortative elements *-ll-* and *-nn-* (see below) and are thus presumably parallel. All of this leads to the supposition that *-anni* was an asseverative particle suitable in jussives as well as indicative forms.

[325] Cf. already JAOS 59. 318 n. 80 for the linking of this form with *tanoža*; see also Goetze, Lang. 16. 135 n. 44.

From *tup-šar-ri-iw-wu-ú-un-ni* Mit. IV 37 we can safely isolate the element -(*u*)*nni* which seems to function like the final element of *tanožiwalla* + (*a*)*nni* (above).

The element *-andi/u* is attested in cohortatives of the type *ḫu-u-ši-el-la--an-ti-in* [326] and *ḫa-u-li-il-la-an-tu* [189]. It is probable that this morpheme is similar in function to *-anni.*

Finally VIII 61 obv. 2 presents the form *ḫa-a-ša-ri-in-na.* Whether there is any connection between the resultant *-inna* and the two morphemes cited above we have no way of deciding.

(e) Miscellaneous

222. The particle *-t/dan.* In the great majority of its occurrences this particle appears after a vowel; since the dental is expressed in single writing it must have been voiced in that position.[327] A clear instance after a consonant is furnished by (*še-e-er-ri-e-dan* [DINGIR^{MEŠ}] *e-e-en-ni-ib-tan* Mit. IV (115-) 116. All the clearly recognizable examples come from Mit.[328] The prevailing orthography is with the sign DAN; for a variant writing cf. *e-ti-i-ta-ni-il--la-ma-an* III 47, alongside *e-ti-i-dan-na-ma-an* ibid. 46.

Owing to the scrupulous observance in Mit. of the distinction between double and single writing of stops there is no danger of confusing this particle with *-ttàn* (subj. pron. suff. 1 p. + *-n, -an,* or *-a-a-an*).[329] This is especially apparent when the two elements happen to occur side by side, e. g.: *at-ta-a-ar-ti-iw--wə-dan tiš-ša-ni-it*[*-ta*]*-an* (88) *tiš-ša-a*[*n*] [330] *su-bi-a-maš-ti-e-ni-dan še-e--ni-iw-wu-uš* KUR *u-u-mi-ni-iw-wu-ú-a wu-ri-*[*i-*]*ta* [331] Mit. III 87 f. "and (*-an*) in the matter of (*-dan*) my father-gift may I (*-tta-*) have an increase, in that matter, (*subiamašten^i-dan*) in view of my country." [332] Here *-tta-* is the goal, whereas the repeated *-dan* indicates circumstance, and the final

326 For the analogous [*ḫu-u*]*-ši-in-na-an-ti* see [190].

327 For an alleged exception see [170 n. 165].

328 In XXVII 34 i 9 ff. the wr. *t/da-an* represents the directive followed by *-n* or *-an*; cf. [153].

329 See above, n. 327.

330 Contrary to Kleinas. Sprachdenkm. 24 there is no reason for assuming a lacuna after *-an*; the usual spacing between words would not have left room for another sign.

331 The transliteration, ibid., gives *wə-ri*[*-e-*]*ta,* although the above reading is admitted as a possibility, n. 11. However, there is no agentive to go with *wəreda.* Furthermore, the preceding dative indicates a prepositional form in *-da.* For the nominalized preposition *wuri-*, which is written with *-u-* in Bogh., cf. [105]. The meaning "in view of" is based on the supposition that the underlying root is the common Mit. verb *wər-* "know, find out"; cf. also [214 n. 309].

332 The idea being "so that my country could see"; literally translated "country--my-to knowledge (?) -its-of."

preposition in *-da* refers to purpose. What danger of confusion there may be concerns the elements *t/dan* and *-t/da*: The initial phonemes are identical; the combination **da + an*[333] would be indistinguishable from *-dan*. What is more, the directive *-t/da* [153] is close in meaning to the general range of *-t/dan*, as we shall see: note especially *ai + da*, *edi + da* [105] : *ai + dan*, *edi + dan* (below); furthermore, both types may coordinate with the dative [235]. Nevertheless, the two morphemes are not interchangeable positionally. For *-t/da*, being a case-element, is restricted to nouns, whereas *-t/dan* occurs with independent particles, verbs, and nouns, hence its classification as an associative. This diversity in position is illustrated by the following instances (wherever possible, the predicate in question is cited in parenthesis).

(a) With particles: *a-i-dan* II 49, 90; *e-ti-i-dan* II 84 (*tadugar-*), IV 106; *e-ti-i-dan-na-ma-an* III 46 (*pal-*), 86; *e-ti-i-ta-ni-il-la-ma-an* III 47 (*pal-*); *e-ti-i-dan-x-*[..]*-an* III 82

(b) With verbs: *pa-aš-še-ti-i-dan* III 116; *su-bi-a-maš-ti-e-ni-dan* III 88; *ú-ru-u-muš-te-e-wa-a-dan* II 9

(c) With nominal forms, e. g.: *ag-gu-dan ni-ḫa-a-ar-ri-e-dan ta-la-me-ni--e-dan* II 61 (*pis-*); *am-ma-ti-iw-wu-*[*ú-*]*-e-ni-dan* I 48; *an-nu-dan šu-e-ni--e-dan* III 108 (*tadugar-*); *at-ta-*(*a-*)*ar-ti-iw-wə-dan* III 50 (*anzannoḫ-*), ibid. 87 (*subiamašt-*); *at-ta-i-ip-pè-ni-e-dan* III 69 (*irnoḫ-*); *e-e-ši-iw-wa-a--aš-tan a-a-wa-ad-du-dan* II 11, cf. III 16 (*oloḫ-*); *ma-a-nu-dan* IV 64 (*pal-*); *pè-ti-ša-a-dan* III 81 (*tan-*); *še-e-ni-iw-wu-ú-e-ni-e-wa-a-dan* IV 46 (*urom-*; cf. *urom + oštcwa- + dan*, above); *še-e-er-ri-e-dan* (116) [DINGIR^{MEŠ}] *e-e-en-ni-ib-tan* IV 115 f. (*šar-*); *ti-ša-a-dan* III 92 (dependent on *pal-*).[334]

It will be observed that *-t/dan* is used frequently with such verbs as *anzannoḫ-* "request," *pal-* "ask," and *šar-* "demand." This points to a prepositional value like "for, about." The same applies to the construction with *pis-* "rejoice." The instances with *tadugar-* "love, show affection" indicate "because"; cf. Mit. III 108 f. "We together, because of all this

[333] I. e., with the connective *-an* or the predicative *-n*.

[334] Although the above list is not meant to be complete, attention should be called to two forms which are listed in Kleinas. Sprachdenkm. with doubtful *-tan*, though neither can possibly involve the particle under review. One is *du-ru-bi-ib-tan* (ibid. 26) Mit. III 118. Since *edi-da-* follows we should expect the noun to be *du-ru-bi-iw-wa*; furthermore, the possessive for "mine" is required by the context, the whole phrase being lit. "trouble/danger-my-to sake-its-for," i. e., "because of my danger." The final sign is marked in the copy as blotched; the reading *-w*[*a*]*-a* is a definite possibility. At all events, *-tan* is not established textually and the particle *-dan* is precluded by the context.

The other instance is *t*[*i-w*]*i-*[*-i-*]*t*[*an*] (ibid. 19) Mit. II 104. We must read, however, *t*[*i-w*]*i*[*-i-y*]*a-*[*an*] and this restoration is consistent with the traces on the tablet; cf. [207 n. 280].

(*annu-dan šuene-dan*), continuously [127 n. 70] love one another." This meaning is especially suitable with *ai-dan* " in the face of " and *edi-dan* " because of." A similar nuance was assumed in the translation of Mit. III 87 f. where -*dan* was rendered " in the matter of." Appproximately the same value seems to be reflected in *tea attaippe* + *ne* + *dan* III 69, lit. " much father-thy-of-attr. part.-about," i. e., " more than thy father."

In conclusion it may be remarked that the range of meaning obtained for -*t/dan* [335] would not be inconsistent with the assumption that this particle consists of the directive -*t/da* + the predicative -*n* ; in that case the meaning would be " it is, because . . . that." But the combined form, if this assumption should be corroborated, functioned as a separate element, which is shown clearly by its position as an associative.

223. The associative element -*z̄*. This suffix is known best from the jussive form of the type *ḫazolez̄* [193 (c)]. The syllabic texts express it by the ambiguous -*š*, but the corresponding alphabetic *ḫzlz̄* [45] leaves no doubt as to the nature of the sound.

In so far as function is concerned, Goetze (Lang. 16. 134) would see in this -*z̄* the marker of 3 sg. imperative and ascribe the same imperative force to forms without interposed -*l*-, e. g., *tadugar-iz̄* Mit. I 19, II 93, IV (113) 121. Accordingly, he adds to this group *ka-ti-iš* (ibid., 135) Mit IV 4 and *pè-te--eš-ta-iš* (ibid. 139) IV 50. It follows that we should include also *ḫi-il-lu-ši-iš* Mit. IV 14, *ni-eš-ši-iš* ibid. I 64, and *pí-su-uš-ta-iš* I 80; *i-su-di-iš* Mâri 5. 6 and *al-lu-lu-da-i[š]* ibid. 7; and finally *e-ti-iš* Mit. III 122.

The last-cited form arouses immediate skepticism as to the correctness of Goetze's interpretation of the suffix. For it is scarcely to be dissociated from the particle *edi-* " concern(ing)," and one cannot see readily the use of an imperative ending with such a word. More serious is the negative evidence of the two Mâri forms. Although the context is obscure (as it is in the case of *edi-z̄*), imperatives are here entirely out of place because in both instances we have an introductory *inu* " as." It thus becomes evident that the jussive function of the type *ḫazolez̄* is determined by other components of the form: the cohortative -*ol*- (or -*i/el(l)*- with transitives) [189] in conjunction with the element -*ae/i*- [193].

In point of fact, it is doubtful whether -*z̄* had any verbal function whatsoever. In *ge-ra-aš-še-n[a-ša-til-l]a-an* [336] *ša-wa-al-la-ša pí-su-un-ni-en tiš-ša-an tiš--ša-an* (80) *pí-su-uš-ta-iš* Mit. I 79 f. the predicate is *pisunnen*; the concluding *pisoštaiz̄* is neither a coordinate of the predicate nor the beginning of a new

---

[335] Cf. Lang. 16. 331.
[336] For this restoration see [167 n. 155].

clause;[337] it appears to be, rather, a cognate adverbial suppletive: "throughout the long years let us rejoice very much in happiness."[338] Note also *ka-ti-iš ḫil-lu-ši-in* Mit. IV 4, where the predicate is evidently the *i*-form *ḫilloži-n* preceded by another term for "speak, communicate" which ends in *-ž*; similarly *ḫi-il-lu-ši-iš ka-tup-pa-a-ni-i-in* ibid. 14 where the sequence *ḫill- -kad-* is the reverse of the above.[339] Finally, *še-e-ni-iw-wu-⟨ú⟩-e-ni-e a-a-i-i-e-e pè-te-eš-ta-iš* Mit. IV 49 f. (cf. Goetze, loc. cit. 139) is not likely to represent an independent clause since no connective is present; the rendering "before my brother very satisfactorily," i. e., "to the complete satisfaction of my brother" will answer the grammatical and contextual requirements; likewise, *tadugariž* proves thoroughly adequate in its respective contexts when rendered "affectionately."

As a provisional interpretation for *-ž* I suggest therefore an adverbial value with the sense of "fully," or the like. It suits not only the Mit. occurrences that are capable of analysis but also the jussive forms mentioned above; *ḫažolež* would thus mean "let be heard fully" and the Amarna gloss *ka₄-ti- -ḫu-li-eš* EA 53. 65, which Goetze was the first to understand in its proper bearing,[340] has a convincing ring when translated "let (it) be down wholly" (*ana šēpēka* "at thy feet"). Incidentally, this interpretation of the particle brings it in accord with the other uses of the element *-ž* which have been encountered thus far: pluralizing particle [142]; emphasizing root-complement with nouns [175 (6)], and with verbs [176 (5)].

224. The elements *-ki* and *-lam* have been discussed above [200]. Both appear to function as negatives and to be used with nominal as well as verbal forms, so that their interpretation as associatives is probable, if not yet certain.

Schematic Recapitulation

225. In a schematic survey of the principal bound forms we have to distinguish only two main categories: (a) suffixes with the noun; (b) suffixes with the verb.

[337] A new clause begins with the next word which carries the connective *-màn*.

[338] Cf. *ana ḫedūti* "for joy, joyfully" EA 27. 97, 29. 157.

[339] In this connection I would call attention to several phrases in Hurro-Akkadian texts which are not paralleled in idiomatic Akkadian usage: *ki-i-me-e ú-ka₄-al-ma ú-ka₄-al* AASOR 16 21. 15, 32. 14 "she shall have complete possession," *la i-ša-at-tar-ma i-ša-at-tar* TCL 9 41. 36 "I! must not write"; and in Tushratta's Akkadian we get *lu-ú a[k-k]á[l] ak-[k]ál-ma-a-ku* EA 29. 156 "I am thoroughly depressed(?)," or the like. What is characteristic of these expressions is not merely the repetition of the respective verbs, which has its analogy in the "infinitive absolute" of Hebrew (cf. AASOR 16 p. 83), but rather the addition of the emphasizing particle *-ma*. The use of the letter might well reflect Hurrian *-ž* of the forms cited above.

[340] See RHA 35. 103 ff.

(a) SUFFIXES WITH THE NOUN

(1) Attributive particles: sg. *-ne*, pl. *-na* [136-41]

(2) Pluralizing particle: *-ž* [142]

(3) Possessive suffixes [143-47]

	Singular	Plural
1 p.	*-i/ef*	*-i/ef-až*
2 p.	*-v*	(**-v-až*)
3 p.	*-i(y)a, -t/di*	*-i(y)a-ž*

(4) Case-relations [148-57]

The case-markers may be attached to a simple stem (e. g., *ene* " god "), a stem + possessive suffix (*en-if* " my god "), or a complex verbal form (e. g., *ar-ož-af-* " given-past-by/of-me ") + the nominalizing particle *-še* + the attributive particles *-ne/a*. These stems are as follows: (*ene-, enif, arožaf-še-ne* +)

	Singular	Plural
Subject-case	zero-suffix	*-až*
Agentive	*-š*	*-žuš*
Genitive	*-we*	*-že*
Dative	*-wa*	*-ža*
Directive	*-da*	*-šta*
Comitative	*-ra*	*-žura*
Locative	**-(y)a*	**-ža*
" Stative "	*-a*	**-ža*

(5) Adjectival suffixes [158-60]

These suffixes may be added to the simple stem, to a stem followed by the abstract-element *-še* [163], or to a stem extended by means of one or more of the nominal root-complements [175]. The suffixes in question are *-ḫe/ḫḫe, -ne, -zi*, and *-ae* [165]

(b) SUFFIXES WITH THE VERB

(6) Positions in the suffix-chain of the verb [178 ff.]

Intensifying elements (*-št-, -id(o)*; class-markers (*-i-, -u/o*); iterative-durative (*-kk-*); negative (*-wa/e*); cohortative (*-l-, -n-*); conjunctive (*-ewa*)

(7) Tense-markers [180-82]

	With-agent-suffix	Impersonal
Perfect	*-ož-*	*-ošt-a*
Future	*-ed-*	*-ett-a*

(8) Determinatives of non-finite forms
Participles *-a, -i, -u* [168-71]
Infinitive *-um, -ummi/e* [172]
Gerund *-ae* [167]
Impersonal element with *-kk*-forms: *-o* [186-87]

(9) Agent-suffixes [194-95]

	Singular	Plural [198]
1 p.	*-af*	*-af-ž̄a*
2 p.	*-u/o*	?
3 p.	*-i(y)a, -a*	?

(10) Suffixes with jussive forms [196, 221]
With agent
1 p. *-i/e*
2 p. *-i*(?)
3 p. —(*en*), pl. (*id*)—(*en*); (deictic *-anni-m, -andi/u*)
Impersonal (*-ai*)*-n*, pl. (*-ai*)*-ž̄a-lla-n -iden* [184]; (*-ž̄* [223])

(11) Subjective pronominal suffixes with non-finite forms [213-18]

1 p.	*-tta-* "I"	*-t/dil(l)a-* "we"
2 p.	??	
3 p.	(*-me/a-*)* "he, she, it"	*-l(l)a/e-* "they"

* Used only as anticipatory element; not joined to verbs.

V. CONSTRUCTION

226. The reasons for arranging our discussion under the separate heads of Morphologic Elements and Construction were given in [96]. In that connection it was made clear that the division to be followed does not correspond exactly to the traditional distinction between Morphology and Syntax; syntactic problems could not be ignored in the presentation of given morphologic elements and, conversely, the order of given bound forms would have to be reviewed under Construction although it is technically a question of morphology. The purpose of the present chapter is to examine the means whereby individual elements are combined into larger units, whether these constitute included phrasal words or clauses and sentences. Accordingly, we shall deal here with the relation of bound-forms to one another, the interrelation of words within a clause, and the combination of individual clauses into a complete sentence.

It goes without saying that the attempted picture will be far from complete or representative. The very limited material at our disposal, its diversified character, its generally poor state of preservation, and our inadequate knowledge of numerous features of form and context, all these are factors that make for a sketchy and uneven presentation. Nevertheless, we are now in a position to bring out a number of salient points. This will be done under the following sub-heads: (1) General results; (2) The Noun; (3) The Verb; (4) Compounds; (5) The Sentence.

(1) General Results

227. From the standpoint of technique Hurrian is a suffixing language. There is no evidence of any other form of affix.[1] The connection between suffix and supporting root is not rigid. In the noun, e. g., other bound forms may be interposed between the so-called case-endings and the root. The same case-endings are employed with terms marking substantives, pronouns, numerals, and prepositions; singular and plural. Moreover, the endings of the head may be repeated under specific conditions with the attribute [238]. In the verb, we find lengthy suffix-chains which are characterized by a fixed order

[1] The suggestion of L. Oppenheim (AfO 12 [1937] 39, 155) that the *-ta-* of personal names like *A-kib-ta-še-en-ni*, *Ar-ta-še-en-ni*, and others may be an independent element prefixed to **še-en-ni* "brother" must be rejected; the second element of these compounds is *taženni* "present" which is abundantly attested. The same writer has deduced also an extensive use of the verbal prefixes from stylistic dislocations in Nuzi Akkadian; cf. ibid. 11 (1936) 62 ff. For the refutation see AASOR 16 pp. 138 f. and cf. BChG 43.

of the component bound forms [178]. All this testifies to a degree of individuality accorded to the suffixes of Hurrian which is not paralleled among the fusional or inflecting languages.[2] The Hurrian suffixes have rather the force of bound particles which impart to the language an agglutinative character [132].

228. Except for subjective personal pronouns the plural[3] is not expressed by separate forms distinct form those of the singular. Instead, a pluralizing particle, -(*a*)*ž*(*a*), is added to the respective singular forms of the noun [142] and of the verb [198]. The attributive pl. particle *-na* is a relational element employed with nouns [138-41].

229. Hurrian recognizes neither gender nor any analogous class-distinctions such as are found, e. g., in Bantu, certain American Indian and Caucasic languages, and the like. For an unsuccessful recent attempt to ascribe to Hurrian distinctions of gender cf. [177].

230. Hurrian is notable for its tendency (a) to relate the various nominal elements in the sentence by prominent use of bound particles; (b) to mark the connection between subject and predicate by means of associative elements; and (c) to conjoin to the verbal concept a large number of bound modifiers. The result of this reliance on multiple concatenation within the sentence is a lack of sharp demarcation between noun, verb, and particle as such. The parts of speech are thus often interchangeable and dependent for their function on their actual position in the sentence [99].[4]

To fix the relation of the various elements in the sentence Hurrian makes prominent use of the attributive particles *-ne* and *-na* which establish the place of the respective nominal components [136-41]. Relation of subject to predicate is stressed, at least in Mit., with the aid of the predicative particle *-n* [203-9]. In addition, Hurrian makes extensive use of non-morphologic associative elements other than *-n* [210 ff.]. Of these, the subjective pronominal suffixes [213-8] may be employed predicatively.

(b) The Noun

231. The possessive pronominal suffixes [143-47] precede the case-endings in the suffix-chain; e. g., *žen* + *if* + *wa* "brother-my-to" [152]. This shows

[2] Cf. [236]. For the terminology cf. Sapir, Language (1921) 146 ff.

[3] Attested in the pl. only by the associatives for "we" [215] and "they" [218].

[4] This lack of concrete values outside the sentence may be responsible for the discrepancies which RŠ Voc. betrays in its use of suffixes. The translators had obvious difficulty in utilizing Hurrian terms for lexical purposes.

that derivational suffixes are placed ahead of the relational elements. The same order is observed with the adjectival suffixes -*ḫ*/*ḫḫe* and -*ne*; cf. [133].

232. The adjectival attribute normally precedes its head. The concept may be expressed by special adjectival suffixes [158-60]; the genitive, e. g., [149 (b)]; apparently also the locative in special circumstances, e. g., "in Egypt (the) land," "Egyptian land" [137(c)].

233. The use of the subject-case in actor-action sentences and as the goal with transitives has been discussed in [149].

234. A special use of the genitive is reflected with the verb *pis-* "rejoice": cf. *an-du-ú-e-* Mit. II 63,[5] and hence also *an-du-ú-a-* [64], *ge-el-ti-i-wə* [176 n. 200].

The same function of the genitive to express reference is attested with the nominalized prepositions *ai-* and *edi-* [105, 128]; e. g., *še-e-ni-iw-wu-ú-e-ni-e a-a-i-e-e pè-te-eš-ti-ten* Mit. III 28 (and similarly, ibid. 29, IV 49 f.) "(it) shall be satisfactory in the presence of my brother," lit. "brother-my-of presence(?)-his-of"; *šu-u-we-ni-e e-ti-iw-wu-ú-e-e* Mit. IV 22 (similarly ibid. 18) "(will say) concerning me," cf. [69]. It is to be noted that in this construction the dependent noun ends in the attributive -*ne* which is not repeated with the following appositive form [137 (3)]. We have here a unique use of the attributive particle, not paralleled even with the otherwise analogous appositive constructions involving the dative and directive (below).

235. The dative is similarly construed with a nominalized preposition in the dative, directive, or -*dan*, to express direction or purpose; but -*ne* is absent in such instances. Cf. ^{d}*e-e-ni-iw-wu-ú-a a-a-i-i-ta* Mit. III 98 "god-my-for presence-his-to," "in the presence of my god (I shall say)"; *at-ta-i-ip-pa* (53) *e-ti-i-i-ta* ibid. 52 f. "father-thy-for sake-his-to," i. e., "concerning thy father"; KUR *u-u-mi-i-ni-iw-wu-ú-a wu-ri-*[*i-*]*ta* ibid. 88 "for my country to see" [222]; *šuk-kán-ni-e-wa-an ti-wi-i-wa-an e-ti-i-dan* Mit. II 84 "because of thy *š.* word." Two datives are probable in *we-e-wə e-ti-i-wə* Mit. III 55 "for thy sake." Especially to be noted in this connection is the paratactic use of the possessive pronoun of 3 p.: "to thy father, for his sake," cf. [69; 207 n. 280]; it should not be confused with the process of suffix-duplication [238].

A special use of the dative seems to confront us with *ul-lu-ḫu-ug-gu-ú-un* Mit. II 104 which occurs twice and is followed each time by two datives; the sense is apparently "different from so-and-so" [207]. The close semantic association of the dative, directive, and *t/dan*-form has already been illustrated

[5] Although the verb (line 64) is lost except for the two obscure signs at the end, some form of *pis-* is required by the parallelism of this passage with Mit. II 54 f.

above. An independent instance is *še-e-ni-iw-wu-ú-a- . . . pa-la-a-ú* Mit. III 92 (and hence also *e-ti-iw-wa pa-la-a-ú* ibid. 91) "I ask from my brother," since *pal-* is commonly construed with *t/dan*-forms, although not without a shift in relation [222].

236. The exclusive use of the agentive to mark the agent with transitive verbs followed by agent-suffix has been stressed in [150, 194]; cf. also [246]. This case is never used as the subject in actor-action sentences.

Where more than one agent is mentioned Mit. uses the agentive suffix (*-š*) each time; the fact that this suffix is subject to assimilation [75] does not, of course, affect the statement; e. g., ^I^*Ma-ni-eš* ^I^*Ge-li-ya-al-la-a-an* IV 20, 21; [^d^*T*]*-e-eš-šu-pa-aš* ^d^*Ša-uš-kaš* ^d^*A-ma-a-nu-ú-ti-la-an* (77) ^d^*Ši-mi-i-ge-ni-e-ti--la-an* (78) DINGIR^MEŠ^ *e-e-en-na-šu-uš* Mit. I 76 ff., cf. [215]. Elsewhere, however, the agentive suffix need be used but once in the sentence; cf. *mu-úš e-ni-wu-úš* "by my exalted god" Mâri 6. 10, 11;[6] *É-a wə-li tu-wə-la-an-e-en Pa-ḫi-ib-bi-ni-im e-ni-iš tu-wə-la-an-e-en* ibid. 1. 31 ff.; from Bogh. note, e. g., ^d^*Ḫé-bat* ^d^*Mu-šu-un-ni* ^d^*É-a* ^d^*Dam-ki-na* ^d^*IŠTAR*^ga^*-aš* ^d^*Na-bar-bi-iš* XXIX 8 iii 40 f. This freedom in the employment of the suffix in question would seem to confirm the suspicion that the force of such elements was that of a "preposition" rather than an inflectional case-ending; cf. [227].

237. The uses of the other cases of Hurrian have been illustrated in [153-6].

238. One of the distinctive features of nominal construction in Hurrian is the process of suffix-duplication [132-3].[7] This should not be confused with the mere repetition of case-elements and associatives with forms which stand in apposition to one another.[8] Prerequisite in the present instance is an attributive construction in which a genitive is dependent on a case-form other than the subject-case; further, the presence of the attributive particles *-ne* or *-na*. When the head is in the subject-case there cannot be, of course, any transfer of suffixes inasmuch as that case has no ending [149]; e. g., *tup-pí-ma-a-an ni-ḫa-a-ri-i-we* Mit. III 36; *tup-pè* (41) *ni-ḫa-a-ar-ri-e-we a-ru-u-ša-uš-še--ni-e-we* ibid. 40 f. Cf. also the pl. construction: DINGIR^MEŠ^*-na a-ar-ti-ni--we*$_e$*-na* ^URU^*Ḫa-at-ti-ni-bi-na* DINGIR^MEŠ^*-na ú-mi-ni-bi-na* ^URU^*Ḫa-at-te-ni--bi-na aš-du-ḫi-na* XXVII 1 ii 71 ff. "the gods, those of the city, those of Hatti, the gods, those of the land, those of Hatti, the female ones," i. e., "the

[6] That this *muž* is not merely an instance of haplology for **mužuš* is shown by [*m*]*u-úš e-ni-ra* ibid. 15 instead of the expected **muž(u)ra enera*.

[7] Cf. Jensen, ZA 14 (1899) 179; Messerschmidt, Mitanni-Studien 3 f.; Friedrich, BChG 3.

[8] See above [236] and cf. Friedrich, op. cit. 18 n. 1.

female deities of the city and country of Hatti." [9] Even this illustration is not properly an instance of suffix-duplication, inasmuch as the repeated *-na* is not a pl. case-ending but merely an attributive particle which relates the genitival and adjectival attributes involved to their respective heads.

To a different category belong the phrases in which the head has its own case-ending. E. g., with the agentive sg. we get: *še-e-na-wə-ša-an* ᴵ*Ni-im-mu-ri-i-aš* (85) KUR *Mi-zi-ir-ri-e-we-ni-eš ew-ri-iš* Mit. I 84 f. Here the head is represented by three appositive forms ("thy brother, Nimmuria, king") all of which repeat the agentive *-s̄* (cf. [236]). In attributive relation to the last noun is the gen. "of Egypt"; it is provided not only with its own gen. ending *-we* but also with *-ne* + *-s̄* of the head. In effect, the attribute is no more than an adjectival form [232] which agrees with its head as to case. If we bear in mind that the "cases" of Hurrian are free from the restrictions in form which characterize the corresponding elements of the inflecting languages proper, the process of suffix-duplication ceases to appear strange.[10] For pl. agentive with gen. sg. cf. DINGIR^{MEŠ}-*na-šu-uš at-ta-an-ni-bi-na-šu-uš* XXVII 42 rev. 9 "by the gods of the father"; cf. [133].

Since a case-ending superimposed upon a gen. form proves thus to refer to the head, we can safely reconstruct the case of the head itself where that form happens to be missing in a fragmentary text. Thus *ašḫožikonnenewe-na-s̄ta* [94 n. 2] testifies to an antecedent pl. noun + pl. directive *-s̄ta,* say, "to the [gods] of the sacrificer(?).

(3) The Verb

239. Hurrian divides its verbs into two sharply differentiated classes. This dichotomy is signalized formally by the class-markers: *-i-* with transitives [119] and *-u/o-* with intransitives [120]. It is expressed also relationally by far-reaching differences in construction. Thus the intransitives cannot take on agent-suffixes [194-97]. Whereas the *i*-class is capable of referring to person by means of these morphologic elements (e. g., *-ya* in 3 p. present), the *u/o*-class is always construed impersonally; its *-a* [169] yields a participial form which requires the support of associative pronouns or a noun in the subject-case to constitute a specific predicate. There is nothing in common, therefore, between the "paradigm" of a finite transitive and of an intransitive, no matter what the tense. Nor do the tense-markers of finite transitives correspond with those of the intransitives; the former use *-ož-* for the perfect

[9] Ibid. 3; but all the instances which Friedrich cites involve plurals in the subject-case and are thus not wholly adequate examples of the process.

[10] For the identical usage in certain Caucasic languages see Dirr, Einführung in das St. d. kaukas. Spr. 354 ff.

and *-ed-* for the future, the latter *-ošt-* and *-ett-* respectively [181-82].[11] When a verb known to be intransitive is found, nevertheless, with the ending *-ož-a* [181], it is apparent that the form in question has been made factitive or causative [122]. In short, the two classes are marked off from one another in form as well as function. For the resulting differences in sentence-type see below [245-6].

For the fixed positions of the various suffixes which may be included in a given verbal form see [178].

(4) Compounds

240. It is not absolutely certain whether Hurrian combined independent words into compounds. The extensive use of root-complements and the presence of a considerable number of associatives would seem to have served much the same purpose. At all events, the available evidence is both scanty and equivocal.

It has long been assumed that *attardi* [173] "bridal gift (for the father)" is composed of *atta(y)* "father" and *ardi* "gift" <*ar* "give" (cf. Messerschmidt, Mitanni-Studien 23); the same construction is apparent in *elardi-* "sister-ship-gift" [173] *zu-ge-et-ta-ar-ti-aš* Mit. IV 100, and a few other forms. But Goetze has recently raised the question (Lang. 16. 135 n. 41) whether *-ardi* is not merely an abstract ending. He may be right, although no such ending is attested otherwise while the derivation from *ar-* gives the precise sense that is required.

There is less basis for interpreting as the second part of compounds the element *-(a)rbu* which occurs in formations like *šinarbu* "two-year-old" and *tumnarbu* "four-year-old," cf. AASOR 16 pp. 131 ff. We do not know of a root **(a)rb-* "age," or the like;[12] on the other hand, both *-(a)r-* and *-p/b-* are well-attested as root-complements [175-6].

The possibility that compounds may be formed with *-uḫli* to designate officials and occupations was indicated in [173]. Whether *-ḫuri*, which is used similarly [ibid.], was a radical element or a suffix is wholly problematic.

241. The problem of compounds is bound to be raised also in connection with personal names. It has lately been broached with due caution by Friedrich,

[11] The two classes meet on common ground when transitives are construed as participles; for then both classes share the actor-action construction. For the common form in *-ož-i* see [181], and for *-ett-a* cf. [182]. It has also been pointed out that *-ošt-* may be used agentively under conditions that are not yet clear [181]. The fact remains, however, that "has given" is *ar-ož-a* (lit. "given-by/of-him"), whereas "has gone" is *itt-ošt-a*; and that *-ed-* has not been found with intransitives.

[12] It could hardly mean "year" in view of the known *šawala-* "year" RŠ Voc. I 13, Mit. I 79.

BChG 13. Although frequent reference to onomastic compounds has been made so far in the discussion (cf. [177]), the term has been applied in a purely formal sense. It is still an open question, therefore, whether *Erwi-žarri* has the general connotation " The lord is king " by virtue of constituting a free syntactic unit of the equational type, or whether it is merely a compound phrase with the value of something like " Lord-king."

Friedrich would solve the problem provisionally by suggesting that the names with -*š* attached to the first element are equational; e. g., *Še-ri-iš-a*-RI and *Še-ri-ša-ta-al* yield *Šeri-š*- whose suffix represents the subject-case. On the other hand, the type *Šimig*(*e*)-*a*RI, which is the prevailing one, might reflect (original) compounds comparable to the Indic *Deva-datta* or Greek Θεόδοτος and thus mean " Sun-given." But this solution will not work. In the first place, it is the initial nominal elements without case-ending that mark the subject [149]. Secondly, such verbal forms as may accompany the endingless nouns in onomastic phrases are invariably participial [168-71, 177] and therefore in actor-action construction. Lastly, the rare -*š* of the type *Šeri-ž-adal*[13] is the same element as in **Eni-ž-tae*: not at all a case-ending (which would be the agentive -*š̄* if Friedrich's argument could be upheld in part) but rather the root-complement -*ž* (which becomes *š̄* only for phonetic reasons [74]) with the force of " much," or the like [177].

If the personal names were indeed construed as phrasal compounds we should need, therefore, other evidence to prove it than that adduced by Friedrich. I believe that such evidence exists although it is circumstantial and hence open to dispute. It is furnished by the atypical treatment of the stem-vowel in numerous nominal elements involved. Thus *aš̄ti* " woman " never has its own stem-vowel in onomastic phrases (i. e., when not used by itself) ; instead we get forms like *Aš̄ta-meri* and *Aš̄tu*(*n*)-*naya* [62]. Similarly *Šimige* becomes -*Šimiga* and **Nuza* appears changed in *Ar-Nuzu, Itḫib-Nuzu,* and the like [ibid.]. Many similar instances could be cited. The important thing is that in either position a nominal element often takes on a final vowel that does not correspond to its own stem-vowel. We have no parallels for such behavior in normal sentence-construction. It follows that the explanation has to be sought in the special conditions that govern onomastic phrases. What

[13] The initial element may plausibly be compared with *šr* RŠ X 4 61 and the Bogh. occurrence cited in Br. 569. I would add also *še-e-er-ri-e-dan* Mit. IV 115 (<**šeri-ne-dan*) which is marked as a divine epithet by its appositive construction with *e-e-en-ni-ib-tan* ibid. 116; *še-e-er-ri-e-wi-in* GUŠKIN Mit. III 67 is obscure as to form, but evidently indicates something desirable, as far as meaning is concerned. The root proves thus a suitable element in personal names. There remains, of course, the possibility that the onomastic *Še-ri-iš* ends in a radical -*š*/*ž*.

these conditions were is open to conjecture; it is not unreasonable, however, to ascribe the results to peculiarities of compound-construction.

(e) The Sentence

242. Our analysis of the Hurrian sentence has to be based almost exclusively on Mit. This source represents a large portion of the entire available material. What is more, it is a single document as against the numerous disconnected and often fragmentary texts from the remaining sources. We can thus judge the contents of Mit. with relative confidence and obtain a basis for evaluating the structure of the sentence. To be sure, the resulting picture is necessarily one-sided. The style of the Mitanni letter differs appreciably from that of the Mâri and Bogh. texts in such matters as the use of the predicative particle *-n* [209] and the connectives [211-212a]. The conclusions which can be drawn at present may apply, therefore, primarily to a limited dialect-area or to a particular speech-type. Nevertheless, it is logical to assume that certain basic features will prove true of the language as a whole.

243. Main clauses are introduced in Mit. normally by means of the connective *-à/an* [211] or the composite form *-màn/-man* [212a]. These connectives are attached to the first radical element in the sentence, either an independent particle or a noun. The relative frequency of such introductions may be judged from a count of the full paragraphs which Mit. marks off with the aid of lines drawn across the column. Out of thirty-six such paragraphs (not counting the first which is in Akkadian), twenty-seven begin with words which include one or the other of the above connectives. In two instances (I 65, IV 69) the initial words (both incomplete) end in *-en*. One paragraph is introduced by *a-i-i-in* (III 44), apparently an interrogative particle. One has *-nin* at the end of the first word (I 74); two paragraphs are damaged at the beginning and only the sign *-in* marks the respective initial words (I 8, 47). In three instances the beginning is lost altogether.

It is clear from this tabulation that main clauses were opened with connectives in the great majority of cases in Mit. This practice is even more noticeable with medial or secondary clauses, so much so that in obscure context a connective is our surest guide as to the correct division of the sentence as a whole.

244. The importance which Hurrian attaches to the grammatical subject of the sentence is apparent from the prominent position which that syntactic element is accorded in the customary word-order. The subject is announced normally at the beginning of the sentence and, except for instances of inversion [253] and inclusion of descriptive attributes [232], may be preceded only by an independent particle. This statement applies alike to actor-action sentences and to goal-agent-action constructions; for subject and goal are represented by the same grammatical form, viz., the subject-case. When the subject is reinforced by an anticipatory pronominal associative, the pronoun comes first; e. g., *undu-màn inna-me-nin ženiffe ašti unetta* Mit. III 21 "And--now-then behold(?)-she-indeed(?), brother-my-of wife arriving will"; the two subjects in this sentence are the anticipatory "she" and "wife." Where special emphasis is deemed necessary the subject may be stated a number of times: in Mit. I 76 ff. *-dil(l)a-* "we" is thus used five times [215]; and in the series of coordinate clauses Mit. IV 117 ff. the same pronominal subject is repeated ten times. All this reflects the effort which Hurrian made to keep the subject in the forefront of the utterance.

245. The agentive, which states the source of action when the goal is indicated simultaneously, is placed normally between the goal (subject-case) and the action-form. E. g., *inu-tta-nin ḫenni ženif-uš tad-ya* (75) *inu-me-nin ḫenni ženif iža-š tad-af* Mit. I 74 f. "As-I-indeed(?) now brother-my-by (am) loved-by-him, as-he-indeed(?) now brother-my me-by (is) loved-by me";[14] *andi-llàn* ^{d}*Šimigene-š ar-ed-a* (107) *ženiffa* Mit. I 106 f. "these Shimige-by given-future-by-him brother-my-to."[15] Once again, however, significant shifts of meaning may be achieved by an inverted word-order, e. g., *ženif-uš-àn ašti šar-ož-a* Mit. III 1 "Brother-my-by wife requested-past-by-him," i. e., "it was my brother who made the request for a wife."[16]

246. The goal-agent-action construction of Hurrian brings up the problem of voice in so far as it affects the transitives in this particular construction. In the discussion so far the passive has been used whenever the analysis called for a literal translation. As the individual morphologic elements were exam-

[14] The correlation of
1 p. pronoun : agent-suffix of 1 p.
as against
substantive : agent-suffix of 3 p.
is closely paralleled in the prepositional phrase; cf.
šuwe-ne ediffe "of me, of my concern" [234]
as against
ženiffa ay-i-da "for my god, to his presence" [235]

[15] Note the position of the indirect object after the verb. However, the order of this particular case-relation may vary considerably.

[16] The normal Hurrian order in the tripartite construction involving goal-agent-actor is reflected in Nuzi Akkadian in violation of the word-order of the latter language. Thus Nuzi uses hundreds of times the equivalent of "A-B-adopted" with A as object and B as subject. Without independent knowledge of the process in question the student of Akkadian would normally assume the opposite relation of the persons concerned.

ined one by one, it became increasingly more evident that the ascription of a passive concept to transitives in tripartite construction is the only interpretation that fits the facts of the structure of Hurrian as a whole. It should be emphasized at this time that each of the numerous elements which enter into consideration was analyzed independently and without specific regard to the concept of the Hurrian transitive. Yet all the evidence has proved to point consistently in one direction. We cannot attempt a variant interpretation of any one distinctive constituent without dislocating thereby the whole structure and raising a series of new problems that are mutually irreconcilable. The cumulative testimony becomes thus decisive. It remains only to gather up the loose ends and let the results speak for themselves. The following points are especially pertinent:

(1) The sharp formal distinction between transitives and intransitives [239].

(2) The use of the subject-case for the actor with intransitives and in other equational sentences, but for the goal with finite transitive forms [149].

(3) The complete parallel in construction between the subject-case and the pronominal associatives; the latter, too, mark the goal with finite transitives, but the subject in the other sentence-types [213 ff.].

(4) Failure of the associative pronoun of 3 p. to combine with verbs.[17] If *-me/a-* really had the value of the objective pronoun "him, her, it" that failure would indeed be strange. We should expect the equivalent of "brother--my said-it, requested-her." But if *-me/a-* could be used only subjectively, the problem disappears. In sentences like "as he, my brother, is loved-by-me," or "and so she will arrive" (cf. [217]) the proper position of the pronoun is at the beginning of the sentence, just where it actually occurs. The 3 p. sg. does not have to be marked with the predicate, particularly where the favorite sentence-type is equational. The use of the corresponding pl. element *-lla/e-* with verbs as well as nouns is accounted for, on the other hand, by the need to indicate number with the aid of a predicative element.[18]

(5) The restriction of the agentive to the goal-agent-action construction [150]. If the *š*-case marked the grammatical subject, how is one to explain the absence of that form in all sentences involving intransitives or non-finite transitive forms, and especially in nominal sentences proper?[19]

[17] See Friedrich, BChG 25.

[18] Not *-na*, which is attributive; cf. [218].

[19] Goetze (Lang. 16. 140) states that the system proposed by him "might very well be rounded out by the inclusion of the nominal sentence, which quite naturally is descriptive of a state of affairs." But this does not explain why the subject of such a sentence should be represented by the objective case or an objective pronoun.

(6) The close connection between the possessive suffixes of the noun and the agent-suffixes, which are used exclusively with finite transitive forms [84, 194]; and the complete etymological and functional independence of these agent-suffixes from the subjective pronominal endings. The problem ceases to exist if we grant that there is an underlying relationship between *en-if* "my god" and *tan-af* "done by/of me, my doing." Then the formal connection within this pair of suffixes and the analogous pairs for 2 p. and 3 p. becomes a matter of course.

(7) The strictly attributive character of the verbal element in *tuppe niḫarrewe arožaf + še + ne + we* [137 (2)] and other similar constructions. This function is assured on formal grounds. The finite verbal form *arožaf* has been nominalized by means of the particle *-še* and can thus be used as a descriptive attribute of the noun *niḫarrewe* (<**niḫari-ne-we*) with which it shares accordingly the termination *-ne-we* (cf. [238]). Now if we view *arožaf* as active "I gave," the complete form will have to be interpreted "(tablet of the dowry) which I gave." [20] But this is impossible for several reasons. The form in question is a single word, construed as a noun and intimately associated with the governing noun through the attributive particle *-ne*. The nominalizing particle *-še* is definitely a derivational element and not a relational one [163-4]. Lastly, Hurrian expresses its relative sentence with the aid of the particle *ya-* [130], not here in evidence. The obvious solution is to interpret the whole phrase in the sense of "tablet of the dowry given(past)-by-me." [21] In other words, the underlying verbal form is passive.

(8) For our last point we may now turn to Nuzi Akkadian where in a number of instances subject and object are interchanged with the result that the text states the very opposite of what the context demands. The passages in question were collected independently several years ago by L. Oppenheim [22] and myself,[23] and both of us arrived at the conclusion that the source of such errors had to be traced back to the influence of their native language upon the Nuzi scribes writing in Akkadian. Specifically, it was a passive verbal concept that was responsible for the curious mistranslations. The argument was suggestive but it lacked the force of direct evidence, which could be provided only by Hurrian itself. Now that we have ample internal testimony pointing in the same direction, the Nuzi mistranslations may be re-examined briefly for purposes of additional illustration.

Let us take as our type-form *ipallaḫ-šunūti* H V 73. 13. The text aims to

[20] Cf. Goetze, RHA 35. 105 n. 12.

[21] The translation as such is unimportant. The main thing is that the form must be an attribute in agreement with its head.

[22] Cf. AfO 11 (1936) 56 ff., especially 61 f. [23] AASOR 16. 131 ff.

instruct the sons of a testator that they honor their mother; but the above term means "she shall honor them." The scribe should have used **ipallaḫū-šī* "they shall honor her." This form constitutes a complete sentence involving

Subject (*i-*)—Action (*plḫ*)—Number (*-ū*)—Object (fem. *-šī*)

Hurrian cannot duplicate, however, a sentence of this kind in a single form so long as the source of action is in the third person.[24] It would have to use three words

Goal ("mother") —Agent ("son-pl.-by," i. e., noun-*na-ž-uš*) —Action + Agent-suffix (verbal stem + *-id-en*)

or, if the goal were carried over from a preceding clause,

Agent—Action— *-n* [205 (7)]

It is plain that the two construction-types, actor-action in Akkadian and goal-agent-action (+ agent-element) in Hurrian, exhibit diametrically opposed orientation. Transition from the one to the other involves, therefore, a radical change in the position of the respective principals. Where the necessary change was not carried out in full, we have to expect the drastic results that we actually find in Nuzi: goal is confused with subject and agent with object. Instead of the children honoring their mother, the mother is made to honor her children. Or, to take another example, the widow who remarries contrary to the provisions of her husband's will is allowed to expel the legal heirs instead of being evicted by them.[25]

The manifest source of these errors in Nuzi Akkadian is thus the passive concept of finite transitives in the underlying Hurrian. It may not be superfluous to stress once again the fact that the mistranslations occur in tripartite constructions which involve verbs with both logical subject and object. It is precisely in these circumstances, and in these alone, that the Hurrian transitives construe as passives. For in all other sentence-types Hurrian uses actor-action construction [247].

247. The prevailing Hurrian sentence-type, however, is not the agentive but the equational. It is bipartite in that the essential elements in it are the subject and the predicate. Its construction is actor-action, as the classification implies. The actor is a noun in the subject-case or a pronominal associative. The predicate may be a noun or an impersonal verbal form, intransitive or transitive. No goal can be included in the latter instance; if one is needed, the agentive construction must be substituted.[26]

[24] With first person indicative we may get Verbal stem-Agent-suffix-Goal; cf. *kebanož-a(f)u-lla(-man)* Mit. III 18 "sent-past-by-me-they(-and)."

[25] Loc. cit. 30.

[26] The explanation which I advanced in JAOS 59. 322 f. was only partially true. I had not realized at the time that the entire group of Hurrian actor-action sentences was equational.

The following examples illustrate the main subtypes of the equational sentence:

(a) Nominal: *undun Manenan ženiffe pašitẖe* [205 (6)] "now then it is Mane who is my brother's envoy"

(b) Intransitive present: *inume ušẖuni šeẖal-a* [205 (9)] "as the silver is clean"

(c) Intransitive perfect: *adinin*[27] *tažen ittošt-a* [205 (4)] "thus the present has gone out"

(d) Intransitive future: *unduman innamanin ženiffe ašti unett-a* [205 (10)] "now then, behold, my brother's wife will arrive"

(e) Intransitive jussive: DINGIR^{MEŠ} *enillàn ženiffena pallaižallaman* Mit. IV 65 "let my brother's gods themselves[28] judge(?)"[29]

(f) Intransitive durative: *tuppiyaž tuppukk-o* Mit. III 45 "their tablets are equal"[30]

(g) Transitive present: *šattilan annudan šuenedan ištanifaža šukkuttoẖa tadugar-i-dillàn* Mit. III 108 f. "we together, because of all this, mutually show affection continually"[31]

(h) Transitive perfect: *unduman ženifen pašož-i* [170a] "now then, my brother having sent (a mission)"

(i) Transitive future: *pašed-i-dan ženifuda* [170] "(and I) shall send to my brother"

(j) Transitive future middle: *aimanim* ... *kulett-a* Mit. IV 59 f. "if he ... will say to himself"[32]

(k) Transitive passive: *H̱až-u-kelde* [171] "Heard is good news" (personal name)

(l) Transitive perfect durative: *ẖillož-i-kkattàn* [186] "I talked at length"

(m) Transitive conditional: *ženifennan ẖillol-ewa* [192] "my brother might say"

(n) Intransitive conditional: *urol-ewa-manin* [192] "should there arise"[33]

The reason for actor-action construction in the nominal sentence (a) and in the various sentences involving intransitives (b-f, n) is self-evident. Nor is it far to seek in the case of the above transitives (g-m). The participial forms in -*i*(g-i), -*a*(j), and -*u*(k) are immediately recognizable as verbal

[27] In these translations I have ignored those associative elements which are without effect upon construction and of little apparent value as to general meaning.

[28] For the use of *-man* as an identifying particle see [212a].

[29] For this value of *pal-* cf. [173 n. 188].

[30] Cf. [128].

[31] For *šukkuttoẖa* "continually(?)" see [127].

[32] See [182].

[33] The subject is uncertain.

nouns [168-71]. The durative form with *-kk-* has the participial marker *-o* with transitives and intransitives alike [187]. This *-o* is preserved in (f) but was changed to *-a-* in (l) for phonologic reasons [186]. There remains only the conditional in *-ewa* (m-n). Since it is in itself impersonal, we cannot but regard it as participial, on the analogy of types (b-l). In other words, all the above examples are nominal, whether the predicate is a substantive or a verbal noun in the form of a participle; [34] it is for this reason that all these predicates are impersonal.[35]

248. When two verbs or verb-derivatives are joined asyndetically, the first has the force of a preverbial complement. E. g., *šuramašten nakken* Mit. IV 42, 51 "let him hasten dismiss," i. e., "let him speedily dismiss"; [36] *tiwena*MEŠ *šu(w)allaman ženifuš kadožašena uriyašena* Mit. IV 30 f. "all the things mentioned desired by my brother," i. e., "all the things which my brother expressly desires"; [37] *aimanin mannubadae olohetta kuletta* Mit. IV 59 f. "if he will . . . thankfully(?) say to himself," cf. [247 (j)]. Whether the same rule was operative in Bogh. is uncertain. At all events, the series of participial forms in XXIX 8 iv 27 f. is not relevant because more than two predicates appear. Moreover, the connective *-ma* is used with the last two forms [212]. The parallel passage ibid. 8 f. is similarly treated.

249. Paratactic clauses involving verbs of the same form-class are characterized in Mit. by the addition of the same associative to each verb. E. g., *mannukkallàn andi unukkalan* IV 2 f. "These will be and come," i. e., "these

[34] It would appear that I have accepted Bork's dictum "Das mitannische Verbum ist durchaus partizipialartig," Mitannisprache 69. That the present results have been reached independently is of little moment in this connection. What is more important is the sweeping character of Bork's assertion without any attempt to prove it. A stray reference to the Caucasic languages cannot settle this or any other problem in Hurrian. Moreover, the agentive construction of Hurrian is not on a par with the equational (cf. the next note). Finally, when Bork speaks about "die bekannte Anarchie des Satzbaues" in Mitanni, Elamite, and Caucasic (loc. cit.) he is in error, especially with regard to "Mitannian." From all that we have seen Hurrian is a model of consistency within the logic of its own system.

[35] The finite transitives (with agent-suffixes) are not impersonal, strictly speaking, inasmuch as they include a reference to the agent in the first, second, or third person. But the agentive verbal form is not in itself predicative. "Given by/of me, you, him," or "giving-my, thy, his" can serve as a predicate only by reason of word-order or, as in Mit., through the mediation of the predicative particle *-n*. Thus even the agentive verb is always in included position unless accompanied by the proper associative element.

[36] See Friedrich, BChG 16.

[37] Note that the first form is in the perfect tense, the second in the present: "he said (that) he desires."

will come to pass"; similarly, *manninin tiwe andi unanin* ibid. 13; note also the sequence *wəžainan . . . peteštenan . . . širennàn* Mit. III 33 f.

250. When the second of two contiguous verbal forms ends in the connective *-à/an* and the first does not, the second clause is subordinate with resultative force. Cf. *ḫiyaruḫḫattan teuna ženifuš kebanuen wurdenittan* Mit. III 73 f. "May I be sent much gold by my brother in order that I be pleased(?)," cf. [214]; similarly *ḫažile pisandištennàn* Mit. IV 43 f. "may I hear so that (I) rejoice" [ibid.], and analogously, *tuppulain tiḫanidennàn* Mit. III 26 f., *innamanin ženiffene ayie peteštetta taridenan šukanne ežene* ibid. 29 f., approximately "behold she will be satisfactory in the sight of my brother so that (even) the distant heavens will . . ." It is to be noted that when the dependent clause consists of more words than the verb alone the word-order is necessarily inverted.

251. When the second verbal element is a participle followed by a connective we get a subordinate construction that carries a wider range of meaning. Cf. *ḫažožafun pisandožittàn* Mit. IV 9, lit. "heard-was-by-me having-rejoiced-I-and," i. e., "I heard with rejoicing"; *anzannoḫožaf kullimàn* Mit. III 51 "I begged saying." In the latter instance no personal pronoun appears, since both forms are transitive and the agent carries thus over from the first form. The function of the participle in this case might well be likened to that of a gerundive: "in saying."

Other examples of the participle-gerundive followed by an associative and appearing in hypotactic clauses are the two forms of *paš* "send" which occur in the same passage at the end of Mit. III:[38] *aimanin šukkommaman durube* (112) *ženiffa* KUR *ominida wəžewa pašinan ženif* (113) *šuda* "if, just the same, a danger to my brother's country should arise, my brother (therefore) sending to me (for aid)—"; *innammaman urowen pašedidan* (117) *ženifuda* "behold, let that never[39] occur, (but) there being in the future a message about it (*-dan*) to my brother—"

From the standpoint of construction the significant feature of both sentences is the collocation of *wəžewa pašinan* in the first instance and *urowen pašedidan* in the other. The subjoined forms are both participial, present and future

[38] For the entire passage cf. JAOS 59. 312 ff. where the general sense was correctly interpreted. But the ascription of a "conjunctive" force to the *i*-form (p. 314) was erroneous. The ending marks the active participle of the transitives, as we have seen [170]. The subordinate connotation is one of the values inherent in the gerundive under special conditions of word-order and in close association with given particles. But the gerundive has to be a participle, and *-i* is the characteristic participial marker of the transitive class.

[39] For the individualizing force of *-mmaman* see [220].

respectively, with a final associative. And in both cases the normal word-order has been inverted. By comparing these two pairs with *anzannoḫožaf kullimàn* (above) from an independent passage we are led to the conclusion that all three illustrate hypotactic uses of the participle-gerundive in Hurrian.

252. It follows that, so far as is known at present, subordinate clauses are not marked by a special form-class of the verb which could not be used also in main clauses. We have seen that the modal element *-ewa* is employed freely in main clauses [192]. The relative sentence, which is introduced by *ya/e-* [130], differs in no way from the other sentence-types in the choice of the predicate. It is worth stressing, moreover, that Hurrian fails to mark direct speech by a special particle (Friedrich, BChG 14 n. 1). In short, external means for differentiating sentence-types are very limited. Coordination is prevailingly paratactic. The only known means of indicating hypotaxis are the employment of the connective *-à/an* with the second of two contiguous verbal forms and the use of the participle-gerundive, but even this form is more widely employed in the main clause.

253. There is some evidence for the device of expressive inversion of the normal word-order. Some illustrations of that practice have already been adduced in connection with the discussion of coordinate verbal forms [250-1]. A significant instance is *wəredalan undu ženifullaman* Mit. III 61 "it is these things, then, that my brother will find out— " Not only is the verb placed here ahead of its agentive, but the favorite sentence-initial *undu* is forced to take second place.[40] Cf. also *kebanedamàn ženifuš* ibid. 117 "my brother will be sure to send."

With nouns we may note inversion in instances like *ženifušàn ašti šaroža* Mit. III 1 "it was my brother who made the request for a wife" [245]; *ženifullàn pašitḫif kozoštiwaen* Mit. IV 40 "let it not be my brother who is responsible for detaining my envoys." Cf. also *ženifudamàn tiwe šukko kulle* Mit. II 12, III 49 "it is to my brother, furthermore, that I would address a word."

254. Hurrian appears to make effective use of its doublets *awenna/e-* [115], *ya/e-* [130], *ma/e-* [217], and *-lla/e-* [218] for purposes of contrast. Cf. *awenne-nin tiwe šurwə yammaman kadilewa* Mit. IV 17 f. "should anyone communicate š. words, as just stated [220] : *awenna-nin kuru šuda yammaman ḫillolewa* ibid. 24 "again, should someone, on the other hand, relate to me

[40] The translations in this section have to be paraphrased. A literal rendering would not convey the added shade of meaning which the inversion in the original imparts, since the word-order of Hurrian differs anyway from ours.

the above—" This contrastive alternation is especially evident with *yalla/e-*; *yalle-nin . . . ammadifuš* Mit. III 52 : *yalla-nin kuru attaifuš* ibid. 55 "such things as my grandfather—" : "again, such things, on the other hand, as my father—"; *yalla-nin : yalle-nin* Mit. I 96-100 "such things . . . as my brother did for my brother's country, and such things . . . on the other hand, as my brother did towards the present—" [41] But in Mit. II 19-22 *yalle-nin* is repeated in a context which reflects coordination rather than contrast. To be sure, this method is not observed throughout. In *inname-nin* Mit. III 21: *innama-nin* ibid. 22 the variation appears to be purely stylistic; note also that we get generally either *ya-me-nin* or *ye-ma-nin* as against a single occurrence of *ye-me-nin* [130]. But the above instances with *kuru* "again" suggest, nevertheless, that the alternation could be utilized to mark juxtaposition.

[41] Cf. Friedrich, BChG 30.

INDEX OF FORMS

All entries are cited in the form in which they are given in the text of this book. Forms in normalized transcription are given without hyphens. Direct transliteration is marked by the use of hyphens. Citations from the alphabetic texts are given in Roman type so as to avoid confusion with normalized syllabic forms.

Double writings of vowels and consonants do not affect the alphabetic listing. Voiced stops are listed with the corresponding voiceless stops (*d* with *t*, etc.). Furthermore, *f*, *v*, and *w* are listed with *p*, *i* and *y* with *e*, *o* with *u*. The symbols *š̄* and *ž* are grouped with *š*, but *s* is listed separately, immediately before *š*.

References are to pages.

INDEX OF PASSAGES

25 = ISTA

CPSIA information can be obtained
at www.ICGtesting.com
Printed in the USA
LVHW081547030419
612835LV00020B/449/P

9 781498 288118